Food, Language, and Society

Food, Language, and Society

Communication in Japanese Foodways

Natsuko Tsujimura

LEXINGTON BOOKS
Lanham • Boulder • New York • London

Published by Lexington Books
An imprint of The Rowman & Littlefield Publishing Group, Inc.
4501 Forbes Boulevard, Suite 200, Lanham, Maryland 20706
www.rowman.com

86-90 Paul Street, London EC2A 4NE

Copyright © 2023 by The Rowman & Littlefield Publishing Group, Inc.

All rights reserved. No part of this book may be reproduced in any form or by any electronic or mechanical means, including information storage and retrieval systems, without written permission from the publisher, except by a reviewer who may quote passages in a review.

British Library Cataloguing in Publication Information Available

Library of Congress Cataloging-in-Publication Data

Names: Tsujimura, Natsuko, author.
Title: Food, language, and society : communication in Japanese foodways / Natsuko Tsujimura.
Description: Lanham : Lexington Books, [2023]. | Includes bibliographical references and index. | Summary: "This book investigates how intricately language, food, and culture interact in Japanese society and culture. Natsuko Tsujimura approaches the language of food in Japanese as a vital component of communication by examining intrinsic mechanisms of the language and the broader social meaning it brings to society"— Provided by publisher.
Identifiers: LCCN 2022046105 (print) | LCCN 2022046106 (ebook) | ISBN 9781498571333 (cloth) | ISBN 9781498571340 (ebook)
Subjects: LCSH: Japanese language—Social aspects—Japan. | Food—Japan. | Language and culture—Japan. | Communication—Japan.
Classification: LCC PL524.75 .T88 2023 (print) | LCC PL524.75 (ebook) | DDC 306.440952—dc23/eng/20221024
LC record available at https://lccn.loc.gov/2022046105
LC ebook record available at https://lccn.loc.gov/2022046106

∞™ The paper used in this publication meets the minimum requirements of American National Standard for Information Sciences—Permanence of Paper for Printed Library Materials, ANSI/NISO Z39.48-1992.

Contents

List of Tables	vii
Acknowledgments	ix
List of Abbreviations	xiii
1 Introduction to Food, Language, and Society	1

PART I: LANGUAGE OF FOOD FROM WITHIN

2 Loanwords	11
3 Mimetics	39
4 The Vocabulary of Food Preparation—Concept and Lexical Process	97
5 Metaphors	133

PART II: LANGUAGE OF FOOD IN SOCIETY

6 Recipes and Cookbooks	167
7 Construction of Gendered Images in Foodways	205
References	249
Index	269
About the Author	287

List of Tables

Table 3.1.	Surveyed cookbooks.	82
Table 3.2.	Token and type counts of mimetics.	83
Table 3.3.	Five most frequently used mimetics in each cookbook.	85
Table 4.1.	Classification of English cooking words. (Lehrer 1969. Reprinted with modification by permission of Cambridge University Press.)	101
Table 4.2.	Classification of Japanese cooking words.	103
Table 4.3.	Summary of semantic components for Japanese cooking words.	117

Acknowledgments

Food and cooking have been my passion for most of my life; it is indeed a privileged passion. Yet, I never even thought of combining it with my linguistics training for scholarly explorations until the second decade of this century. The critical steppingstone that motivated me for this new line of research was the opportunity to teach on the language of food in 2014 as part of the Themester courses that the College of Arts and Sciences of Indiana University offers every fall semester. The theme of the 2014 Themester was "Eat, Drink, Think: Food from Art to Science." It was a eureka moment for the union of linguistics and food. Putting together course materials for the undergraduate class was not an easy task but it was a process that I enjoyed very much. All together I taught the course under the title "Tasting Food in Japanese: Food, Language, and Linguistics" three times at Indiana University, each time adding new materials while eliminating less successful ones. I am certain that I benefited from my students far more than they from me. The interest they enthusiastically showed, opinions on reading materials and stories they shared with me and the class, and especially the new range of perspectives on food and beyond that they brought to my attention were like fresh air inspiring me for additional research. Without those undergraduate students' curious minds, I would not have written this book. And, I am grateful to the College of Arts and Sciences for the institutional opportunity that sowed the seeds to broaden my scholarly journey.

My research on the language of food relied greatly on archival work in Japan. The National Diet Library and the library of the Ajinomoto Foundation for Dietary Culture each house an enormous number of documents that are indispensable to carry out investigations on a wide scope of topics revolving around foodways. At both libraries, not only did I find virtually all the sources that I needed to examine but additional information was made available to me that has enhanced and expanded the level of my inquiry. I am indebted to the service that these libraries and their staff provided.

I am a newcomer to Food Studies, a cross- and multi-disciplinary area that pertains to a wide gamut of subject matters revolving around foodways. The Association for the Studies of Food and Society, an academic organization that brings together scholars and practitioners who are concerned with foodways, has been an instrumental platform for me to present my ongoing research, testing the waters before launching full-fledged proposals. For the past decade since I became a member, I have learned a great deal about Food Studies through my attendance at the ASFS's annual meeting, where I also presented my own research. The materials in part II of this book, in particular, gained much from the scholarly exchanges I witnessed and experienced. The ASFS's conferences, its journal, *Food, Culture & Society*, and webinar and zoom lectures they organize have constituted vital resources for my scholarly growth in recent years. Parts of this book have been also presented at other conferences including the 25th Japanese/Korean Linguistic Conference (Hawai'i, 2017), Conference on the Language of Japanese Food (Toronto, 2018), the 2nd Cultural Linguistics International Conference (Germany, 2018), and the annual conference of the American Name Society (Texas, 2017; New York, 2019). I thank the audiences of these meetings for their comments and discussion.

My sincere thanks go to an anonymous reviewer of the manuscript, who provided constructive criticisms and valuable suggestions to improve its content and presentation. Part II of the book especially benefited from the reviewer's comments in shaping and strengthening my discussion regarding sociocultural implications of the language of food.

In publishing this book, I received financial support from various offices at Indiana University for archival research in Japan, conference presentations, and expenses incurred related to publication. I wish to thank the Department of East Asian Languages and Cultures and the East Asian Studies Center. I am also grateful to the Office of the Vice Provost of Research at Indiana University Bloomington, who offered me partial funding through the Retired Faculty Grant-in-Aid Program.

Working with the staff at Lexington Books was an important and pleasurable aspect of writing this book. Jana Hodges-Kluck, Senior Acquisitions Editor of Lexington Books, took up the original proposal. Although she moved to another department, she made sure that the transition went smoothly. Along with the great care that she provided to my first book with Lexington Books, I am grateful to her in attending to the initial stage of the production with superb professionalism. Sydney Wedbush, Assistant Acquisitions Editor, also answered a number of questions concerning the current book before she moved on. Alexandra Rallo, Associate Acquisitions Editor, has overseen that the manuscript moved forward without much delay, and I appreciate her clear, succinct communications to that end. Ryan Dradzynski, Assistant Acquisitions Editor, took great care of formatting the manuscript. I am very fortunate to have worked with these individuals on the Lexington Books staff.

Stuart Davis has been a big fan of my book project and paid close attention to it from the beginning to the end. As is customary, he read several draft versions numerous times and offered me thoughtful and useful feedback. His professional expertise and constant encouragement as well as his "oishii" to my cooking no doubt kept me and my book project going. I wish my mother had seen the completion of this book. She is a virtual co-author as someone who can really talk about the joy and virtue of food and cooking.

List of Abbreviations

ACC	accusative particle
C	consonant
GEN	genitive particle
N	syllable-final (coda) consonant
NOM	nominative particle
TOP	topic marker
Q	geminate consonant in mimetic words
V	vowel
*	ungrammatical

Chapter One

Introduction to Food, Language, and Society

We often take for granted the language we speak every day to communicate with others. However, language plays an essential role in every aspect of our lives including in our food culture. People can express their experiences with food—both positively and negatively—through a variety of words, expressions, and narratives. To illustrate, there are so many ways in which apples are described. Consider the following descriptions of apples in Japanese, compiled in Kawabata and Huchinoue (ed. 2006, 133) from a variety of sources.

(1) 果物の籠には青林檎やバナナが奇麗につやつやとならんでいた。

"Neatly lined up in a fruit basket were shiny green apples and bananas."

(2) 夕闇の中にリンゴの香りが濃密にただよっている。

"The aroma of apples densely floats in the dusk."

(3) 睦子さんが紅玉をむいてくれた。蜜がぎっしり。さわやかな甘みと酸味、みずみずしい果汁が口いっぱい広がった。

"Mutsuko peeled a Kogyoku [Jonathan apple] for me. It was filled with sweet spots. A refreshing sweetness and tartness, succulent juice spread all over my mouth."

(4) ガラスの鉢に盛られ、食事がのどを通らない時もシャリシャリした冷たい食感が心地よく、白い果肉を口に入れるたび果汁が体に沁み入る。

"They [apples] are served in a glass bowl. Even when I don't have much appetite, their crisp and cold sensation is pleasant, and each time I put the white flesh in my mouth, the juice seeps into my body."

(5) リンゴが熟すと、おばあさんが籠にもいで、ひとつずつ、ていねいに地下室の棚にならべた。積み重ねると、下のが傷むからねえ。ぼくたちが、おなかをすかせて地下室にリンゴを取りに行くと、いつもおばあさんが、うしろからどなった。くさったのから、食べるんだよ。おばあさんがケチだったせいで、ぼくは子供のとき、リンゴというといつもくさったのしか食べなかったような気がするよ。

"When the apples were ripe, the old lady picked them into a basket and one by one, gently arranged them on the shelf in the basement. For, piling them up would bruise the bottom ones. When we went to the basement hungry to fetch some apples, she always yelled from behind, 'Eat the rotten ones first.' I feel as if I only ate rotten apples growing up because she was so frugal."

(1–4) describe apples in terms of sensual reactions: visual in (1), olfactive in (2), taste in (3), and texture and mouth feel in (4). In addition, the depictions in (2–4) dynamically capture the sensual reactions in motion. The narrative around apples in (5) speaks to unforgettable memories that food can bring to the storyteller.

The questions of how and where food and food experiences are described (and by whom) provide abundant opportunities for investigating the intriguing relationship between language and culture from cross- and multi-disciplinary perspectives (e.g., Fisher 1968; Cotter 1997; Lakoff 2006; Hosking 2010; Gerhardt et al. 2013; Jurafsky 2014; Szatrowsky 2014; Riley and Paugh 2019). Linguistics, in which language is studied for its systematic regularity, has much to contribute to the language of food since unconcsious knowledge of language underlies and interacts with our dietary life in surprising and unexpected ways. It enables us to understand why certain choices of words and phrases are more appealing to members of a community.

To exemplify the role that linguistic regularity plays, take the way in which words are formed, i.e., morphology, for instance. One of IHOP's menu items, *wafflicious*, and the name of a Turkish-style wrap stand in Austin Texas, *Kebabalicious*, are creatively shaped. Yet, they are not coined randomly. Instead, they are following the same word-formation mechanism of blending by substituting the first syllable of *delicio*us with *waffle* and *kebab*. This is in fact the same systematic pattern in which *ginormous* (*gigantic* and *enormous*), *motel* (*motor* and *hotel*), and *camcorder* (*camera* and *recorder*) are generated. Native speakers—both proprietors and customers—are aware how to interpret *wafflicious* and *Kebabalicious* and appreciative of the humor underlying the names.

Another example is found in the recipe name, "Hand Salad with Yogurt-Lemon Dressing."[1] At first, I took it as a joke, paralleling "hand salad" to potato salad, bean salad, egg salad, tomato salad, and the like. These garden variety compound names are formed with the first noun describing the primary ingredient of the salad. This is indeed a common pattern also observed with names of soups, stews, and pies, among others. Yet, the reputable magazine in which this recipe is posted certainly would not suggest a human body part for the main ingredient of a salad. It is explained that the "salad" is basically a lettuce-and-dip dish. That is, "hand" is not an ingredient but a sort of utensil with which the "salad" is consumed, namely, eat by hand. By breaking a familiar pattern of compounding, the recipe name indeed grabs attention. It is important to understand, though, that the eye-catching effect emerges only because we acknowledge the systematic pattern that holds between the two (or more) words that are put together into compounds.

The language of food is even more powerful in our communication when we realize that words for taste descriptions and food-related expressions are frequently extended to the evaluation of non-food items and concepts. Common English expressions like <u>*sweet* dreams</u>, <u>*bitter* experience</u>, and <u>*it's icing on the cake*</u> illustrate how much these linguistic extensions are entrenched in our daily life. We also see that vocabulary items like *tart*, *apples*, and *cantaloupes*, when referring to females and their body parts, echo sexism in society. Such extensions, regularly processed by means of metaphors, are inevitably shaped by our cultural beliefs and social constructs that are not necessarily shared by speakers of other languages of the world. The language of food, thus, offers a window through which we can witness the role that culture plays in human communication.

This book approaches the language of food in Japanese as a vital component of the communication venue and examines it both at a micro level (linguistic perspective) and at a macro level (sociocultural perspective). Food discourse in Japanese assumes a culture whose food preparations and presentations have had an enormous influence not only on its own people but on global food culture. The Japanese culinary tradition and the Japanese language, thus, offer an excellent context for a (socio-)linguistic examination of how food—and foodways in general—relates to language and people in the society. The Japanese context can help provide further background for looking at other cultures and their people through the language of food.

Although I use linguistic methodology in analyzing the language of food, both narrowly and broadly, I do not regard linguistic analysis of the language of food as forming an independent subfield of linguistics, namely, so-called "culinary linguistics" (Gerhardt et al. 2013). Subfields of linguistics including applied linguistics, computational linguistics, anthropological linguistics, and forensic linguistics have each developed their own unique ways of applying linguistic concepts and methodology that are specific to and cater toward these narrowly-defined areas. For instance, forensic linguistics applies linguistics to the context of the law and the judicial system and procedures. On the other hand, linguistic investigations of food-related matters do not seem to aim at capturing systematic patterning or reaching generalizations that pertain to the language of food. Instead, researchers, including myself, have used the language of food as a data source, just as they could examine the language used in sports or fashion for analysis. For the same reason that we do not have subareas like "sports linguistics" or "fashion linguistics," I do not subscribe to the independent subarea of linguistics called "culinary linguistics." Instead, I would claim that research on food through the lens of linguistics is fruitful because the analytical tools in the sub-disciplinary areas within linguistics provide concepts and terminology that are critical and beneficial to investigating numerous ways in which food interacts with language (Tsujimura 2022b; see also Cook 2012; Szatrowsky 2014; Toratani 2022).

The book is divided into two thematic parts. Part I centers on the language of food at a micro level by analyzing its structure and meaning aspects by way of linguistic concepts and terminology. Specific topics to be examined for linguistic analysis are loanwords related to food and cooking, mimetics, the lexical properties of cooking vocabulary, and metaphors. The topic of loanwords, discussed in chapter 2, emerges from the globalization and glocalization of food, which often occur alongside with linguistic adoption and adaptation of naming of food. When a food term is borrowed into another language, the original term almost necessarily changes in pronunciation from that of the source language so as to fit the phonetic and phonological system of the borrowing language. Furthermore, its original meaning is sometimes not kept intact, but instead the term receives a new, innovative meaning that departs from the original meaning. Often added to the linguistic process of borrowing are aspects of cultural differences and people's perceptions. Drawing samples from conventionalized loanwords as well as those on restaurant menus and recipes in cookbooks and websites, the chapter describes loanwords of food that have been borrowed into Japanese, discussing their linguistic patterning and sociocultural implications brought to the speech community.

Chapter 3 examines the range and effects of the mimetic vocabulary in food discourse including, but not limited to, descriptions of taste, cooking processes, restaurant menus, and advertisements. Japanese holds an extensive inventory of mimetic words as is demonstrated by their ubiquitous appearances in a variety of topics beyond foodways and transcending genres of communication. Mimetic expressions create vivid images in the minds of the language users. As such, they are particularly convenient in giving accurate instructions for cooking processes, making precise reference to differing cooking temperatures (e.g., low~mid~high heat) and manners of cooking (e.g., simmering, quick stir-frying, desired crispiness after frying). They also appear widely in food packaging as a direct means to appeal to consumers. The outstanding selling features of products, such as texture (e.g. crisp, fluffy, plump, creamy), are frequently expressed by mimetics. Language-specific tools like mimetics are exceptionally advantageous in the domain of the language of food, where concise descriptions that immediately relate to human senses greatly contribute to communicating gastronomic experiences among the language users.

Chapter 4 investigates the semantic aspect of cooking verbs and explores linguistic patterns in which verb meaning is constructed. We may encounter difficulty in translating recipes in one language to another. The general English word *cook*, for example, can correspond to several more detailed terms in another language depending on what is being cooked, what a given food is cooked with, or at what temperature, among other factors. Taxonomies of cooking terms and of taste terms in languages point to systematic ways in which semantic components are organized, giving rise to crosslinguistic variation. In Japanese, verbs to mean "cook" are classified according to whether fat is used, whether a food is cooked in water, or whether a food is cooked in water and other ingredients such as soy sauce and sugar. A different set of criteria is adopted for the taxonomy of cooking terms in other languages. In Russian the amount of liquid in which a food is cooked plays an important role in distinguishing among verbs under the general term for "to cook" (DiVirgilio 2010). This suggests that criteria for information leading to a taxonomy of food terms are in a tight connection with conceptual differences underlying the culinary tradition of each culture. The chapter also illustrates the regularity in which linguistic mechanisms common to the Japanese language are deployed to expand cooking vocabulary productively and creatively.

Metaphors, the subject of chapter 5, are an effective tool to describe taste of food accurately and to make the food enticing to those who eat it or conversely to discourage them from consuming it. As I have mentioned some examples earlier, taste descriptors are also extended to non-food domains as metaphors. Adjective pairs like *sweet* and *bitter* that describe opposite food tastes are metaphorically extended to non-food items, preserving the same opposite relation, as in *sweet memory* vs. *bitter experience*, and maintaining the conceptual relation that *sweet* is good and *bitter* is bad. Primarily framed in the Conceptual Metaphor model (Lakoff and Johnson 1980), the chapter gives a descriptive catalog of metaphors of and for food effectively used in our communication. By looking into conceptual threads around which individual instances of food metaphors coalesce, we are able to witness social and cultural values, norms, and stereotypes on which metaphorical expressions are built.

Part II of this book consists of macro-level investigations of the role that food and food-related matters play in communication and culture. Our attention is shifted more to the language of food situated in a social and cultural context although the micro-level examinations in part I explicitly and implicitly remain to serve as vital foundational components of communication. The language of food is examined broadly as food discourse that reflects social and cultural norms and echoes the need for their reconsideration as response to changes in the society. In this part, cookbooks and other related venues of food narratives such as advertisements and comic books are surveyed, and their implications to the nature of interpersonal communication and identity construction are discussed. Under such a tenet, chapter 6 provides a diachronic and synchronic examination of cookbooks. A consideration of the social background of female cookbook authors displays ways in which such authors build and share a common identity with their readers through the cookery discourse. As a case study, one of many cookbooks by Katsuyo Kobayashi is closely analyzed. The interesting range of her language use in the cookbook is illustrated as an effective communicative means to build an identity as a working woman and to share it with her audience.

Chapter 7 further extends the macro-level investigation to consider the social and cultural implications that food items and home cooking bear to gender roles and gender identity. Gendering food, such as meat with men and salad with women, mirrors concepts and norms that exist in our daily life and persists through social and cultural reinforcement. Home cooking is another example of gendering since it has been assumed to be women's responsibility in hegemonic societies. Men who cook at home, then, pose a challenge to hegemonic masculinity and present an opportunity to examine new images of male identity that are receptive of social transformations. This chapter explores ways in which gender images, especially masculine images, are reflected and portrayed in food discourse. In so doing, it is essential to take into consideration how social changes have influenced conventional gender roles and their perceived images.

Given the diversity and the interdisciplinary nature of research in food studies, the two thematic parts in this book are intended to bind together two perspectives—linguistic and sociocultural—for analyzing the language of food as communication. That is, the language of food in Japanese is studied through the lens of cognitive science and of cultural studies for a better understanding of its form and its use in the society. As the discussion aims to show in the chapters to follow, the exploration of these topics benefits from each of the two approaches but more productively from the intersections of the two. The book is intended for those interested in these matters.

Prior knowledge of linguistics is not assumed and a sufficient level of explanation is provided in the text when necessary. For the majority of sample sentences in the text, where matters of Japanese language are consequential, I provide the Japanese original, its transliteration (i.e., in Romanization), and its English translation. When the content of the message, namely, what is said, is more of the focus, I show the Japanese original and its English translation, without the transliterated text.

NOTE

1. The recipe appears on Bon Appetite's website, https://www.bonappetit.com/recipe/hand-salad-with-yogurt-lemon-dressing.

Part I

LANGUAGE OF FOOD FROM WITHIN

Chapter Two

Loanwords

Contemporary society witnesses numerous instances of globalization and glocalization, and food represents a quintessential example of these phenomena. When the world becomes increasingly borderless with ubiquitous travel, food items and cuisine of one culture are introduced to another, but they are rarely reproduced in exactly the same form or manner as they are in the source culture. For example, ingredients that are called for in the original preparation may not always be available and inevitably need to be substituted for or dispensed with. Cooking utensils and methods that are utilized in the original also may not be familiar to and accessible in a new setting. However, these culinary gaps are often ingeniously modified to fit the new environment, so that glocalized cuisine is given a new, innovative life. It is interesting, furthermore, that the glocalized version may strike one as being less authentic compared to the original, but its adapted and popularized form in the new culture sometimes receives a renewed meaning of authenticity, as has been discussed widely in relation to types of cuisine that have evolved—and continue to do so—since they were first brought to the US.[1]

The processes of introduction and acclimatization associated with globalization and glocalization in foodways remarkably parallel the paths that are taken when words are borrowed from one language to another: adoption and adaptation of loanwords form an equivalent dichotomy. Following Haspelmath (2001), I will use "donor language" for the language from which a word is borrowed, "source word" for the original word in the donor language that is borrowed, and "recipient language" for the language into which the word is borrowed. When a food term is borrowed into another language, it is virtually inevitable to see its pronunciation changed to be consistent with the phonetic and phonological system of the borrowing language. Furthermore, it is sometimes the case that its original meaning becomes lost, and instead receives newly assigned meanings that are different from the original meaning. Often added to this process of linguistic adoption and adaptation are aspects of cultural differences and people's perceptions, resulting in new terms that are innovative and appealing to recipient language users for marketing purposes. This chapter describes food-related loanwords borrowed into Japanese and discusses linguistic mechanisms and sociocultural implications.

1 LOANWORDS IN JAPANESE LEXICAL STRATA

Loanwords comprise one of the four vocabulary classes that constitute the lexical strata of Japanese. The four strata are Native, Sino-Japanese, Mimetic, and Loanword. Loanword—lexical borrowing from languages other than Chinese—is also a type of word formation process that is actively used in the Japanese lexicon (Irwin 2011, 2016; Tsujimura 2014). Two surveys on loanwords in magazines that the National Institute for Japanese Language and Linguistics (NINJAL) conducted 38 years apart attest to an exponential increase in the number of loanwords, both token and type, as it is reported in Irwin (2011, 14–18). Based on magazine samples published in 1956 and those in 1994, these surveys classified the data into four vocabulary categories: native/mimetic, Sino-Japanese, foreign, and hybrid. The number of loanword tokens (i.e., the "foreign" category) counted as 3 percent of the entire vocabulary of the samples in 1956 whereas the proportion increased to 12 percent in the 1994 survey. As for the type count, a surge from 10 percent to 35 percent was witnessed during the same time span.

There has been a variety of donor languages contributing to the inventory of loanwords throughout the history of Japanese. According to Irwin (2011), lexical borrowing started in the mid-16th century from Portuguese. Donor languages since then include Dutch, Russian, French, German, and English, but since the 20th century the heaviest borrowing has been from English. Examples of food-related loanwords from these languages except for English are shown in (1).

(1) a. Portuguese: pan "bread," kasutera "sponge cake," tenpura "tempura," bōro "crunchy cookie"
  b. Dutch: bīru "beer," hoppu "hop," shiroppu "syrup," sahuran "saffron"
  c. Russian: wokka "vodka," ikura "salmon roe," piroshiki "piroshki," borushichi "borscht"
  d. French: mayonēzu "mayonnaise," pīman "green pepper," consome "consommé," guratan "au gratin"
  e. German: baumukūhen "cake with a cross section of concentric rings," yōguruto "yogurt," gumi "gummi," kafein "caffeine"

Loanwords do not emerge in a vacuum. After all, they are not original to a given recipient language but are adopted for valid reasons. Haspelmath (2001) maintains that a need for a new concept as well as prestige are primary motivations for lexical borrowing. When a concept or an object does not exist in the recipient culture, it is necessary to adopt the source word that names it. The loanwords in (1) illustrate lexical borrowing based on such necessity given that the food items named by them did not exist in the Japanese food culture prior to the borrowing. Prestige is a more complex attitudinal factor that has to do with social and identity constructs, and as such exhibits intricate sociolinguistic and sociocultural consequences (Zwicky and Zwicky 1980; Lakoff 2006; Jurafsky 2014). For example, menu or recipe items like *terīnu* "terrine," *foagura* "foie gras," *karupaccho* "carpaccio," and *akuapattsa* "acqua pazza" are not everyday dinner table terms that are comprehensible to each Japanese person. It suggests that those who are familiar with these terms, at the very least, have an interest in, or knowledge of, French and Italian cuisines. Furthermore, if these names (especially the first two) appear in menus, the restaurants are most likely not inexpensive or family-style. As Lakoff (2006) explains, the language of menus and recipes reflects an identity construct that demonstrates restaurant owners' and patrons' social and economic class, the degree of knowledge and sophistication, and the level of education. In this respect, it is indeed "we are what we eat."

The prestige associated with loanwords has sociocultural consequences, one of which is demonstrated by their use as a marketing strategy in order to create novelty and sometimes false sophistication. Zwicky and Zwicky's (1980) survey of English-language restaurant menus reveals that attempts to cut and paste loanwords without genuine linguistic knowledge of them end up with macaronic names of dishes like "Le Crabmeat Cocktail," "Turtle Soup au Sherry," and "Flaming Coffee Diablo, Prepared en Vue of Guest." Although it may be an example less directly strategized for effects of prestige, Mister Donut in Japan sells a donut variety under the names *pon-de-ringu*, *pon-de-kokutō*, and *pon-de-sutoroberī*, which are all based on the Portuguese word *pão de queijo* "Cheese bread." *Pão de queijo* has been borrowed into Japanese with the pronunciation *pon-de-kējo*. *Pon-de-ringu* combines the first part of the Portuguese loanword *pon-de* with the English loanword *ringu* "ring," representing a common round donut shape with a hole in the middle. *Pon-de-kokutō* and *pon-de-sutoroberī* are formed by substituting *ringu* with the Sino-Japanese word *kokutō* "brown sugar" and the English-based loanword *sutoroberī* "strawberry." These substitutions reflect different flavors of the same line of donut products. The novelty with a hint of western flair supplied by the loanwords, however macaronic they may be, is intended to catch consumers' attention more effectively than marketing these donuts simply as a family of *dōnatsu* "donut," which is by now an extremely common and conventionalized word in Japan. In addition to product names, similar macaronic phenomena appear ubiquitously in other venues of foodways like recipe names. We will discuss further examples in the next section, but a quick perusal of the popular recipe website Cookpad (cookpad.com) shows ample examples (loanwords are underlined): *penne*-*ando*-*chīzu* "penne and cheese," *misoshiru-kara-no supa*-*guratan* [miso.soup-from-GEN spaghetti-gratin] "spaghetti au gratin made of miso-soup," and *mentaiko-to tōhu-no kurīmī reisei pasuta* [spiced.cod.roe-and tofu-GEN creamy cold pasta] "creamy chilled pasta with spicy cod roe and tofu."

2 LOANWORD ADAPTATION

Just as unfamiliar food items and cuisines take some adjustments before becoming sufficiently acclimated to a new culture, so too do loanwords. This is because no two languages have identical linguistic systems. As a result, a series of adaptations must be carried out at different linguistic levels, ranging from phonetics, phonology, morphology, and semantics, to orthography. For instance, a brief look at a sound-based adaptation applied to common Japanese food names on English menus illuminates their consistent stress-accent pattern: súshi, sashími, sukiyáki, wasábi, yakitóri, and sáke, where the vowels indicated by an accent marker receive stress in English. While English signals phonetic prominence by stress, Japanese employs a different pattern known as the pitch-accent system. It suffices to mention that the prominence patterns of these food names are realized in Japanese as the contouring of high pitch and low pitch, rather than stress on a certain syllable. For example, sushí and wásabi are Japanese accentual realizations. Looking at the loanwords in English, notable is the systematic stress placement on the penultimate syllable, i.e., the second syllable from the end. This stress placement is indeed a predominant pattern of English nouns that consist of more than one syllable. Thus, the disparity in marking prominence is adjusted by following the linguistic system of the borrowing language, as the above-mentioned English stress on the Japanese food names illustrates.

The most obvious adaptation in Japanese loanwords is adjustments of sound segments. When Japanese does not have a sound that is in a source word, it is replaced by the most similar one, either in the place or manner of articulation (Lovins 1975; Irwin 2011, 2016; Tsujimura 2014; Kubozono 2015). Examples of English-based loanwords into Japanese are given in (2). The phonetic representations of the source words are given in the middle column to indicate their actual pronunciations in Japanese, and [:] marks an elongated vowel. The rightmost column lists substituted sound segments upon borrowing the words from English to Japanese.

(2) source word   Japanese   substitution: English → Japanese
- a. <u>v</u>ani<u>ll</u>a   [baniɾa]   [v] → [b], [l] → [ɾ]
- b. <u>f</u>ork   [Φo:ku]   [f] → [Φ]
- c. smoo<u>th</u>ie   [sumu:ʝi:]   [ð(i)] → [ʝ(i)]
- d. jui<u>cy</u>   [ʝu:ʃi:]   [s(i)] → [ʃ(i)]

The substitution of [v, l, f, ð, s] in English by [b, ɾ, Φ, ʝ, ʃ], respectively, shows the gap in the phonetic systems of the two languages. In Japanese [s] is available as in *suika* "watermelon" and *sake* "sake," but when it is followed by [i] as in (2d), the standard phonological rule in the language applies and changes the sequence to [ʃi]. As a consequence, the loanword becomes consistent with the general sound patterns of the recipient language, so that they sound more like Japanese rather than "foreign."

Another type of sound adaptation is by vowel insertion or vowel epenthesis, which is made necessary due to the structure of the basic phonological unit in Japanese, i.e., mora (Irwin 2011; Tsujimura 2014; Kubozono 2015; Otake 2015). Each mora takes the form of a vowel that may or may not be preceded by a consonant ((C)V), a coda nasal (i.e., a nasal sound that is not followed by a vowel), or a geminate consonant (i.e., the first of two identical consonants).[2] A word must consist of a single or multiple mora(s). A consequence of the mora structure is that consonant clusters, i.e., a sequence of consonants without an intervening vowel, are not allowed in Japanese except for a coda nasal and a geminate consonant. Additionally, a word cannot end with a consonant unless it is a coda nasal. It follows that when a source word has a consonant cluster, a vowel must be inserted to break the sequence of two or more consonants. When a source word ends with a consonant, a vowel must be added unless the final consonant is a coda nasal.

The variety of epenthetic vowel patterns is illustrated in the loanwords in (3). The items in the middle column are given in Romanized transliteration and those in the rightmost column are phonetic transcriptions of the same words with inserted vowels indicated by the underline.

(3) source words   Japanese
- a. cream   k<u>u</u>rīm<u>u</u>   [k<u>u</u>ɾi:m<u>u</u>]
- b. steak   s<u>u</u>tēk<u>i</u>   [s<u>u</u>te:k<u>i</u>]
- c. stew   shichū   [ʃ<u>i</u>ču:]
- d. dressing   d<u>o</u>resshing<u>u</u>   [d<u>o</u>reʃʃing<u>u</u>]
- e. toast   tōs<u>u</u>to   [to:s<u>u</u>to]
- f. salad   sarad<u>a</u>   [saɾad<u>a</u>]

The words in (3a–d) begin with consonant clusters while (3e) has one at the end of the word. Insertions of [u] in (3a, b, e), of [i] in (3c), and of [o] in (3d) intervene between two consonants. The inserted vowels create morals of the CV pattern. All but (3c) end in a consonant in the source language, and for each word-final consonant, a vowel is added: [u] in (3a, d), [i] in (3b), [o] in (3e), and [a] in (3f). For both consonant clusters and word-final consonants, Kubozono (1995) and Irwin (2011) give generalizations as to which vowel is inserted to follow which consonant: [o] after [t, d], [i] after [č, ǰ], and [u] in other environments. The loanwords in (3) comport with these generalizations to some degree, but there are also outliers like [i] after [k] in (3b), and [a] after [d] in (3f). Although the generalizations hold of loanwords for the most part, Irwin (2011) explains that the historical time when lexical borrowing took place and the type of donor language seem to contribute to the lack of consistency with the more general patterns.

Deletion of phonetic segments is also observed in the process of loanword adaptation (Smith 2006; Irwin 2011). Some examples are given in (4).

(4) source words   loanwords

  a. mash<u>ed</u> potato   masshu poteto   [maʃʃu poteto]
     dri<u>ed</u> fruits   dorai hurūtsu   [dorai Φuru:tsu]
     boil<u>ed</u> cabbage   boiru kyabetsu   [boiru kʲabetsu]

  b. ton<u>gue</u>   tan   [tan]
     roa<u>st</u>   rōsu   [ɾo:su]³
     restauran<u>t</u>   resutoran   [ɾesutoɾan]

  c. <u>A</u>merican   meriken   [meriken] (as in *meriken-ko* [American-powder] "flour")

The *-ed* suffix of adjectival passives is dropped in loanwords like those in (4a). These modifiers without *-ed* are further extended to create new words including *masshu suīto poteto* "mashed sweet potato," *masshu karihurawā* "mashed cauliflower," and *dorai miruku* "dried milk." They also combine with Japanese native words, sometimes reversing the order, as are demonstrated by recipe names including *kabocha masshu* [pumpkin mashed] "mashed pumpkin," *dorai shōga* [dried ginger] "dried ginger," *ringo dorai* [apple dried] "dried apple," *boiru asari* [boiled clams] "boiled clams," and *ebi boiru* [shrimp boiled] "boiled shrimp." Note that drying and boiling are not new concepts in Japanese cooking, and there are indeed corresponding native verbs that refer to them, *hos(u)* "to (sun)dry" and *yude(ru)* "to boil," as in *hoshi-shītake* "dried shitake mushroom" and *yude-tamago* "boiled egg." Each of the terms under (4a) is borrowed as a set phrase that names a type of food with a specific method of preparation. But once adapted to Japanese, they are reanalyzed for more productive word formation. The names of the dishes with *masshu, dorai, boiru,* and the like are often of Western style. In that light, the use of these loanwords describes the food and food preparation more closely to the original forms. At the same time, they are likely to appeal to the younger generations whose exposure to English and other foreign languages and cultures is increasing. I should hasten to add that *huraido poteto* "fried potato" and *huraido chikin* "fried chicken" maintain the *-ed* suffix, pronounced as [do], rather than *hurai poteto* and *hurai chikin*. Additionally, *hurai* is used for foods that are dusted with breadcrumbs and deep fried, as in *kaki hurai* "fried oysters" and *ebi hurai* "fried shrimp," where the first word of each example belongs to the (Japanese) native vocabulary. The recipe name *boirudo eggu* "boiled egg" is found on an online recipe site, but this seems to be a bit of an extreme case since the native compound *yude-tamago* refers to the exact same thing and is very commonly used.[4]

(4b) and (4c) are alike in that the deleted segment is at the edge of the word. Deletion at the right edge is not particular to loanwords but is quite common especially with coda consonants in casual speech. In contrast, deletion at the beginning of a word, as in (4c), is rare. When flour was introduced from the US to Japan in the Meiji era, the English word *American* and the Sino-Japanese *ko* "powder" were compounded in order to distinguish the American flour from its domestic equivalent, *komugi-ko* [wheat-powder]. The deletion involved in *meriken* is likely to have resulted from aural perception of the English pronunciation of the word in 19th century Japan since the unstressed word-initial vowel does not receive any prominence. However, in the contemporary Japanese food vocabulary, *amerikan*, without deletion and by itself, refers to lightly roasted, lightly brewed coffee. Also, the compound word *amerikan-doggu* [American-dog] is a common name for corn dogs.

One consequence of vowel epenthesis in loanwords as shown in (3) is that a loanword becomes long and thus creates a ground for clipping. It should be noted, however, that clipping is actually a very common word formation pattern that is prevalent across vocabulary types in Japanese. Clipping when applied to loanwords, then, can be regarded as an adaptation to the general linguistic system employed in Japanese rather than a special maneuver reserved for loanwords. Listed in (5) are loanwords in both full and clipped versions.

(5)
source words	loanword – full	loanword – clipped
chocolate	chokorēto	choko
sandwich	sandoicchi	sando
asparagus	asuparagasu	asupara
mayonnaise	mayonēzu	mayo
ice cream	aisu kurīmu	aisu
potato chips	poteto chippusu	potechi
lemon squash	remonsukasshu	resuka
Mister Donut	misutā dōnattsu	misudo

Single words like the first four examples in (5) are typically shortened by deleting the last few moras. Compounds are clipped by taking a—typically first—few moras of each member, as the last three examples in (5) illustrate. Of the compound examples, *aisu* for *ice cream* departs from the common pattern, but it is particularly interesting in that it creates ambiguity between a reference to ice cream products and iced beverages like iced coffee and tea. To refer to ice cubes, on the other hand, the native word, *kōri*, is regularly used.

Clipped loanwords become bases for a further expansion of food vocabulary. An example has previously been mentioned regarding *pon-de-ringu*, Mister Donut's products in section 1. To further illustrate, *mayo* in (5) can be compounded with native words, together indicating mayonnaise as an added flavor or ingredient. For instance, *ume-mayo* "(pickled) plum flavored mayonnaise," *shio-mayo* "salted mayonnaise," and *negi-mayo* "mayonnaise with scallions" are all formed by native words compounded with *mayo*. *Ume* in *ume-mayo* refers specifically to *ume-boshi* [plum-dried], very salty and sour pickled plums that are considered one of the most traditional types of Japanese pickling. So, the hybrid of a native word and a (clipped) loanword demonstrates a well-adjusted harmony of a Western sauce (mayonnaise) and a food item that is deep seated in the local food culture and tradition (pickled plums). Additionally, although it is a compound that consists of two loanwords, *tsuna-mayo* "(canned) tuna with mayonnaise" has gained enormous popularity, especially among younger people. It is essentially the same as tuna salad in the North American food scene but has come to be frequently used as a filling for rice balls. It is no exaggeration that *tsuna-mayo* rice balls are ubiquitously found in shelves of convenience stores in Japan. This adaptation to the rice culture is a testament to an ingenious and insightful way of glocalizing new food items and customizing them to the taste customary to the Japanese people.

Vocabulary expansion with loanwords further informs us that food adaptation is not limited to ingredients. For example, the loanword *sando* based on *sandwich* in (5) generates *tamago-sando* "egg sandwich" and *kyūri-sando* "cucumber sandwich." It also combines with other loanwords (or native words) to indicate the way sandwiches are made or served. For example, *arenji-sando* [arrangement-sandwich] "sandwich with varied ingredients and in different serving styles," *hotto-sando* [hot-sandwich] "hot sandwich," and *ōpun-sando* [open-sandwich] "open-faced sandwich" illustrate that newly adapted words run the gamut in their areas of references. Similarly, recipe names like *oyatsu-sando* [snack-sandwich] "sandwich for snack" indicates that the sandwich is relatively light and suitable as a snack between meals. So, loanword adaptation and subsequent vocabulary expansion signal the degree to which people are flexible and creative in localizing a foreign cuisine into a new type of food experience while preserving what is customary in their own food culture.

Besides phonological (sounds) and morphological (word forms) adaptations, semantic adjustments with loanwords are sometimes inevitable. As mentioned in endnote 4, Smith (2006) discusses two bases for lexical borrowing: "auditory borrowing" based on auditory perception of the original pronunciations and "orthographic borrowing" based on the spelling in the donor language. Due to these bases, some source words surface as two similar but non-identical forms, which Smith calls loan doublets. Interestingly, not only do some doublets have different pronunciations, but they are also associated with slightly dissimilar meanings. Illustrations with food-related loanwords are given in (6).

(6) | source word | loan doublets | meaning in Japanese |
| --- | --- | --- |
| a. roast | rōsu | sirloin |
| | rōsuto | roast |
| b. lemonade | ramune | soda pop |
| | remonēdo | lemonade |
| c. cocoa | kakao | cocoa tree |
| | kokoa | hot chocolate |
| d. curry | karē | curry |
| | karī | authentic Indian curry |

The two meanings to which each doublet refers are related but sufficiently distinct. In (6b) *ramune* is a carbonated clear beverage that resembles 7-Up and does not contain lemon juice. More significantly, though, the name points distinctively to its container. There is a small glass marble as a stopper between the bottle top and the liquid, and when we tilt the bottle to drink the soda, the glass marble makes a clinking sound. If a carbonated beverage is not packaged in a standard glass bottle, it is not a *ramune*. So, *ramune* ended up having a very narrow sense, compared with the meaning of the source word.

The distinction regarding *curry* in (6d) may not be widely made, perhaps only relevant in a limited context. It is fair to say that Japanese *karē* is one of the most popularized food items that originate in another culture, but its adapted version—much thicker than Indian curries—is also known to be quite a departure from its original form. Its variant, *karī*, which I believe is an instance of auditory borrowing, appears sparsely, and is intended to refer to a curry dish that is more faithful to authentic Indian versions. For example, *Nakamuraya jun indo-shiki karī* [Nakamuraya pure Indian-style curry] "authentic Indian-style curry by Nakamuraya" is the name of curry products marketed by an old establishment, Nakamuraya.[5] The line of packaged curries with a variety of ingredients (e.g., vegetables, chicken) is distinguished from the more common Japanese adaptation, and *karī* as opposed to *karē* is an attempt to mark the products' authenticity. In an even narrower context, *karī* is compounded with *sūpu* "soup," deriving *sūpu-karī*, featuring its soupy texture. The pronunciation *karī* is phonetically closer to the source word than *karē*, and highlights an intended flair of genuineness. Recall that prestige is one of the motivations of borrowing words from another language. Use of loanwords, especially when they are pronounced more faithfully to source words like *karī*, can serve as a strategic tool for appealing to the target clientele. Those in the clientele group are likely to have a projected culinary and linguistic sophistication that pertains to Indian cuisine. Furthermore, they may be considered to belong to a certain social, cultural, and economic class of people.

Another semantic phenomenon observed with loanwords is semantic shift in which meaning becomes narrowed to specified references, or conversely, generalized to include broader senses.[6] In American English, for example, *biscotti* means small rectangular cookies that are twice-baked typically with almonds or other nuts in them. In its donor language, Italian, *biscotti* subsumes all kinds of cookies, and what *biscotti* in American English denotes is called *cantucci* in the donor language. So, the original meaning of *biscotti* became narrower to equate to a specific type of cookie.

Irwin (2011) draws an example of semantic narrowing from *raisu* "rice." Rice is a staple in Japan, and as such there is no need for borrowing another word to name it. In fact, Japanese already employs two words that correspond to *rice* in English: *gohan* for cooked rice and *kome* for the grain form before cooking. As Irwin characterizes, *raisu* refers to cooked rice that is served on a plate as an accompaniment of curry and Western-style dishes like hamburger steak and pork cutlet.[7] So, *raisu* has a much narrower sense than what *rice* in English denotes. Examples of narrowing also include *jūsu* "juice," *ikura* "salmon roe," and *miruku* "milk." *Jūsu* means only fruit and vegetable juice to be consumed as a beverage and does not include other uses such as lemon juice to be added for cooking. Instead, *remon-jiru*, a compound of the loanword *remon* "lemon" and the native word *shiru* "juice, soup," is commonly used for the latter purpose. As for *ikura*, the source word *ikra* in Russian includes fish roe in general, but the meaning has narrowed specifically to salmon roe when the word was borrowed and adapted into Japanese (Irwin 2011). To refer to milk, the Sino-Japanese word *gyūnyū* is still prevalently used, with occasional use of its loanword counterpart, *miruku*. However, in this case, too, we see semantic narrowing. In Japanese, *miruku* is used for cream as in "cream and sugar" for coffee. So, at Japanese coffee shops and restaurants, *miruku* is the standard word for cream. In fact, it is far less common in Japan to drink coffee with milk unless café-au-lait or café-latte is ordered. Finally, I might add *esunikku hūdo* "ethnic food" to the list of examples of semantic narrowing. Even in the US, where multiple ethnicities are represented in the culinary domain, the term "ethnic food" means different things depending on the individual. In Japan *esunikku hūdo* "ethnic food" largely refers to cuisines of Southeast Asia, particularly Thai, Indonesian, and Vietnamese foods (Hatanaka 2020).

The process of adoption and adaptation of loanwords can sometimes take an unexpected path, resulting in odd outcomes. The Japanese flavoring liquid *ponzu* is one such example. According to Vos (1963), its source word is *pons* in Dutch, which means alcoholic and non-alcoholic punch in the donor language. Vos further explains its Japanese version *ponsu* as follows: "[i]n the beginning of the Meiji era *ponsu* was a well-known remedy against colds; it consisted of squashed bitter oranges (*daidai*), to which sugar was added" (p. 368). In his follow-up, Irwin (2011, 38) further elaborates that *ponsu* eventually lost its medicinal use and instead was served as "a simple juice." The current form was then created by mixing it with ingredients like rice vinegar, soy sauce, and kelp. An intriguing aspect is that even at this later stage, *ponsu*, a single word in the donor language, was linguistically re-analyzed into two parts, *pon-su*. Since *su* is homophonous with Japanese *su* "vinegar," the character for vinegar (酢) was allocated to the second part of *pon-su* (ポン酢). Furthermore, as is common with compounds in Japanese, the sequential voicing (Rendaku)—the phenomenon that changes a voiceless consonant to its voiced counterpart at the beginning of the second segment of a compound—applies to -*su* of *pon-su*, generating the pronunciation of [pon-zu]. The linguistic path from *ponsu* to *pon-zu* exhibits an interesting historical transition to which the systems of phonology, morphology, and semantics of the language contributed in an intriguing way. It seems even more remarkable that the origin of *ponzu* is not common knowledge among Japanese people today.

On occasion loanwords can be recycled in that they, as adapted forms, are re-borrowed into an original donor language. Outside the food vocabulary, *anime* and *karaoke* are examples of such re-borrowing. The source word for *anime* is *animation* in English. It was borrowed into Japanese and adapted as *animēshon*, which subsequently underwent clipping to derive *anime*. At the same time, *anime* has come to be used under a more narrowly defined meaning to refer to a specific genre of movies and TV. The clipped word *anime* is then borrowed back to English under the form and meaning different from the original English source word *animation*. *Karaoke*, in Japanese, is a compound consisting of two parts, *kara-oke*: *kara* is a native Japanese word to mean empty, and *oke* originates from the English word *orchestra*, which was subsequently shortened. The compound, literally meaning "empty orchestra," refers to the entertainment tool that offers tunes and written lyrics showing at the bottom of the screen so that people can sing to them. The new concept (i.e., the instrument) and the label to name it as a whole have been borrowed (partially back) to English. This time, though, *karaoke* has been adapted to the phonological patterns of English for its pronunciation including the stress placement on the penultimate syllable.

In the language of food, *katsu* represents a similar case of loanword recycling. It originates from the English word *cutlet* and was phonologically adjusted to *katsuretsu*, which subsequently was clipped to *katsu*. Typically, *katsu* is a breaded and deep-fried pork chop, but chicken or beef may be used instead. In Japanese restaurants in North America, it has gained popularity, as is suggested by its frequent listing in menus under *katsu*, rather than *cutlet*. A quick perusal of English-language internet recipe venues informs that *katsu* is extended to fish as its ingredients, as the recipe names like "Crispy Fish Katsu" (https://www.blueapron.com/) and "Salmon Katsu" (https://www.pbs.org/) evince. In Japan, however, fish that is cooked by the same method (i.e., breaded and deep-fried) is not called *katsu* but *hurai*, another loanword from the English *fry*. So, we have *aji-hurai* "fried mackerel," *shiromi-zakana-no hurai* [white-fish-GEN fry] "fried white fish," *ebi-hurai* "fried shrimp," and *kaki-hurai* "fried oyster," but none of these are subsumed under *katsu*.[8] So, *katsu* as a loanword in English has a broadened meaning whose core semantic component focuses on the cooking method of deep-frying after breading, and the type of primary ingredients is not as restricted as what *katsu* means in Japanese. The (partially) recycled loanword, thus, has developed a renewed definition in the original donor language.

Although it is not strictly parallel to the example of *katsu* above, the reverse direction between Japanese and English is also found, as is demonstrated by *gurīn-tī* "green-tea." The English word *green-tea* is a literal translation of Japanese *ryokucha* (緑茶: green-tea). *Ryokucha* and *green-tea* are consumed at home and restaurants. Its powdered ground form called *maccha* is used typically for the tea ceremony, but also serves as a flavor for ice cream and a variety of beverages, Japanese sweets, and baked goods. Even though *ryokucha* is still a very commonly used word in Japan, its English translation, *green-tea*, is borrowed into Japanese as *gurīn-tī*. However, the loanword *gurīn-tī* in Japanese seems to refer more specifically to *maccha*, the concentrated powdered variety. For instance, in 2017 Starbucks Japan introduced a new beverage under the product name *sheikun appuru gurīn-tī* "shaken apple green-tea"—a cold drink that is made of maccha powder and apple juice (Yamaguchi 2017).[9] Outside Starbucks, beverage names like *gurīn-tī rate* "green-tea latte" as well as recipe names including *yōguruto-no gurīn-tī-gake* [yogurt-GEN green-tea-poured] "green-tea poured over yogurt" (https://cookpad.com/recipe/5796307) and *gurīn-tī-pan* [green-tea bread] "green-tea bread" (https://cookpad.com/recipe/5251226) mostly call for maccha powder rather than unground green tea leaves or brewed (liquid) tea. In this example, then, *gurīn-tī*, as a loanword in Japanese, has a narrower sense than its Japanese counterpart from which it has been translated. Note that along with *gurīn-tī*, *maccha* is frequently used in Japanese food and beverage scenes, and that *gurīn-tī* sometimes refers to brewed tea. The situation is somewhat similar to the coexistence of *gohan* "cooked rice," *raisu* "cooked rice served on a plate," and *kome* "rice grain," but divisions among *gurīn-tī*, *maccha*, *ryokucha* "green-tea, both leaves and brewed," and *ocha* "tea in general, all forms" are perforated, allowing substantial overlap among them.

We have thus far focused on loanwords that are nouns in both donor languages and Japanese. Generally, it is common that lexical borrowing targets major vocabulary items like nouns, verbs, adjectives, and adverbs, whereas function words and affixes are less likely to be borrowed as independent (free) morphemes.[10] However, drawing on their examinations of recipe names at the Cookpad site (https://cookpad.com), Shimada and Nagano (2017, 2018) observe that English-based loanwords *in* "in," *on* "on," and *uizu* "with" frequently appear on the online recipe site. Their examples are transliterated and presented in Romanization, but my own glance at the same website confirms that the loanwords are written either in English or in the katakana (or even hiragana although less frequently) syllabary of Japanese. There are two differences between the donor and recipient languages that are relevant to the adaptation of these English prepositions. First, Japanese is a language with postposition rather than preposition, which affects word ordering. Second, more important to our current discussion, spatial relations between two items (e.g., X is in Y; X is on Y) are expressed in Japanese by relation nouns. Thus, *X is in Y* and *X is on Y* in English correspond respectively to *X-ga Y-no naka* and *X-ga Y-no ue*, where *naka* and *ue* are nouns that mean "(place) inside" and "(place) above." Crucially, the relative orders between Y and *in/on* in English and between Y and *naka/ue* in Japanese are reversed: *in/on Y* in English vs. *Y-no naka/ue* in Japanese. When the English loan preposition appears in recipe names, some instances maintain the English word order while others reveal a pattern that cannot be attributed to either English or Japanese word order. In fact, the untraceable word order is confusing as to which food item is inside or on top.

In (7–10), examples of recipe names with オン・おん・*on* are in (7–8), and those with イン・*in* are in (9–10), all taken from the Cookpad website.[11] The recipe names in (7) and (9) take the English word order pattern, whereas in (8) and (10), the word order does not seem to resemble either the donor language or the recipient language. In each example set, the preposition in (a) is displayed in the Japanese katakana syllabary while the preposition in (b) is written in English, following the presentation mode of the recipe site. The English translations of the recipe names are my own, after consulting the photos, captions, and cooking instructions, so that the intended spatial relations are accurately interpreted.

(7) with オン・おん・*on*: English word order pattern

    a. シチューオンライス
       shichū on raisu
       stew on rice
       "stew on rice"   (https://cookpad.com/search/シチューオンライス)

       アボカドオントースト
       abokado on tōsuto
       avocado on toast
       "avocado on toast"   (https://cookpad.com/recipe/6789791)

    b. ポテトグラタンonバゲット
       poteto guratan on bagetto
       potato au gratin on baguette
       "potatoes au gratin on baguette"
           (https://cookpad.com/dining/recipes/3138683)

       テリヤキチキンonオニオンライス
       teriyaki chikin on onion raisu
       teriyaki chicken on onion rice
       "teriyaki chicken on onion-rice"
           (https://cookpad.com/recipe/6109528)

(8) with オン・おん・*on*: unusual word order pattern

    a. 黒ごま豆腐オン枝豆
       kuro-goma-dōhu on edamame
       black-sesame-tofu on edamame
       "black-sesame tofu topped with edamame [=boiled green soybeans]"
           (https://cookpad.com/recipe/4837473)

       ハンバーグおんチーズ
       hanbāgu on chīzu
       hamburger on cheese
       "hamburger steak topped with cheese"
           (https://cookpad.com/recipe/4992128)

    b. たまごマヨonチーズ
       tamago mayo on chīzu

   egg mayonnaise on cheese
   "(boiled) egg with mayonnaise [=egg salad] topped with cheese"
           (https://cookpad.com/recipe/6162100)

   塩昆布キャベツonジャコ
   shio-konbu kyabetsu on jako
   salted-kelp cabbage on dried.young.sardine
   "salted kelp and cabbage topped with dried young sardine"
           (https://cookpad.com/recipe/5769113)

(9) with イン・*in*: English word order pattern
  a. チーズイン味噌汁
   chīzu in misoshiru
   cheese in miso.soup
   "miso soup with cheese in it" (https://cookpad.com/recipe/6146123)

   フルーツインティー
   hurūtsu in tī
   fruits in tea
   "tea with fruits in it" (https://cookpad.com/recipe/5815631)

  b. 椎茸in煮込みハンバーグ
   shītake in nikomi hanbāgu
   shiitake in stewed hamburger
   "stewed hamburger steak with shiitake mushrooms in it"
           (https://cookpad.com/recipe/6212760)

   なめ茸inだし巻き卵
   nametake in dashimaki-tamago
   nametake in dashi.rolled.egg
   "[Japanese-style] rolled omelet with nametake mushrooms in"
           (https://cookpad.com/recipe/6086923)

(10) with イン・*in*: unusual word order pattern

  a. 豆腐バーグインモッツァレラ
   tōhu-bāgu in mottsarera
   tofu.burger in mozzarella
   "tofu-burger with mozzarella in it"
          (https://cookpad.com/recipe/5742398)

   もずく酢インみょうが
   mozukusu in myōga
   seaweed.vinegar in myoga.ginger
   "vinegar marinated seaweed with myoga ginger in it"
          (https://cookpad.com/recipe/6213916)

  b. 抹茶風卵焼きin青汁
   maccha-hū tamago-yaki in aojiru

green.tea-like omelet in chlorophyll.juice
"green-tea-flavored omelet with chlorophyll juice in it"
(https://cookpad.com/recipe/6192793)

チーズケーキinキャラメルりんご
chīzukēki in kyarameru ringo
cheesecake in caramelized apple
"cheesecake with caramelized apples in it"
(https://cookpad.com/recipe/6195424)

In (7) and (9) the syntactic structure of each example follows exactly the pattern of noun phrases in English. The recipe names and each part are either native words, loanwords, or their combinations. This means that recipe names as a whole do not occur in English. Instead, they are constructed from phrases of which オン・おん・*on* and イン・*in* are loanword members. Consequently, we can view that the English word order has also been borrowed.[12] Of these examples, furthermore, *shichū on raisu* "stew on rice" in (7a) seems particularly popular and prevalently used. Not only is it a recipe name that recurs on various online recipe sites, but a food company (the House Foods Corp.) markets a roux version under the same name. Additionally, the "*chīzu in* X" pattern, as demonstrated in the first example in (9a), is also widespread, and similar names with a large variety of substitutions for X are easily found. Examples include *chīzu in omuretsu* "omelet with cheese in it," *chīzu in hanbāgu* "hamburger steak with cheese in it," and *chīzu in korokke* "croquette with cheese in it." In this function, *chīzu in* may be considered a standardized unit to simply mean that cheese is inside.

The names in (8) and (10) are linguistically more curious. If their modification structure were analyzed on par with that of (7) and (9), food preparers would encounter unexpected (and unwanted) outcomes. For instance, *kurogoma-dōhu on edamame*黒ごま豆腐オン枝豆 in (8a) would mean that the tofu is placed on top of edamame, rather than the other way around. Worse yet, for *chīzu-kēki in kyarameru ringo* チーズケーキinキャラメルりんごin (10b), one would hardly be able to picture a cheesecake inside a caramelized apple. Accompanying photos and the instructions are absolutely necessary to lead to how these names are to be understood. There do not seem to be linguistically coherent reasons to explain the word order in (8) and (10), especially since there is no ground for motivating the distinction between (8) and (10) on the one hand, and (7) and (9) on the other. Although logical criteria to distinguish between the two patterns are yet to be found, I surmise that オン・おん・*on* and イン・*in* of the recipe names in (8) and (10) may serve as postpositions—the lexical category employed in Japanese—simply judging from their location in the phrases. Importantly, though, all the examples arranged in this inexplicable word order start with references to what the recipe is about, namely what is the type or category of the food preparation, providing the most essential information about the recipe. For instance, the recipe names *kurogoma-dōhu on edamame* and *hanbāgu on chīzu* in (8a) inform the readers that they should expect to make a type of *(kurogoma-)dōhu* "(black-sesame) tofu" and a type of *hanbāgu* "hamburger steak." Likewise, in (10), *maccha-hū tamago-yaki in aojiru* is a kind of *(maccha-hū) tamago-yaki* "(green-tea-flavored) omelet" and *chīzu-kēki in kyarameru ringo* is a kind of *chīzu-kēki* "cheesecake." Notwithstanding the confusing word arrangement, the most basic information seems to be communicated, aided further by visual aids and the prose description.[13] At the same time, the use of the unorthodox phrasal structure may well simply be motivated by an attempt to draw attention with a casual and even humorous nuance under the naming practice.[14]

Although it may be considered an extrinsic factor for patterns of loanword adaptation, the role that orthography plays cannot be ignored, especially considering macaronic effects. Creative and humorous use—with occasional silliness—of the orthographical mixture no doubt draws attention from those who are looking for new ideas to be brought into their personal kitchens, even though the recipes in and of themselves do not rise to a level of innovation. The recipe names in (11–13) illustrate such an orthographical language play with loanwords and mock-loanwords.

(11) GBSポテト
GBS poteto [GBS=garlic, butter, shoyu "soy sauce"]
GBS potato
"potato with garlic, butter, and soy sauce"
(https://ameblo.jp/wanwan2005/entry-11838303425.html)

(12) a. TKG [=tamago kake gohan]
"cooked rice with a raw egg poured over"   (Kurashiru 2020)

b. 塩味TKG
shio-aji TKG
salt-taste TKG
"cooked rice with a raw egg poured over, salt-flavored"   (Ibid.)

c. だしバタTKG
dashi-bata TKG
broth-butter TKG
"cooked rice with a raw egg poured over along with dashi-broth and butter"   (Kikkoman n.d.)

(13) a. トマトジュースdeアクアパッツァ
tomato jūsu "de" akuapazza
tomato juice "de" acqua pazza
"acqua pazza made with tomato juice"
(https://cookpad.com/recipe/3592078)

    b. オーブンDEラタトゥユ（フランス料理）
       ōbun DE ratatouyu (huransu-ryōri)
       oven DE ratatouille (French cooking)
       "ratatouille in oven (French cooking)"
                                  (https://cookpad.com/recipe/1389014)

    c. 2分de柿シャーベット
       nihun de kaki-shābetto
       two.minutes de persimmon sherbet
       "2-minute persimmon sherbet" (to cleanse the palate for French cooking)
                                  (https://cookpad.com/recipe/4154773)

GBS poteto in (11) was originally created by Koji Aita whose blog site has received popularity, and the recipe name has been widespread in other cooking venues. GBS looks as if it were an abbreviation of English words, but it is in fact partly so. G and B respectively stand for garlic and butter, but S is taken from the initial letter of the Japanese word for soy sauce, *shōyu*. So, GBS is an abbreviation of words from two languages put side by side. Another abbreviated recipe name in (12), TKG, is based on an already existing Japanese dish name, *tamago-kake gohan* [egg-pouring (cooked) rice] "cooked (white) rice with a raw egg poured over it." Like S for *shōyu* in GBS in (11), each of TKG is Japanese, written in Romanization. This type of abbreviation practice is not too common in Japanese foodways, but TKG has widely been used, as its extensions to (12b) and (12c) indicate.[15]

In (13) the use of "de" has a double meaning based on two similar sounding words. One is a preposition borrowed from French *de* (e.g., *la soupe de tomates* "tomato soup," *un verre de vin* "glass of wine"), and the other is a Japanese native postposition to indicate ingredients, instruments, or time (e.g., *batā-de itameru* [butter-with fry] "fry with butter," *nabe-de yuderu* [pot-in boil] "boil in a pot," *gohun-de yakeru* [five.minutes-in get.fried] "get fried in five minutes"). (13a) informs us that the acqua pazza dish has tomato juice as an ingredient, which departs from a standard recipe that typically calls for water. The ratatouille recipe in (13b) is cooked in an oven as opposed to a more commonly used pot as the kitchen utensil in which the ratatouille is cooked. The recipe even goes out of its way to specify parenthetically that it is of French cooking, and also to capitalize DE in the name for emphasis. (13c) is an example in which *nihun de* "in two minutes" features quick cooking. A side comment for this recipe adds a note that the sherbet dish is a good accompaniment for cleansing the palate after (or during) a French meal, which is routine in the French (fine) dining experience. With respect to French and Japanese syntax, the placement of *de* as the French preposition and that of *de* as the Japanese postposition are contrastive vis-à-vis the noun that each modifies. Judging from the meanings of these recipe names, however, it is evident that the Romanized de/DE embedded in the Japanese orthography is meant to be interpreted as Japanese postposition *de* with its Japanese pronunciation rather than the original French *de*. But simply by using the non-Japanese script, it gives a superficial French-ness to the recipes. That is, substituting de/DE in (13) with *de* in the hiragana syllabary (i.e., で) does not make any difference as far as the general descriptions of the recipes are concerned. The nuanced pretentiousness stemming from the prestige associated with French cuisine is clearly the intended eye-catching effect. At the same time, I should hasten to add that the bilingual pun created by *de* with the orthographical aid brings out more of a humorous tone than a social identity with the upper-class or culinary sophistication. This is sufficiently demonstrable from the easily accessible, popular nature of the website at which the recipe names in (13) are posted.[16]

The examples in (11–13) have an appearance of a macaronic mishmash, but they represent the scope of the globalization of world cuisines. Simultaneously, they reveal Japanese people's efforts to make foreign cuisines as accessible and adjustable as possible, so that they can alleviate hesitation and intimidation in approaching an unfamiliar food experience. However messy it may be from the linguistic viewpoint, the humorous use of language and orthography certainly serves well as a casual, welcoming tool for expanding one's cooking repertoire and creativity.

3 CULINARY GLOBALIZATION AND LOANWORD PERCEPTION

The issue of identity emerges in discussions of food and society across a variety of disciplines. For example, Bourdieu's (1984) view of associating taste (including taste for food) and social class is well cited in sociology and beyond. From an anthropological perspective, Ochs et al. (1996, 8) summarize food as part of identity construct: ". . . conduct with regard to food defines persons and groups. What one eats, how one eats, when and with whom are guided by understandings of one's identity within society; or to put it another way, alimentary conduct helps to define one's identity within society." In a similar vein, Lakoff (2006) claims that "culinary preferences and sophistication" enter a group of canons that serve as what she calls "minor identity."[17] Here I consider the practice of naming food in recipes, menus, and related venues to be part of "conduct with regard to food" in the sense of Ochs et al.'s quotation above. Since we have been focusing on loanwords, we shall examine implications that loanwords may have to matters concerning identity in these naming practices.

According to Irwin (2011), the first stage of lexical borrowing started in Japan with Portuguese in the mid-16th century. An increase in the number of donor languages and loanwords took place in the 19th century, and during the 20th century loanwords from English have resulted in heavy borrowing. Although initially motivated by the necessity to label new concepts, loanword names for food items and cooking methods undeniably have a prestigious tone and a sense of sophistication. For example, the sentiment can be detected in earlier food writings like Gensai Murai's *Shokudōraku*, which was originally written and popularized in 1903. When we see foreign names in contemporary menus and recipes, unless they are widely conventionalized, they are perceived with prestige, sophistication, and perhaps exoticism. These accompanying perceptions are closely connected to constructing identity norms that define individuals who choose to consume (e.g., as restaurant patrons) or prepare (e.g., as foodies at home) food items labeled by loanword names. As Zwicky and Zwicky (1980) explain, restaurants with fancy French-sounding menus use them as a strategy to impress with the purported sense of class consciousness and linguistic sophistication.

Conversely, however, loanwords (and foreign words) can be perceived negatively and even with hostility. What has come to be known as "Pastagate" in Canada illustrates such negative reactions. According to Hobbis's (2017) explanation of the event, Quebec's language police, Office québécois de la langue française (OQLF), warned an Italian restaurant that Italian words like *pasta*, *antipasti*, and *calamari* on their menu should be replaced with their French counterparts. Notwithstanding sensational oppositions to this warning as detailed by Hobbis's article, the OQLF's nationalistic attempt is to maintain the dominance of the French language even in menus of restaurants that specialize in foreign cuisines. Given the ubiquity of loanwords that are recognized in Japanese food-related communication, the antagonistic view of loanwords in support of linguistic nationalism as in Pastagate seems moot in the Japanese food scene today. On the other hand, loanwords and especially their exponential increase from the 20th century to date have not always been welcomed with consistently favorable views.

Irwin (2011, 195–200) summarizes various Japanese public opinion polls on attitudes toward loanwords (not limiting to a specific area like food) that were conducted from the late 20th century to the early 21st century by national agencies like Bunkachō Bunkabu Kokugoka (BBK) "Agency for Cultural Affairs, Culture Bureau, National Language Division," Nippon Hōsō Kyōkai (NHK) "Japan Broadcasting Corporation," and National Institute for Japanese Language and Linguistics (NINJAL). The following points are relevant to our discussion.[18] First, when asked about desirability of loanwords, around 40 percent of the responses were "undesirable" and a little over 40 percent were "no opinion," suggesting that responders generally did not have favorable opinions about loanwords. Furthermore, the undesirable view was more likely held by older people while "desirable" and "no opinion" correlated with the younger age cohorts. Second, the "desirable" responders were asked to provide their reasons, by choosing one or more of the following five: (i) "Some things can only be expressed using a loanword"; (ii) "Loanwords are easy to understand"; (iii) "Japanese has always been borrowing words"; (iv) "Loanwords enrich Japanese language and culture"; and (v) "Loanwords have style." Overall, (i) was the strongest reason (nearly 70 percent), followed by (ii) (30 percent~40 percent), while (v) was not considered a common reason for the favorable view (around~less than 10 percent). Third, the reasons for the "undesirable" view were asked, based on the following five choices, again allowing for multiple responses: (i) "The intrinsic goodness of Japanese is being lost"; (ii) "Loanwords are hard to understand"; (iii) "Japanese language and culture become corrupted"; (iv) "Using loanwords just seems like posing"; and (v) "I hate loanwords." Commonly selected were (i) (hovering around 50 percent) and (ii) (around 55 percent on average), while each of (iii) and (iv) was at around the 30 percent mark. Finally, respondents were asked which topic or subject areas pose serious problems with comprehending loanwords. They recognize computer and technology, government and economics, and health and welfare as more problematic than fashion, music, sports, and cuisine.

In interpreting these results in the context of our current discussion, three relevant points seem to me to emerge. First, perceptions regarding desirability of loanwords have strong correlations with the age factor: the older the respondents, the less accepting they are of loanwords. Arguably, progressive internationalization, more exposure to foreign languages and cultural artifacts, and their easier access through on-site experiences and through a wider range of social media have contributed to paving a steady path to a perception that loanwords are no longer distant and belonging to "others." Not only the "desirable" view but particularly the "no opinion" responses supported by the younger cohort seem to suggest that they regard loanwords as a regular matter rather than a cause for concerns.

Second, regarding the reasons for the "desirable" view, (i) ("Some things can only be expressed using a loanword") corresponds to the necessity factor underlining lexical borrowing, motivated for appropriating a new concept (Haspelmath 2001). In contrast, the reason for the "desirable" view under (v) ("Loanwords have style"; around~less than 10 percent) and the reason for the "undesirable" view under (iv) ("Using loanwords just seems like posing"; around 30 percent) address the prestige aspect of motivating loanwords. The polls show that necessity to name something new is a dominating reason for a favorable perception of loanwords whereas prestige or sophisticated airs—a nuance associated with them—is not thought to be a value of significance. It is indicative that loanwords are perceived to be a linguistic tool of practical function, instead of a label that signals some sociocultural or socioeconomic standing.

Third, loanwords in cuisine are not viewed as overly difficult to understand. Loanwords related to consumption and preparation of food do not pose a serious hindrance in communication, but instead are considered more easily reachable and manageable. On the one hand, the nationalistic attitude toward loanwords parallel to Quebec's Pastagate is indeed detectable: "[t]he intrinsic goodness of Japanese is being lost" (around 50%) and "Japanese language and culture become corrupted" (30%) are thought to be primary reasons that loanwords are "undesirable." On the other hand, putting together the three points above, Japanese society, which continues to experience culinary globalization, seems to take the predominant attitude that loanwords are a matter of functional necessity and convenience to the extent that what loanwords name are transparent to language users. And, crucial to aiding linguistic transparency seems to be the prevalent use of visuals made increasing available, thanks to a wide variety of media and advancement of technology. It makes sense, then, that younger generations are leading in the favorable and pragmatic attitude toward food-related loanwords given their propensity to become acclimated to media and technology.

We can assess likely manifestations of the observations made thus far by examining loanword use in restaurant menus in Japan. To that end, I compare menus of two restaurants: a popular chain family restaurant, Coco's Restaurant, and a high-end Italian restaurant in Tokyo, Ristorante Acqua Pazza.[19] Coco's offers a wide spectrum of dishes of both the Japanese-style and the Western-style. Spaghetti and pizza items obviously include loanwords originating from Italian: *supagetti* "spaghetti," *peperonchīno* "pepperoncino, red pepper," *guranapadano chīzu* "Grana Padano cheese," *mottsarera* "mozzerella cheese," *boronēze* "Bolognese," *gorugonzōra* "gorgonzola cheese," and *pittsa marugerīta* "pizza margarita." Loanwords whose origins are other than Italian include: *rōsuto chikin* "roasted chicken," *chedā chīzu* "cheddar cheese," *gārikku batā* "garlic butter," *karibu chikin janbaraya* "Caribbean chicken Jambalaya," *shīzā sarada* "caesar salad," *kariforunia tako sarada* "California taco salad," *ahījo* "(small) garlic; a dish cooked in garlic oil," *kesadīya* "quesadilla," *kōn sūpu* "corn soup," *toripuru konbo ranchi* "triple combo lunch," *foagura* "foie gras," *toryuhu* "truffle," and *supaishī bīhu karē* "spicy beef curry." These names reflect sound adaptations and are all written in the katakana syllabary.

As expected of an Italian restaurant, the menu of Acqua Pazza is filled with loanwords from Italian, again phonetically adjusted and written in the katakana syllabary. The names of their savory offerings consist of: *akua pazza* "acqua pazza," *karupaccho* "carpaccio," *mottsarera chīzu* "mozzerella cheese," *kachokabarro chīzu* "caciocavallo cheese," *huritto* "fried," *bānya kauda* "bagna cauda," *ringuine* "linguine," *tariorīni* "tagliolini," *supagettīni* "spaghettini," *bongore bianko* "vongole bianco," *vapōre* [It. vapore] "steam," *ossobūko* "osso buco," *rizotto* "risotto," and s*arusa verude* "salsa verde, green sauce." The dessert section includes *jerāto* "gelato" and *doruche* [dolce] "sweet." The menu also informs us that *bejitarian* "vegetarian" and *vīgan* "vegan" are accommodated.

Both menus show quite an extensive list of loanwords, but Coco's menu shows a surprising number and range of loanwords, both conventionalized and relatively recent ones, especially given that it is a family restaurant. Items like *rōsuto chikin* "roasted chicken," *chedā chīzu* "cheddar cheese," *gārikku batā* "garlic butter," and *kōn sūpu* "corn soup" have been recognized for a long enough time to be conventionalized and hence transparent to a wide background of patrons. In contrast, other loanword names indicate international variety in cuisine types and ingredients that enter into Japanese menus more recently (perhaps within the past 50 years), gaining increasing familiarity: Italian[20] (e.g., *peperonchīno* "pepperoncino, red pepper," *mottsarera* "mozzerella cheese," *boronēze* "Bolognese," *gorugonzōra* "gorgonzola cheese"), Mexican and Spanish (e.g., *tako* "taco," *ahījo* "a dish cooked in garlic oil," *kesadīya* "quesadilla"), and Cajun cooking (e.g., *janbaraya* "Jambalaya"). Of further interest is that loanwords that are too specialized for a common use, such as *guranapadano chīzu* "Grana Padano cheese," or considered to be served at expensive restaurants, like *foagura* "foie gras" and *toryuhu* "truffle," show up on Coco's menu. The sustained use of the range of loanwords while simultaneously broadening their inventory at a popular family restaurant seems to point to a natural consequence of globalization of dining experience and a more casual and willing attitude toward it. As briefly mentioned above, restaurant menus, especially those at family restaurants, are frequently accompanied by photo presentations of their offerings. Even if (part of) loanword names of meals are not familiar to patrons, what they expect of the menu items are at least visually shown, if servers' verbal response is not available or informative enough. From the restaurant proprietor's viewpoint, however, the loanword references like *guranapadano chīzu* "Grana Padano cheese," *foagura* "foie gras," and *toryuhu* "truffle" may indeed be intended to impress customers, although it seems unlikely that a family restaurant does serve foie gras and truffle. In that sense, these loanwords in Coco's menu may take advantage of the prestige factor. At the same time, though, knowing that expensive ingredients like foie gras and truffles cannot be lavished, if offered at all, at family restaurants, the prestige associated with the borrowed names, especially coming from French, can possibly be interpreted more with humorous reactions to the false pretense.

Acqua Pazza, as expected, presents its menu containing loanwords that are largely from Italian. Characteristic of an Italian (i.e., ethnicity-specific) restaurant, narrowly defined references like *ringuine* "linguine," *tariorīni* "tagliolini," and *supagettīni* "spaghettini" are used, rather than bundling them under *pasuta* "pasta" or *supagetti* "spaghetti." Furthermore, *kachokabarro chīzu* "caciocavallo cheese," which would hardly be known to average Japanese diners, adds a local (of Italy) flare and authenticity as well as authority. The only borrowed word that seems to me to stand out in this menu is *vapōre* "steam," which is perhaps a term that is unlikely to be transparent to many, if not most, restaurant goers. It is interesting to find out that steam cooking meant by *vapore* in Italian is not a traditional method of cooking and has only recently been incorporated in Italian cookery.[21] Moreover, in terms of techniques, *vapore* does not seem to refer to any special process or utensil that would distinguish itself from the standard steaming. Steaming is a process that is quite common in Japanese cooking, and the Japanese verb *musu* describing the same method frequently appears in food naming and culinary discourse. So, there is no particular reason that the loanword *vapōre* is mentioned for necessity or convenience in Acqua Pazza's menu. Instead, it illustrates an instance where prestige supersedes necessity, although in this case, the prestige is only perceptual to augment the Italian-ness of the restaurant.

From the orthographical perspective, Acqua Pazza's menu demonstrates a combination of conservative and innovative transcriptions. As I have reviewed in the previous section, the pronunciation of [v] in a donor language is adapted to [b] in Japanese to compensate for the phonetic differences. However, the adapted pronunciation of [b] for [v] by Japanese speakers can be transcribed in two different ways: one reflecting [b] and the other [v] (e.g., *benisu*ベニス vs. ヴェニス "Venice," *baiorin*バイオリン vs. ヴァイオリン "violin"), although the former has been recommended by the government since the mid-20th century. According to Sakamoto (2002), who surveyed the transcriptions of loanwords corresponding to [b] and [v], newspapers primarily use the conservative pattern reflecting [b], while internet writings, as in Yahoo and Google, adopt both, with an approximately equal split. Acqua Pazza's menu shows both patterns: *bongore*ボンゴレ "vongole" and *bejitarian*ベジタリアン "vegetarian" corresponding to [b]; and *vapōre* ヴァポーレ [vapore] "steam," *vīgan*ヴィーガン "vegan," and *verude*ヴェルデ [verde] "green" assume the underlying [v]. A quick online search for these loanwords indicates that both orthographic patterns are represented for "vongole," "verde," and "vegan" but only the [b] pattern for "vegetarian" and "vapore." The orthographic option of the ヴ-[v] arguably gives the impression or perception related to higher education or linguistic sophistication. Whether intentional or not, the use of the more progressive orthography is in tandem with the high-end outlook and a cosmopolitan air that the restaurant projects. As for the [b] pattern for "vongole" (ボンゴレ) and "vegetarian" (ベジタリアン), they are listed in general Japanese dictionaries, which suggests that their borrowing took place earlier than the other words discussed here. As such, they are fairly solidly conventionalized with the conservative orthography. All in all, maintaining the more conservative orthography does not change the general image of the restaurant.

In conclusion, as the examination in this chapter evinces, the number, type, and range of loanwords are likely to increase commensurate with the rate at which the world's cuisines influence Japanese food culture. As a consequence, the deluge of loanwords in foodways will no doubt continue. The loanword phenomenon is not simply a linguistic matter but rather speaks much to the ways in which the society and the people think about themselves and others. Thus, the study of loanwords in foodways sheds interesting light to how the society evaluates and re-evaluates the new in relation to what is already in place.

NOTES

1. The topic of authenticity in foodways has been rigorously and contentiously debated. For instance, the term "authenticity" itself is extremely difficult to define since what is authentic varies widely depending on an individual's perspectives as well as sociocultural background (Abarca 2004; Pilcher 2012; Portnoy 2015, 2017). A more recent view of authenticity as it pertains to cuisines is insightfully expressed by Jonathan Gold, a food critic who received the Pulitzer Prize in 2007. Asked in an interview about Mexican restaurants in West Los Angeles, Portnoy (2017) reports, Gold "did not consider these places to be inauthentic. Instead, he argued that they are authentic representations of what Mexican food has evolved into over centuries of Mexican presence in Southern California."

2. A coda nasal and a geminate consonant correspond respectively to the kana syllabary of 「ん・ン」 and 「っ・ッ」.

3. The source word *roast* surfaces as two loanword pronunciations, [ro:su] and [ro:suto], and they are assigned specific meanings of "sirloin" and "roast meat," respectively. I will discuss more instances of this type of doublets later.

4. The same site (cookpad.com) even includes the recipe name, *yude-tamago boirudo eggu* "boiled egg boiled egg," which seems to go overboard in the use of loanwords for recipe names, especially since the recipe is simply about boiling eggs.

One example of *boirudo* other than *boirudo eggu* is *boirudo fisshi* "boiled fish," as it is referred to in Gensai Murai's *Shokudōraku*, which was a newspaper serial published in *Hōchi Newspaper* for a year starting in 1903. There are several references to

36   *Chapter Two*

names of Western cuisines, and some of the loanwords in this serialized novel show spellings (in the katakana syllabary) that are different from their contemporary equivalents. For instance, *fisshi* "fish" in *Shokudōraku* corresponds to *fisshu* in its modern-day form. Other examples include *potēto* (not *poteto*) "potato," *kahē kēki* (not *kōhī kēki*) "coffee cake," and *korun stacchi* (not *kōn sutāchi*) "cornstarch." Exact accounts for these differences are not obvious to me, but it could be possible that Western-style cuisines and food items were introduced to Meiji Japan (1868–1912), and the earlier spellings may reflect aural perceptions of the source words rather than being based on their orthography in the donor language(s). Smith (2006) discusses "doublet" forms of loanwords resulting from perception-based and orthography-based borrowing.

    5. https://www.nakamuraya.co.jp/pavilion/products/pro_001.html.

    6. According to Irwin (2011), narrowing is more commonly observed in semantic shift of loanwords.

    7. It seems to me, furthermore, that a free-standing *raisu*—as opposed to compounds with it—mostly, if not always, means cooked white rice.

    8. The only exception to this may be *ebi-katsu* "shrimp cutlet." However, virtually all the recipes for *ebi-katsu* I have found in Japanese instruct us to process shrimp by butterflying it, or by mixing chopped shrimp with other ingredients including a binding agent. What is known as *ebi-hurai*, in contrast, preserves the whole deveined shrimp throughout the cooking process.

    9. The franchise additionally sells maccha powder sticks separately under the name *Starbucks VIA Matcha*.

    10. Thomason (2001) summarizes the extent of lexical borrowing into a borrowing scale, which shows how the degree of contact (casual, slightly more intense, more intense, intense), the scale of lexical borrowing, and the borrowers' linguistic and social factors correspond to each other. Based on her borrowing scale, Irwin (2006) identifies the degree of contact applicable to Japanese as the "slightly more intense" or the "more intense" category. According to this estimate, the scale of lexical borrowing for Japanese is expected to extend to all vocabulary types.

    11. The data presented in (7–10) are collected from the Cookpad website (https://cookpad.com) to maintain the same data source as Shimada and Nagano's. However, similar types of samples are found in other online recipe sites that are affiliated with large food corporations like Ajinomoto and Kikkoman (e.g., https://park.ajinomoto.co.jp; https://www.kikkoman.co.jp/index.html).

    12. Shimada and Nagano (2018) analyze that *on* as a loanword is used on par with Japanese deverbal nouns like *nose* "put on," without "affect[ing] the syntax of Japanese." According to this analysis, *shichū on raisu* in (7a) would be parallel to *shichū-nose raisu* [stew-put.on rice]. Their analysis does not distinguish between the English pattern in (7) and (9) and the unusual pattern in (8) and (10). Based on a similar example they provide, *kurogoma-dōhu on edamame* in (9a) would be *edamame-nose kurogoma-dōhu* [edamame-put.on black sesame tofu]. Note that their analysis of *shichū on raisu* in (7a) maintains the English word order while that of *kurogoma-dōhu on edamame* in (9a) shows a rearranged word order. Shimada and Nagano offer no clear criterion as to when the word order of a sequence remains intact and when it

undergoes the adjustment. They further claim that "[b]orrowed *in*, not borrowed *on*, can behave like an original preposition, participating in modifying a preceding noun." It is not clear to me which pattern they are commenting on, but contrary to what they say, the examples in (7–10) indeed suggest that *on* and *in* as loanwords demonstrate non-uniform patterns, sometimes following the English word order and sometimes showing an innovative order.

13. One outlier to these observations is *chō-kurīmī! on tama pote-sara* 超クリーミー！オンたまポテサラ [super-creamy on egg potato-salad] "super-creamy! potato salad topped with an egg [fried, sunny-side up]" (https://cookpad.com/recipe/4380911). Not only the *on tama pote-sara* portion of this name starts with the loanword preposition *on*, but the type of the food appears at the end of the phrase.

14. Borrowing of prepositions is not limited to *on* and *in*, as is indicated by Shimada and Nagano's discussion of *with* in their analysis. Nor is it restricted to English. I find examples of French *avec* "with" (phonologically adapted in Japanese as *abekku* when pronounced or written in the Japanese syllabary) incorporated in recipe names like *aojiru-de tōnyū mushi-pan avec mugi-choko* [chlorophyll.juice-with soy.milk steamed-bun avec barley-chocolate] "soy milk steamed bun with chlorophyll juice (powder) and chocolate-coated barley (in it)" (https://cookpad.com/recipe/2259473). The word order regarding the preposition *avec* maintains that of French.

15. Outside food-related areas, the word formation by abbreviation of Romanized Japanese words is found in NHK [=nippon hōsō kyōkai] "Japan broadcasting company," but more examples are found in popular culture. For instance, KY [=kūki yomenai "air cannot.read"] "cannot read the room" (i.e., unable to figure out what is going on) and JK [=joshi kōkōsei "female high.school.student"] "female high school student" are prevalent among younger language users.

16. The Cookpad provides a user-friendly recipe site. It offers an extensive range of recipes with affordable ingredients and cooking procedures that are easy to follow.

17. In contrast, aspects of major identity include those like race, gender, and sexual preferences (Lakoff 2006, 143).

18. Loanwords in these polls are meant to include not only words that have been borrowed from source languages, but also those whose meanings have been adapted so much so that they do not correspond to the original meanings in source languages.

19. I consulted the menus of these two restaurants at: https://www.cocos-jpn.co.jp/menu/index.html and https://acqua-pazza.jp/menu/. Typical of a family restaurant, Coco's offerings are economical: no dish costs more than $15, and the majority of their main meals are available for less than $10. At Ristorante Acqua Pazza, the prices of a la carte dishes range roughly from $15 for an appetizer dish (antipasto) to $50 for a meat dish. The restaurant also offers a 6-course lunch and a 6-course dinner, starting at around $100 and $130, respectively. Based on this price information, I consider Ristorante Acqua Pazza to be a "high-end" restaurant.

20. Italian food has been popular, and loanwords like *supagetti* "spaghetti," *pasuta* "pasta," *lazania* "lasagna," and *piza* "pizza" already are widely recognized and used. For *piza* (ピザ), the pronunciation of [pittsa] and its corresponding orthography (ピッツア) reflect a more recent effort to be closer to the source word. On the Coco's menu

I consulted, the former ([piza] ピザ) appears as a category under the heading of *piza/saido-menyū* [pizza side-menu] "pizza/sides," while the latter ([pittsa] ピッツァ) is used as part of individual food items, as in *mīto pittsa* "meat pizza."

21. At least two online sources confirm this information, https://memoriediangelina.com/glossary/ and http://passionepercucina.blogspot.com/2013/01/italian-cooking-terms-z.html.

Chapter Three

Mimetics

The most rudimentary and straightforward vocabulary items in English/Japanese to describe gustatory tastes are probably *sweet/amai, sour/suppai, salty/shoppai~shiokarai, bitter/nigai,* and *umami* (savory). To these, some would add *pungent/karai* and *astringent/shibui*. But, our food culture offers far richer experiences than what these words can manage to cover. In the highly informative society we live in, communicating our gustatory, culinary, and alimentary knowledge among one another in an effectual manner is not only necessary but pleasurable, whether the communication be of personal or commercial motivation. We casually exchange "food diaries" with friends, families, and even strangers, in person as well as through multiple forms of media including food blogs and Instagram. In so doing, our intention is to express in detail our excitement and disappointment and to share with others our food encounters as real as possible. In business settings (e.g., restaurants, manufactured products, cookbooks and recipes), informing and tempting are crucial to success in sales, and ingenuity in linguistic manipulation contributes much to achieving those goals (Zwicky and Zwicky 1980). Whatever food scenes might surround us, we take advantage of the expressive linguistic gears which language users deploy for creative and communicative food discourse, despite the apparent dearth of descriptive vocabulary items noted above.

Information regarding foods and food-related activities runs the gamut from ingredients to attributive tastes, and research has shown that the nature of information has a great influence on people's experience in foodways. Zwicky and Zwicky's (1980) examination of restaurant menus illustrates how "tasty adjectives" including *rich, crisp, special, generous, natural,* and *zesty* are used to tempt patrons. Wansink et al.'s (2005) study further demonstrates that food names in cafeteria menus with adjectives and other descriptors (in italics) like "*Traditional Cajun* Red Beans & Rice," "*Succulent Italian*

Seafood Filet," "*Tender* Grilled Chicken," "*Homestyle* Chicken Parmesan," "*Satin* Chocolate Pudding," and "*Grandma's* Zucchini Cookies" generated from patrons more positive evaluations about food tastes as well as overall eating experiences than the identical names without the descriptive expressions. On the other hand, inclusion of a particular ingredient like soy ("contains 10g of soy protein" vs. "contains 10g of protein") has been found to influence the taste negatively (Wansink et al. 2000). These studies point to a propensity that consumers and patrons have in order to form particular images about food items familiar to them.

One such image that has been investigated from a cross-disciplinary perspective is that of brand names. The research reported in Allison and Uhl (1964) and Hoyer and Brown (1990), for instance, reveals that brand labels positively bias the taste. Allison and Uhl show that while the beer drinkers in a blind comparison test could not identify the brand of beer they customarily consume, the rating that they give to their brands increased once the names were identified. In similar findings with peanut butter, Hoyer and Brown explain that even when a known brand of peanut butter is judged to have a lower quality, the participants of the study nevertheless chose the known brand over a higher-quality, unknown brand. These investigations suggest the power of brand names and brand images on people's perceived sense of taste. They further shed interesting light on the type of words that serve as an appealing or repelling factor in naming food-related products.

Equally relevant to understanding the relationship between cognition (word) and perception (taste) is the way in which verbal descriptions are framed. For example, the same ground beef can be described as either "75% lean" or "25% fat," but the subjects of Levin's (1987) study (also Levin et al. 1985) rated the "75% lean" meat more favorably than the "25% fat" meat in leanness, quality, greasiness (i.e., less greasy), and good taste. Thus, the same product can give consumers perceived differences depending on descriptive frames—percent-lean vs. percent-fat—in which the target object is presented to the audience. The follow-up experiment of Levin and Gaeth (1988) replicated Levin's study with an additional sampling session. Verifying the earlier result, they add that the presentation of the attributive information of percentage-lean vs. percentage-fat before sampling influenced the subjects' evaluation more robustly than a post-sampling presentation of the information. Nevertheless, they also comment that the bias triggered by the attribute labeling (i.e., the framing influence) is reduced when the subjects actually sampled the meat. Although this last point may come intuitively as no surprise, it still confirms the undeniable relevance of direct personal experience that taste sampling offers in making judgments about one's sensory reactions.

Thus far, we have been largely focusing on effects that cognitive input (e.g., words and phrases) has on our sense of taste. But, as it is frequently pointed out, taste can be influenced by other senses or linguistic descriptors referring to other senses. The relation between smell and taste, for instance, has been a well-established link. Color, belonging to the vision sense, has also been demonstrated to influence taste perceptions in taste discrimination tests (e.g., Hoegg and Alba 2007). Given that preparation and consumption of food is indeed a multi-sensory experience, then, our judgments and evaluations pertinent to food are likely to be controlled or aided by interactions of sensory reactions. In explaining the "sensuality of products" and the relevance of considering sensory and sensual appeal in the field of marketing, Krishna (2010) states, "[o]ur senses being primal, we react immediately and subconsciously to them, unlike to a brand name or an attribute, both of which are learned" (p. 4), and "our senses are innately linked to our perception of products and services" (p. 2)[1] Under this general premise, it has been shown that taste perceptions are robustly affected in advertisements by evoking multiple senses as opposed to a single sense (e.g., Elder and Krishna 2010).

Consolidating all these research findings, we arrive at three power structures that play a significant role in communicating about food: power of personal gustatory experience (e.g., sampling, direct stimulus of taste perception), power of words (e.g., "tasty adjectives," brand names, framing effects), and power of sensual/sensory appeal (e.g., sensory marketing, single- and multi-sensory effects on taste). Food experience amounts to visceral reactions to the sensate and affective. Is there any mechanism in language that makes it possible for us to express these reactions as if it were a surrogate that subsumes the three powers? I argue that mimetics, richly available in Japanese, are a linguistic tool that plays just such a role. One of the characteristics that uncouples the mimetic vocabulary from the non-mimetic prosaic word class is its sensory and sensual orientation. As such, mimetic words appeal to our senses and affects. In communicating about food and food-related activities, they are able to present vivid images that are coalesced around perceptual reactions, whether they be shape, color, texture, smell, sound, or of course taste. A powerful fountain of expressiveness, mimetics are an efficacious linguistic means to take the language user to a virtual dining or cooking experience without the actual gustatory or culinary undertaking. In that light, the mimetic vocabulary makes an enormous contribution to a wide range of food discourse.

I will spend this chapter on the effectiveness of mimetics in various aspects of communication around food, but sufficient for now is a brief presentation of (1), which is an advertisement slogan created by Osaka Kintetsu Railway (Otsubo 1989). "Q" stands for a geminate, i.e., part of a long consonant identical with the one immediately following it.[2] For Romanized transliterations of mimetic words are indicated by repeated vowels rather than [:] in this chapter.

(1) ジューッときたら、グイッと行きたいね

JuuQ-to　　　　　kitara,　　　　**guiQ**-to　　　　　iki-tai-ne.
mimetic-quotative　when came　*mimetic*-quotative　go-want-particle

"When it goes 'juuQ,' I want to go 'guiQ.'"

The bold-faced words in (1), *juuQ* and *guiQ*, are mimetics. The sentence may sound cryptic, but any adult Japanese would understand what it is all about; and Japanese speakers reach a uniform interpretation. Otsubo (1989) explains that (1) corresponds to its fuller, less cryptic, version, ジューッと肉が焼けて来たら、グイッと飲みたい "When the meat is getting cooked, 'juuQ,' I want to drink (beer), 'guiQ.'" In this longer version, contextually clearer verbs are provided (i.e., *yaku* "cook, roast" and *nomu* "drink") along with an intended object (i.e., *niku* "meat"). The first mimetic *juuQ* stands for the sound of cooking meat as it sizzles, and importantly, it is the image of meat rather than that of seafood or vegetables that the mimetic evokes. Furthermore, the sound connects to a narrower set of cooking methods that induce dripping fat, such as grilling and griddling with a direct fire. The direct contact of meat fat and fire naturally produces smoke and smell. So, the single word of *juuQ*, without any verbal indication to identify the type of activity, generates the image of sizzling meat while simultaneously appealing to the domains of vision, audition, and olfaction.

As for *guiQ*, it depicts the manner of drinking liquid quickly and perhaps audibly or in a large amount, paralleling the English *gulp* as opposed to *sip*. Particularly ensuing the scene of sizzling meat set up by *juuQ*, the liquid is an alcoholic beverage, beer being the most fitting. Moreover, the use of direct fire for cooking meat, consumption of meat, and beer drinking are all gendered as males. Putting together all the images that these two individual mimetic words evoke in this context, it is surmised that the line in (1) is part of a dialogue uttered by a male speaker to another. Most importantly, as elliptical as it is, (1) does not merely sends us an explicit overall idea about the pairing of sizzling meat and beer consumption. It also affords a virtual experience of reliving or imagining a scene filled with multi-sensory stimuli that are enacted by these two mimetic words. So, the mimetic vocabulary can carry out the three powers mentioned above in a concise individual word form. This is why mimetics serve as an expedient linguistic tool for speaking of visceral experiences like taste of food.

Below, I shall begin by explaining the linguistic nature of the mimetic word class, and then illustrate in detail the roles that mimetics play in food discourse from various perspectives. Samples of mimetics for the expository purpose are primarily drawn from the language—both oral and written—used for descriptions and evaluations of food taste and for cooking instructions and commentaries. However, given that communication is the broader theme of this book, I shall also discuss ways in which mimetics participate in advertisements that extend to product names and catchphrases.

1 THE SEMANTIC NATURE OF THE MIMETIC VOCABULARY

The mimetic vocabulary constitutes an important word class in the Japanese lexicon, and its membership is large. Similar types of vocabulary in other languages of the world have been described and analyzed (e.g., Basque, Chichewa, Finnish, Korean, Pacho, Quechua, Tamil, and Turkish) under the terms like ideophones, onomatopoeia, and expressives. As in these languages, Japanese mimetics have been discussed from a variety of disciplinary perspectives, attesting to their relevance to a wide range of scholarly investigations. The extent of rigorous linguistic examinations is reflected by the rich literature on the topic (e.g., Hamano 1986, 1998; Kakehi and Tamori 1993; Kita 1997; Tamori and Schourup 1999; Nasu 2002; Akita 2009). For a terminological distinction, I will use "prosaic" to refer to the vocabulary that is not mimetics.

Mimetic words in Japanese are generally divided into two classes, *giongo* "onomatopoeia" and *gitaigo* "mimesis," on semantic grounds. However, to give a bit finer cataloging for exposition, I follow Martin (1987), Shibatani (1990), and Akita (2009), among others, in adopting the three-way distinction: phonomimes (*giseigo* 擬声語/*giongo* 擬音語), phenomimes (*gitaigo* 擬態語), and psychomimes (*gijōgo* 擬情語). Phonomimes overlap with what is known under the term onomatopoeia. They imitate audible sounds including those made by animate and inanimate beings as well as those that emerge in surroundings. Phenomimes, which have the largest membership in Japanese mimetics, depict static and dynamic conditions and manner (e.g., states of natural surroundings, manner of human actions). Psychomimes symbolize emotions, feelings, and pains. Representative examples in (2) are taken from Akita (2009, 12–13) with minor changes in transcriptions and English translations. As before, I use "Q" to represent a geminate consonant. Additionally, "N" stands for a coda (i.e., syllable-final) consonant.[3]

(2) a. Phonomimes: bakiQ "crack," buubuu "oink-oink," gorogoro "thunder," kotoN "plonk," kusukusu "chuckle," putsuQ "snap," shuQ "swish," chariN "clink," waNwaN "bow wow," doshiN "thud"

b. Phenomimes: shiQtori "moist," niyari "grinning," nebaneba "sticky," chokomaka "bustling restlessly," koNgari "toasted lightly brown," koNmori "swelling," pikaQ "shining," poiQ "tossing," subesube "smooth," suQkari "completely," jirori "staring sharply," zuraQ "lined up"

c. Psychomimes: biQkuri "surprised," gaQkari "disappointed," haQ "noticing," kurakura "dizzy," puNpuN "smelling," ukiuki "feeling happy and lighthearted," zoQ "fearful," zukiQ "feeling one's head/tooth throb"

While there are several morphological patterns in which mimetic words frequently appear, such as reduplicated forms and the CVCVQ pattern, the variety of formal representations that the examples in (2) demonstrate indicates that the mimetic vocabulary cannot be defined exclusively by its formal properties. (cf. Akita 2009)

There are several linguistic characteristics that separate mimetics from prosaic words. Although more will be mentioned in the discussions to follow, I single out the semantic differences. Semantic characterizations of mimetics and their equivalents in other languages that researchers have tried to capture coalesce to their vividness of sensual images that mimetics evoke. This aspect sharply distinguishes mimetics from what Diffloth (1972) calls the "cognitive mode of meaning" in characterizing prosaic words. Comparing the rhetorical power of ideophones (i.e., mimetic equivalents) to a bland food taste, Samarin (1970, 157) comments, ". . . take them [=ideophones] out, and the narration becomes as tasteless as oatmeal without salt." Voelts and Kilian-Hatz (2001) further generalize the semantic nature of mimetics and ideophones into a "special dramaturgic function," which is to "simulate an event, and emotion, a perception through language" (p. 3).

A little more formally, Kita (1997) articulates the semantic difference in terms of two distinct dimensions to which mimetic and prosaic words belong: the affecto-imagistic dimension for mimetics and the analytical dimension for prosaic words. Kita's definitions of the two dimensions are in (3).

(3) a. Affecto-imagistic dimension: the level at which language has direct contact with sensory, motor, and affective information (Kita 1997, 380)

b. Analytical dimension: the level of decompositional and hierarchical representation in terms of decontextualized semantic partials (Ibid., 409)

Kita's analytical dimension in (3b) is in tandem with Diffloth's characterization of prosaic words as the cognitive mode of meaning in viewing that what is represented by a prosaic word becomes rationalized into a concept. In contrast, the affecto-imagistic dimension in (3a) and other researchers' insight into the semantic function of mimetics come together on their direct association with the sensate and affects. Indeed, mimetics and prosaic words are both linguistic symbols. Yet, mimetics present the sensate and affects without the mediation of the rationalization process. Mimetics are immediate (i.e., im-mediate, in the sense of Armstrong [1975]) presentations of what is perceived, and consequently, their "meanings" are visceral images that give the language user the "in-it" feeling, to borrow the term in Feld (1988). That is, those images bring forward the feeling as if one were living *in* the very sensual and affective experience. In contrast, prosaic words represent (i.e., re-present) the perceived in the form of rationalized concepts by which one can speak *of* the experience. The cognitive mode of meaning in Diffloth's term, thus, equates to the "of-it" notion (as opposed to "in-it" feeling) of what is perceived. As I argued elsewhere (Tsujimura 2022a), the two sets of pairing, presentation-immediation-"in-it" vs. representation-mediation-"of it," I believe, shed light on the essential semantic difference between the mimetic and prosaic vocabulary.[4]

I should hasten to add that I am not claiming prosaic words cannot achieve the same level of direct, sensual reactions. As Lodge (1990) argues, verbal (i.e., prosaic) narratives can successfully create "the sense of reality in fiction, the illusion of access to the reality of personal experience" (p. 144). Metaphors, for one, are an effective force to that end, and are certainly an operational rhetorical device in a variety of Japanese communication, including food discourse. Although I have focused on contrastive semantic features between mimetic and prosaic words, it should be reminded that both classes of vocabulary are necessary in communication, but their contributions are different. Mimetics speak of senses whereas prosaic words speak of ideas/concepts. That said, an uncontested advantage of mimetics over prosaic words is that a single mimetic word is able to attain a very robust vivacity and the "in-it" feeling, whereas the same degree of rhetorical effectiveness is usually reached by multiple prosaic expressions that consist of words and phrases.

To appreciate the vivacity that individual mimetics exude, we may draw an example from product names, which aim at instant, intuitive appeal to consumers as a marketing strategy. The (a) examples in (4–10) are names of food products with mimetics, in bold, discussed in Tamori (2002, 19–21; my translation), whereas in (b) I provide prosaic alternatives to the mimetic words in the corresponding (a) examples.

(4) a. **gizagiza**-potato (potato chips)
[mimetic]-potato
"potato chips with ridges"

b. nokogiri-no ha-no yōna potato
saw-GEN teeth-GEN like potato
"potato chips like the teeth of a saw [=serrated]"

(5) a. **korokoro**-kōya (cubed dehydrated tofu)
    [mimetic]-dehydrated.tofu (*kōya-dōhu*)
    "cubed dehydrated tofu"

   b. chīsai   saikoro-no   yōna   kōya
      small   dice-GEN   like   dehydrated.tofu
      "dehydrated tofu like small dice"

(6) a. **hokuhoku**-masshupoteto (potato salad)
    [mimetic]-mashed.potato
    "warm, soft, and flaky mashed potato (salad)"

   b. atatakaku   yawarakaku   hukasitate-no   masshupoteto
      warm   soft   just.steamed-GEN   mashed.potato
      "mashed potato (salad) made of warm, soft potatoes that have just been steamed"

(7) a. **karikari**-okoshi (snack for squirrels and hamsters)
    [mimetic]-millet.and.rice.cracker
    "crisp millet and rice cracker"

   b. katai mono-o   kamikudaku toki-no   yōna   oto-ga   suru
      hard thing-ACC   crunch   when-GEN   like   sound-NOM   make
      okoshi
      millet.and.rice.cracker
      "millet and rice cracker that makes sounds like when you crunch a hard thing"

(8) a. **sukusuku**-kizzu-aisu (ice cream)
    [mimetic]-kids'-ice.cream
    "ice cream for kids that promotes (kids') rapid growth"

   b. genki-yoku   seichō-suru   yōna   kizzu-aisu
      healthy-well   grow   like   kids'-ice.cream
      "ice cream for kids that makes them grow healthy if they eat it"

(9) a. **gungun**-sōsēji
    [mimetic]-(processed).sausage
    "(processed) sausage that promotes (children's) rapid growth"

   b. (taberuto)   hayaku   genki-yoku   seichō-suru   sōsēji
      (if eat)   fast   health-well   grow   (processed).sausage
      "(processed) sausage that will make you grow and become healthy if you eat it"

(10) a. **sarasara**-su · su · su (fruit juice with natural black vinegar)
     [mimetic]-vinegar · vinegar · vinegar
     "vinegar that helps smooth blood flow"

b. (chi-ga)   yodominaku nagareru yōni-naru su・su・su
   (blood-NOM) smoothly   flow   begin.to vinegar・vinegar・vinegar
   "vinegar (in the fruit juice) that makes the blood begin to flow smoothly"

Admittedly, in my effort to find expressions as close in meaning to the mimetics as possible, I ended up resorting to frequent similes with *yōna/yōni* "like," as in (4b, 5b, 7b, 8b, 10b). Furthermore, in all the pairings, the advertising phrases in (b) are much longer, and perhaps wordy, than those with mimetics in the (a) variants. It should be clear that mimetics can afford a high degree of expressiveness despite the parsimony of words. This is an ideal for creating catchy and impactful product names.

The mimetics in the (a) examples of (4–6) depict static states of the products, while those in (7–10) evoke images of dynamic actions and events. The mimetic *gizagiza* in (4a) and *korokoro* in (5a) activate the vision sense, immediately presenting a serrated shape of potato chips and a small square shape of dehydrated tofu pieces, respectively. The visual appeal triggered by the mimetics gives rise to those graphic images. The similes *nokogiri-no ha-no yōna* "like the teeth of a saw" in (4b) and *chīsai saikoro-no yōna* "like small dice" in (5b) figuratively, through analogy, associate the shape of potato chips with the serration of a saw and with the shape of dice. The association is mediated by prosaic references to the teeth of a saw and small dice, whose attributive physical appearances verbally describe potato chips and tofu pieces. The mimetic *hokuhoku* in (6a) typically connects with just cooked (and thus warm), flaky food items like potatoes, pumpkins, and chestnuts. In this example, the mimetic evokes an image of freshly cooked potatoes as a major ingredient of a potato salad product. The warmth, softness, and flakiness are felt through the vision and touch (texture) sensations that *hokuhoku* appeals to. Note also that these visual and tactile images apply also to the state of potatoes during the cooking process: the flakiness, for example, depicts the texture observed upon mashing still warm potatoes that have just been cooked. In the prosaic alternative in (6b), each of these enticing traits is literally spelled out.

The example in (7a), *karikari*, depicts the sound that domestic squirrels and hamsters as pets make when they crush the snack with their teeth. Along with the crunchy sound, the mimetic refers to a solid and dry texture. The cross-modal references as a highlighted selling point of the millet and rice cracker for small pets readily connect to people's experiences with the crispiness of rice crackers, for which we envisage the same sound and texture. In (7b), the exact type of sound and texture that *karikari* can identify in one word has to be explained in simple but multiple words. Even then, the prosaic description seems hardly able to produce the perceptual reactions that arise from *karikari*.

The mimetics in (8–10), repeated below, do not refer to intrinsic properties of the products that they characterize (i.e., ice cream, sausage, vinegar, fruit juice), but nevertheless focus on benefits to human growth and health that attract the consumers.

(8) a. **sukusuku**-kizzu-aisu (ice cream)
   [mimetic]-kids'-ice.cream
   "ice cream for kids that promotes (kids') rapid growth"

   b. genki-yoku   seichō-suru   yōna   kizzu-aisu
      healthy-well   grow   like   kids'-ice.cream
      "ice cream for kids that makes them grow healthy if you eat it"

(9) a. **gungun**-sōsēji
   [mimetic]-(processed).sausage
   "(processed) sausage that promotes (children's) rapid growth"

   b. (taberuto)   hayaku   genki-yoku   seichō-suru   sōsēji
      (if eat)   fast   health-well   grow   (processed).sausage
      "(processed) sausage that will make you grow and become healthy if you eat it"

(10) a. **sarasara**-su · su · su (fruit juice with natural black vinegar)
    [mimetic]-vinegar · vinegar · vinegar
    "vinegar that helps smooth blood flow"

    b. (chi-ga)   yodominaku nagareru yōni-naru su · su · su
       (blood-NOM)   smoothly   flow   begin.to   vinegar · vinegar · vinegar
       "vinegar (in the fruit juice) that makes the blood begin to flow smoothly"

Sukusuku in (8a) refers to a continuous healthy physical growth of humans, and *gungun* in (9a) broadly depicts a fast movement. The product *kizzu aisu* "ice cream for kids" is meant to attract children, and we can quickly infer the relation of *sukusuku* to the ice cream. That is, the product is marketed to enhance children's healthy physical development. The relation between *gungun* and sausage in (9a) is similarly conjectured. The fast speed evoked by the mimetic word connects the sausage to a dietary source of healthy growth for the youth. Again, the prosaic rephrasing in (8b) and (9b) conveys the same message, but the mimetics function as if they exert dynamic force in depicting the manner of children's growth. It may be likened to viewing human growth (e.g., in height) in a fast-forwarded film.

The name of the fruit juice in (10a) appears enigmatic since the product is not a vinegar but a fruit juice with black rice vinegar. The product name does not even include the word *jūsu* "juice." The amino acid in black rice vinegar is known to improve blood flow. The mimetic *sarasara* depicts a very smooth manner of water flow (or liquids of a similarly loose texture). As a modifier for vinegar, *sarasara* refers to the manner of unobstructed blood flow as a health benefit of an important ingredient (i.e., vinegar) of the juice product

The image of blood flowing freely without blood clots is a visual (and perhaps tactile) image to which *sarasara* evokes. The prosaic rephrasing in (10b) would inform consumers of this expected benefit in the verbal explanation. However, in (10a), in addition to the concise yet full vividness of the mimetic, the pulsing effect of *su-su-su* "vinegar-vinegar-vinegar" is especially effective in this example, supplementing the rhythm that the reduplicated mimetic form of *sarasara* carries. All in all, comparisons between product names with mimetics in the (a) versions and their (b) alternatives with prosaic explanations bring out the sharp differences in the extent of immediate sensual appeal and highlight the mimetics' role as the shortest channel of marketing messages to consumers.

In efforts to re-evaluate mimetics and ideophones in the world's languages, research has unearthed much linguistic evidence against approaches that decenter their linguistic significance, particularly in the past 40 years or so for Japanese. The frequency of their appearance in diverse discourse genres and their rhetorical role in expressive descriptions that are detected in food communication represent additional validation of the importance of mimetics. For example, Ikawa (1991) compiled words that express "sensation in food" (食感覚) from written sources such as a dictionary, a comic book with a food theme, and advertisements in newspapers and magazines. The collected words were classified according to the five senses, and in terms of their vocabulary type, they belong to all four vocabulary strata—native, Sino-Japanese, loanword, and mimetic. In the touch domain, in particular, 67 of the total 140 entries (47.86%) are mimetics. Their references range from temperature, hardness/softness, sliminess, dryness/wetness, to density, attesting to the wealth of fine-grained verbal expressions in food discourse. Also in oral discourse, Noda (2014) reports on a frequent use of mimetics to describe food texture in naturally occurring conversation.

To give another example, Hayakawa et al.'s (1997) investigation into the property of food sheds further light on multi-sensory deployment in characterizing "oiliness" in food. Among verbal descriptions of taste, the researchers of this study recognized that *aburakkoi* "oily, greasy," for instance, is one of the expressions whose exact meanings are not as clear-cut as it may seem. This is because lipid contents are not always a reliable gauge for food items that are considered *aburakkoi*. Hayakawa et al. asked 30 food researchers in a university lab to name verbal expressions that would describe foods or dishes that contain fats and oils. The list of collected words counts 28 in total, and half of them are mimetics. The descriptive expressions they collected, displayed in (11), are divided into the mimetic and prosaic classes. The numbers in parentheses to the right of the expressions indicate the ranking in frequency of the participants' answers. In (11a) -*shita* (the past tense form of the verb *suru* "do") suffixed to mimetics makes each expression refer to an "oily, greasy" state.

(11) a. Mimetic descriptors (15 words)

    betobeto-shita (1)   "sticky"
    gitogito-shita (3)   "(looking) greasy"
    kotteri-shita (4)   "rich"
    sakusaku-shita (5)   "crisp"
    karari-to-shita (7)   "crisp"
    nettori-shita (8)   "moist and sticky"
    shittori-shita (9)   "moist and soft"
    torori-to-shita (10)   "thick and creamy"
    giragira-shita (12)   "glittering"
    nurunuru-shita (14)   "slimy"
    karikari-shita (17)   "crisp and dry"
    baribari-shita (22)   "crisp and hard"
    nechinechi-shita (26)   "sticky and unpleasant"
    sappari-shita[5] (27)   "refreshing"
    tsurun-to-shita (28)   "smooth and slippery"

b. Prosaic descriptors (13 words)[6]

    aburakkoi [油っこい] (2)   "greasy, fatty, oily"
    aburakkoi [脂っこい] (6)   "greasy, fatty, oily"
    maroyaka-na (11)   "mild, mellow"
    shitsukoi (13)   "heavy"
    abura-ga notta (15)   "fatty and tasty"
    aburagitta (16)   "greasy, oily"
    kuchidoke-ga yoi (18)   "melt in the mouth"
    kōbashii (19)   "aromatic"
    nameraka-na (20)   "smooth"
    omoi (21)   "heavy"
    karui (23)   "light"
    kudoi (24)   "heavy, strong"
    koku-ga aru (25)   "having body"

Among the mimetic descriptors in (11a), *gitogito* "(looking) greasy" and *giragira* "glittering" are based on the vision sense; *sakusaku*, *karikari*, and *baribari* differ in nuanced crispiness that is attributed to an interaction of sound and texture (hearing and touch); and the remaining expressions refer to texture. Within the prosaic word list, *kuchidoke-ga yoi* "melt in the mouth" and *nameraka-na* "smooth" refer to mouth-feel; and *kōbashii* "aromatic" describes an olfactory feature. The way in which Japanese people describe greasy/oily/fatty foods in words as is demonstrated in this study illuminates their reliance on sensual reactions in expressing food taste and tastiness. The study lends support to the view that mimetic words pave a direct path to the networking of the senses in communicating gastronomic experiences. Research reports like these further confirm that mimetics are no less relevant than prosaic words as a linguistic tool that is convenient to deploy in speaking of taste.

In terms of their morphological features, mimetics surface in a few common patterns that correlate closely with their semantic characteristics that we have discussed thus far. Pairings like *pakuN~pakuQ(-to)~pakuri~pakupaku* and *dotaN~dotaQ(-to)~dotari~dotadota*, for example, share the base *paku* (generally for opening the mouth wide) and *dota* (generally for a loud falling or striking sound), based on which alternant forms are generated. Frequently occurring variant forms are recognized by the final -N, -Q, and *-ri* as well as reduplication, and subtle meaning differences are detected among them. Hamano (1998, 104–107) discusses the semantic distinctions among the four morphological patterns, as is summarized in (12). The semantic characterizations in (12) are somewhat vague, and clear distinctions between (12a) and (12c) are particularly difficult to articulate. Yet, Hamano demonstrates the delicate nuances by the examples in (13a–c); and I have added (13d) for a comparison. The English translations are expected to elucidate the delicate undertone in each morphological schema. The Romanization in (13) is slightly modified from Hamano's original.

(12) a. CVCVN: e.g., pakuN, dotaN, potaN
      the action involves elastic objects or is accompanied by a reverberation

   b. CVCVQ: e.g., pakuQ(-to), dotaQ(-to), potaQ(-to)
      the movement is carried out forcefully or vigorously in a single direction

   c. CVCV*ri*: e.g., pakuri, dotari, potari
      quiet ending of the movement

   d. CVCV-CVCV: e.g., pakupaku, dotadota, potapota
      continuous, stative, distributive, or repetitive movement

(13) a. Namida-no   tsubu-ga   **potaN**-to   tsukue-no   ue-ni   ochita.
        tear-GEN   drop-NOM   desk-GEN   top-to   fell
        "A *large teardrop fell* on the desk top."

   b. Namida-no   tsubu-ga   **potaQ**-to   tsukue-no   ue-ni   ochita.
      tear-GEN   drop-NOM   desk-GEN   top-to   fell
      "A *large teardrop fell* on the desk top and *splashed*."

   c. Namida-no   tsubu-ga   **potari**-to   tsukue-no   ue-ni   ochita.
      tear-GEN   drop-NOM   desk-GEN   top-to   fell
      "A *large teardrop fell and rolled to a stop* on the desk top."

d. Namida-no tsubu-ga   **potapota**-to tsukue-no   ue-ni   ochita.
   tear-GEN   drop-NOM   desk-GEN   top-to fell
   "*Large teardrops kept falling* on the desk top."

The fundamental semantic content shared by the base (e.g., *paku, dota, pota*) remains to be the core affecto-imagistic meaning across variants, while the frames in which the individual variants appear distinguish one nuance from another. Not all mimetics have a systematic set of variants signaled by -N, -Q, -*ri*, and reduplication, but when a base appears in at least two or more forms, the differences in nuance as Hamano lays out in (12) tend to be sustained. Supplied by this morphological machinery, the mimetic vocabulary can expand to furnish additional ways of expressing sensual and affective depictions in more granular detail.

Mimetics and ideophones in languages other than Japanese play an important role in the food domain as well. Strauss (2005) and Strauss et al. (2018) demonstrate that Korean ideophones/mimetics appear extensively in food commercials on television and online recipes. Ideophones that symbolize texture and touch qualities of food items include *pasak pasak (hata)* "(be) crunchy, crispy," *wulthung pwulthung (hata)* "(be) bumpy," and *chokchok (hata)* "(be) moist with dew, (be) slightly damp." They are illustrated by Strauss's examples of (14), taken from Strauss (2005, 1447).

(14) a. **pasak pasak** kephi sunayk
      "crunchy coffee snack" [Nongshim Coffee Snack]

   b. **wulthwung pwulthwung** kephi sunayk
      "the solid, bumpy coffee snack" [Nongshim Coffee Snack]

   c. **chokchok** hakey sapsita
      "let's live moistly" (i.e., with our thirsts quenched) [Kaul Taychwu Date Flavored Drink]

The ideophonic expressions in (15) are some of the terms used for cooking instructions that appear in Strauss et al.'s (2018, 239) data base of Korean online recipes along with their explanations of the terms.

(15) a. comwulcomwul: "squish squish" in squeezing ingredients to mix together with hands

   b. chwungchwung: "chop chop chop" – quickly and into small pieces

   c. phalphall: "the sight of liquid at full boil"

   d. thathathatha: "sound of hitting lightly; in cooking context, it evokes the sound of stir-frying"

It is evident from these examples that Korean ideophones are also based on perceptual appeals to the vision, texture (touch), and hearing senses.[7]

Reporting on elicitation tasks, Dingemanse (2011) stresses the important role that ideophones play in precisely pointing out sensory images in Siwi, a language in the Niger-Congo family spoken in eastern Ghana. Dingemanse (2011, 81) lists Siwi ideophones that depict taste and flavor in (16).

(16) a. saaa   "cool sensation (e.g., ginger)"
     b. sùùù   "burning sensation (e.g., pepper)"
     c. tsuà`î`ĩ   "elastic"
     d. màgàdã̀`ã̀`   "hard to swallow"
     e. sikitii   "tough, hard to chew"
     f. tìtìrìtìì   "sticky like a cat's tongue"

The words in (16) illustrate that while they refer to general tactile sensations, (16c–f) particularly depict mouth-feel reactions. Furthermore, it seems that ideophonic expressions have specific (or a specific set of) food items with which they tightly associate, as with ginger and pepper in (16a, 16b).

A significant consequence of the visceral nature of mimetics is that they can enrich the vocabulary for describing and evaluating food taste and preparatory processes. They provide an efficacious linguistic shortcut for discriminating and characterizing one's palate as well as giving accurate culinary instructions with remarkable precision. Mimetic words can indeed hit the bullseye in the variety of discourse that deals with food consumption and food preparation.

2 DESCRIPTION AND EVALUATION OF TASTE

Our perception of food taste being *oishii* "good-tasting" and *mazui* "unpalatable" ramifies into fine-grained components that correspond to individual sensual and sensory reactions. Endorsing this view, Kakehi (1989) explains that the taste of sake is expressed by a sum of multiple sensual appeals. He includes the following for illustration: touch (e.g., *kime-no komakai/arai* "fine/coarse texture"), narrow sense of taste (e.g., *amai* "sweet," *karai* "dry"), smell (e.g., *kabi-kusai* "musty," *yakumi-shū* "spicy"), vision (e.g., *yamabuki-iro* "bright golden yellow," *shiro-boke* "white Japanese quince"), and hearing (e.g., *onkyō-kōka* "sound effect" – for creating ambience) (p. 54). Although Kakehi's examples above are prosaic expressions, as I have argued previously, the mimetic vocabulary contributes to communicating similarly particularized taste experiences in a single word. Its rich membership further offers a large selection pool from which language users can choose so that an exact word sharply identifies personal reactions.

We can find multiple mimetic words in all sense categories relevant to taste depictions, but among them, mimetics appealing to the sense of touch, in particular, are copiously exemplified. It comports with the strong overall tendency to describe food taste in terms of texture, inclusive of all vocabulary types and expressions. Indeed, such a tendency has been widely noted in Japanese food discourse (e.g., Hayakawa 2003, 2013; Hayakawa et al. 2005; Noda 2014; Kindaichi 2016; Ohashi 2016; Ota 2000; Sugiyama 2016). It suggests that texture is a critical "ingredient" in constructing a concept of tastiness in Japanese food culture, as is demonstrated by scholarly investigations.[8] For example, Muto (2003) classifies 183 food-related mimetics (both taste and cooking) according to the four senses—touch, vision, hearing, and taste. Touch is a large category, and includes temperature, pain (e.g., felt in the mouth and nose), texture (e.g., against teeth, tongue, general mouthfeel), sliminess, dryness-wetness, elasticity, and softness-hardness.[9] Some examples of her classification are shown in (17–20). Representative food items with which Muto associates the mimetic expressions are indicated in square brackets. Examples in (17–20) focus on mimetics that relate to food consumption rather than food preparation, the latter of which I will discuss in section 4. The meanings of the mimetics as food-related expressions are based on Kakehi et al. (1996) unless indicated otherwise.

(17) touch

hokahoka [cooked rice] "the state in which food is hot and looks tasty"
kiin [beer] "a piercing or ringing pain in the ears"
piriQ [hot pepper] "the state of feeling a sharp momentary pain or sensation, as from an electric shock, spicy food, etc."
tsuun [wasabi] "the state of feeling a stinging sensation"
shakishaki [lettuce] "the state of food, especially fruit and vegetables, being crisp"
nurunuru [fermented soy beans] "the state of being slimy or slippery"
pasapasa [(stale) bread] "the state in which something has lost its moisture or taste"
shiQtori [sponge cake] "the state of agreeably moist or damp"
puripuri [shrimp] "the state of being plump and chewy"[10]
kachikachi [popsicle] "the state of an originally soft or liquid substance becoming very hard"
gunyagunya [*kon'nyaku* (konjac)] "the state of lacking firmness or rigidity"

(18) vision

poroporo [pilaf] "the manner in which an object having become dry crumbles easily"

guchagucha [rice porridge] "the state in which something loses its original form"
barabara [(no-fat) scrambled egg] "the state of something which should be intact being broken into pieces"
doN'yori [soup] "the state of being dull, clouded, or gloomy"

(19) hearing

korikori [abalone] "the sound made when scratching or chewing something hard"
zakuzaku [frozen orange] "a loud crunching sound made when rough or hard particles are pressed or stirred"
shuwashuwa [beer, soda pop] "a sound of effluent bubbles in carbonated drinks"[11]
tsurutsuru [soba, udon] "a repeated loud slurping sound made when eating wet food noisily"

(20) taste

saQpari [salad] "the state of being plain or unadorned"
aQsari [vinegared dish, clear soup] "the state in which color, taste, make-up, etc., is simple or light"
kiriri [dry sake] "the manner of fastening something tightly"
maQtari [custard] "the state of being mild in taste"[12]

These samples give a quick glance at a wide range of evoked images that characterize specific attributes of particular food items. Many refer to positive features, but mimetics like *pasapasa*, *kachikachi*, and *gunyagunya* in (17) and all in (18) generally point to undesirable states. The mimetic *nurunuru* in (17) along with others such as *nebaneba*, *neQtori*, and *nechanecha* all depict slimy, slippery, or sticky feels, those typical of bananas, honey, okra, and grated Japanese yams, for instance. As Hayakawa (2003) summarizes as "food culture of stickiness," there are a number of food items in Japan whose glutinous contents are favored and valued for their health and nutritional benefits. Japan is known for its rice culture, and the most prevalently used short-grain rice in fact counts as the most representative of the sticky, glutenous texture. Just like the taste of green tea discussed in Suter et al. (2020), the sticky food texture is part of the culturally constructed food taste. It stands to reason that several mimetic words mentioned above are readily available to depict those exact textures.

The BMFT Kotobarabo [language lab] (Ohashi 2015, 2016) engaged in a longitudinal study that examined people's judgments of words that evoke the sense of deliciousness in food. The survey team called these words *shizuru-wādo* "sizzle word." There are 102 words, combining mimetic (80 items) and prosaic expressions (22 items) that were pre-selected to be *shizuru-wādo*, and the participants were asked to choose which word they regard as inciting deliciousness.[13] The team repeated the study every 3 years from 2003 until 2015, over the time span of 12 years. The 1800 participants range from 15 to 69 years old, balanced both in age and sex.[14] (21) summarizes the mimetics that are among the top 10 *shizuru-wādo* in the years of 2003, 2009, and 2015. The numbers in parentheses indicate the ranking (including both mimetic and prosaic expressions) for each year. The mimetics in boldface were selected in all of the three years as well as 2006 and 2012.

(21) a. 2003: sakuQ-to (4) "crisp," **sakusaku** (5) "crisp," **mochimochi** (6) "chewy," **hokuhoku** (7) "warm and flaky," shakishaki (8) "crisp"

b. 2009: **mochimochi** (2) "chewy," **sakusaku** (5) "crisp," **hokuhoku** (6) "warm and flaky," toroori (7) "meltingly soft," shakishaki (8) "crisp"

c. 2015: **mochimochi** (1) "chewy," mocchiri (3) "chewy," **sakusaku** (5) "crisp," **hokuhoku** (6) "warm and flaky," toroori (7) "meltingly soft," sakuQ-to (9) "crisp"

SakuQ-to in (21a) and (21c) is a morphological variant of *sakusaku*, and *mocchiri* in (21c) is also related to *mochimochi*, confirming strong associations between the particular textures these mimetics identify and "delicious" images that they evoke.

Of a number of interesting findings that Ohashi reports, the range of variation observed with mimetics seems to me to suggest that a few sociolinguistic factors (e.g., time span, gender, age) are at play. First, over the 12 years of the study, the ranking of *shizuru-wādo* has changed, and words that took upward paths are mimetics while the trend of significant decrease is more prevalent among prosaic expressions. (22–23) summarize these notable changes in ranking, based on Ohashi (2015, 55). I include only the results of 2003, 2009, and 2015.

(22) *shizuru-wādo* that moved upward in ranking

	2003		2009		2015
mochimochi "chewy"	6	→	2	→	1
moQchiri "chewy"	11	→	3	→	3
toroori "meltingly soft"	22	→	7	→	7
huwahuwa "fluffy"	38	→	12	→	11

(23) *shizuru-wādo* that moved downward in ranking

	2003		2009		2015
koshi-no aru "chewy, elastic"	2	→	9	→	12
shitazawari-no yoi "pleasant to the palate"	10	→	26	→	24
hagotae-no aru "al dente, chewy; crunchy"	12	→	30	→	28

The contrast between mimetics and prosaic expressions is robust. Interestingly, *koshino-aru* in (23) and *mochimochi/moQchiri* in (22) refer to a very similar texture, typical of noodles, bread, and rice cakes; and *shitazawari-no yoi* in (23) seems at least inclusive of the texture that *toroori* in (22) depicts. In that light, while the identified textures remain to be strongly connected to an enticing taste, the way in which it is verbally expressed is shifted from prosaic to mimetic.

Second, the report notes that female speakers use mimetic expressions more than males, and to the extent that I can gather, the type of mimetics seems different between males and females. For instance, all the mimetics in (22) as well as *tsurutsuru* "smooth and slippery" and *puripuri/purupuru* (also their morphological variants) "plump, chewy, elastic" are consistently selected by females. In contrast, mimetics that males choose are *shuwashuwa* "a sound of effluent bubbles in carbonated drinks," *gokugoku* "gulping down," *zaQkuri* "loud crunching," and *nebaneba* "sticky" (Ohashi 2015, 21, 92). The mimetics of female choice speak of generally soft textures, whereas the first three selections by males are sound-based. *Gokugoku*, moreover, refers to the manner of drinking a large quantity of liquid, rather than explicating a food texture. So, the locus of emphasis on identifying the favorable tenet that leads to a pleasurable taste sense appears to vary depending on the gender.

Third, we also see some variation across age groups. The women in the study are divided into 6 groups, and their mimetic choices are listed in (24), based on Ohashi (2015, 21).

(24) a. 15–19: *pururun* "soft and elastic," *huNwari* "soft and fluffy," *sakuhuwa* "crisp and fluffy," *zakuQ-to* "loud crunching," *zakuzaku* "loud crunching"

b. 20–29: *toroori* "melting soft," *mochiQ-to* "chewy," *mochimochi* "chewy," *huwahuwa* "fluffy," *juwaa* "oozing," *juwaQ-to* "oozing," *karikari* "crunchy"

c. 30–39:   moQchiri "chewy," kariQ-to "dry and crisp," tsuruQ-to "smooth and slippery," puripuri "plump and chewy," puriQ-to "plump and chewy," nebaneba "sticky"

d. 40–49:   huwatoro "fluffy and melting soft," toroQ-to "melting soft," sakusaku "crisp," karaQ-to "dry and crisp"

e. 50–59:   hokuri "warm and flaky," hoQkori "warm and flaky," tsuru-tsuru "smooth and slippery"

f. 60–69:   shiQtori "moist"

Females of all age groups favor mimetics, as *shizuru wādo*, that evoke some softness and smoothness in food texture. Yet, the younger the speakers are, the more frequently words of crispiness and crunchiness are chosen, such as *zakuQ-to, zakuzaku, karikari,* and *kariQ-to*. In (24d) women of the 40–49 age range have selected another mimetic of crispiness, *sakusaku*. However, in contrast with the other four crunchy mimetics (i.e., *zakuQ-to, zakuzaku, karikari,* and *kariQ-to*), *sakusaku* corresponds to a lighter sound and texture like that of the wafer part of Kit Kat. Together with the fact that women over 50 years old favor mimetics of soft and smooth feel, the variation based on age demonstrated in (24) may mirror age-appropriate diet habits.

Let us turn to how mimetics are used in a variety of food discourses in spoken and written Japanese of varied sources (e.g., YouTube videos, essays, novels, articles and ads in newspapers and magazines, food packaging). To begin, (25) is an utterance by a female high-school student upon consuming *tamago-kake gohan* "raw egg over a bowl of cooked rice" with coke. Recall that *tamago-kake gohan* as TKG was discussed in chapter 2, and it is a very common dish, especially for breakfast.

(25) 生卵で口が**マッタリ**したところをコーラが**シュワーッ**と流れるのが気持ちいい

Namatamago-de kuchi-ga **maQtari**-shita tokoro-o kōra-ga **shuwaaQ**-to nagareru-no-ga kimochi ii.

"It gives a pleasant feeling when coke passes [like **shuwaa**] through the mouth, washing away the richness [**maQtari**] of a raw egg"

(Hayakawa 2007, 44–45)

The first mimetic *maQtari* characterizes the rich, somewhat slimy mouth feel that a raw egg, especially the yolk, leaves behind. The second mimetic *shuwaaQ* corresponds to the sparkling of the carbonated drink. In this context, furthermore, *shuwaaQ* has an image of a dynamic stimulus in the mouth. As the coke flows through the oral cavity, its tiny sparkling bubbles cleanse the sliminess of the egg away, giving a refreshing sense.

(26–28) are found in YouTube video clips broadcasted by cooking specialists.

(26) 表面カリッとしてて、中すごいほくほくしていますね。

Hyōmen **kariQ**-to shite-te, naka sugoi **hokuhoku** shite-imasu-ne.

"The surface is crisp [**kariQ**], and the inside is fluffy [**hokuhoku**]."

(Jo 2021)

In this video, a former restaurant chef, Jiro Jo, shows how to make a potato galette with cheese inside. At the end of his hands-on instructions, he tastes the galette he has just made and gives the comment in (26). Upon hearing *kariQ* and *hokuhoku*, the viewer will ascertain contrastive textures between the outside and the inside of the galette. The browned potatoes that had direct contact with the frying pan have produced a crisp surface. Contrastively, in the inside, the combination of shredded potatoes and cheese maintains a desired level of moisture and a hot and fluffy consistency, reminiscent of a freshly baked potato just out of the oven.

The examples in (27–28) are taken from a cooking demonstration by Ryuta Kijima and his guest.

(27) パサつかせないで、できたてホカホカを何かおいしく食べれるような鶏胸を茹でる料理を紹介したいと思います。

Pasa-tsuk-ase-nai-de, deki-tate **hokahoka**-o nanka oishiku tabe-reru-yō-na tori-mune-o yuderu ryōri-o shōkai-shi-tai-to omoimasu.

"I would like to introduce a recipe for boiled chicken breast that is not dry [**pasa**] and can be enjoyed while piping hot [**hokahoka**]." (Kijima 2021)

(28) 胸肉だと思えない。ぷるっとしてじゅわっとして。

Mune-niku-da-to omo-e-nai. **PuruQ**-to shite **juwaQ**-to shite.

"I can't believe it's a chicken breast. It's elastic [**puruQ**] and juicy [**juwaQ**]." (Ibid.)

(27) is an introductory remark by Kijima, a cooking specialist, for a chicken dish. It is a common understanding that cooked chicken breasts tend to be dry in texture. This is signaled by the first compound word in (27), *pasa-tsuka-seru* "make dry," where *pasa-* is a mimetic base of *pasapasa*, *pasaQ*, and other similar derived forms. These mimetics generally suggest negative qualities and refer to an undesirable rubbery texture resulting from lack of sufficient moisture. Kijima's recipe is expected to yield a moist chicken breast dish that ameliorates such a cooking challenge. The second mimetic,

hokahoka, does not speak directly to inherent attributes of the chicken breast, but nevertheless, adds an enticing benefit to the recipe. Together, the viewer will imagine a taste of a hot and juicy chicken dish as an outcome. (28) confirms that the imagination is in fact realized. Tasting the dish, the guest comments that the chicken breast uncharacteristically has preserved bounciness and succulence. Expressed in terms of mimetics, *puruQ* and *juwaQ*, by someone who is actually tasting it, this verbal depiction provides the viewer with a virtual experience of feeling the texture of the cooked chicken breast.

Authors of essays on food and restaurant guides are fastidious about specifics of positive and negative recommendations and reasons for their evaluations. Mimetics are a convenient linguistic and rhetorical tool to sharpen their reference points and to communicate directly with the senses of the audience. The passages in (29–30) are written by food professionals—an essayist and a food stylist, respectively. (31) is from a collection of humorous essays written by an essayist and comic artist.

(29) ただ、実際に持ち帰って、時間が経ってから家で食べると、**じゅわ〜っと**油が染み出て、かなり厳しい。あれはやっぱり、立って**ささっと**食べるからこそ気にならない。何より、おつゆの味と衣の厚みが融合して、食べているうちに**もろもろ、もわぁっと**なってきて、こくがだんだんと深くなってゆく。あれが立ち食いそばの醍醐味だと気づきました。

Tada, jissai-ni mochi-kaette, jikan-ga tatte-kara ie-de taberu-to, **juwaaQ**-to abura-ga shimidete, kanari kibishii. Are-wa yappari, tatte **sasaQ**-to taberu-kara-koso ki-ni naranai. Nani-yori, otsuyu-no aji-to koromo-no atsumi-ga yūgō-shite, tabete-iru uchi-ni **moromoro, mowaaQ**-to natte-kite, koku-ga dandan-to hukaku natte-yuku. Are-ga tachigui-soba-no daigomi-da-to kizukimashita.

"But, when I buy it (=tempura soba) for a take-out and eat it sometime later, the grease oozes out [**juwaaQ**] and it's not tasty at all. After all, the grease (of the tempura) doesn't bother me all the more because I quickly [**sasaQ**] eat it while standing. More than anything, the taste of the broth and the thickness of the batter harmonize; as I eat it, it [the broth-soaked batter] becomes soft [**moromoro**] and shapeless [**mowaaQ**] and gradually the flavor deepens. I realized that is the genuine delight of stand-up soba."

(Hiramatsu 2015, 156)

The four mimetics in the commentary on tempura soba at a stand-up soba restaurant in (29) make the narrative into a dynamic presentation of a soba-eating scene. The manner of the grease oozing out from a deep-fried tempura batter onto the soba broth is identified as *juwaaQ*, which evokes a visual image of glistening oil specks floating on the broth. Note, too, that the tilde used for emphatic vowel lengthening, じゅわ〜っ, rather than its more standard counterpart of a horizontal bar, as in じゅわーっ, may be regarded as iconic of slow oozing of the grease that suggests lack of freshness in the take-out soba. The juxtaposition of *moromoro* and *mowaaQ* details that first the tempura absorbs the broth into a soft mass and then swells up before starting to lose its firm shape. Note that the morphological shapes of these two mimetics are consistent with the semantic generalizations in (12) discussed earlier. *Moromoro* takes the reduplicated pattern of (12d), CVCV-CVCV, that iconically implies a repetition of a movement, and the continued absorption of the broth indicated by *moromoro* is compatible with the interpretation underlying the morphological template. The presence of the mimetic final Q of *mowaaQ*, although slightly diverging from CVCVQ, is suggestive of a forceful movement, referring specifically to the quick saturation of the broth.

The state of a deep-fried food that tops a bowl of soup depicted in (29) is very similar to the description in (30).

(30) …コロッケそば。**ぐずぐず**にならない程度にコロッケをおつゆに浸し、崩しながら食べる幸せといったら！

... korokke-soba. **Guzuguzu**-ni naranai teido-ni korokke-o otsuyu-ni hitashi, kuzushi-nagara taberu shiawase-to ittara!

"... soba with croquette. Dipping the croquette in the broth just enough not to get it crumbled [**guzuguzu**] and then eat it while breaking it. What happiness it brings to me!" (Takahashi 2012, 121)

Upon dipping a croquette in the soba broth, the writer uses *guzuguzu* as a gage of texture to be avoided. The state of *guzuguzu* refers to the croquette that has soaked up the broth and starts falling apart. Once the writer catches the moment right before that, she has the leisure of being engaged in breaking it as she likes. These depictions of tempura (batter) in (29) and croquette in a bowl of soba in (30) have an effect that can be likened to bringing a video camera up close to the noodle bowl and filming in slow motion. And, these dynamic film-like scenes surely take us on a journey of a virtual dining experience, however imaginary it may be.

In his essay on American food culture, Higashi (2016) expresses a fastidious opinion about egg dishes he observes with American breakfast. In particular, he defines his ideal of egg dishes by way of mimetics, as in (31).

(31) …中が**トロリ**としたオムレツや、**しっとり**とした舌触りの優しいスクランブルエッグなど望むべくもない。

... naka-ga **torori**-to shita omuretsu-ya, **shiQtori**-to shita sita-zawari-no yasashii sukuranburueggu-nado nozomu-beku-mo nai.

"... it is impossible to ask for an omelet that is melting [**torori**] inside or delicate scrambled eggs that feel moist [**shiQtori**] to the tongue."

(Higashi 2016, 53)

In his view, omelets should not be fully cooked so that he can taste the rich and creamy mixture of the yolk and white oozing out as he puts a bite in his mouth. This is the *torori* state. Scramble eggs are cooked further than the *torori* state but still maintain the soft and moist, though not crumbly, texture of *shiQtori*. Higashi is indeed not alone in holding these ideals, as *torori* and *shiQtori* are customary mimetics that cooccur with omelets and scrambled eggs in Japanese cooking and dining discourse.

Mimetics are also effective in calling up food memories. In (32), for instance, the author, Sadao Shoji, reminisces about his childhood in the early Showa era (1926–1989), when eggs were considered to be a valuable food item. A single boiled egg that he was allowed to take to a school excursion or to an athletic meeting is vividly portrayed.

(32) 大切に割って、大切に殻をむくと**ツルツル**の白身が現れてネ、それに塩を少しつけて**パクリ**とやると、**ホクホク**した黄身が**サクリ**と割れて口の中に拡がって…

Taisetsu-ni watte, taisetsu-ni kara-o muku-to **tsurutsuru**-no shiromi-ga arawarete-ne, sore-ni shio-o sukoshi tsukete **pakuri**-to yaru-to, **hokuhoku**-shita kimi-ga **sakuri**-to warete kuchi-no naka-ni hirogatte . . .

"Upon gently cracking [the boiled egg] and gently shelling it, the slick [**tsurutsuru**] egg white appears; when I snap up [**pakuri**] the slightly salted egg, the flaky [**hokuhoku**] yolk crisply [**sakuri**] breaks, spreading all over in my mouth . . ." (Shoji 1984, 295)

Just as in (29), the process of consuming the single, previously boiled egg is detailed at multiple moments, each of which is characterized by the mimetics for varying textual sensations. The *tsurutsuru* surface is not only shiny but moist, simultaneously appealing to visual and textual senses; the *pakuri* motion reflects Little Sadao's anticipated excitement to have the rare opportunity to eat something precious; and finally, the first *hokuhoku* and then *sakuri* mouth-feel vivifies his pleasure of savoring the flaky egg yolk crumbling in the mouth.

Despite its prevalence and effectiveness in food discourse that we have examined thus far, the mimetic vocabulary has not always been taken seriously for research consideration. Tamori (1993) explains that one of the reasons has to do with "childishness" associated with the word class, and its formality (or alleged lack thereof) has been investigated (Schourup 1993). However, newspapers, which use the formal writing style, show a liberal number of mimetic examples even in articles that report scientific experiments. (33) is one such instance.

(33) 米をゼリーのような**ぷるぷる**の感触にした「米ゲル」を食品総合研究所（茨城県つくば市）が開発した。…失敗したと思ってしばらく放置していたが、数日後も**ぷるぷる**の状態を保っていたため、本格的な研究に着手した。…卵などを混ぜてシュークリームの生地を作ると、**パリッ**とした感触がいつまでも保たれ、うどんを作るとコシが強い。

Kome-o zerī-no yō-na **purupuru**-no kanshoku-ni shita "kome-geru"-o Shokuhin Sōgō Kenkyūjo (Ibaraki-ken Tsukuba-shi)-ga kaihatsu-shita. . . . shippai-shita-to omotte shibaraku hōchi-shite-ita-ga, sūjitsugo-mo **purupuru**-no jōtai-o tamotte-ita-tame, honkakuteki-na kenkyū-ni chakushu-shita. . . . tamago-nado-o mazete shūkurīmu-no kiji-o tsukuru-to, **pariQ**-to shita kanshoku-ga itsumademo tamot-are, udon-o tsukuru-to koshi-ga tsuyoi.

"The Food Research Institute (Tsukuba City, Ibaraki) has developed 'kome-geru' [rice-gel], which is made by turning rice into an elastic, bouncy [**purupuru**] texture like jelly. . . . Although they had left it untouched thinking that they failed, they launched full-blown research since it had remained elastic and bouncy [**purupuru**]. . . . A cream puff dough made of it (=kome-geru) and eggs, among others, maintains the crisp [**pariQ**] texture for a long time; udon using it has a strong body (=chewiness)."

("Okome Henshin" 2015)

In this experiment, the development of a gel-like texture as it is particularized to be *purupuru* is a goal of the researchers. Judging from the context, the *kome-geru* "rice gel" is expected to serve as an ingredient of, or additive to, food items. The metaphorical reference to jelly (or gelatin) alone could describe the texture, but *purupuru*, mentioned twice in the passage, makes one recall the mild elastic resistance that a gelatin dessert has. Simultaneously, *purupuru* evokes the visual image of a gentle quiver from the *kome-geru*. Another mimetic *pariQ*, symbolizing a crisp rather than stale texture, augments an additional layer to discriminating exact kinds of tactile sensation that the agricultural research reportedly essentializes in this newspaper article.

In a similar vein, (34–35) appeared in Asahi Digital, which is a well-respected news venue.

(34) ヤマサとマルマンがつくった「辛みそ揚」は、魚肉のうまみと**しゃきしゃき**したゴボウの歯ごたえに、甘みとこくのある辛さが後を追う。練り物に発酵食品を混ぜると、**ぼそぼそ**した食感になることがあるが、「辛みそとの相性は抜群」とヤマサの佐藤社長。

Yamasa-to Maruman-ga tsukutta "Kara-miso-age"-wa, gyoniku-no umami-to **shakishaki**-shita gobō-no hagotae-ni, amami-to koku-no aru karasa-ga ato-o ou. Nerimono-ni hakkō-shokuhin-o mazeru-to, **boso-boso**-shita shokkan-ni naru koto-ga aru-ga, "kara-miso-to-no aishō-wa batsugun"-to Yamasa-no Satō-shachō.

"'Kara-miso-age,' crafted by Yamasa and Maruman, features the flavor of fish meat and the crisp [**shakishaki**] firmness of burdock roots, with an aftertaste of sweet and rich spiciness. Combining fish-paste products and fermented foods sometimes produces a dry, crumbly [**bosoboso**] mouth-feel, but '[the fish-paste product] is well suited with spicy miso,' says President Sato of Yamasa." (Matsushita 2021)

(35) まきの釜でゆでた手打ちの麺には、もちっとした弾力とこしがある。

Maki-no kama-de yudeta te-uchi-no men-ni-wa, **mochiQ**-to shita dan-ryoku-to koshi-ga aru.

"Handmade noodles in a pot boiled over wood fire has springy [**mochiQ**] elasticity and body." (Okubo 2019)

(34) is an article that reports on a new food product that has resulted from the collaborative venture of two large food companies. (35) is part of a series that features local attractions in Kyoto. It is worth noting that the language used in these examples is not intended for advertisements and yet the use of mimetics makes the content more comprehensible than without them, and importantly, they are far from giving the "childish" undertone that Tamori mentions. The mimetics in these examples, particularly, *shakishaki* in (33) and *mochiQ* in (34), are widely acknowledged attributes of burdock and udon, respectively. The familiar collocation, thus, is beneficial to overall readability.

Fiction writing takes advantage of mimetics to enrich the vivaciousness in food depictions. It is interesting to note that writers vary in frequency of mimetic use: some are more prone to them than others. Moreover, despite my initial expectation that novels on food themes see a wider variety of mimetics, individual preferences seem to dictate this rather than a general pattern. Personal propensity for mimetics notwithstanding, a broad range of aspects pertinent to food items is depicted with mimetics in this genre of writing every bit as vividly as in others. The mimetic word in each of the examples from novels in (36–39) below targets a very distinctive facet of a given food that contributes to the characterization of overall taste and food experience. All the mimetics in (36–37) simulate diverse sensations that the food items give within the mouth.

(36) じゅっと煮汁が染み出した。**こっくり**と甘く煮ふくめられた油揚げ、硬めに炊かれたすし飯が**ほろり**と崩れていく。

JuQ-to nijiru-ga shimi-dashita. **KoQkuri**-to amaku ni-hukumer-areta abura-age, katame-ni tak-areta sushi-meshi-ga **horori**-to kuzurete-iku.

"The (seasoned) liquid suddenly oozed out [**juQ**]. The deep-fried tofu that has absorbed full-bodied [**koQkuri**] sweetness in simmering broth and the al-dente sushi rice falls into small pieces [**horori**]." (Yuzuki 2013, 10)

(37) 歯でかむと、まず「**もちっ**」とした弾力を感じる。更に歯に力を加えるとスパゲティの中心が一瞬強固な抵抗を示す。だがその抵抗はあくまで一瞬の物であって、次の瞬間、歯は「**しゃっきり**」とスパゲティを食い切っている。

Ha-de kamu-to, mazu "**mochiQ**"-to shita danryoku-o kanjiru. Sara-ni ha-ni chikara-o kuwaeru-to supageti-no chūshin-ga isshun kyōko-na teikō-o shimesu. Daga sono teikō-wa akumade isshun-no mono-de atte, tsugi-no shunkan, ha-wa "**shaQkiri**"-to supageti-o kui-kitte-iru.

"Upon biting, I first feel elasticity '[**mochiQ**].' When I further add force to my teeth, the middle of the spaghetti momentarily responds with stubborn resistance. But, the resistance is only temporary, and at the next moment, my teeth bite through the spaghetti '[**shaQkiri**].'" (Kariya 1991, 42)

The narrative excerpt in (36) serves to illustrate dynamic in-mouth actions, to which mimetics add liveliness and on-the-site feel. The protagonist's description of consuming an inarizushi piece (i.e., sushi rice wrapped in a seasoned, deep-fried tofu) transitions in slow motion. It starts from the first bite, which lets out the rich sweetness of the tofu wrap (*juQ*), to a subsequent bite that disassembles the packed sushi rice (*horori*). The suddenness of the liquid emission presented by the mimetic comes from the final Q of *juQ*, just like the forcefulness associated with the CVCVQ pattern discussed in (12b). The sweetness of the deep-fried tofu assessed by *koQkuri* results from slow and delicate cooking that produces a deep flavor.

Turning to (37), the mastication of a single bite of a strand of spaghetti depicted in this example is temporally sliced into two seemingly long stages. The first mimetic *mochiQ* is the texture that is felt with the teeth upon reaching the firmness of al-dente pasta. The final Q-ending of the mimetic adds a sense of forcefulness, comporting with the elasticity and resistance mentioned in the passage. The resistance is broken by *shaQkiri*. Somewhat oddly, this mimetic generally refers to a crisp texture, like that of pickles or the sound of biting into them (Ono 2007).15 Applied to pasta in (37), however, *shaQkiri* spotlights the perfect, al-dente texture of the spaghetti, although a hint of exaggeration might be indisputable.

The next two examples contain mimetics—*tsuntsun* in (38) and *nurunuru* in (39)—that illustrate the types of bodily sensation that food items bring about outside the oral cavity.

(38) 唐辛子の香りはするけど、**ツンツン**しないし、とってもまろやか。

Tōgarashi-no kaori-wa suru-kedo, **tsuntsun** shi-nai-shi, tottemo maroyaka.

"The aroma of the red peppers is noticeable, but it does not sting [**tsuntsun**]; it is mild." (Yuzuki 2013, 152)

(39) 指と口のまわりがすぐに**ヌルヌル**してくる。カニの肉は**しっとり**として、舌が一瞬震えるほど冷たく感じられる。

Yubi-to kuchi-no mawari-ga sugu-ni **nurunuru** shite-kuru. Kani-no niku-wa **shiQtori**-to shite, shita-ga isshun hurueru-hodo tsumetaku kanjirareru.

"My fingers and around my mouth quickly become slimy [**nurunuru**]. The flesh of the crab is moist [**shiQtori**] and feels cold as if my tongue instantly shivers." (Murakami 1998, 149)

Tsuntsun in (38) signifies a customary reaction of strong spices (e.g., wasabi, mustard) and pungent odor (e.g., vinegar, ammonia), and as such the mimetic reflects a sharp, perhaps pulsing, sensation felt through the nostrils. A prosaic equivalent would be *hana-o tsuku* "lit. stab/prick the nose" or *hana-o shigeki-suru* "stimulate the nose," but they do not match the visceral reaction that the mimetic *tsuntsun* evokes. *Tsuntsun* can discriminate the ways in which the stimuli travel through the nasal cavity, thereby bringing about explicit sensations. In (39), a few lines before the passage gives contextual information that the protagonist was served stone crab with hot butter and a mustard sauce, but the overpowering taste of the crab makes him forget which sauce he opted for. Whichever sauce it was, his fingers and around the mouth are smothered with butter fat or mustard. The mimetic *nurunuru* brings out an image of glistened and sticky fingers and face, which leads to the smoothness and richness (or heaviness)—both texture and taste—of the sauces. Indeed, it does not paint an elegant dining scene. Instead, coupled with the moist (*shiQtori*) crab that is said to have a defined taste, the meal as a whole pictures a robust and succulent experience.

Finally, mimetics constitute an expedient and efficacious tool in devising product names and catchphrases for marketing. In (40) are phrases that appear on food packages, where mimetic words shorten paths to sensual descriptions of the products.

(40) a. さくさく抹茶　　　　とろり抹茶
sakusaku-maccha　　　**torori**-maccha
"crisp-green tea"　　　　"creamy-green tea"
　　　　　　　　　　　　　　　　[Meitō Sangyō: chocolate product]

b. もちふわ　匠の逸品
mochi-huwa takumi-no ippin
"chewy and fluffy artisan masterpiece"　　　[Kōbeya: bread product]

c. パリッとスリット
pariQ-to suritto
"crisp (rice cakes) by a slit-process [so that a sheet of rice cakes will be (easily) split]"
　　　　　　　　　　　[Satō Shokuhin Kōgyō: dehydrated rice cake]

d. 栗きのこ　釜めしの素　—　ほくほく栗としゃきっときのこ
kuri-kinoko kamameshi-no moto — **hokuhoku**-kuri-to **shakiQ**-to-kinoko
"chestnut-mushroom base for kamameshi — flaky-chestnut and crisp-mushroom"
　　　　　　　　　　　　　　　　[Marumiya: base for mixed rice]

The chocolate product named *Uji-maccha* "Uji green tea" comes in three green tea flavored chocolate varieties, two of which have the labels given in (40a). Both names are compounds comprising mimetics, *sakusaku* and *torori*, and the prosaic word for green tea, *maccha*. The first mimetic, *sakusaku*, depicts a very light, crisp texture of small rice puff bits blended in green tea chocolate. The second, *torori*, evokes an image of a rich and smooth green tea filling oozing out when biting into the chocolate shell. The two mimetics essentially provide information about the distinguishing textures, but simultaneously appeal to the hearing sense through a crisp sound and to the visual image of the running soft center. (40b) is the name of a bread product. In the Japanese food culture, chewiness and fluffiness are ideal features of bread for toast, and variants composed of the bases *mochi* and *huwa* (e.g., *mochimochi~mochiQ~moQchiri* and *huwahuwa~huwaQ~huNwari*) widely characterize these desirable textures. Recall that mimetic variants of *mochi* and *huwa* have scored very high as *shizuru wādo*, i.e., words that evoke the sense of deliciousness in food, as summarized in (22). As part of a product name, (40b) capitalizes on the familiarity of the terms, and economically compounds them into a single mimetic word.

　　The mimetic *pariQ* in the name of a dehydrated rice cake in (40c) highlights a perfectly crusty surface that the rice cake is expected to produce once it is heated. At the same time, the crunching sound of *pariQ* signifies a crisp texture. The ingenuity of this product name, however, lies in a rhythmic effect of rhyming that the mimetic *pariQ-to* (*-to* being the quotative particle) and the loanword *suritto* "slit" together induce. According to the explanation on the package, the term *suritto* "slit" refers to *suritto kakō* "slit process." Dehydrated rice cakes are generally sold as small individual pieces (around the size of 3"x2"), but the product *pariQ-to suritto* is processed in such a way that four pieces of the standard size are connected into a larger sheet. The dividing slits make it easier for a consumer to separate them even by hand rather than a knife. The mimetic *pariQ* simulates a crunching sound, and when it is suffixed by the quotative particle *-to* in order to make it adverbial, it rhymes with *suritto*. That is, the pronunciations of [pa-ri-t-to] and [su-ri-t-to] share the identical final three moras, [ri-t-to]. So, not only does the mimetic evoke the sensual reactions in the hearing and touch dimensions that showcase the product's attribute, it also contributes to making the rhythmic name reverberate to the consumers' ears.

Kamameshi in (40d) refers to cooked rice mixed with assorted vegetables as well as chicken or seafood. To make the cooking process easier, the package contains cooked ingredients (chestnuts and mushrooms in this case) and a dashi base. The flakiness of the chestnuts is immediately transparent upon hearing/seeing *hokuhoku*; and *shakiQ* of the mushrooms assures the product preserves the juiciness and the firmness from the characteristic fiber that gives a pleasant mouth-feel, totally free of mushiness. Similar to (40c), furthermore, the second part of the phrase, *hokuhoku-kuri-to shakiQ-to-kinoko*, strikes me as rhythmically skillful in that *hokuhoku-kuri-to* and *shakiQ-to-kinoko* are even-balanced in terms of the number of moras, i.e., seven moras each. In this regard, the language of the food packaging in (40c) and (40d) both make great use of mimetics not only for immediately ascertainable information about the products but also for their rhythmic nature as a marketing strategy.

Following up on the aspect of rhythmic effects of mimetics in marketing, (41) presents an advertisement catchphrase for *shōchū*, strong distilled spirits based on rice, wheat, and potatoes, among others ("CatchCappuccino," 2009).

(41) とくとく   **tokutoku**   "glug-glug"
    注いで、   sosoide   "pour"
    グビグビ   **gubigubi**   "gulp-gulp"
    飲もう。   nomō   "let's drink"

"Let's glug and gulp (*shōchū*)"   [Nikaidō: shōchū]

Ways in which products are marketed are not limited to showcasing their intrinsic characteristics related to taste and associated elements like texture and aroma. The two mimetics, *tokutoku* and *gubigubi*, speak to external factors that invite consumers to pay attention to the product. *Tokutoku* is an onomatopoeia that imitates the glugging sound that a liquid makes when poured from a bottle with a narrow opening. *Gubigubi* corresponds well with the English word *gulp* as a manner of drinking, but it more narrowly implies a way of consuming alcohol. So, the apposition of these two mimetics generates an image where the sound of *shōchū* being poured with the *tokutoku* sound spontaneously instigates the chain reaction of gulping it. Furthermore, the reduplicated form in which both mimetics appear is iconic with the sound of continuous alcohol flow (*tokutoku*) and with the repeated gulps (*gubigubi*). The mimetics participate in forming a rhythmic slogan that has a lasting effect on our auditory memory. Together they help call forth a view and sound of *shōchū* poured into a glass segueing into a scene of a satiable agent drinking it. In all, the catchphrase interspersed with *tokutoku* and *gubigubi* in (41) is easily intoned and hence readily remembered, while spurring multi-sensual reactions to the target product.

Perhaps, for the English speaker, the catchphrase in (41) would be somewhat reminiscent of the famous 1970s US television commercial for the antacid Alka-Seltzer whose catchphrase was "pop pop fizz fizz, oh what a relief it is." "Pop pop" is an onomatopoeia for the sound of a tablet going into a glass of water, and "fizz fizz" is another onomatopoeia for the sound of the tablet dissolving in water. This, along with the rhythmic nature of the whole utterance, made the phrase easily remembered once it was heard.

3 COOKING INSTRUCTIONS

Cooking instructions, whether oral or written, exemplify another venue of communication on food where mimetic use is widely noticed. Many of the cooking-related mimetics are conventionalized, often with commonly collocated prosaic words. One of the most familiar mimetics is *saQ-to* "quickly" upon calling for a swift action, like stir-frying, washing, and mixing. Another is *koNgari*. Cooccurring with *ageru* "to deep-fry," *koNgari* signals a brown color and a crisp texture as a benchmark for ideal deep-frying. In oral cooking instructions, the pervasiveness of the mimetic vocabulary is readily witnessed by paying attention to the exchange between a host and a cook on a daily TV cooking show. I informally observed a 20-minute cooking program broadcasted by Nippon Hōsō Kyōkai "Japan Broadcasting Corporation" (NHK) for four days in one week. Different male and female cooks and chefs are invited daily to introduce 2 to 3 dishes, and a host interacts with the cook/chef of the day while assisting him/her. Without exception, mimetics are actively used in two-person dialogues to describe the taste and texture of ingredients as well as to describe the manner of the cooking process and the resulting state. The rate of mimetic use between the four host-cook/chef pairs (i.e., eight individuals) in a single 20-minute broadcast time ranged from 6 types and 6 tokens to 8 types and 12 tokens. This frequent use of—or heavy reliance on—mimetics in a type of culinary discourse that is constrained by a limited air time comes as no surprise given their ability to pack miniscule particulars in a single word.

I give an example of mimetics that refer to processes of cooking in liquid. Individual English verbs like *boil*, *simmer*, *stew*, *seethe*, *braise*, and *jug* are different primarily in heating temperature, duration of cooking, and/or special utensils required. These distinguishing features are thus internally lexicalized as part of the meanings of the verbs. That is, the semantic differences among these verbs are attributed to lexical properties of individual verbs. Japanese employs the verb *niru* to refer to the common process of cooking food in liquid (usually seasoned), but mimetics that collocate with *niru* make relevant distinctions: *kotokoto niru*, *kutsukutsu niru*, and *torotoro niru* all indicate slow cooking at a low temperature, similar to *simmer* in English; *gutsugutsu niru* and *hutsuhutsu niru* imply a higher temperature like *boil*; and *guragura niru* stands out as a rigorous cooking process at the highest temperature. Thus, the manner in which in-liquid cooking varies is expressed via mimetics that occur externally to the verb *niru*.

It should be noted that the way in which the in-liquid cooking process of *niru* is externally manifested by a variety of mimetic words is not limited to cooking terms, but instead it follows a more general linguistic pattern of Japanese. To illustrate, the same role that mimetics play recurs in expressing types of walking and types of pain. As (42) and (43) demonstrate, the generic verbs, *aruku* "walk" and *itamu* "hurt," are accompanied by a constellation of mimetics that detail motions and painful conditions.

(42) chokochoko aruku "waddle"
 tokotoko aruku "trot"
 tobotobo aruku "plod"
 yotayota aruku "stagger"
 tekuteku aruku "trudge"
 doshidoshi aruku "lumber"
 burabura aruku "stroll"
 yochiyochi aruku "toddle"

(43) zukizuki itamu "throb"
 hirihiri itamu "smart"
 shikushiku itamu "gripping"
 chikuchiku itamu "prick"

piripiri	itamu	"tingle"
gangan	itamu	"splitting"

As we have argued, mimetics are rich in detailed information presented in visceral terms, and their linguistic distribution thoroughly agrees with the way of furthering communication beyond food discourse.

Cookbooks, recipe collections, and cooking shows provide a practical guide to create a dish. A composite network of information that is assembled into cooking instructions discusses the size and amount of ingredients, the estimated duration and temperature of cooking processes (e.g., frying, boiling, cooling), the manner of cooking activities (e.g., rinsing, cutting, cooking with heat), and the expected state of finished dishes. In each of these areas, mimetics aptly and intuitively give directives to make the cooking process comprehensible. The instructions in (44) are for making miso soup, and important advice at critical stages is in effect summarized by differentiating several mimetics.

(44) a. 昆布が**ゆらり**と動いて、湯が**くつくつ**し始めたら、すぐに昆布を取り出す。

Konbu-ga **yurari**-to ugoite, yu-ga **kutsukutsu** shi-hajime-tara, sugu-ni konbu-o tori-dasu.

"When the seaweed moves slightly [**yurari**] and the (hot) water is about to boil [**kutsukutsu**], immediately take out the seaweed."

(Watanabe 2015, 38)

b. お味噌汁は**ぐらぐら**煮立たせては絶対ダメよ。**ぐらっ**ときた煮えばなを注ぐのよ。

Omisoshiru-wa **guragura** ni-tat-asete-wa zettai dame-yo. **GuraQ**-to kita niebana-o sosogu-no-yo.

"You must absolutely NOT boil miso soup rigorously [**guragura**]. Be sure to pour it (into a bowl) at the onset of boiling [**guraQ**]."

(Ibid., 39)

(44a) is at the initial step of making a seaweed-based dashi, a broth. Essential to this step is the exact timing of removing the seaweed. The crucial moment is gaged by the mimetic *yurari*, which refers to the slight and slow swaying of the seaweed. This is immediately followed by the "beginning of *kutsukutsu*," the instant at which the water is just about to boil gently. (44b) directly records an oral instruction by a cooking expert Tokiko Suzuki. She advises with caution that miso soup not be kept rigorously boiling but instead be served at the very outset of the boiling point. The timing of removing the soup from the heat is vitally critical, and the contrastive morphological forms of the two mimetics (*guragura* vs. *guraQ*) that share the common base, *gura*, is remarkably helpful to determine the exact moment. As the semantic undertones of the morphological templates in (12) indicate, the reduplicated form *guragura* suggests a continuous state of rigorous boiling, whereas *guraQ* (CVCVQ) signals a single forceful event, corresponding to the onset of the boiling. With the nuances that are attributed to the morphological forms, *guragura* and *guraQ* in (44b) provide useful visual benchmarks to be mindful about.

Informing about the appropriate timing can be important to preventing food from being over- or under-processed. While suggested times can be given numerically, an alternative of stipulating a reference point by mimetic words is a very common practice in cooking instructions in Japanese, as (45–49) demonstrate. Many of those mimetics indicate sounds and visible textural changes.

(45) カツオを入れ、**ジュッ**と美味しそうな音がしたら大成功です。

Katsuo-o ire, **juQ**-to oishisō-na oto-ga shi-tara daiseikō-desu.

"Put the bonito piece (in a frying pan); when you hear the delicious sizzling sound [**juQ**], it's a great success."　　　　(Okuzono 2012, 57)

(46) **ブクブク**してきたら大きくかき混ぜ、**ふんわり**し始めたら火を止め、…

Bukubuku shite-ki-tara ōkiku kaki-maze, **huNwari** shi-hajime-tara hi-o tome, . . .

"When (the egg mixture) starts bubbling [**bukubuku**], give it a rough stir; when it starts to be fluffy [**huNwari**], turn the heat off, . . ."　(Kobayashi 2008, 61)

(47) ドウの固さは**ダラダラッ**と垂れるくらい、**ドテン**としてはいけません。

Dou-no katasa-wa **daradaraQ**-to tareru-kurai, **doteN**-to shite-wa ikemasen.

"The density (texture) of the (pancake) dough should be thick drips [**daradaraQ**], not a heavy drop [**doteN**]."　　　　(Takamine 2012, 197)

(48) 鍋にバターを溶かして玉葱を炒め、**しんなり**したら弱火にして小麦粉をふり入れ、2分程さらに炒める。

Nabe-ni batā-o tokashite tamanegi-o itame, **shiNnari** shi-tara yowabi-ni shite komugiko-o huri-ire, 2-hun-hodo sara-ni itameru.

"Melt the butter in a pot and sauté the onions; when the onions are softened [**shiNnari**], lower the heat, sprinkle the flour, and sauté them further for about 2 more minutes."　　　　(Kobayashi 2014a, 130)

(49) パリパリにこうちょっと少し長めに炒めたほうが、…

Paripari-ni kō chotto sukoshi nagame-ni itameta-hō-ga, . . .

"It's better to stir-fry (the ground meat) a little longer to get crispness [**paripari**] like this, . . ." (Chin 2008)

The mimetics *juQ* in (45) and *bukubuku* in (46) are onomatopoeia; and *bukubuku* additionally relates to the visual perception of bubbles formed by the eggs. In both cases, the moments signaled by *juQ* and (the onset of) *bukubuku* are not long-lasting and thus should be captured instantly. To that end, intuitive appeals to the hearing and vision senses may well be a more informative means to avoid missing the right timing. The second mimetic of (46), *huNwari*, points to a soft and fluffy texture. The transition from *bukubuku* to *huNwari* is also important to note: *bukubuku* arouses an image of a wet surface before the eggs set while *huNwari* is fluffy and moist but not wet.

The mimetics in (47), *daradaraQ* and *doteN*, generally depict moving objects, but their contrast in this context gives a precise cautionary reminder regarding the texture of the pancake batter. The morphological frames of the mimetics make a contribution to the preciseness. *DaradaraQ* and *doteN* refer, respectively, to drips of thick liquid and a fall of a heavy object, based on which the thickness or density of the batter can be visually imagined. Morphologically, a combination of reduplication and the final suffix of -Q in *daradaraQ* gives rise to the sense of a motion of "short-duration," according to Akita (2009, 195). That is, the consistency of the batter is loose enough to run but not to the extent of a fast continuous flow. In contrast, *doteN*, fitted in the form of CVCVN in (12), bears a nuance of reverberation. It evokes an image that the batter is stiffened into a denser mass, like a glob of mashed potatoes, and when it is dropped, it would have a reverberating impact, whether in sound or in motion. So, *daradaraQ* is a desired consistency of the batter, whereas *doteN* would not make fluffy pancakes.

In the last two examples, *shiNnari* in (48) and *paripari* in (49) provide visual indexes as to how long the ingredients are to be cooked. *ShiNnari* is a very common mimetic to depict (generally) vegetables like thinly sliced onions, cabbage, and mushrooms when cooked in heat and oil. They reach the *shiNnari* state after they absorb heated oil and lose their original firmness although still maintaining moisture. In contrast, *paripari* depicts a crisp texture, and in the context of (49), suggests that the continuously stir-fried ground meat loses much of its juice and becomes dry and crumbly. The clear visual images that the mimetics bring to our mind serve as graphic guides (although virtual) to the benchmark that should be looked for during the cooking process. Prosaic equivalents of *shiNnari* and *paripari* are available: the adverbs *yawarakaku* "softly" can replace *shiNnari* in (48); and *chotto sukoshi nagame-ni* "(stir-fry) a little longer" that Chef Chin says in the video in (49) gives some guidance but how much longer is left unsaid without the mimetic. The mimetic and prosaic expressions complement each other in (49), but nevertheless, the mimetics in both examples unequivocally generate informative images of the states that the onions and the meat are expected to attain without additional qualifiers.

The next set of examples in (50–53) illustrates detailed explanations as to how motions and actions in cooking should be carried out.

(50) きゅうりは…塩を振りかけて**ゴロゴロ**と転がし、**さっ**と水で洗って水気を切ります。ビール瓶か肉叩き、なければスリコギできゅうりをまわしながら、初めは「**トントン**」と、次第に「**バンバン**」と強く叩いてきゅうりが半分ほど破裂したら、…

Kyūri-wa . . . shio-o huri-kakete **gorogoro**-to korogashi, **saQ**-to mizu-de aratte mizuke-o kirimasu. Bīru-bin-ka niku-tataki, nakereba surikogi-de kyūri-o mawashi-nagara, hajime-wa "**tonton**"-to, shidai-ni "**banban**"-to tsuyoku tataite kyūri-ga hanbun-hodo haretsu-shitara, . . .

". . . after salting and rolling [**gorogoro**] the cucumbers (on a cutting board), rinse them quickly [**saQ**] and drain. With a beer bottle, a meat tenderizer, or otherwise a wooden pestle, lightly hit [**tonton**] the cucumbers first and then hit them hard [**banban**], so that they burst, . . ."

(Takamine 2012, 149)

(51) …キャベツ、人参、みょうが、青じそなどの野菜を**ザクザク**と刻み、大ぶりなボウルに入れる。そして塩壺から二つかみ分の塩を**さらさら**と振りかけ、手のひら全体を使い、**ぎゅっぎゅっ**と野菜を揉んでいく。

. . . kyabetsu, ninjin, myōga, aojiso-nado-no yasai-o **zakuzaku**-to kizami, ōburi-na bouru-ni ireru. Soshite shiotsubo-kara huta-tsukami-no shio-o **sarasara**-to hurikake, te-no hira zentai-o tsukai, **gyuQgyuQ**-to yasai-o monde-iku.

". . . after coarsely chopping [**zakuzaku**] the vegetables including the cabbage, carrots, myoga, and shiso, put them in a large bowl. Then sprinkle [**sarasara**] two handfuls of salt in the salt jar over them, and rub them firmly [**gyuQgyuQ**] by using the entire palm." (Watanabe 2015, 38)

(52) … 最後にサニーレタスを**ホワッホワッ**と葉っぱをつぶさぬように和える。

. . . saigo-ni sanīretasu-o **howaQhowaQ**-to happa-o tsubusanu-yō-ni aeru.

". . . at the end, mix the lettuce gently [**howaQhowaQ**], trying not to crush the leaves." (Kobayashi 2008, 77)

(53) 強火で**さっ**と、いや、**ささっ**と炒めるという感じに、**しんなり**しすぎないように火を通します。

Tsuyobi-de **saQ**-to, iya, **sasaQ**-to itameru-to iu kanji-ni, **shiNnari** shi-suginai-yō-ni hi-o tōshimasu.

"Over high heat, stir-fry [the kale] quickly [**saQ**], or rather, very quickly [**sasaQ**], so that it will not become too wilted [**shiNnari**]."

(Nagao 2021, 71)

There are a few onomatopoeic expressions in this set of examples: *tonton* and *banban* in (50), and *zakuzaku* and *sarasara* in (51). In (50), while *banban*—a sound of forceful hitting like banging—cooccurs with the prosaic adverb *tsuyoku* "hard," *tonton*—a sound of gentle hitting like tapping—stands by itself. Yet, these two mimetics alone adequately inform us of the different degrees of pressure to be applied to the cucumbers. The sequence of the *tonton* hitting followed by the *banban* hitting is auditorily imaginable and makes it straightforward to expect for the cucumbers ultimately to burst into pieces even without the prosaic elaboration. *Zakuzaku* in (51) evokes a sound of roughly or coarsely cutting up crisp and fibrous vegetables. Additionally, the *zakuzaku* manner of cutting implies that it does not involve a fine, methodical result like julienne or even thinner strips—a kind of cavalier action that strikes one as less stressful. Another onomatopoeia in (51), *sarasara*, refers to a light sound of dry granular objects like sand falling. Applied to cooking, this mimetic prompts visualization of the salt's falling not as a mass but as a continuous thin flow, as its reduplicated form infers. Two handfuls of salt are to be added to the vegetable mixture by the action denoted by the prosaic verb *hurikakeru* "sprinkle," but the qualification by *sarasara* makes sure that the salt is scattered evenly over the mixture. Even though the flow of the salt may actually not be heard, the manner in which the salt is added is guided by the visual image that the mimetic evokes.

As briefly mentioned earlier, *saQ* in (50) and (53) is a very common mimetic in cooking instructions although it is widely used beyond cooking. *SasaQ* in (53) is an emphatic form of *saQ*, but in this example, the minimal (linguistic) contrast between the two is relevant to the cooking process. The instruction first says *saQ-to* "quickly," but it is subsequently corrected to *sasaQ-to* to warn about a swifter action. The difference between *saQ-to* and *sasaQ-to*, in fact, is not so much about the exact duration as about drawing the reader's careful attention not to overcook the vegetable.

GyuQgyuQ in (51) and *howaQhowaQ* in (52) offer guidance of the hand movement in their respective contexts, but they refer to varying degrees of pressure to be applied to the vegetables. The basic cooking processes that are adopted here are prosaically described by *(tenohira zentai-o tsukai) momu* "rub (by using the entire palm)" in (51) and *(happa-o tsubusanu-yōni) aeru* "mix (trying not to crush the leaves)" in (52). The rubbing motion in (51) is further elaborated on by *gyuQgyuQ*, which calls for an action of firmly pressing down the vegetables. The reduplicated form indicates the action is repetitive, and each pressing motion is forceful, as the ending -Q of the base *gyuQ* suggests. The prosaic description in (52) warns the reader not to crush the lettuce leaves, but *howaQhowaQ* presents an exact image of the hand movement. According to a mimetic dictionary (Ono 2007), *howaQ* is characterized as "the manner in which softness or warmth hangs over." In the context of (52), we are instructed to scoop up the lettuce leaves gently and drop them softly, and repeat the cycle a few times. The motion is as if we pick up freshly fallen snow on our rounded palms and scatter it to the ground. The Q-ending of the base *howaQ* does not strictly suggest a forceful action in this case, but instead, the light lettuce leaves are abruptly but fluffily dropped back into the bowl. In addition, the reduplication signals a repetition of the same cycled motion several times. These two cases demonstrate that while the prosaic instructions describe base-line motions, the mimetic elaborations steer us to the precise manner in which the motions should be carried out.

Mimetics for the amount and size of ingredients are less common than those for other aspects of cooking instructions because tools like measuring spoons and cups are readily available and widely adopted. Yet, examples like those in (54–56), if not by exact measurements, give intuitive guidelines. We start with the ingredients list in (54) written by Hideko Takamine, an accomplished actress who was actively engaged in writing essays especially later in her life.

(54) サラダオイル（少々）
sarada-oil (shōshō)   vegetable oil (a small amount)
清酒（少々）
seishu (shōshō)   sake (a small amount)
醤油（**タラタラ**、くらい）
shōyu (**taratara**, kurai)   soy sauce (approximately **taratara**)
みりん（**タラリッ**）
mirin (**tarariQ**)   mirin (**tarariQ**)

(Takamine 2012, 61)

The list in (54) is a part of the compilation of her short essays on food and cooking that accompanies recipes. The extremely abbreviated amount information in this list of ingredients is obviously not dictated by strict measurements, but it gives a glimpse of her philosophy of cooking. As a lay person in the culinary domain, she claims that she can only share rough estimates—"eye estimate"—of ingredients that are subject to change according to her mood and health condition of the day. She goes on to say that the reader should consult her own "tongue" according to which her favorite tastes should be found (p. 6). Clearly, "a small amount" for vegetable oil and sake as well as the amounts of soy sauce and mirin given only in terms of mimetics (*taratara* and *tarariQ*) may not be helpful to everybody, especially the novice. Yet, how much soy sauce and mirin are called for is intuitively made out by the contrast between *taratara* and *tarariQ*. These mimetics share the base, *tara*, which generally illustrates the manner of a liquid dripping. The morphological frames of the mimetic forms make a slight difference in the amount of the liquids (soy sauce and mirin, in this case). The reduplication of *taratara* suggests a continuous flow of soy sauce. In contrast, the combination of the *-ri* ending and the final Q in *tarariQ* evokes the liquid drop being quickly added but not resulting in a splash. In brief, *taratara* is a thin stream of soy sauce, whereas *tarariQ* indicates one drop of mirin. Despite the sense of continuous flow of soy sauce that the reduplicative form generally implies, we figure that the recipe does not require a large quantity of the two liquids. Takamine in the instruction further guides us with the following reminder: *shiru-ga jabujabu shinai-yōni* . . . "so that the liquid does not end up with *jabujabu* . . ." (p. 61), where another mimetic *jabujabu* infers a pool of liquid. So, even a novice cook at the very least ascertains approximate quantities of the liquid ingredients based on the relationship among *taratara*, *tarariQ*, and *jabujabu*.

Hitahita points to the amount of a liquid and is quite common in cooking instructions. (55) is part of basic key points relevant to in-liquid cooking. They are scrupulously explained to help novice cooks.

(55) 火の通りが早い具材なら、少なめの**ヒタヒタ**、反対に時間がかかる具材は**たっぷり**の水で煮ます。
ヒタヒタ：具材の表面がところどころ水から出る。
かぶる位：具材全体が**ぎりぎり**水に浸る。
たっぷり：具材が完全に浸り、さらに２割水を足す。

Hi-no tōri-ga hayai guzai-nara, sukuname-no **hitahita**, hantai-ni jikan-ga kakaru guzai-wa **taQpuri**-no mizu-de nimasu.
hitahita: guzai-no hyōmen-ga tokoro-dokoro mizu-kara deru.
kaburu kurai: guzai zentai-ga **girigiri** mizu-ni hitaru.
taQpuri: guzai-ga kanzen-ni hitari, sara-ni 2-wari mizu-o tasu.

"Ingredients that are quickly cooked will be boiled in a smaller quantity of water, just enough to cover them [**hitahita**], whereas ingredients that take longer to be cooked will be boiled in plenty [**taQpuri**] of water.
[**hitahita**]: the surface of the ingredients is above the water here and there.
at the level of covering: all the ingredients are barely [**girigiri**] covered under the water.

[taQpuri]: once the ingredients are completely immersed in the water, add 20% more water" ("Amakarai Okazu" 2014, 21)

The amount of water varies depending on how fast each ingredient is cooked, but the first sentence in (55) suggests a general two-way division marked by mimetic words: *hitahita* for fast-cooking and *taQpuri* for long-cooking. Subsequently, these two mimetics are further defined along with *kaburu kurai* "at the level of covering," which too is widely used in cooking instructions. *Hitahita* and *taQpuri* are prosaically elaborated on, but once these cooking definitions are kept in the mind of the beginner cook, the mimetics are clearly advantageous for their ability to evoke relevant visual images in a single word. Interestingly, the definition of *kaburu kurai* uses a mimetic word, *giri-giri*, which refers to a level that is maximally close to a limit or a boundary. Altogether, (55) provides, in concrete and visual terms, an excellent essential guide not only to cooking techniques but to cooking vocabulary helpful to grasp them. Mimetics play an important role to that end.

The mimetic *korokoro* in (56) below also appeals to the visual sense regarding the size and shape of the shrimp.

(56) エビは…**コロコロ**に切って酒と塩をふる。

ebi-wa . . . **korokoro**-ni kitte sake-to shio-o huru.

". . . cut the shrimp into dice [**korokoro**] and sprinkle sake and salt over them." (Kobayashi 2008, 61)

The recipe does not say anything about how the shrimp is to be cut, except that the cutting outcome should be *korokoro*, which calls to mind a small, round object rolling over, resembling dice. Applied to shrimp, we figure medium-sized shrimp should be diced or cubed into 3 to 4 pieces. Moreover, the target shape underlying *korokoro* is akin to a dice-like object, and the direction of cutting is horizontal rather than vertical. Again, the single mimetic word is economically informative.

To reiterate diverse roles that mimetics can play in descriptions of cooking process, (57) presents a parade of four mimetic words contributing to different dimensions of food preparation.

(57) 続いて鍋に胡麻油をひき、そこへカボチャを**コロンコロン**。軽く炒めてしょう油と砂糖と日本酒で味付けし、さらに上から、カボチャが**ひたひた**になるほどの水を足し、だしの素を**サササッ**と加え、蓋をしてしばし**クツクツ**煮込む。

Tsuzuite nabe-ni goma-abura-o hiki, soko-e kabocha-o **koroNkoroN**. Karuku itamete shōyu-to satō-to nihonshu-de aji-tsuke-shi, sara-ni ue-kara, kabocha-ga **hitahita**-ni naru-hodo-no mizu-o tashi, dashi-no moto-o **sasasaQ**-to kuwae, huta-o shite shibashi **kutsukutsu** nikomu.

"Next, put sesame oil in the pan, and add the pumpkin cubes [**koroN-koroN**] to it. After stirring them lightly and seasoning them with soy sauce, sugar, and sake, pour water enough to cover the pumpkin [**hitahita**], quickly [**sasasaQ**] add powdered soup stock, cover the pot, and simmer [**kutsukutsu**] for a while." (Agawa 2012, 139)

The first, *koroNkoroN*, is a variant *korokoro* in (56). The accompanying "reverberation" that the "N" in *koroNkoroN* signals, as stated in (12), leads to the interpretation that the size of the cut-up pumpkin is larger than the shrimp pieces in (56). The amount of water specified in terms of *hitahita* suggests that some of the pumpkins emerge just above the water line. The three repetitions of *sa* in *sasasaQ* seem somewhat comical due to their underlying sense of exaggeration, but the message of a prompt action is clearly conveyed. Finally, *kutsukutsu* informs us that the pumpkins are to be cooked slowly at low heat.

In addition to instructions that directly touch on cooking processes, useful tips on how to select ingredients, cautionary advice, and notes on supplementary knowledge also constitute an important element in cooking narratives. Examples are given in (58–61). Once again, mimetics play a valuable role in this type of communication.

(58) **ゴリゴリ**だったり、**グチャグチャ**だったりではそれこそ台なし、歯ざわりと色を大切にしましょうね。

Gorigori-dattari, **guchagucha**-dattari-dewa sorekoso dainashi, hazawari-to iro-o taisetsu-ni shimashō-ne.

"It will be ruined if (the peas) are hard [**gorigori**] or mushy [**guchagucha**], so I want to stress the importance of firmness to the teeth and color."
(Takamine 2012, 37)

(59) この時、火力を強くして一挙にいためる方がよい。弱い**だらだら**火では、美味しく出来上がらないから、注意が肝腎だ。

Kono toki, karyoku-o tsuyoku shite ikkyo-ni itameru-hō-ga yoi. Yowai **daradara**-bi-dewa, oisiku deki-agaranai-kara, chūi-ga kanjin-da.

"At this point, it is best to turn the heat up and stir-fry (the ingredients) all at once. With low and slow [**daradara**] heat, they won't be tasty. It's important to pay attention." (Dan 1975, 80)

(60) 黒パンは**フカフカ**していない**ズッシリ**としたものを選び、…

Kuropan-wa **hukahuka** shite-inai **zuQshiri**-to shita mono-o erabi, . . .

"As for rye bread, get one that is dense [**zuQshiri**] rather than fluffy [**hukahuka**] . . ." (Takamine 2012, 221)

(61) 蓋を閉めて熱がこもると、**パリッ**と焼けた皮が**ブヨ**ってなっちゃうし。

Huta-o shimete netsu-ga komoru-to, **pariQ**-to yaketa kawa-ga **buyoQ**-te nacchau-shi.

"When covered with a lid, it [bento box] gets fraught with heat, and the crisp [**pariQ**] (fish) skin becomes soggy [**buyoQ**]." (Abe 2020, 91)

The two mimetics in (58) illustrate polar textures of peas that are both to be avoided: *gorigori* presents the mouth-feel of undercooked peas while *guchagucha* is the mushy texture resulting from overcooking. Even though the precise cooking time is not offered, an ideal consistency is negatively defined by the two images induced by the mimetics in this cautionary remark. The mimetic *daradara* in (59) is different from the use of the same word in (47). Instead of referring to a flow of a semi-liquid batter, *daradara* in (59) characterizes a slow, continuous cooking. Compounded with the prosaic word *hi* "fire, heat," *daradara-bi* "daradara-heat" is likely Dan's coinage. The *daradara* in the compound is metaphorically interpreted based on its rather negative sense of something dragging on without a substantial result or a person's lethargic state. *Daradara* in this context cautions that a slow (implying long) cooking at a low temperature is not suitable. It is also interesting and almost humorous that *daradara-bi* "*daradar*a-heat" sounds full of ill-feeling, expressing Dan's personal contempt toward the inappropriate cooking process. The bread selection in (60) specifically speaks of rye bread. Generally, favorable qualities of white bread for toasting are *hukahuka* and *huwahuwa* for softness or *mochimochi* and *moQchiri* for chewiness. *ZuQshiri* usually refers to a heavy weight, but it infers a dense texture when applied to bread. In (60) rye bread is a base for canape, and in order to withstand its savory topping, dense (*zuQshiri*) rather than fluffy (*hukahuka*) texture is recommended. (61) is uttered by the owner of a lunch-box business. She shares the common-sense knowledge that unvented steam could ruin the crispness of a broiled fish skin, which adds savor. The difference between *pariQ* and *buyoQ* is recalled as mouth-feel, crunchy vs. soggy. Consequential changes in appearance that the steam causes, from favorable *pariQ* to unwanted *buyoQ*, are instinctively imaginable in the face of these mimetics.

4 COOKBOOK SURVEY OF MIMETICS

Ohashi's (2015) survey, discussed in section 3 above, reports that women use mimetics more frequently in identifying "delicious" tastes, i.e., as *shizuru wādo* "sizzle word." As far as food and taste descriptions are concerned (section 2), however, the likelihood of frequent use of mimetics does not seem to be dictated so much by gender as by individual variation. In this section, I examine whether male and female recipe writers differ in their use of mimetics and whether any possible change is observed over time.

I have surveyed 21 cookbooks published over the span of 87 years from 1927 to 2014. Eleven of them are authored by females and 8 by males. The remaining two, published in 1927 and 1928, are compilations of recipes that resulted from Japan's first cooking program broadcasted on radio by NHK in 1925. Compiled by NHK, these two cookbooks do not list the authors, and their gender is unknown. There are other printed cookbooks available prior to the 1920s, but they are not included in this survey because the archaic language requires special skills to decipher. Those that are authored by females are represented in each of the decades between the 1940s and the 2010s, and multiple cookbooks by two authors, Ai Kidosaki (1986, 1987) and Katsuyo Kobayashi (1995, 2011), are included in the survey. The female authors in this study have been well known to the public through their professional activities in various media including TV programs, blogs, and publications of cookbooks. I was unable to find a well-balanced set of cookbooks by male authors that would be evenly distributed throughout the same time period on par with those by female authors. One of the reasons seems to be that the information about cooking, particularly home-cooking, that is featured on media outlets for the general public is led primarily by females. This is in line with the prevalent gender role of the society to date that a woman is supposed to cook for her family—a familiar ideology that has been common at least throughout much of the 20th century. I will explore this topic in chapter 7. Table 3.1 summarizes the information of the authors and the publication dates.[16]

The structure of a recipe and the visual presentation of essential components of a recipe have evolved over time, and they could vary widely depending on the author. Whitman and Simon (1993, 3) list the following elements relevant to forming a recipe although not all of them are always included: title, headnote, ingredients list, instructions, servings (yield) line, note, and variation.[17] All of the cookbooks I surveyed include titles, ingredients list, and instructions.[18] The use of notes and comments varied depending on the author, ranging from sparse to constant use. Notes are sometimes included in instructions, especially in the earlier cookbooks. Independent headnotes started to appear in the cookbooks after the mid 1960s in my dataset, but in more recent cookbooks in general, headnotes that give the author the opportunity to give personal anecdotes regarding the dish are becoming more standard. Headnotes can thus provide a useful window for a glimpse at how the author personalizes his/her recipes. It is important for our purpose that the

Table 3.1. Surveyed cookbooks.

Cookbook Title/Author	Gender of Author	Year of Publication
Cooking for Four Seasons		1927
Everyday Cooking		1928
Sawasaki, Umeko	F	1941
Egawa, Tomi	F	1957
Tatsumi, Hamako	F	1960
Tatsumi, Yoshiko	F	1978
Kobayashi, Katsuyo	F	1980
Kidosaki, Ai	F	1986
Kidosaki, Ai	F	1987
Kurihara, Harumi	F	1992
Kobayashi, Katsuyo	F	1995
Okada, Shiori	F	2007
Kobayashi, Katsuyo	F	2011
Army Cookbook	M	1937
Doi, Masaru	M	1969
Shiota, Maruo	M	1997
Deguchi, Kazumi	M	2002
Aita, Koji	M	2006
Nishi, Junichiro	M	2007
Kokubun, Taichi & Kobayashi, Kentaro	M	2009
Doi, Yoshiharu	M	2014

use of mimetics is examined in the same part of a recipe, and for this reason, I counted mimetic expressions only in cooking instructions, which all of the 21 cookbooks uniformly include. Although the discourse from which mimetics are collected is undeniably about food (e.g., taste, cooking process, presentation), all mimetic words have been counted for the purpose of analysis, whether or not they pertain directly to food.

Table 3.2 summarizes the token and type counts of mimetic expressions that appear in the instruction part of a given cookbook. The 21 cookbooks show a wide disparity in the number of recipes included. To achieve an evenness in this aspect, the token and type numbers of mimetics have been divided by the number of recipes in each cookbook, so that the mimetic-to-recipe ratio is measured uniformly across the 21 cookbooks examined in this study. Notwithstanding individual variation in using mimetics in cookbooks, women generally use more mimetic expressions by the number (tokens)

Table 3.2. Token and type counts of mimetics.

	Gender	Year	# of Pages	# of Recipes	Type	Token	Type/Recipe	Token/Recipe
Cooking for Four Seasons		1927	263	306	54	207	0.1764706	0.67647059
Everyday Cooking		1928	428	298	62	195	0.2080537	0.65436242
Sawasaki, Umeko	F	1941	219	119	40	79	0.3361345	0.66386555
Egawa, Tomi	F	1957	134	150	46	105	0.3066667	0.7
Tatsumi, Hamako	F	1960	220	154	110	242	0.7142857	1.57142857
Tatsumi, Yoshiko	F	1978	223	101	91	147	0.9009901	1.45544554
Kobayashi, Katsuyo	F	1980	91	63	76	127	1.2063492	2.01587302
Kidosaki, Ai	F	1986	114	142	61	199	0.4295775	1.40140845
Kidosaki, Ai	F	1987	100	67	92	178	1.3731343	2.65671642
Kurihara, Harumi	F	1992	112	126	13	54	0.1031746	0.42857143
Kobayashi, Katsuyo	F	1995	103	104	52	139	0.5	1.33653846
Okada, Shiori	F	2007	96	119	38	105	0.3193277	0.88235294
Kobayashi, Katsuyo	F	2011	79	68	29	68	0.4264706	1
Army Cookbooks	M	1937	325	248	6	36	0.0241935	0.14516129
Doi, Masaru	M	1969	254	214	16	67	0.0747664	0.31308411
Shiota, Maruo	M	1997	80	59	12	34	0.2033898	0.57627119
Deguchi, Kazumi	M	2002	94	64	9	27	0.140625	0.421875
Aita, Koji	M	2006	96	189	32	95	0.1693122	0.5026455
Nishi, Junichiro	M	2007	80	64	8	22	0.125	0.34375
Kokubun and Kobayashi	M	2009	144	83	35	109	0.4216867	1.31325301
Doi, Yoshiharu	M	2014	111	76	39	98	0.5131579	1.28947368

and more variety of mimetics (types) in cooking instructions. Furthermore, although the limited samples may prevent us from reaching larger generalizations, as far as the cookbooks written by males are concerned, more recent publications tend to contain a higher degree of mimetic use, such as in cookbooks by Kokubun and Kentaro (2009) and Doi (2014). In contrast, variation among cookbooks by female writers seems to reflect more of individual preferences for mimetics than the chronological factor. Among the cookbooks by female authors, Kidosaki (1987) and Kobayashi (1980) lead the group in the number and variety of mimetic use, followed by the mother-daughter pair, H. Tatsumi (1960) and Y. Tatsumi (1978). Of these cookbook writers, Kobayashi particularly stands out for her creative use of mimetic expressions throughout her recipe writing, as I will detail it in chapter 6.

It may be helpful to compare the survey results in table 3.2 with another study that observes the use of mimetics in recipes. Harada (2012) examines cooking instructions of the magazine *Shuhu no Tomo* "The Housewife's Friend," which was one of the three major women's magazines in wide circulation in the 20th century.[19] Her data were compiled based on one issue of the magazine in every 10 years from 1917 to 2008. Each issue has different numbers of recipes, but she calculated the token and type counts of mimetics, using the measure of ratio that I adopt in my survey. Her examination informs us that the highest numbers of 1.9 token and 1.2 type per recipe are observed in 1928, whereas 1998 marks the lowest use of mimetics in cooking instructions, reporting 0.5 token and 0.1 type per recipe. Although Harada concludes that mimetics in cooking instructions as is demonstrated in the magazine were on the decline, her survey report does not show a consistent decrease in the use of mimetics at an even pace over the period of 90 years. Additionally, in her study we cannot confirm female authorship in the magazine throughout the 90 years under investigation.

Returning to my survey of cookbooks, table 3.3 tallies the five most frequently used mimetic expressions that appeared in each of the 21 cookbooks examined. The top 20 mimetic words of the table indeed have strong associations with food and cooking. The English translations are provided that are consistent with the context. Most of them predominantly refer either to food items (largely texture) or to the cooking process, as is evident from their collocations. For instance, the second most frequent mimetic, *hitahita*, is a measurement term as exemplified earlier in (55) and refers to the level of liquid. *Kotokoto*, collocating with the verb *niru* "cook in liquid," offers a gauge for a low heating temperature by referring to a simmering state for some duration of time, similar to *kutsukutsu* in (57). *KaraQ-(to)* is almost always used (or implied) with the verb *ageru* "deep fry," depicting the resulting texture that is crisp (and brown) and not soggy. Note that *saQ-(to)* "quickly," *zaQ-(to)*

Table 3.3. Five most frequently used mimetics in each cookbook.

saQ-(to) "quickly"	18
hitahita "just enough liquid to cover"	10
koNgari "crisp"	9
shiNnari "soft, limp"	9
zaQ-(to) "quickly"	7
karaQ-(to) "crisp"	5
kotokoto "simmering"	4
jiQkuri "thoroughly"	4
kariQ-(to) "crisp"	3
saQpari "plain and refreshing"	3
dorodoro "(liquid) thick and sticky"	3
torori "soft and glutinous"	3
dorori "(liquid) thick and sticky"	3
parapara "sprinkle lightly"	3
hutsuhutsu "(liquid) boiling"	3
koNmori "bulging upward"	2
saQkuri "(mix) lightly"	2
suQ-(to) "quickly, easily"	2
pariQ-(to) "crisp"	2
poroporo "dry and crumbling"	2
aQsari "simple and light"	1
uQsuri "faintly"	1
karari "crisp"	1
kiQchiri "exactly"	1
guragura "boiling vigorously"	1
kurukuru "round and round"	1
zakuzaku "chopped into large pieces"	1
zaQkuri "roughly"	1
sarasara "loose, dry"	1
soQ-(to) "softly"	1
torotoro "soft and glutinous"	1
paQ-(to) "quickly"	1
barabara "sparsely scattered"	1
biQkuri "surprised"	1
piQtari "tightly"	1
piN-(to) "stretched tight"	1
huNwari "light and fluffy"	1

"quickly," *jiQkuri* "thoroughly," *koNmori* "bulging upward," and *suQ-(to)* "quickly and easily" (as well as possibly *parapara* "sprinkle lightly") have high familiarity in elaborating on a broad range of manner of actions far beyond the food dimension. However, even after disregarding these several mimetics, 70% of the mimetic expressions in table 3.3 that the cookbook authors frequently use are specialized to various aspects of food, ranging from texture, taste, and the cooking process to the expected desirable appearance. It suggests that the mimetic vocabulary plays an important role as a useful and efficacious vehicle by which the recipe writers can speak of food in communicating to their readers.

Moreover, the sustained use of a relatively narrow set of food- and cooking-related mimetics over time is consistent with Harada's (2012) findings. She reports that *saQ-(to)* "quickly," *koNgari* "crisp," *shiNnari* "soft, limp," *zaQ-(to)* "quickly," *karaQ-(to)* "crisp," and *karari* "crisp" are most frequently used; and that additionally *hitahita* "just enough liquid to cover," *torori* "soft and glutinous," *hoNnori* "slightly," *poQchiri* "small amount," and *toroQ-(to)* "soft and glutinous" are also regularly used although they are on the decline. All but one of the items (i.e., *karari*) in Harada's first group appear among the first 20 items in table 3.3. Despite its seeming infrequency, *karari* is a variant of *karaQ-(to)*, making the overlap virtually complete. As for the second group of mimetics, a majority also appear in table 3.3. Thus, common mimetics that partake in the language of recipes appear to form a relatively narrow set and not overly diverse, particularly when compared against the total number of words comprising the mimetic vocabulary as a whole. It means that those that are of recurring use in recipes may be codified as part of a technical language, specific to the food dimension. Nevertheless, they are "technical" terms which non-technical, novice people can effortlessly relate to by the visceral nature that the mimetic vocabulary class inherently has.

5 SOUND SYMBOLISM AND INNOVATION OF MIMETICS

One of the interesting aspects of words like mimetics, ideophones, and onomatopoeia in the world's languages is sound symbolism: the association between sound with meaning is not arbitrary (Hinton et al. 1994). The Frequency Code, as discussed in detail by Ohala (1994), for instance, claims that high frequency (pitch) sounds (e.g., vowels such as /i/ that are produced at the front of the mouth) are associated with small, thin, and light things, while low frequency sounds (e.g., vowels like /u/ that are made at the back of the mouth) are associated with the opposite meanings. The hypocoristic forms in English, such as *Jenny*, *Billy*, and *Stephie*, are one example illustrating the Frequency Code. The smallness as it is related to the terms of endearment is attributed to the front vowel /i/ of these nick names.

Not surprisingly, the non-arbitrary aspect of sound symbolism has been a topic of marketing research that pertains to food, given the large influence of language on consumers (e.g., "power of words") that was mentioned at the beginning of this chapter. In particular, much research has investigated the ways in which sound symbolism in brand names influences people's perceptions of products, as is reported in, for example, Klink (2000, 2001), Yorkson and Menon (2004), Ngo et al. (2011), Jurafsky (2014), and many more. This line of inquiry extends to the language of food from a variety of angles. Based on the Frequency Code, Yorkson and Menon (2004) report on experiments to test sound symbolic effects that product names of ice cream might have on people. One group of participants were told that a new ice cream product is being introduced under the brand name *Frish*, and another group under *Frosh*. It follows from the Frequency Code that a back vowel (as in *Fr<u>o</u>sh*) symbolizes bigger, heavier, slower, and duller objects. Applying this generalization to the names of ice cream, the researchers hypothesized that *Frosh* would be perceived as smoother, creamier, and richer than a name with a front vowel, *Fr<u>i</u>sh*. The participants were asked to read a prepared press release of the ice cream and to evaluate the product for its smoothness, creaminess, and richness. The results were borne out, attributing potential consumer's judgments to sound symbolism. This and the line of other research mentioned earlier confirm that the impact which language has on the marketing and advertisement of food cannot be underestimated.[20]

In more general terms, Hamano (1998) extensively investigates for Japanese what range of sound-meaning associations exist in mimetic words. Recall that earlier in (12) we have observed some instances illustrating that semantic characteristics are attributed to specific sounds or morphological forms in mimetics. Another type of sound symbolism as it is relevant to Japanese mimetics has to do with the voicing feature of consonants. Consonants contrast in the presence (voiced) or absence (voiceless) of vibration of the vocal chords, as with [b] vs. [p], [g] vs. [k], and [z] vs. [s]. Hamano claims that a voiced initial consonant of a mimetic base correlates with the semantic characteristic of "heavy/large/coarse/thick" whereas its voiceless counterpart is associated with the opposite sense of "light/small/fine/thin." In addition, the "coarseness" of a voiced consonant further extends to a nuance of "incompleteness." The two sets of contrast in (62) and (63), taken from Hamano (1998, 83, 85, with minor change in notation), illustrate the semantic correlations.

(62) a. Supurinkurā-no mizu-ga   *paQ*-to   kakatta.   [paQ]
        sprinkler-GEN   water-NOM   was.sprayed.on
        "A *splash* from the sprinkler sprayed on me."

   b. Mizu-o   *baQ*-to   kakerareta.   [baQ]
        water-ACC   was.poured
        "He threw (*a bucket of*) water (*and I was drenched*)."

88   Chapter Three

(63) a. Kono   hōrensō-wa   saQ-to   nite-arimasu.   [saQ]
         this   spinach-TOP   boil-exist
         "This spinach has been boiled *quickly*."

     b. Kono   hōrensō-wa   zaQ-to   nite-arimasu.   [zaQ]
         this   spinach-TOP   boil-exist
         "This spinach has been boiled *briefly* (and *incompletely*)."

It should be recalled that in section 3, I discussed several mimetics that cooccur with the prosaic verb *niru* "cook in a liquid": *kotokoto*, *kutsukutsu*, and *torotoro* for slow cooking at a low temperature; *gutsugutsu* and *hutsuhutsu* for cooking at a high temperature; and *guragura* for vigorous boiling. Of these, *kutsukutsu* and *gutsugutsu* contrast in voicing of the initial consonant of the base, kutsu (voiceless) vs. gutsu (voiced). The guidelines of the slow vs. vigorous cooking certainly reflect the sound symbolism underlying the contrastive voicing features of the minimally different pair of mimetics.[21]

Research on the sound symbolism of voiced vs. voiceless consonants of Japanese mimetics has been explored to examine how it influences people's judgments of food taste and texture (e.g., Sakamoto and Watanabe 2016; Shinohara et al. 2017; Kumagai et al. 2022; Uno et al. 2022). Sakamoto and Watanabe (2016), for one, report on their experiment in which participants were asked to drink 24 liquid samples that had been altered for taste and texture, and then to describe gustatory sensations in mimetic words. The study results show that the mimetics with the initial voiceless consonants of /s, h, ʃ/ correspond to a good taste and texture, whereas those with the voiced consonants of /g, b, z, d/ are associated with a bad taste and texture. They suggest as an implication of the study that mimetics may further index emotional evaluations like "pleasant" and "unpleasant" that consumers hold of products. In another experimental work, Shinohara et al. (2017) confirm that voiced consonants in mimetics give rise to an image of hard texture in food whereas voiceless counterparts are associated with a soft texture. They also found that the effects of sound symbolism were perceived by Japanese speakers but not by English speakers. Based on this observation, they conclude that sound perceptions and their semantic symbolism are subject to crosslinguistic variability.

Native speakers of Japanese are not consciously aware of the linguistic account for the systematic relation between sound and meaning. Yet, the regularity with which the sound symbolic phenomena are detected in the mimetic vocabulary mirrors the speaker's subconscious knowledge of the language. In fact, utterances that are built upon the systematic sound symbolic relation occur in our food discourse without being acknowledged as such. On the 2017 airing of the TV cooking show *Kyō-no Ryōri* "Today's Cooking," Yoshiharu

Doi (a cooking expert) recommended the *kotokoto* cooking because the ingredient (chestnuts) would fall apart in the *gotogoto* cooking. The two mimetics make a clear and intentional contrast in terms of the degree of heating. The *gotogoto* cooking at high heat would be too strong for the chestnuts, so the use of a lower temperature is advised. The level of a bubbling boil, *gotogoto*, and that of a slow simmer, *kotokoto*, reflect the meanings to which the voiced and voiceless consonants correspond as a pair. Both mimetics are common in cooking, but Mr. Doi could have chosen *gotogoto* (boil) vs. *kutsukutsu* (simmer) or *gutsugutsu* (boil) vs. *torotoro* (simmer) without changing the content of the instruction. However, the selection of the minimally contrastive pair—goto vs. koto—in this case is particularly intuitive and transparent to his audience.

Another illustration can be drawn from a TV reporter's utterance on a morning show, in which he reports the taste of a new udon noodle product. In describing the texture, he came up with an innovative mimetic *kumikumi*, and elaborated on his first impression by explaining that the texture is like chewing on *gumi*, a Japanese loanword based on German *gummi(baer)* "gummy bear." Crucially, instead of *gumigumi*, which would more directly correspond to the gummy texture, he opted for *kumikumi*, a voiceless counterpart of *gumigumi*. The audience instinctively figures that the consistency he tried to depict is chewy yet somewhat less resisting than with gummy bears. It is consistent with the commonly accepted standard of stickiness, elasticity, or firmness to the bite for udon noodles, just as other mimetics like *mochimochi* and *shikoshiko* identify. In this case, however, adlibbing a novel mimetic seems to add a new way of interpreting and appreciating the udon taste through its texture that is totally transparent to the viewers. The intuitive sense that motivated the reporter's creative word choice, thus, is not random but cohesive throughout the mimetic vocabulary, and his audience certainly shares his intended nuance.[22] It further indicates that the underlying, although subconscious, knowledge about sound symbolism is mutually recognized by the participants in this food communication.

The voicing feature of consonants that shows symbolic meaning may have some correlation with Japanese people's judgments of *shizuru wādo* "sizzle word" in Ohashi's (2015) survey summary discussed earlier in section 2. Contrastive of the list of mimetics in (21) that Japanese speakers consider to be *shizuru wādo*, Ohashi notes that those in (64), all mimetics, ranked low as *shizuru wādo*. I have supplied a food-related meaning for each mimetic word in (64).

(64) gotsugotsu "hard, coarse, rough"
      dorodoro "thick, sticky state of semi-liquid"

zarazara	"coarse, rough"
jarijari	"rough materials (like sand) rubbing"
dorori	"thick, sticky state of semi-liquid"
garigari	"a loud crunching sound"

Recall that the participants in this study were asked to choose words that they consider to evoke the sense of deliciousness from the list of pre-selected words that the survey team had prepared. In that light, the mimetics in (64) should not be regarded as the study participants' voluntary choice of words that are associated with "un-deliciousness." Instead, these pre-selected words ranked low among the total of 102 words, relative to those in (21), for instance. Citing the voiced consonants of the mimetics in (64), Ohashi (2015, 26) explains for the low ranking of them as follows: they reflect a strong "friction" that accompanies the textures they present, leading to an unpleasant reverberation. Although not in linguistic terms, Ohashi's reasoning attributes the "un-deliciousness" to the voiced consonant.

On the other hand, the relatively low ranking of the mimetics with voiced initial consonants in (64) may receive another interpretation, when put in a slightly different context. It should be remembered that the distributions of favorable mimetics that women chose as *shizuru wādo* was given earlier in (24) based on age groups. The list is repeated below.

(24) a. 15–19: purupuru "soft and elastic," huNwari "soft and fluffy," sakuhuwa "crisp and fluffy," **zakuQ-to** "loud crunching," **zakuzaku** "loud crunching"

b. 20–29: toroori "melting soft," mochiQ-to "chewy," mochimochi "chewy," huwahuwa "fluffy," **juwaa** "oozing," **juwaQ-to** "oozing," karikari "crunchy"

c. 30–39: moQchiri "chewy," kariQ-to "dry and crisp," tsuruQ-to "smooth and slippery," puripuri "plump and chewy," puriQ-to "plump and chewy," nebaneba "sticky"

d. 40–49: huwatoro "fluffy and melting soft," toroQ-to "melting soft," sakusaku "crisp," karaQ-to "dry and crisp"

e. 50–59: hokuri "warm and flaky," hoQkori "warm and flaky," tsurutsuru "smooth and slippery"

f. 60–69: shiQtori "moist"

Bold-faced mimetics have voiced initial consonants. The two mimetics in (24a) and the two in (24b), respectively, share the same base, *zaku* and *juwa*. It seems notable that younger people consider them among the higher ranked groups of mimetics that appeal to the sense of deliciousness, whereas they are not the choices by older age cohorts. The loud crunching sound and its associated coarseness symbolized by *zakuQ* and *zakuzaku*, as well as the forceful emission of smell or flow of liquid referred to by *juwaa* and *juwaQ*, are indeed consistent with Hamano's (1998) characterization of voiced initial consonants. Additionally, hard consistency, coarse surface, and emission or flow of thick substance coalesce around similar images. Importantly, these images are not necessarily negative but perhaps differently reacted to. That is, putting together the sound symbolic meanings with the age stratification, the evoked images stemming from "force" can be interpreted to mirror exertion of youthful energy. The solid bite of a hard-baked rice cracker or any other crunchy food item, as can be depicted by *garigari*, for instance, is perhaps more welcomed to the youth than to aging populations who are likely to favor food with a tender feel that is particularly easy on the teeth. The image that succulent juice oozing out of a sizzling steak in the manner *juwaQ* and *juwaa* in (24b) presents is also more appetizing to meat-eating youth than to older age groups who are mindful about its implications to health. The meaning symbolized by a particular sound can often be subjectively and flexibly construed according to individuals and circumstances. On the other hand, once younger age groups become older and then likely to change their food (especially texture) preferences and dietary choices, their perceptions of which words describe tastiness would evolve. Thus, changes in physical condition and capacity related to aging may well alter one's sense-based reactions and subsequently the verbal expressions describing one's sensual experiences.

As we have previously suggested, mimetics are a linguistic tool that is remarkably convenient as a marketing strategy for two palpable reasons: the direct sensual appeal stemming from the affecto-imagistic dimension, and the brevity of word form. It stands to reason that the restaurant industry pays much attention to what type of wording should appear more effective in menus (e.g., advice on the names of menu items, their descriptions and explanations). Citing how important choice of words is to attracting patrons' attention, a book on how to create menus (Nikkei Resutoran 2014, 168) emphasizes that mimetics help concretely convey what deliciousness entails. Under the heading "a word collection for menus," for instance, the manual lists mimetics in (65a) to be included in the names of food offerings. They highlight particular mouth-feels. The expression in (65b) is also suggested for a caption.

(65) a. uma-toro   "delicious-melting" [uma < umai "delicious" (prosaic)]
     sakusaku   "light, crisp"
     huwahuwa   "fluffy"
     purupuru   "soft and elastic"

    moQchiri   "chewy, elastic"
    hukahuka   "fluffy"

b. **suuQ**-to   tokeru
   suuQ-quotative   melt
   "melt smoothly"

The words in (65a), except for the first in the list, are free-occurring mimetics, but I surmise that they are to be combined with another word denoting a feature ingredient: e.g., **sakusaku** *huraido chikin* "crisp fried chicken" and **purupuru** *ebi-chiri* "chewy shrimp in chili sauce." Note that the mimetics in (65a) have been repeatedly discussed in previous research results and in our examples of food discourse, and it certainly confirms how seriously the mimetic vocabulary is taken by business owners and patrons.

As vivid as the images that mimetics evoke, many existing ones that are of frequent use are conventionalized and they might lose their immediate sensual impact. Trendiness of some mimetics in food discourse also evolves over time, as the transition in (22–23) attests to. However, speakers' linguistic ingenuity maintains a high level of expressiveness in food descriptions and evaluations. The mimetic vocabulary has an easy access to projected images, so coinage partakes in marketing efforts as a practical and efficacious path for drawing consumers' and patrons' attention and enticing their curiosity. The ultimate goal of food narratives is to figure out how best to arrive at productive interpersonal communication through the topic of food, and mimetics, existing and innovative alike, make a great contribution to that end. We have already observed an example of novel mimetics like *kumikumi*, which a TV reporter invented in describing the udon texture, as well as *uma-toro* in (65a), which combines the prosaic adjective *umai* "delicious" with the mimetic *torotoro* or *torori* "smooth, melting."

In a similar vein, Hayakawa (2007, 44–45) observes a few innovative mimetics that are attested. One is *koQsari*, which is a blend of two mimetic words, *koQteri* "rich" and *aQsari* "simple, light." It seems contradictory to put together these two mimetics that present virtually opposite taste qualities, but the blended mimetic refers to the taste of ramen noodles that is somewhere between *koQteri* and *aQsari*. A ramen specialty restaurant in Tokyo has on its menu *koQteri rāmen*, *aQsari rāmen*, and *koQsari rāmen*. *KoQteri rāmen* features its rich soup: the caption says *toroQ-to shita sūpu* "soup that is toroQ," where *toroQ* is a mimetic that speaks to its thick consistency and rich flavor. In contrast, *aQsari rāmen* comes in a soup with soy sauce base and tastes lighter. *KoQsari rāmen* is made with half of *koQteri rāmen* and half *aQsari rāmen*, so that the taste is literally a blend of the two (Kaishiden 2013).

Another instance of a coined mimetic that Hayakawa comments on is *punipuni*, which is based on *puripuri*. She explains that the sound of *ni* expresses a unique stickiness and is incorporated to *puripuri*, which displays elasticity typical of gelatin, ultimately generating *punipuni*. She does not elaborate on the sound symbolism that underlies the relation between *ni* and stickiness, but *punipuni* seems to represent the texture that is elastic and sticky, just like some mochi products. Indeed, an online search (https://cookpad.com) finds recipe links for mochi made of potatoes and cornstarch (*punipuni jagaimo-mochi* "punipuni potato-mochi," by izumealove), rice flour dumplings (*oyatsu punipuni shiratama* "punipuni rice flour dumplings for snack," by mihochi), and cake with mochi in it (*mochi-iri punipuni kēki* "punipuni cake with mochi in it," by @rieco). Supposedly, all of these dishes yield a combined texture of elasticity and stickiness.

Taking into consideration many aspects of mimetics that are accommodated in the system of language, the Panasonic advertisement for a juicer in (66) is a witty and stylish slogan. The four lines do not seem to cohere into a meaningful message, each apparently pointing to an individual facet of some relevance to the juicer. Yet, as cryptic as it may appear, the catchphrase skillfully incorporates elements of word play and rhythmic tones in delivering an advertising message.

(66) ビタミンは bitamin-wa "vitamins-TOP"
  ゴクゴク、 **gokugoku** "gulp-gulp"
  濃く濃く、 kokukoku "thick-thick"
  しぼりたて。 shiboritate "just squeezed"

"For vitamins (of fruits and vegetables), gulp [**gokugoku**] a thick juice that is freshly squeezed" (Panasonic n.d.)

The first line starts with a health benefit of using the juicer, namely, vitamin intake. The advertisement then moves on to consumption of the juice, which is foregrounded by the sound and manner of the drinking act that the sole mimetic *gokugoku* depicts. *Gokugoku* mimics the sound of continuously drinking a large amount of liquid. Its implicit nuances are a thirsty condition, a refreshing taste, and arguably masculinity underlying the energetic manner of drinking.

The third line, *koku-koku*, is a repetition of the gerundive form (*koku*) of the prosaic adjective *ko-i* "thick," and emphasizes that the machine-squeezed juice is succulently thick, rather than watery and insipid. A rhythmic transition from *gokugoku* to *koku-koku* is achieved by what is termed as moraic assonance (Tsujimura and Davis 2009). Assonance in English rhyming—a type of imperfect rhyme—is characterized by having stressed vowels match but the following consonants do not (Zwicky 1976). Examples include *wine* vs. *times* and *sleepin'* vs. *dreamin'*, where the vowel in each pair is identical but what follows it is not alike. A similar pattern of rhyming practice is prevalent in Japanese especially in Hip Hop lyrics, but due to the difference in phonological systems of the two languages, the concept of assonance is applied to the domain of mora, which is an essential phonological unit in Japanese. Briefly put, moraic assonance is exemplified by pairs like *somari* vs. *tobari*, in which the vowels are identical in each corresponding mora (a unit roughly equivalent to syllable) even though the immediately preceding consonants are not: the vowel sequence is [o-a-i] in both but the accompanying consonants differ, [s-m-r] vs. [t-b-r].

With this rhyming pattern in mind, the mimetic *gokugoku* and the prosaic *koku-koku* in (66) is considered to rhyme as an instance of moraic assonance. Additionally, the same number of moras in each of *gokugoku* and *koku-koku*, i.e., 4 moras, enhances the rhythmic effect. The last line *shiboritate* "just squeezed" in a prosaic phrase showcases the handiness with which a freshly squeezed juice is made available at any time. The individual line may be fragmental, but when intoned in the mora counts of 5-4-4-5 interspersed with the two rhymed lines, this catchphrase not only has multi-sensory appeals but communicates well with consumers through the brief, coded language.

Gustatory experiences are by nature very visceral and hence personal. Communicating such individual experiences seems a great deal more productive if linguistic and rhetorical delivery comports with the subjective nature of the message. In that light, it is no exaggeration that the mimetic vocabulary contributes much to food discourse through a mosaic of sensual reactions inherent to the word class.

NOTES

1. A summary of cross-disciplinary research on taste perception and consumption is given in Krishna and Elder (2010). Also see Rozin and Hormes (2010) on sensory marketing from a psychological perspective; and Ward and Simner (2003) and Simner and Ward (2006) on their study with synesthetes for an interaction of a perception (taste) with a concept (word). Moriguchi (2015), in his brief, somewhat informal, remarks on sensory marketing, echoes the relevance of the sense of touch (tactile sensation) and interactions among senses, in particular, as future issues to be explored by the food industry.

2. A geminate consonant corresponds to the hiragana and katakana syllabary of 「っ」 and 「ッ」 in writing.

3. A coda nasal sound corresponds to the hiragana and katakana syllabary of 「ん・ン」 in writing.

4. In ruminating on ways to reconfigure the difference between the two types of vocabulary, I have been influenced by the literature in anthropology, aesthetic studies, and music including Armstrong (1971, 1975), Goodman (1976), and Feld (1988). The idea presented here is further elaborated on in Tsujimura (2022a).

5. Although Hayakawa et al. (1997) do not seem to consider *sappari-shita* to be a mimetic word, it is listed in Kakehi et al.'s (1996) mimetic dictionary. I follow Kakehi et al.'s classification and place *sappari* under (11a).

6. The first two words in (11b) are of the same pronunciation but differ in the Chinese character assigned to them. Hayakawa et al. (1997) explain that judging from the food items with which the participants chose to associate them, the first word of the two refers to greasiness typical of liquid oil (as in tempura, French dressing, and fried chicken) whereas the second relates to solid oil (as in bacon, fat of meat, and broiled eel).

7. Strauss (2005) and Strauss et al. (2018) found that Japanese demonstrates less mimetic expressions than Korean in TV food commercials and online recipes that they examined. As the next two sections in this chapter show, however, the use of mimetics is quite extensive and productive in Japanese food discourse.

8. In their interesting article, Suter et al. (2020) report on a comparative study that investigates the history and culture of non-alcoholic beverage consumption between Japan and Australia. Part of their concluding remarks touches on the issue of "the culturally and historically constructed nature of taste" (p. 343). The emphasis on texture as a key element leading to the concept of tastiness in Japanese food scenes seems to me to suggest that cultural and historical considerations are called for in unpacking what people consider to be good-tasting and unpalatable in different languages.

9. The 183 words in Muto's study include a few that are not mimetics. For example, she treats *atsuatsu* "piping hot" and *tsubutsubu* "lumps" as mimetic words, but they are reduplicated forms of prosaic words, *atsui* "hot" (adjective) and *tsubu* "grain" (noun). A large number of mimetics take the reduplicated form, but reduplication is a common morphological process of word formation that is adopted for the purposes of emphasis and plurality. I surmise that Muto erroneously took the reduplication of *atsuatsu* and *tsubutsubu* as a sign of mimetics.

10. The meaning definition of *puripuri* that Kakehi et al. (1996) provide characterizes human body parts, especially those of women. The one I give here is based on general dictionaries including *Kojien*.

11. Kakehi et al. (1996) do not include *shuwashuwa* in their mimetic entries. The definition is based on another mimetic dictionary by Ono (2007).

12. As indicated by custard being a typical food with which Muto associates *maQ-tari*, the mimetic, when used as a taste word, refers to rich and full-flavored mouthfeel rather than simply "mild."

13. The report does not make it clear exactly what the participants were instructed to do, e.g., whether they were to choose a specified number of words and rank them, or were simply to choose an unspecified number of words from the list. Also, an earlier version of the report (Ohashi 2010) states that the corresponding word list for the 2003 survey includes 77 words (59 mimetics and 18 prosaic expressions, on my

count), which suggests that the word lists were not identical throughout the multi-year project.

14. This information is the background of the study conducted in 2015 and provided in Ohashi (2015). The participants' background information is not available in Ohashi (2016).

15. In (34) *shakishaki*, which shares the base *shaki* with *shaQkiri* in (37), depicts the consistency of burdock roots. These variants with the base *shaki* typically refer to the crisp and moist texture characteristic of fruits and vegetables (e.g., apples, cucumbers, celery, lettuce).

16. For convenience, the titles "Cooking for Four Seasons," "Everyday Cooking," and "Army Cookbook" are given in English in tables 3.1 and 3.2. Their Japanese titles are *Shiki-no Ryōri*, *Hibi-no Ryōri*, and *Guntai Chōrihō*, respectively.

17. Following Labov's (1972) narrative framework, Cotter (1997) analyzes recipes, dividing their parts somewhat differently from Whitman and Simon (1993). In this book I adopt Whitman and Simon's terminology for ease of reference.

18. Japanese cookbooks utilize photographs to illustrate the appearance of completed dishes and/or step-by-step cooking processes more widely than English-language cookbooks. Out of the 21 cookbooks I surveyed for this study, black-and-white photographs were used as early as Egawa's 1957 cookbook. According to Halloran (2014), photographs did not appear in cookbooks written in English until the 1980s.

19. The other two women's magazines are *Hujin no Tomo* "Ladies' Friend" and *Hujin Kurabu* "The Women's Club." These magazines started before the war, and continued circulation during and after it. They are considered important to the history of women in Japan.

20. Maurer et al. (2006) and Jurafsky (2014) report on similar studies that demonstrate the effect of language on people's judgments.

21. It is important to keep in mind, however, that pairs like *kutsukutsu* vs. *gutsugutsu* are not systematically found. For example, a voiceless counterpart of *guragura* "vigorous boiling," i.e., *kurakura*, does not refer to slow cooking, although it depicts a dizziness. Nor does a voiced counterpart of *torotoro* "simmer," i.e., *dorodoro*, symbolize cooking at a high temperature, although *dorodoro* in cooking can refer to a thick semi-liquid texture. So, in order to detect a clear effect of sound symbolism, a minimally contrastive phonetic pair within a narrowly defined semantic field should be taken into consideration.

22. See Uno et al. (2022) and Kumagai et al. (2022) for experimental studies on sound symbolism relevant to Japanese food texture.

Chapter Four

The Vocabulary of Food Preparation—Concept and Lexical Process

As globalization of foodways progresses, we come to the realization that an individual food item or a food preparation process named in one language and its translation equivalent in another language may not always represent the same object or concept. We have discussed one example in chapter 2, drawing on the English word *rice* and its translation equivalents in Japanese. Another example is found with "steamed rice" for cooked rice, the term used on English menus at Japanese (and Chinese) restaurants in the US. In my own conception as a native Japanese, making *gohan* "cooked rice" does not involve steaming, which is roughly translated as *musu* in Japanese. Steaming or the process of *musu* requires an ingredient to not be submerged in water, but cooking rice, whether in the Japanese or English context, assumes that the water completely covers the grain. In fact, this process is more in line with boiling. Furthermore, rice cooking in Japanese culinary culture is not complete until after the rice absorbs all the water AND is let sit in the residual steam and moisture for 10 to 15 minutes without removing the lid. This last step is referred to as *murasu*. These rice cooking stages are collectively named by the verb *taku*. I will discuss it in more detail later, but this example suggests that culinary processes are not necessarily conceptualized in a uniform fashion across cultures. In addition, such disparities bear interesting consequences to the way in which concepts relevant to food preparation are lexicalized into individual verbs.

    The primary goal of this chapter is to demonstrate that the organization of words for food preparation is subject to linguistic analysis by deploying a small set of semantic features. Concepts pertinent to food preparation are represented by individual verbs in some cases whereas in others they are periphrastically expressed (e.g., by a combination of a verb and an expression external to it). We will see that languages may differ as to what linguistic tools and mechanisms are employed in mapping concepts onto linguistic expressions. Our examination verifies that the organization of individual words and periphrastic expressions to describe various aspects of food preparation is not random but highly regular and systematic, and that culture-specific concepts are fully accommodated by invoking language-specific tools that are commonly adopted in semantic domains beyond foodways. I will demonstrate these linguistic contributions to the vocabulary of food preparation based on cooking verbs, where "cooking" is narrowly conceived of as food preparation with heat. At the end of the chapter, I will briefly discuss cutting verbs available in Japanese.

1 COOKING VERBS—LEXICALIZATION AND SEMANTIC COMPONENTS

Drawing from analytical measures of distinctive features in phonology, Lévi-Strauss (2013) attempted to examine cooking methods by applying the methodological concept to the cooking vocabulary. Here I shall focus only on the aspect that is of direct relevance to our discussion. Lévi-Strauss analyzes the three cooking methods of roasting, boiling, and smoking by assigning a positive or negative value of the semantic features, [+/-air] and [+/-water]. In the binary feature assignments, roasting is characterized as [-air] [-water], boiling as [-air] [+water], and smoking as [+air] [-water]. This three-way distinction has come to be known as the culinary triangle.

In evaluating to what extent the culinary triangle can be universally applied, Lehrer (1972) advances a lexical analysis of cooking words in several languages (including Japanese) that semantically dissect the cooking vocabulary into componential specifications like [+/-air] and [+/-water].[1] More elaborate than Lévi-Strauss's semantic features, the set of meaning components that Lehrer employs ranges from those that are thought to be cross-linguistically applicable (e.g., [+/-water], [+/-fat], [+/-direct heat]) to those that are commonly, but not universally, characteristic (e.g., [+/-submerge], [+/-long cooking time]). It further includes semantic components that are more restricted to specific utensils and ingredients (e.g., [+covered pot] for *braise*, [+barbecue sauce] for *barbecue*). Combinations of these components are shown to be helpful in identifying how concepts of cooking activities are represented as lexical forms while distinguishing among them. The semantic approach to word meaning under componential analysis is of great relevance to typological investigations of lexicalization patterns that languages exhibit. Meaning components are internally specified as part of the meaning of a word in some languages whereas in other languages, the same components are externally expressed as collocates. By looking at the way in which semantic components are lexicalized internally or periphrastically, we can acquire a better understanding of typological regularities and variation. In addition, the taxonomy of the cooking vocabulary resulting from componential analysis is considered valuable to discerning semantic relations like hyponymy and incompatibility among individual terms of food preparation in a language. Analyzing semantic features along these lines, thus, suggests broader implications to the general lexical organization of language.

My semantic analysis of Japanese cooking verbs below takes a similar componential approach to Lehrer's as a methodological foundation. I will, however, make necessary modifications that are motivated by the concepts and linguistic expressions that highlight and accommodate crosscultural and crosslinguistic differences. As noted earlier, the cooking vocabulary to be analyzed in this section is restricted to verbs that denote the use of heat.

I begin with some of the semantic components that Lehrer (1969, 1972) considers to play major roles in classifying English cooking words. Specifications of positive vs. negative values in (1) highlight core concepts that characterize individual cooking actions and have linguistic representations as meaning components. The italicized verbs for sampling are marked for each feature.

(1) a. use of water (wine, milk, etc.): *boil ~ grill*
   [+Non-fat liquid] v. [-Non-fat liquid]

   b. use of fat: *fry ~ boil*
   [+Fat] v. [-Fat]

   c. direct or radiated heat v. conducted heat: *broil ~ bake*
   [+Direct] v. [-Direct]

   d. vigorous v. gentle cooking action: *boil ~ simmer*
   [+Vigorous] v. [-Vigorous]

   e. long v. short cooking time: *stew ~ parboil*
   [+Long time] v. [-Long time]

   f. large amount v. small amount of some substance: *deep fry ~ sauté*
   [+Large] v. [-Large]

   g. additional special parameters:
   [+To soften] → *stew*
   [+Rack or sieve] → *steam*
   [+Alcohol] → *flamber*
   etc.

The bifurcation of the required use of non-fat liquids like water and broth minimally separates *boil* from *grill*. Likewise, *boil* and *simmer* are distinguished from each other by indicating whether the cooking method involves a vigorous action or not, i.e., [+Vigorous] for *boil* and [-Vigorous] for *simmer*. In addition to the primary features like (1a–f), some of the cooking methods are identified for narrower, more specific characteristics, including unique purposes (e.g., *stew*) as well as necessary utensils (e.g., *steam*) and ingredients (*flamber*). These special features are unary with only the positive specification. The summary of the feature specifications for cooking words in English that Lehrer (1969) provides further includes stipulations as to whether a verb can collocate with a liquid or solid ingredient as an item to be cooked. For example, we can boil both liquids and solids, as in *Peter boiled water/potatoes*. However, only solid ingredients but not liquids can be stewed, e.g., *The chef stewed beef/*milk*. In contrast, liquids are the only ingredients that can be reduced, e.g., *The wine/*cod is being reduced*. So, to reflect these collocational restrictions, *boil* is assigned [+Liquids] and [+Solid], stew [-Liquids] and [+Solids], and *reduce* [+Liquids] and [-Solids].

The organization of English cooking verbs developed by Lehrer (1969, 1972) is laid out in table 4.1. The list in (2) exemplifies how the verbs are componentialized. For brevity, only the semantic components that are assigned to each of the verbs classified under "$boil_1$," are presented.

(2) $boil_1$ [+Non-fat liquid] [-Fat]
       $boil_2$ [+Non-fat liquid] [-Fat] [+Vigorous action]
       simmer   [+Non-fat liquid] [-Fat] [-Vigorous action]
       stew   [+Non-fat liquid] [-Fat] [-Vigorous action] [+Long cooking time] [+To soften]
       poach   [+Non-fat liquid] [-Fat] [-Vigorous action] [+To preserve shape]
       braise   [+Non-fat liquid] [-Fat] [-Vigorous action] [+Lid]
       parboil   [+Non-fat liquid] [-Fat] [-Long cooking time]
       steam   [+Non-fat liquid] [-Fat] [+Vigorous action] [+Rack, sieve, etc.]
       reduce   [+Non-fat liquid] [-Fat] [+Vigorous action] [+Reduce bulk]

As Lehrer (1969) notes, the taxonomy of cooking words in table 4.1, which results from componential analyses of the individual verbs like those in (2), indicates semantic relations of incompatibility and hyponymy among them. For instance, words that are divided by vertical lines in the same row are incompatible with each other (e.g., $boil_1$, *fry*, *broil*, and *bake*). Words separated by horizontal lines indicate hyponymy. So, *braise* is a hyponym of *stew* while *sauté* is a hyponym of *fry*.

Turning to the Japanese cooking vocabulary, *ryōri-suru* "cook" is the broadly conceived word to refer to general cooking preparation and subsumes

Table 4.1. Classification of English cooking words. Source: Lehrer 1969. Reprinted with modification by permission of Cambridge University Press.

Cook								
boil₁				fry		broil		bake
simmer	boil₂			sauté pan-fry	French-fry deep-fry	grill	barbecue charcoal	plank	roast	shirr	scallop
poach	stew	parboil	steam	reduce							
	braise										

more specific verbs that name a variety of activities for cooking methods. Lexical items that I examine below include *wakasu* "boil (water)," *niru* "cook," *yuderu* "boil," *yugaku* "parboil," *taku* "cook (rice)," *musu* "steam," *hukasu* "steam," *ageru* "fry," *itameru* "stir-fry," *yaku* "roast/broil," *aburu* "grill," *iru* "parch/roast," and *kogasu* "char." Note that I have temporarily given English glosses here as rough estimates for equivalent meanings, but their underlying concepts and nuanced meanings will be detailed below in the course of discussion. As with the English taxonomy in table 4.1, all these Japanese cooking verbs in my analysis assume the use of heat, i.e., [+Heat]. When the distinction of direct or indirect heat is pertinent, it will be so specified. The classification of Japanese cooking verbs is based in part on Tsujimura (2018a, forthcoming) but has been modified and further extended to include additional words that had not been analyzed previously. To begin, the organization of the Japanese cooking verbs that I consider is presented in table 4.2.

The major division I draw has to do with the use of water and that of fat. It is worth noting that the use of water, indicated by the features of [+/-Water], is more narrowly specified than the use of non-fat liquid, which is one of the primary features in Lehrer's analysis. Contrastive with more inclusive liquid options, singling out water as part of cooking processes turns out to be relevant to culinary concepts underlying the cooking vocabulary in Japanese. The parameters concerning water and fat separate the 13 verbs into four categories: [+Water] [-Fat] (*wakasu, niru, yuderu, yugaku, taku, musu, murasu,* and *hukasu*), [-Water] [+Fat] (*ageru, itameru, yaku*), [-Water] [-Fat] (*yaku, aburu, iru*), and [-Water] (*kogasu*). The last category is unmarked for the use of fat. These four groups are divided by double vertical lines in table 4.2 for expository purposes.

[+Water] [-Fat]

While sharing the features [+Water] [-Fat], *wakasu, niru$_1$,* and *musu* are interpreted to be incompatible with one another in the sense that each does not imply the other. For example, *wakasu* does not imply *niru*, and *niru* does not imply *musu*. The vertical positioning divided by a horizontal line suggests the hyponym relation between the two terms. The hyponym relation is demonstrated by *yuderu* and *yugaku*, for instance: *yugaku* is a type of *yuderu*, so it is a hyponym of *yuderu*. By the same token, *hukasu* is a hyponym of *musu*.

I explain the members of the [+Water] [-Fat] category from left to right. *Wakasu* is a unique word in that water is the sole item to be processed by heat. That is, its purpose is exclusively boiling water, and as such, the process does not allow for any ingredients. This distinct characteristic is marked as

Table 4.2. Classification of Japanese cooking words.

				ryōri-suru						
wakasu	niru₁			musu	ageru	itameru	yaku₁	yaku₂	iru₁	iru₂	kogasu
	yuderu	niru₂	taku (+murasu)	hukasu				aburu			
		yugaku									

wakasu	niru₁			musu	ageru	itameru	yaku₁	yaku₂	iru₁	iru₂	kogasu
	yuderu	niru₂	taku (+murasu)	hukasu				aburu			
		yugaku									

[-Ingredient] to isolate it from other members under the [+Water] [-Fat] category and also from the remaining verbs in table 4.2. Furthermore, in order to reach the boiling point, a rigorous heating action is necessary. The verb is, thus, marked as [+Vigorous action]. The selection of direct object for *wakasu* is restricted to *(o-)yu* "hot water," not allowing *mizu* "cold water": *(o-)yu-o wakasu* [hot.water-ACC boil] "boil (hot) water" vs. ungrammatical **mizu-o wakasu* [cold.water-ACC boil] "boil (cold) water." The direct object that cooccurs with the verb is what is produced by the heating process instead of an item that is expected to undergo a change in shape or condition. The English verb *boil* contrasts with *wakasu* in this respect. In *boil water*, the water refers to cold water whose temperature is expected to change as a result of the process. These two patterns in the semantic nature of direct objects correspond to verbs of creation and verbs of change of state in the lexical semantics literature (e.g., Levin 1993). In both Japanese and English, the verbs in *ie-o tateru* [house-ACC build] "build a house" and *sukāto-o nuu* [skirt-ACC sew] "sew a skirt" belong to verbs of creation. Their direct objects, i.e., "house" and *sukāto* "skirt," refer to what have been created as a result of building and sewing actions, respectively. In contrast, the verbs in *ki-o kiru* [tree-ACC cut] "cut a tree" and *ninniku-o tsubusu* [garlic-ACC crush] "crush garlic" are change of state verbs, denoting that each of the cutting and crushing actions changes the original condition of a tree or garlic. That is, a tree is not created by cutting, nor is garlic by crushing. Thus, *wakasu* is grouped together with *tateru* "build" and *nuu* "sew" as belonging to the lexical semantic class of creation verbs.

Although less frequently encountered, *wakasu*, as a cooking verb, seems to allow for cooccurrences with other liquids than water in limited contexts. In social media sites, we occasionally find examples like *gyūnyū-o wakasu* [milk-ACC boil] and *ocha/mugicha-o wakasu* [tea/barley.tea-ACC boil]. However, the meaning of *wakasu* in the first example seems more in line with warming rather than boiling, and in the second, *wakasu* has the general sense of preparing tea rather than referring to a specific phase of the tea-making process. Given that a larger selection of direct objects beyond milk and tea is not detected, [+Vigorous action] and [-Ingredient] sufficiently characterize semantic components relevant to *wakasu*.[2]

The next verb, $niru_1$, covers a general concept of cooking with heat and water, and accordingly exhibits more wide-ranging references than other verbs in this category. It is contrastive with *musu* as to whether the cooking process requires ingredients to be covered with the water. *Musu* can be regarded as a translation equivalent to *steam* in English, as briefly mentioned earlier, and ingredients are not expected to have direct contact with the water. With $niru_1$, on the other hand, ingredients to be cooked are submerged in the water. This

The Vocabulary of Food Preparation—Concept and Lexical Process 105

difference is notated by [+Submerge] for *niru₁* and [-Submerge] for *musu*. Although *niru* is considered to extend rather widely to cooking processes with heat and water, it can also be branched out to its slightly narrower definition. For this reason, I divide *niru* into two variants, more general vs. more specific, and refer to them as *niru₁* and *niru₂*. *Niru₂*, along with *yuderu* and *taku*, are types of *niru₁* and thus are hyponyms of *niru₁*.

These three hyponyms share with *niru₁* the components of [+Water], [-Fat], and [+Submerge] but are further particularized by additional parameters. With *niru₂*, the liquid used for this method is not just water but with additional flavoring agents. For instance, liquids typical of Japanese-style dishes include *dashi* "stock," soy sauce, sugar, sake, mirin, and a blend of any of them. In fact, these liquids can be with or without water. The *niru* cooking process as a whole is intended to make ingredients tender or a preferred doneness. Additionally, when a seasoned liquid is used in *niru₂*, the (non-liquid) ingredients are expected to absorb the flavor and taste of the liquid mixture. This special distinction between the two *niru*'s is made by marking *niru₂* with [+Special cooking liquid]. Given the purposes of *niru*, cooking time varies depending on (non-liquid) ingredients and also on individual preferences as to how deeply the seasoning is absorbed (i.e., how strong- or mild-flavored resulting tastes are aimed at). The verb *niru* is generally a change of state verb, cooccurring with names of solid ingredients, as in *kabocha-o niru* [pumpkin-ACC cook] "cook pumpkins" and *butaniku-o niru* [pork-ACC cook] "cook pork." Although less common, however, it seems that the verb is able to serve as a creation verb as well. The dictionary *Meikyō Kokugo Jiten* gives the example of *shichū-o niru* [stew-ACC cook] "cook a stew" and specifically notes that *shichū* "stew" is a dish resulting from the cooking process. Other acceptable examples of the creation verb use may include *nikujaga-o niru* and *kobumaki-o niru*, where *nikujaga* "meat and potatoes cooked in soy sauce and sugar" and *kobumaki* "kelp roll with fish in it (cooked in soy sauce and sugar)" are names of popular dishes rather than raw ingredients before cooking.

Turning to *yuderu*, it generally corresponds to what English *boil* means but the liquid must be water.[3] The cooking water is brought to a boil, but after that, the water temperature may be retained or lowered as long as at least slow bubbles keep showing. Ingredients to which *yuderu* applies range from vegetables, beans, eggs, to meat and poultry. A hyponym of *yuderu*, *yugaku* is a type of *yuderu*, sharing the component of [+Submerge] and the requirement of water as the exclusive cooking liquid. What separates the two, however, is the cooking time and the purpose of the process. The cooking time needed for *yuderu* depends on ingredients since its primary and general purpose is to make them tender or into a preferred doneness. In contrast, similar to parboiling in English, *yugaku* requires only a quick action of submerging an ingredient in boiling water. A longer duration would end up with the process of *yuderu*. As for the purpose of the process, *yugaku* is to remove strong, sometimes bitter, tastes that are experienced with leafy vegetables like spinach. As a consequence, the range of ingredients to which *yugaku* applies is more restricted than with *yuderu*. Meats and fish often have strong smell or sliminess, but it is extremely odd, if accepted at all, to use *yugaku* to describe the process of removing it. A more suitable word for that purpose applied to meats and fish is a compound verb *yu-dōshi-suru* [hot.water-pass. through-do], which describes pouring hot water over those ingredients. The feature of [-Long cooking time] and an additional special parameter of [+To remove harsh taste] characterize the cooking process *yugaku*. In a number of Japanese-language cookbooks, *yugaku* is replaced by *(saQto) yuderu* "boil quickly," where *saQto* "quickly" consists of the mimetic *saQ* followed by the quotative particle *-to*. The substitution of *saQto yuderu* for *yugaku* may be a way to avoid the somewhat technical nuance that *yugaku* has. Both *yuderu* and *yugaku* are change of state verbs with uncooked ingredients as their direct objects: for example, *jagaimo-o yuderu* [potato-ACC boil] "boil potatoes" and *hōrensō-o yugaku* [spinach-ACC parboil] "parboil spinach." They cannot be creation verbs, disallowing their cooccurrence with direct objects that correspond to cooked items resulting from the processes.

At this point, one may wonder if $niru_1$ and $niru_2$ are both needed and how $niru_1$ differs from *yuderu*. With respect to $niru_1$ and *yuderu*, I should point out that there is a compound, *mizu-ni*. The compound consists of the noun *mizu* "(cold) water" and *ni*, which is the stem of the verb *niru*. As a whole, *mizu-ni* is a noun that refers to a food product that has been cooked in (hot) water, i.e., by the process of *yuderu*. *Mizu-ni* occurs in the phrase *X-no mizu-ni* "(water-)boiled X," where X is a primary ingredient, and is often seen in labels of canned foods. Examples include *saba-no mizu-ni* "boiled mackerel," *hotate-no mizu-ni* "boiled scallops," *asari-no mizu-ni* "boiled clams," *daizu-no mizu-ni* "boiled soybeans," *takenoko-no mizu-ni* "boiled bamboo shoots," and *masshurūmu-no mizu-ni* "boiled mushrooms." Since mackerel, scallops, clams, soybeans, bamboo shoots, and mushrooms in these instances are boiled in water, one might expect their labels to be more like *X-no mizu-yude*, where *yude* is the stem form of the verb *yuderu*. However, no such examples are found. Furthermore, although the form *X-no mizu-ni* (e.g., *saba-no mizu-ni*) is perfectly natural as the attested product labels show, its verb phrase equivalent *X-o mizu-de niru* [X-ACC water-by/with cook] "cook X in water" (e.g., **?saba-o mizu-de niru*) seems anomalous, if acceptable at all. Another contrast should be made between *saba/daizu-o niru* [mackerel/soy.beans-ACC cook] and *saba/daizu-o yuderu* [mackerel/soybeans-ACC boil], neither of which is specified for the type of liquid, i.e., simple water or a special cooking liquid. In this situation, however, the default interpretation of the former (i.e., *X-o niru*) is such that mackerel or soy beans are cooked in seasoned liquids whereas the latter (i.e., *X-o yuderu*) is that the ingredients are boiled in water. The contrastive interpretations focusing on the type of cooking liquids are underscored by *yude-tamago* [boil-egg] and *ni-tamago* [cook-egg]. A *yude-tamago* is made by cooking a raw egg in boiling water, i.e., a boiled egg. In order to make a *ni-tamago*, an egg is first boiled (i.e., making *yude-tamago*), and then the *yude-tamago*, usually shelled, is further cooked in a seasoned liquid so that the flavor of the liquid soaks into the boiled egg. These differences strongly suggest that the parameter [+Special cooking liquid] is a significant semantic component that is lexically incorporated in one variant of *niru* while at the same time reserving the possibility that the action of *niru* may refer to a water-only process. This is one motivation for keeping $niru_1$ and $niru_2$ separate on the one hand, while at the same time, making a distinction between $niru_1$ and *yuderu* on the other. That is, $niru_1$ is inclusive of both the water-only process and the use of special liquid; $niru_2$ highlights, and hence is reserved for, the use of special liquid; and *yuderu* is characterized for the exclusive use of water. These relations make $niru_2$ and *yuderu* hyponyms of $niru_1$.

There is another reason for *niru* to be superordinate to *yuderu*. It has to do with the fact that *niru* is considered to be one of the five essential elements in Japanese traditional cuisine, *washoku*. They are *ageru* "deep-fry," *niru* "cook in liquid," *musu* "steam," *yaku* "roast/broil," and *kiru* "cut" (for raw ingredients). Of these, *niru* and *musu*, both under the [+Water] [-Fat] category, are represented as part of the essentials. In contrast, *yuderu*, per se, is not included, even though *yuderu* can certainly be a common method used at a more preparatory stage. So, the concept of *niru* is arguably more broadly construed than that of *yuderu* even though the practical action could be more narrowly specified.[4]

Let us turn to *taku* and *musu*. I will start with *musu* since it is relevant to the discussion of *taku*. As mentioned earlier, *musu* is basically equivalent to *steam* in English. It separates itself from $niru_1$ and its hyponyms by the feature [-Submerge]. The main cooking agent of *musu* is a sufficient amount of steam resulting from vigorous water boiling, so the verb is further specified for [+Vigorous action]. The steaming technique further requires cooking utensils like a rack and a sieve, and also a lid to prevent the steam from escaping. I follow Lehrer's analysis in adding the additional parameters of [+Rack, sieve][5] and [+Lid].

Hukasu is characterized by the same set of components for *musu*, and the process and relevant utensils of *hukasu* are indeed identical to those of *musu*. As subtle as it may seem, however, the only difference is that *hukasu* collocates with a limited number of ingredients that include potatoes and pumpkins. Contrastively, the method of *musu* can be applied to any food items, ranging from vegetables to meat and fish. This difference may ultimately be attributed to very similar but nuanced purposes of the two. *Hukasu* is narrowly designated for making ingredients tender by applying steam to them, whereas *musu* is designated for putting heat through ingredients regardless of whether they become tender. For example, a whole fish and shumai (Chinese dumplings) are cooked by *musu*, rather than *hukasu*, because transforming them from being raw to a cooked condition is the intended end result. Their textures are actually somewhat soft to begin with, so a change in texture is not relevant as far as these ingredients are concerned. On the other hand, when potatoes and pumpkins undergo the process of *hukasu*, their expected outcomes are tender textures by default. Notwithstanding this subtle difference in purpose, however, cookbooks and online recipe sites that I have perused largely use *musu* instead of *hukasu* even when ingredients are potatoes and the purpose is to steam them to a tender texture. So, *hukasu* can be replaced by *musu*, but importantly, not the other way around. The unidirectionality suggests a hyponymous relationship between the two verbs. Concerning collocate possibilities for direct objects, both *musu* and *hukasu* are change of state verbs, *satsumaimo-o musu/hukasu* [sweet.potato-ACC steam] "steam sweet potatoes." In addition, *musu* can function as a creation verb because it is possible to interpret the direct object *shūmai* in *shūmai-o musu* [Chinese.dumplings-ACC steam] to refer to a finished dish.

I have given a brief comment on *taku* at the outset of this chapter. The verb is basically reserved for rice-cooking, as the virtually exclusive collocation with *gohan* "cooked rice" or *kome* "rice grain" shows: *gohan-o taku* [(cooked).rice-ACC cook] "cook (cooked) rice" or *kome-o taku* [rice.(grain)-ACC cook] "cook rice (grain)."[6] These two collocation patterns indicate that *taku* can be either a creation verb or a change of state verb. Earlier, I anecdotally noted that calling cooked rice "steamed rice," as in English-language menus, sounds peculiar to me because what is referenced as steaming in English does not quite match the process of cooking rice. Detailed examinations of the process involved in cooking rice below should make it clear as to why *taku* is indeed an intriguing verb that cannot simply be equated with English *steam* or Japanese *musu*.

The rice-cooking process represented by *taku* is divided into two stages. In fact, this observation has led Lehrer (1972, 163) to analyze that *taku* consists of *niru* temporally followed by *musu*. She illustrates the two stages componentially as in (3).

(3) Time1: [+Water], Object (rice) [+Submerged]
    Time2: [+Water], Object [-Submerged]

In standard Japanese, *taku* is kept for rice cooking, so the specification of rice as the unique ingredient in (3) is necessary. During Time1 the rice grains that are submerged in (cold) water are brought to a boil and then simmered in a reduced heat until the water is fully absorbed. This part of the process is equivalent to what *niru₁* denotes. Even *yuderu* fits the description, but the critical difference is that *yuderu* does not assume the cooking water is absorbed at the end. This makes the classification of *taku* under *niru₁* more appropriate. The componential representation of Time2 is intended to be parallel to that of *musu* according to Lehrer's explanation. However, the process during Time2 is somewhat different from what we have analyzed for *musu* above in at least two respects.

First, since by Time2 the rice has absorbed the cooking water, the [+Water] [-Submerged] of Time2 in (3) would require a very distinct type of interpretation from the same set of features assigned to *musu*. That is, for *musu*, water must be present rather than absorbed, and moreover, it would have to be separated from the ingredient, i.e., rice, by cooking utensils like a rack and a sieve. Contrary to this assumption, rice-cooking does not call for such utensils. Second, *musu* is marked for [+Vigorous action] because the water must be boiled hot enough to release continuing steam. This obviously means that the liquid has to be heated. Crucially, however, the process during Time2 takes place AFTER the heat has been turned off. The heat relevant to the process at this stage is simply residual rather than an external application. The so-called steaming period is for the cooked rice to further absorb the mixture of heat, steam, and moisture that has remained from the first stage of more active cooking. It is intended to make the cooked rice fluffy, moist, and chewy. Although the use of electric rice cookers has been widely adopted today, it is not rare to see in cooking guides of various sorts in Japanese that recommend cooking rice in an earthen pot. On such occasions, the instructional language firmly emphasizes that the second stage is a critical step toward making ideal cooked rice. The verb that refers to this second phase is *murasu*. The stage of *murasu* is part of the process of *taku*, adding a finishing touch to the overall rice cooking.

For the entire time of *taku*, which subsumes *murasu*, a lid is a required utensil. The verb *taku* is, thus, marked for [+Lid]. Note that I do not consider *murasu* to be an independent verb that partakes in the current taxonomy because *murasu* should be regarded as a (static) process after the heat has been turned off. This stands out as a sharp contrast with the other verbs in that they consistently call for dynamic actions by a human actor and the use of heat to activate cooking processes. So, *murasu* is included in table 4.2 as a composite part of *taku* but does not have a status as an individual cooking verb on par with others in my current examination.

Incidentally, *murasu* also describes the steeping process during brewing coffee and making tea, but just as with rice-cooking, the verb refers to a period in which no human involvement is observed. For example, in preparing (manual) drip coffee, a first small batch of hot water is poured over ground coffee, quickly making a foamy mass. As the foam starts subsiding, the coffee grinds absorb the moisture and emits an aroma. This absorption process is named by *murasu*, during which no human action is taken except for waiting. In the case of brewing tea, hot water is poured into a pot that contains tea leaves. We subsequently let the leaves soak the water and open, whereby the tea leaves are in the state of *murasu*. In English, *steep* or *let sit* would be its equivalents. It is important to point out that even on the occasions of preparing pour-over coffee and a cup/pot of tea, *murasu* constitutes one (passive) part of the whole process. In other words, although it refers to a critical phrase of food/drink preparation in order to bring the flavor to an ideal level, *murasu* does not stand by itself and remains auxiliary as a word of food and drink preparation.[7]

In some dialects of Japanese, *taku* is used in the same sense as *niru*. In the western part of Japan, which is referred to as the *Kansai* region and includes, for instance, Osaka, Kyoto, and Kobe, *taku* is used as the equivalent of what *niru* means in the eastern area. So, *kabocha-o taku* "cook pumpkins," *mame-o taku* "cook beans," and *daikon-o taku* "cook daikon" are commonly heard in the Kansai area. In the eastern region, on the other hand, *taku* is exclusively used for rice-cooking, and thus *niru* and *taku* are considered to be different cooking methods.

(4) summarizes componential analyses of the eight [+Water] [-Fat] verbs.

(4) wakasu   [+Water] [-Fat] [+Vigorous action] [-Ingredient]
    niru$_1$ [+Water] [-Fat] [+Submerge]
    niru$_2$ [+Water] [-Fat] [+Submerge] [+Special cooking liquid]
    yuderu   [+Water] [-Fat] [+Submerge]
    yugaku   [+Water] [-Fat] [+Submerge] [-Long cooking time] [+To remove harsh taste]
    taku   [+Water] [-Fat] [+Submerge] [+Lid] [+Rice]
    musu   [+Water] [-Fat] [-Submerge] [+Vigorous action] [+Rack, sieve] [+Lid]
    hukasu   [+Water] [-Fat] [-Submerge] [+Vigorous action] [+Rack, sieve] [+Lid] [+Potato, pumpkin]

[-Water] [+Fat]

The next group of cooking verbs, *ageru*, *itameru*, and *yaku$_1$*, share the features of [-Water] [+Fat], the mirror image of the previous class. *Yaku$_1$* and *yaku₂*, although the same word, contrast in the major component of [+/-Fat], *yaku₁* being [+Fat] whereas *yaku₂* [-Fat]. For this and additional reasons to be discussed later, they are treated separately in the taxonomy. First, *ageru* is equivalent to English *deep-fry* and *French-fry*, the two being synonyms according to Lehrer (1969). In the method of *ageru*, ingredients, whether they are battered or not, are cooked in a large amount of liquid fat. Since the fat covers ingredients, *ageru* is marked for [+Submerge]. Lehrer assigns [+Large amount of fat] to *deep-fry* and *French-fry*, which is analyzed as hyponyms of *fry*, but claims that [+Submerge] is presupposed rather than componentialized because there is no contrastive English verb that is marked with [-Submerge (in fat)]. This account seems puzzling since *sauté* and *pan-fry* are also hyponyms of *fry*, and *sauté* is further specified as [-Large amount of fat]. It is thus not clear why *sauté* (as well as *pan-fry*, for that matter) cannot be componentialized as [-Submerge]. Submerging ingredients in liquid fat is parallel to water submersion for the verbs in the first category we have previously discussed. I continue to use [+Submerge] for *ageru* to keep conceptual and terminological consistency between the present and previous categories.

Regarding direct object choices, *ageru* shows a variety of raw ingredients and names of finished dishes, serving both as a change of state verb and as a creation verb. *Ageru* as a change of state verb is illustrated by *nasu/tōhu-o ageru* [eggplant/tofu-ACC deep.fry] "deep-fry eggplants/tofu." In contrast, *katsu/tenpura/harumaki-o ageru* [cutlet/tempura/spring.rolls-ACC deep.fry] "deep-fry katsu/tempura/spring rolls" exemplify the creation verb use. As briefly mentioned above, food items that are to be processed by *ageru* can be either breaded, battered, or no coating, but when ingredients, often vegetables and fish, are deep-fried as is (i.e., without coating), the compound *su-age* [bare-deep.frying] indicates the no-batter cooking manner more exactly, as in *yasai-o su-age-ni suru* [vegetable-ACC *su-age*-to do] "deep-fry vegetables without coating/batter."

Itameru differs from *ageru* in that it requires only a little fat to cook ingredients with and is thus assigned the feature [-Submerge]. In addition, *itameru* typically needs the stirring action so that ingredients do not become stuck to a pan and burned. This is parallel to English *stir-fry*, which is naturally specified for the additional parameter of [+Stir]. So, *itameru* is incompatible with *ageru* in two contrasting features of [-Submerge] and [+Stir]. It is generally understood that ingredients that are processed by the *itameru* action are small in size to make the stirring easier. That is, a large chunk of meat like a steak, for instance, is not subject to this cooking method, but instead *yaku₁* is the suitable process, as we will discuss below. *Itameru* is a change of state verb, as in *yasai/niku-o itameru* [vegetable/meat-ACC stir.fry] "stir-fry vegetables/meat." The unacceptability of phrases like **gomokusoba-o itameru*, where the direct object is the name of the Chinese noodle cooked with assorted vegetables, meat, and/or seafood, suggests that *itameru* does not have the use as a creation verb.

I have briefly mentioned earlier that *yaku* has two variants, $yaku_1$ and $yaku_2$, and that they are analyzed as incompatible rather than hyponyms, even though they are an identical verb. The division is motivated by the fact that *yaku* refers to either a process that assumes the use of fat, [+Fat] (i.e., $yaku_1$), or another that assumes without it, [-Fat] (i.e., $yaku_2$). Presumably related to the difference in [+/-Fat], furthermore, the type of heat also distinguishes between the two. Like all the verbs that we have discussed thus far, $yaku_1$ uses heat that is transmitted through cooking utensils. The most general medium for $yaku_1$ is a frying pan, which makes heat application to ingredients indirect, [-Direct heat]. On the other hand, $yaku_2$ involves an open fire, referred to as *jikabi* "direct fire." That is, ingredients are cooked by applying direct heat (i.e., flame) to them, [+Direct heat]. Since the use of fat and the choice of direct or indirect heat constitute essential components, it seems more appropriate to treat two methods of *yaku* significantly distinct and thus to consider them semantically incompatible instead of regarding one as a type of the other. I will discuss $yaku_2$ in more detail under the next category.

Similar to *itameru* but distinct from *ageru*, $yaku_1$ does not call for a large amount of fat with which ingredients are cooked, i.e., [-Submerge]. $Yaku_1$ is further distinguished from *itameru* because stirring is not needed, hence [-Stir]. In fact, cookbook instructions, whether explicitly or implicitly, suggest that ingredients not be stirred during the process of $yaku_1$. It further follows from the absence of the stirring action that the surface of an ingredient becomes brown. Recall that *itameru*, in contrast, involves stirring so that ingredients do not become burned in a pan. Implicit in the stirring action is that the ingredients in the pan for *itameru* are cut into relatively small pieces. The lack of stirring with $yaku_1$ presupposes that the ingredient is larger than the size for *itameru* and is often in one piece, such as a piece of steak or a fillet of fish. Even sliced (not chopped) vegetables like eggplants and lotus roots are cooked in the $yaku_1$ method. Common instructions of $yaku_1$ as in (5) reflect no or little stirring and surface browning as consequential aspects of the process.

(5)　フライパンに植物油と、バターの半量を入れてれんこんを並べる。**時おりヘラで押さえながら弱火で焼き、焼き色がついたら返して、**残りのバターをいれる。

Huraipan-ni shokubutsuyu-to, batā-no hanryō-o irete renkon-o naraberu. **Tokiori hera-de osae-nagara yowabi-de yaki, yaki'iro-ga tsuitara kaeshite,** nokori-no batā-o ireru.

"Put vegetable oil and half of the butter in a frying pan, and place (thinly sliced) lotus roots in it. Fry them at low heat while **occasionally pressing them down with a spatula; turn them over when they are brown**, and add the remaining butter." (Kato 2019, 152)

Attention should be paid to the instructions to press down the sliced lotus roots by a spatula, and to turn them over once the surfaces of the vegetable slices become brown. They are perfectly congruent to the surface browning that [-Stir] entails. In the cookbook from which (5) is cited, recurrences of similar expressions are consistent with meager stirring of $yaku_1$ which produces browned surfaces. For instance, *yaki-iro-o tsukete* [fried-color-ACC add] "to brown" and the mimetic word *koNgari*, both describing golden brown, regularly collocate with $yaku_1$.

In light of the [-Stir] feature of $yaku_1$, the names of the popular dishes *yaki-soba* and *yaki-udon* are curious. They are prepared by a great deal of stirring that is better described by *itameru*, even though the names consist of the stem form of *yaku*, i.e., *yaki*. Furthermore, the instructional language in recipes for *yaki-soba* and *yaki-udon* invariably is replete with the verb *itameru*. Given the set of components that construct the meaning of *yaku* above, the actual stir-frying process carried out in making *yaki-soba* and *yaki-udon* is clearly incompatible with what the names suggest. The only exception is a type of *yaki-soba* that is served with a topping in thickened sauce, commonly known as *an-kake* [thickened.sauce-pour]. For this dish, untangled Chinese noodles are placed over an oiled frying pan without stirring them. Once the bottom of the noodle bunch is browned, then they are turned over. The cooking verb for this process is $yaku_1$, and it cooccurs with mimetics like *koNgari* for brownness and *pariQ* for crispness as well as the afore-mentioned *yaki-iro-o tsukete* "to brown." Additionally, some accompanying photographs of this type of *yaki-soba* that illustrate some of the cooking phases make it clear that $yaku_1$, not *itameru*, is the technique to be followed in these recipes. The topping sauce, usually a mixture of chopped vegetables and meat pieces, is cooked in liquid and subsequently thickened by a starchy agent (e.g., corn starch). The crispness of the noodles, resulting from the $yaku_1$ action, and the moisture from the topping are expected to offer a nice blend of texture that is different from the standard *yaki-soba*, i.e., the type that requires constant stirring. So, despite that the dish is labeled by their compounded names with *yaki-*, it is clear from cooking instructions that the method to be used for the standard *yaki-soba* and *yaki-udon* is *itameru* that involves continuous stirring. In this way the names *yaki-soba* and *yaki-udon* reflect an exceptional use of *yaki*.

As for direct object options, $yaku_1$ can take either resulting dishes or ingredients to be processed. For example, *okonomi-yaki-o yaku* "make an as-you-like-it pancake" and *sutēki-o yaku* "pan-fry a steak" represent the use of *yaku₁* as a creation verb. As a change of state verb, *yaku₁* can take a variety of ingredients, ranging from meat, fish, and vegetables, as in *niku/sakana/nasu-o yaku* "fry meat/fish/eggplant." As I have noted above, the size of collocated meat and fish strikes me as larger than for *itameru*.

(6) summarizes semantic components assigned to *ageru*, *itameru*, and *yaku₁*. Note that browning surface is not considered to be a purpose of *yaku₁* but it is a consequence of [-Stir].

(6) ageru   [-Water] [+Fat] [+Submerge]
    itameru   [-Water] [+Fat] [-Submerge] [+Stir]
    yaku₁   [-Water] [+Fat] [-Submerge] [-Direct heat] [-Stir]

[-Water] [-Fat]

The third class of cooking verbs, comprising *yaku₂*, *aburu*, *iru₁*, and *iru₂*, assumes the use of neither water nor fat. *Yaku₂* contrasts with *yaku₁* by the use of direct heat, [+Direct heat], and has *aburu* as its hyponym. *Iru* is divided into two variants, *iru₁* and *iru₂*, based on distinct purposes that are to be analyzed as incompatible. Starting with *yaku₂*, the use of direct heat, i.e., direct exposure to a flame, distinguishes it and its hyponym, *aburu*, from all the other verbs in our analysis. To highlight the feature of direct heat, a more specialized compound noun *jikabi-yaki* [direct.heat-cook] may be used, as in *jikabi-yaki-ni suru* "cook in direct heat." This cooking method typically requires a gridiron on which ingredients are placed and have direct contact with a flame. English seems to exhibit more variety of words that correspond to a comparable method, including *grill*, *toast*, *broil*, and perhaps *plank*. Representative food items suitable for *yaku₂* include rice cakes, corn, (sweet) potatoes, and (whole) fish. They serve as direct objects of *yaku₂* as a change of state verb.[8] The surface of the ingredients become brown due to the direct contact with a flame. I consider the surface browning to follow from the direct exposure to a flame.

Aburu is a type of *yaku₂*, making substantial use of a flame. Unlike *yaku₂*, its direct application of a flame does not require utensils like a gridiron. A common way of activating this method is to pass an ingredient over a flame or put it near a flame. Some ingredients, such as fish, may be skewered before applying the cooking process for safety reasons. Although less common in home-cooking, a gas burner may be a convenient kitchen tool for this method. *Aburu* and *yaku₂* differ also in the duration of the cooking process. The purpose of *yaku₂* is to make ingredients cooked through by direct heat, and so, the time required for the process depends on the ingredients. In contrast, the purpose of *aburu* is not so much to change the textures of food items as to bring out flavors and aromas that are characteristic of ingredients. This cooking process is also used to brown the surface of ingredients, similar to the technique that is used to create a brown surface for crème brulee. Together with these specific purposes, the cooking time is brief, [-Long cooking time], as an elongated process would end up burning the ingredients. Representative foods for releasing flavors and aromas are *nori* "seaweed," *surume* "dried squid," and *himono* "sun-dried fish." Crispiness generally results from the *aburu* action. Sliced raw fish like sashimi can be subject to *aburu* to induce a brown surface, leaving the inside of the fish raw. The verb collocates with the food items mentioned above as direct objects, making *aburu* a change of state verb. I am unaware of instances of *aburu* as a creation verb.

Just as is with *yaku*, I divide *iru* into two separate yet parallel methods, rather than treating one as more specific than the other. Unlike $yaku_2$ and its hyponym *aburu*, however, *iru* does not involve direct heat, [-Direct heat], and consequently makes use of utensils like a frying pan or a pot. I distinguish between iru_1 and iru_2 based on two non-overlapping purposes. One, for iru_1, is to cook ingredients until the moisture is greatly reduced. Given this purpose, we expect the ingredients to inherently contain liquid contents, such as tofu, eggs, and *konnyaku* "konjac." The other purpose, for iru_2, is to bring out flavor and aroma of such food items as beans, seeds, and nuts. For both iru_1 and iru_2, stirring is required, i.e., [+Stir], to prevent the ingredients from burning, although a golden color of the dried ingredients usually follows from the process of iru_2. Since *iru* does not generally use fat (especially for eggs and *konnyaku* for iru_1 and ingredients in general for iru_2), it is sometimes referred to as *kara-iri* [dry-*iru*] "dry roasting" to underscore the [-Water] [-Fat] aspect of this process. English *roast* or *parch* may match iru_2 although there does not seem to be a single English verb that captures what is involved in iru_1. Both iru_1 and iru_2 are change of state verbs, collocating with the ingredients mentioned above as their direct objects. There are recipe names (i.e., the names of resulting dishes) that highlight the *iru* process, such as *iri-tamago* [*iri*-egg], *iri-dōhu* [*iri*-tofu], and *iri-goma* [*iri*-sesame.seed], where *iri*- is the stem of *iru*. However, *iritamago-o iru*, *iri-dōhu-o iru*, and *iri-goma-o iru* sound extremely odd and redundant at best, which suggests that *iru* does not serve as a creation verb.

The componential analyses of the four verbs that have been discussed in the [-Water] [-Fat] category are summarized in (7). Different sets of ingredients have been mentioned for iru_1 and iru_2 in our discussion, but they are in tandem with the respective purpose of each process. In that light, the nature of the ingredients is presupposed by the cooking purposes, making it unnecessary to parameterize specific ingredients.

(7) yaku₂   [-Water] [-Fat] [+Direct heat] [+Gridiron]
    aburu   [-Water] [-Fat] [+Direct heat] [-Long cooking time] [+To bring out flavor, aroma] [+To brown surface]
    iru₁   [-Water] [-Fat] [-Direct heat] [+Stir] [+To eliminate liquid]
    iru₂   [-Water] [-Fat] [-Direct heat] [+Stir] [+To make aromatic]

[-Water]

Finally, *kogasu*, roughly equated with the English *burn*, *char*, and *blacken*, seems somewhat misleading as a cooking term because it has the connotation of an accidental failure in the cooking procedure. Needless to say, *kogasu* is analyzed here as a method that has its intended purpose and expected results. Although the verb literally denotes burning, it seems to have a nuanced meaning in the cooking field, which is confirmed by the language of recipe instructions. In recipes *kogasu* or its equivalent in the softer and politer style *kogashimasu* should be expected, but in reality, we rarely see these two verbal forms. What we see more commonly instead is compounded food names that consist of its stem, *kogasi-*, as in *kogashi-negi* [*kogashi*-leek], *kogashi-batā* [*kogashi*-butter], *kogashi-miso* [*kogashi*-miso], and *kogashi-jōyu* [*kogashi*-soy.sauce]. Viewing the instructions as well as occasionally accompanying photos and YouTube videos, it becomes clear that these food items are not burned or blackened but instead browned with an appetizing aroma.

Recall that in our earlier discussion of *yaku₁*, we have noted that *yaki-iro* [*yaku*-color] is used in (5) to refer to the golden-brown color resulting from the *yaku₁* process. We also encounter *koge-iro* to describe a similar surface. Note that *koge* in *koge-iro* is the stem of *kogeru*, which is an intransitive counterpart of *kogasu*. So, the golden-brownness associated with *yaku₁* is interpreted on par with the surface appearance that results from *kogasu*. Importantly, it is not a burned surface that *yaku₁* and *kogasu* intend to yield. We have further commented that *yaku₁* frequently occurs with the mimetic word *koNgari* "golden brown" to describe the same golden appearance. *Yaki-iro*, *koge-iro*, and *koNgari*, thus, point to the uniform visual result following the procedures of *yaku₁* and *kogasu*. As I noted earlier, the verb *kogasu* alone does not have a frequent appearance as an instructional word, but compounded forms that include *koge-* (e.g., *koge-iro*, *koge-me*) and *kogashi-* (e.g., *kogashi-negi*) are of frequent use. For that reason, I consider *kogasu* to have sufficient relevance to the taxonomy of cooking terms. *Kogasu* is componentialized as in (8).

(8) kogasu   [-Water] [+To brown surface]

Table 4.3 summarizes the distribution of semantic components that have been assigned to the cooking verbs with the use of heat. These components

Table 4.3. Summary of semantic components for Japanese cooking words.

	Water	Fat	Submerge	Long Cooking Time	Stir	Direct Heat	Vigorous Action	Other relevant parameters
wakasu	+	-					+	-Ingredient
niru$_1$	+	-	+					
niru$_2$	+	-	+					+Special cooking liquid
yuderu	+	-	+					
yugaku	+	-	+	-				+To remove harsh taste
taku (+murasu)	+	-	+					+Lid +Rice
musu	+	-	-				+	+Rack, sieve +Lid
hukasu	+	-	-				+	+Rack, sieve +Lid +Potato, pumpkin
ageru	-	+	+					
itameru	-	+	-		+			
yaku$_1$	-	+	-		-	-		
yaku$_2$	-	-				+		+Gridiron
aburu	-	-		-		+		+To bring out flavor and aroma +To brown surface
iru$_1$	-	-			+	-		+To eliminate liquid
iru$_2$	-	-			+	-		+To make aromatic
kogasu	-							+To brown surface

are lexicalized in the verbs, serving as critical semantic parts that construct their meanings.

2 PERIPHRASTIC EXTENSIONS

2.1. Compounding

Each of the cooking words that have been componentialized in the previous section forms an individual verb. Put differently, the semantic components that individually or collectively distinguish one verb from another are represented internally to each lexical form to construct its meaning. In addition to these individually lexicalized words, meaning components can also be represented external to the words. In Japanese, compounding is a commonly utilized word formation process to that end, further enriching the cooking vocabulary. The compounding pattern that I consider to be interesting is two-word compounds that consist of the verbs that are semantically incompatible in our taxonomy (table 4.2). The particular compound formation that I single out below takes the pattern of W(ord)1-W(ord)2, where W2 is represented by the stem form of *niru* and *yaku*, i.e., *ni* and *yaki*. W1-*ni* and W1-*yaki* are categorially nouns, and they can function as verbal phrases when appearing in the sequence of W1-*ni (ni) suru* and W1-*yaki (ni) suru* [W1-*ni/yaki* (into) do]. Examples are shown in (9): (9a) and (9b) are examples of W1-*ni* and W1-*yaki*, respectively.

(9) a. mushi-ni [musu-niru] "steam-cook (in liquid)," age-ni [ageru-niru] "deep.fry-cook (in liquid)," itame-ni [itameru-niru] "stir.fry-cook (in liquid)," iri-ni [iru-niru] "cook.down-cook (in liquid)"

b. mushi-yaki [musu-yaku] "steam-fry," age-yaki [ageru-yaku] "deep.fry-fry," iri-yaki [cook.down-fry] "cook down-fry"

It should be remembered that the first members of these compounds hold incompatible relations with the second members, i.e., horizontal placement in table 4.2. The nature of incompatibility is due to conflicting componential specifications that are summarized in table 4.3. For example, regarding *mushi-ni* in (9a), *musu* is [-Submerge] but *niru* is [+Submerge]; and for *mushi-yaki* in (9b), *musu* is [+Water] while *yaku* is [-Water]. So, it appears anomalous to juxtapose two words that are lexicalized for opposite semantic values. Contrary to the expectation, the compounds in (9) are widely used as logical cooking vocabulary.

There are two ways of interpreting these apparently inconsistent relationships between W1 and W2: one in which altered concepts of W1 and W2 are amalgamated into a somewhat new notion of a cooking method, and the other in which the processes denoted by W1 and W2 are ordered in temporal sequence. Let us start with the first type. Relevant examples are demonstrated by *mushi-ni* and *iri-ni* in (9a) as well as *mushi-yaki*, *age-yaki*, and *iri-yaki* in (9b). Regarding *mushi-ni* and *mushi-yaki*, recall that *musu*, from which *mushi* of these compounds is derived, is componentialized as [+Water] [-Fat] [-Submerge] [+Vigorous action] [+Rack, sieve] [+Lid], and the conceptual amalgamation of these components accounts for the presence of unescaped steam. Crucially, it is the existence of steam, rather than how steam is produced, that is maintained as the altered notion of *musu* relevant to the compound words of *mushi-ni* and *mushi-yaki*. For example, in a recipe called *buta-renkon* "pork and lotus roots," the instruction given after a few preparatory stages includes *mushi-ni*, as in (10).

(10) 煮立ったらふたをして弱火にし、3〜4分間**蒸し煮**にする。

Nitat-tara huta-o shite yowabi-ni shi, 3〜4-pun-kan **mushi-ni**-ni suru.

"Once (the liquid) is brought to a boil, cover it [=frying pan], turn the heat down, and cook it in **mushi-ni**." (Izawa 2015)

The steam is created by the boiled liquid, which consists of four tablespoons of water and sake. The liquid mixture is consistent with [+Special cooking liquid] of *niru*. By covering the pan, the steam is locked in. As the last part of the sentence in (10) indicates, the instruction identifies the method as *mushi-ni*.

Mushi-yaki is processed virtually in the same fashion, although the amount of liquid strikes me as less than *mushi-ni*, which accordingly may produce a brown surface typical of $yaku_1$. (11) is a segment of a recipe for pan-fried Chinese cabbage with miso-flavored meat sauce. After pan-frying Chinese cabbage halves in a little oil, the recipe calls for *mushi-yaki*.

(11) ふたをして弱火で6〜7分間**蒸し焼き**にして器に盛る。

Huta-o shite yowabi-de 6〜7-hun-kan **mushi-yaki**-ni shite utsuwa-ni moru.

"Cover it [=frying pan] and cook it in **mushi-yaki** for 6-7 minutes; plate it." (Ichise 2014, 8)

This recipe is accompanied by a photo illustration that corresponds to the step in (11), and there is no ambiguity as to how *mushi-yaki* is understood. It is also clear from the photo that the cabbage surface is brown, as expected of the $yaku_1$ technique. In this particular recipe, no liquid is added to the pan to create steam, but instead the Chinese cabbage is expected to release a sufficient amount of moisture to that end.

Although not included in (9), I should note that *mushi-yude* also appears in the form of *mushi-yude-ni suru* as part of cooking instructions. *Yuderu*, like *niru*, assumes submersion of ingredients in a boiling liquid, specifically in boiling water. Instead of covering ingredients with a lot of water, however, *mushi-yude* uses a reduced amount of water than in *yuderu*, which with a lid, creates steam that cooks ingredients. So, in this compound, the concept of *musu* and that of *yuderu* both undergo conceptual modifications. The amount of water required for *mushi-yude* varies depending on the ingredients and recipe, but it ranges from 2 to 3 tablespoons to half a cup of water for a half head of a small Chinese cabbage. This amount is clearly far from enough for full submersion that is required of *yuderu*. A frying-pan is a common utensil for *mushi-yude*. With the different conceptualization of *musu*, the compounds *mushi-ni*, *mushi-yaki*, and *mushi-yude* parallel the English verb *braise*, although *braise* was borrowed from French. As far as steam-related cooking words are concerned, it is interesting to note that English relies on a loanword to deal with a new concept while Japanese makes use of the prevalent word formation process of compounding to accommodate concepts that may not dictate the one that has been lexicalized as individual verbs.

As for *age-yaki*, the first member of the compound, *ageru*, lexicalizes the component of [+Submerge] in a large quantity of fat. This characteristic, of course, goes against *yaku*, for which fat may be used (i.e., for $yaku_1$) but not to the extent that ingredients are fully submerged in it. In *age-yaki*, ingredients are battered as with *ageru*, but the amount of frying oil required is far less than what is called for in *ageru*, although perhaps more than the amount used for $yaku_1$. Furthermore, as expected of $yaku_1$, ingredients are not frequently stirred but turned over once, and the surface is browned. *Age-yaki* seems to be widely used today as an alternative cooking method of *ageru*, in consideration of health benefits. As such, the *age-yaki* process is adopted to dishes that are usually known for the *ageru* method, such as *katsu* "deep-fried pork cutlet" and *kara'age* "fried chicken," as it is evidenced by a number of recipes (in various media) and online video demonstrations. For instance, a YouTube clip (Mamadays 2020) for making *kara'age* "fried chicken" is captioned as **age-yaki** *dakede sakusaku, jūshī kara'age* "simply **age-yaki** makes crisp, juicy fried chicken." In the instructions the "deep" frying stage calls for only 3 tablespoons of oil, a significantly less amount than for submerging ingredients for *ageru*. The video is also unambiguous about not stirring the chicken pieces. In these respects, the method is essentially the same as $yaku_1$ and the chicken is fried golden brown. So, the compound *age-yaki* changes the concept of *ageru* by the use of less fat while keeping the semantic components of $yaku_1$ intact.

Finally, with *iri-ni* and *iri-yaki*, W1 is the stem of *iru* and refers to the concept of *iru*$_1$ in these compounds, and *-yaki* of *iri-yaki* corresponds to *yaku*$_1$. Sparsely occurring, these compounds are not as clear-cut as other cases considered thus far, in that they seem to have a meaning very similar to *niru* or *itame-ni*. Also, unlike the earlier samples, *iri-ni* and less commonly *iri-yaki* occur as part of recipe names rather than being included in cooking instructions that would take the forms of *iri-ni (ni) suru* "lit. do iri-ni" and *iri-yaki (ni) suru* "lit. do iri-yaki." *Iru*$_1$ is componentialized as [-Water] [-Fat], whereas *niru* is marked for [+Water] and *yaku*$_1$ for [+Fat]. Thus, these characteristics with opposite values need to be negotiated in interpreting each of the compounds. So far as I can ascertain, the meaning of *iri-ni* is constructed by combining the hallmark feature of each member: the liquid reducing element of *iru*$_1$, and *niru*'s method of cooking in a seasoned liquid. Putting together, *iri-ni* means cooking ingredients in a seasoned liquid until the moisture is evaporated or greatly reduced. For example, the instruction of the recipe named *takenoko to konnyaku-no* **iri-ni** "**iri-ni** of bamboo shoots and konnyaku" emphasizes the reduction of the liquid mixture in that process, as in (12).

(12) ... 調味料を入れ、煮汁がなくなるまで、中火で**炒り煮**。

   ... chōmiryō-o ire, nijiru-ga nakunaru-made, chūbi-de **iri-ni**.

   "... add the seasoning (liquid) and cook in **iri-ni** at medium heat until the liquid is gone." (sanono230 2021)

The instruction of *chōmiryō-o ire* "add the seasoning (liquid)" corresponds to a special cooking liquid necessary for *niru*$_2$ rather than the liquid inherently contained in the ingredients. The instruction of *nijiru-ga nakunaru-made* "until the liquid disappears" elaborates on the liquid reducing purpose of *iru*$_1$.

The compound *iri-ni* appears in another recipe name *gobō-no yōhū* **iri-ni** "Western-style **iri-ni** of burdock." The third step of this recipe instruction asks that a seasoning liquid consisting of white wine, water, and soup base granule be added to the stir-fried vegetables. Immediately after that, the direction of (13) follows.

(13) 強火にして、たえず混ぜながら汁気がなくなるまで**炒り**あげる。

   Tsuyobi-ni shite, taezu maze-nagara shiruke-ga nakunaru-made **iri**-ageru.

   "Turn the heat up, and complete the **iru** process until the liquid is gone while constantly stirring." (Ishizawa 2004, 79)

This instructive language does not include *iri-ni* itself except for the recipe name, but the amalgamated process of *iru*$_1$ and *niru*$_2$ is evident. Here, the cooking verb *iru* appears in another compound *iri-ageru*, where *-ageru* is not to be confused with *ageru* "deep-fry" as the cooking verb in our taxonomy. Instead, *-ageru* in *iri-ageru* in (13) is an aspectual verb to indicate "finish/complete doing something."[9] (13) ensures that the liquid be entirely evaporated by further noting *shiruke-ga nakunaru-made* "until the liquid is gone" and advising that the ingredients be continuously stirred, *taezu maze-nagara* "constantly stirring." These two cues point to the crucial semantic components of iru_1, i.e., [+To eliminate liquid] and [+Stir]. As with the previous example, the moisture to be eliminated by the cooking process is the special cooking liquid that defines $niru_2$. As for *iri-yaki*, to the extent that I am able to discern, its cooking process is not particularly different from that of *iri-ni*.

To sum up thus far, the recurring pattern of the first type of compound relationship indicates that the cooking process denoted by a compound as a whole showcases notable components of each of the compound members and unites them into a new or modified cooking technique, while relaxing other feature specifications.

The second way of explaining the semantic relationships between the two compound members is as a temporal sequence, namely, "W1 before W2" or "W1 and then W2." The compounds *age-ni* and *itame-ni* in (9a) follow this pattern. With these compounds, *ageru* "deep-fry" or *itameru* "stir-fry" is applied first, and then the ingredients are cooked by the *niru* method. Unlike the first type of compound relation, the concepts of *ageru*, *itameru*, and *niru* as individual verbs remain the same as we have discussed in section 1. In addition, forming a temporal sequence, each of these compounds refers to two processes rather than one. An example of *age-ni* is found in *nasu-no* **age-ni** [eggplant-GEN age-ni] "**age-ni** of eggplants" (Kurihara 1992, 34). The recipe first calls for deep-frying sliced eggplants. Once cooked tender, they are transferred to a heated liquid mixture of soy sauce, mirin, sugar, chili bean sauce, and vinegar. So, it is evident that the *ageru* and *niru* processes individually take place, one preceding the other. Likewise, the recipe for *takenoko-to shin-kyabetsu-no* **itame-ni** "**itame-ni** of bamboo shoots and new cabbage" (Chiba 1996) makes clear that *itame-ni* is interpreted to consist of two distinct but sequential processes. The third step of this recipe states that all the vegetables are to be stir-fried with olive oil in a frying pan (*itameru*). The instruction of the fourth, and the last, phase states that the liquid mixture of dashi, mirin, and soy sauce should be added when the color of the vegetables becomes brightened. It continues to instruct the reader to cover the pot and cook (*niru*) the vegetables at low temperature for a few minutes. In each example, the two cooking processes referred to by the members of the compound are temporally partitioned and sequenced without any overlap. The concepts of the two verbs that form the compounds are not altered in any sense. Interestingly, a pair of individual cooking methods, sequenced one after another, is nevertheless viewed as a single cooking style called *age-ni* and *itame-ni*.

We have thus far examined two-word compounds in which both members are the cooking verbs that we have organized into the taxonomy. These primary cooking words are also productively compounded with other verbs that are not generally regarded as cooking terms in their own right. Some examples are presented in (14), which consist of *ni-*, the stem form of *niru*, as W1 and non-cooking verbs as W2. The W2 members in (14), once compounded, usually lose their basic meanings that they have as independent verbs. Instead, they add different meanings that are metaphorically or functionally extended to elaborate on the cooking process denoted by W1. In square brackets, I give the basic meaning of the second member when it stands alone.

(14) ni-komu   [be packed]   "to boil well, to stew"
     ni-tateru   [raise]   "to boil up"
     ni-tsumeru   [pack]   "to boil down, to reduce"
     ni-kaesu   [turn]   "to reboil"
     ni-kobosu   [spill]   "to boil and then throw away the liquid (usually followed by another round of boiling)"

     ni-shimeru   [soak]   "to boil x hard (down)"
     ni-dasu   [put out]   "to extract the essence by boiling"
     ni-tsukeru   [attach]   "to boil x hard with soy (and sugar)"

Notice that *ni-komu* and *ni-tsumeru*, in particular, correspond to English *stew* and *reduce*, respectively. Even though slow cooking and making liquids thicker or concentrated exist as concepts pertinent to cooking in both languages, the linguistic strategy to verbally express these cooking notions is different. English incorporates (i.e., lexicalizes) relevant semantic components in individual words, whereas Japanese, making use of compounds, expresses the same components externally as the second member. That is, what seems to be a lexical gap in one language may well be compensated for by deploying common linguistic mechanisms available in the language.

In order to discern the role that compounds of the type illustrated in (14) play, let us revisit table 4.3. Among the components other than "other relevant parameters," all the semantic features are represented for both positive and negative values, except for [Long cooking time] and [Vigorous action]: the former has representations of its negative value (i.e., *yugaku* and *aburu*) while the latter is represented by its positive value (i.e., *wakasu*, *musu*, and *hukasu*). In the first compound of (14), *ni-komu* "to boil well, to stew," the second member *komu* adds the intensifying sense to W1. Consequently, *ni-komu* has the nuance of the process of *niru* being elongated, on par with [+Long cooking time]. Furthermore, it seems uniform that long cooking, at least with liquids, implies relatively low heat, which corresponds to [-Vigorous action]. That is, the second member *-komu* in *ni-komu* plays a role that augments the componential features of [+Long cooking time] and [-Vigorous action]. The compound type demonstrated in (14), thus, serves as a linguistic tool by which semantic components that are not lexicalized are nevertheless supplemented periphrastically.

Beyond V(erb)-V(erb) compounds that consist of the cooking words we have analyzed in tables 4.2 and 4.3, we encounter additional compounds that detail various fine-grained aspects of cooking methods. I illustrate them based on *yaku* since this verb is well represented. The first pattern of compounding is utensil-oriented. It should be remembered that special utensils (e.g., a lid for *taku*, a rack for *musu*) have indeed been included as relevant parameters in characterizing Japanese cooking words. We have specified [+Gridiron] for $yaku_2$, but the compounds in (15) further illustrate the variety of utensils with which the *yaku* method can be carried out. They are N(oun)-V(erb) compounds, where the first member noun refers to cooking utensils or tools that are specifically or characteristically called for. The second member is the stem form of *yaku*, but as a whole, these N-V compounds are considered to be nominalized and function as nouns.

(15) ami-yaki "gridiron/grate-$yaku_2$," kushi-yaki "skewer-$yaku_2$," sumi-yaki "charcoal-$yaku_2$," nabe-yaki(-udon) "(clay-)pot-yaku(-udon noodle)"

The last compound in (15), *nabe-yaki*, is best known for the dish name *nabe-yaki-udon* today, but a clay-pot is understood to be used for cooking and serving this noodle dish. It is curious, however, that the method of cooking is labeled by *yaku* although *niru* is more suitable to identify the process of making this dish since ingredients (usually at least udon noodles and vegetables) are cooked in a soup, i.e., a special cooking liquid.

The compounds in (16) describe the manner that further qualifies the *yaku* process. They are V-V compounds except for *maru-yaki*, which is a N-V compound.

(16) kasane-yaki "layer-yaku," tsutsumi-yaki "wrap-yaku," maru-yaki "whole [lit. circle, full]-yaku," tsuke-yaki "marinate-yaku," teri-yaki "marinate [lit. shine]-yaku"

Tsutsumi-yaki can mean two types of wrapping: one is equivalent to cooking in parchment paper (i.e., en papillot), and the other is to wrap an ingredient with another ingredient (i.e., stuffing). The first member of *maru-yaki*, i.e., *maru* "lit. circle," does not have a literal reference to any food or food-related object, but it suggests that the entire ingredient like a chicken is processed, generally preserving the whole shape rather than cutting it up to pieces. *Tsuke-yaki* and *teri-yaki* are virtually the same in that the *yaku* process is applied after ingredients are marinated in soy sauce or a soy sauce-based liquid. *Teri* in *teri-yaki* is the stem of the verb *teru* "shine," and indicates that the marinade for *teri-yaki* contains mirin and/or sugar whose sugar content serves as an agent to make the surface shiny.

In a way, the first members of the compounds in (15–16) are not absolutely necessary in giving cooking instructions. Yet, when appearing as part of recipe names, they certainly provide concise, "at a glance" information that highlights critical or attractive aspects of expected cooking processes without having the recipe user peruse the entire instructions. In a similar vein, there are many compounds, especially with *yaki* (*yaku*) and *ni* (*niru*) as their second member, that inform what sort of flavor is expected by way of naming seasonings (e.g., salt, miso) and tastes (e.g., sweet, delicious). Examples include *shio-yaki* "salt-yaki," *amakara-ni* "sweet.salty-ni," *uma-ni* "delicious-ni," *miso-ni* "miso-ni," and *saka-ni* "sake-ni,"[10] among others. Expanding the cooking vocabulary is straightforwardly accommodated by compounding with remarkable productivity, flexibility, and creativity. It is a testament that compounding is indeed a standard word formation process that is habitually used in broad areas of Japanese including the cooking field.

2.2. Mimetics

As we have discussed in chapter 3 (section 3), mimetics serve as an equally versatile linguistic mechanism in enlarging the range of cooking expressions. Although, like compounds, descriptive contents that mimetics contribute to detailing cooking processes are added externally to the individual cooking verbs as their periphrastic modifiers, mimetic expressions increase nuanced specificity to the base-line definitions of the lexicalized cooking vocabulary. For instance, the verb for in-liquid cooking, *niru*, collocates with several mimetics that differentiate the degree of boiling. Cooking in a vigorously boiling liquid is expressed by *guragura*, and with slightly less vigor, brisk boiling or bubbling is described by *gutsugutsu* and *hutsuhutsu*. At the level of a slow boil, *kotokoto*, *kutsukutsu*, and *torotoro* are used to modify a lower, although still boiling, temperature. The last three mimetics further imply a slow and sustained cooking like stewing, parallel to *simmer* in English. Mimetics, thus, play a role as shorthand for details that would otherwise need lengthy prose descriptions. Furthermore, the collocation of *guragura* with *niru* amounts to adding the [+Vigorous action] feature; and, juxtaposing *kotokoto*, *kutsukutsu*, or *torotoro* with *niru* is parallel to the compound *ni-komu* in (14) in augmenting [+Long cooking time] and [-Vigorous action]. So, periphrastically, mimetics participate in particularizing a given cooking process represented by the lexicalized cooking vocabulary.

The contribution that mimetics make to cooking communication in practice is commented on in Fukutome (2014). She notes that although college students seem to understand the general process of cooking ingredients (e.g., leafy vegetables) in boiling water, some students show difficulty in recognizing a boiling point in an actual cooking practicum. She further reports that mimetics which describe various boiling stages (e.g., *gutsugutsu*, *hutsuhutsu*) are easier to comprehend in practical scenarios, and their inclusion in home economics classes is suggested as pedagogically advantageous. Another point of interest in Fukutome's study is that the college-age Japanese speakers in her research seem to exhibit variability in perceiving some of the above-mentioned mimetics that typically occur with *niru*. In one of her experiments, she showed the participants video samples of various stages of water boiling, and asked what expressions, including mimetic words, they would use to describe the boiling phases. Focusing on three mimetics for our discussion, *gutsugutsu*, *guragura*, and *hutsuhutsu*, the participants used *gutsugutsu* to describe the most rigorous, rapid boil where the water temperature was 99.9° C(elsius) (=211.82°F), *guragura* for 99°C (=210.2°F), and *hutsuhutsu* for the lowest temperature of 94°C (=201.2°F). On the one hand, the results confirm that the mimetic vocabulary is easily accessible to speakers in recognizing practical references, as evidenced by its prevalent use in cooking instructions. On the other hand, given that the findings are somewhat different from the interpretation of these mimetics that I have given earlier, individual mimetic words are also subject to variation in their actual interpretation, especially depending on the age cohort.

One of the most widely occurring mimetics in cooking instructions is *satto* [saQ-to] "quickly," an adverb mentioned earlier in the context of its collocating with *yuderu*.[11] In fact, *saQ-to* is not limited to the cooking field and its broad application is so conventionalized that it is likely unrecognized as mimetic. So, whenever a quick action is called for in cooking processes, *saQ-to* is an extremely convenient adverb. For our purpose, however, I want to point out that *yugaku*, one of the basic cooking verbs, seems to have relatively uncommon usage in practice, and its replacement by *saQ-to yuderu* is noticeably more prevalent in the language of cooking instructions especially in recent days. Recall that *yugaku* is a hyponym of *yuderu*, and the distinction between the two has to do with a brief cooking time of *yugaku* together with its intended purpose of removing harsh tastes inherent to leafy vegetables like spinach. Given that boiling ingredients in water is shared by both verbs, it is reasonable to equate *yugaku* to *saQ-to yuderu* without losing or changing its practical consequences. In fact, the substitution is quite customary in cookbooks. In a cookbook that features vegetables (Kusaba 2017, 118–19), all of the four recipes for spinach that require what I view as the *yugaku* action contain the language, *nettō-de saQ-to yuderu* [hot.water-in saQ-to boil] "quickly boil in hot water."

The same collocation pattern is widely used in cookbooks including the one compiled by Yoshiharu Doi. Doi received professional culinary training and has been active broadly in cooking and nutrition education. For him, the terminological distinction between *yuderu* and *yugaku* must be of basic technical knowledge that is not insignificant. In Kato (2019, 61), in which Doi is responsible for its recipe selections, the caption for a garland chrysanthemum salad characterizes the greens as having *nigami* "bitter taste." So, the boiling process of *yugaku* would be suitable for this leafy vegetable. Instead of using *yugaku*, however, the instruction states, *saQ-to yudete* "boiling [it] quickly," where *yudete* is the gerundive form of *yuderu*. Note that the instructions of cookbooks are sometimes written by editorial staff even though culinary specialists (like Doi) are fully responsible for and engaged in devising the recipes. In that light, I surmise that *saQ-to yuderu* may not necessarily be Doi's choice of words. On the other hand, the substituted phrase, especially given its widespread use, is a likely attempt to make the terminology less technical-sounding and more user-friendly. Just as the gap between cooking concepts and cooking vocabulary observed with younger generations mentioned in Fukutome's study, some of the cooking terms, especially those that are analyzed as hyponyms in table 4.2 (e.g., *yugaku*, *hukasu*, *aburu*), are possibly underused. To the extent that the concepts themselves still survive, however, mimetics are indeed an effective and accessible linguistic means to supplement the basic set of verbs with relevant nuances.

3 CUTTING VERBS

English exhibits a variety of lexicalized verbs for cutting as they apply to the cooking field, although some are loanwords from French. They include *slice, julienne, mince, chop, cube, dice, sliver, shave, carve, pare, peel,* and *score*. In addition, *chiffonade* is a noun, also a French loan, but it is becoming common as a verb, as cooking instructions in media outlets attest to that trend. Japanese, in contrast, uses the unique verb of cutting, *kiru* "cut," but not surprisingly, relies on a wide use of compounding to distinguish among different manners of cutting. The usual form is W1-W2, where W2 is *kiri*, the stem form of *kiru*. Due to the Rendaku phenomenon (i.e., sequential voicing),

W1-*kiri* is phonetically realized as W1-*giri*. W1-*kiri*, which is categorically a noun, is used in the pattern of W-*kiri-ni suru* for its verbal function.

In demonstrating examples of compounds for cutting, I divide the semantic relationships between W1 and *kiri* into two types: one in which W1 refers to the manner of cutting or (actual) resulting shapes, as in (17), and the other in which W1 describes resulting shapes via metaphor, illustrated in (18). In square brackets I indicate the form and meaning of W1 before compounding.

(17) W1=the manner of cutting or resulting shape

    a. usu-giri   [usui "thin"]   "slice thin"
    b. atsu-giri   [atsui "thick"]   "slice thick"
    c. koguchi-giri   [koguchi "a small cut end"]   "cut across into small chunks"
    d. zaku-giri   [zaku "assorted vegetables"]   "cut into rough pieces"
    e. butsu-giri   [butsu – mimetic?]   "cut into rough (larger) pieces"
    f. sogi-giri   [sogu "sliver"]   "shave, sliver"
    g. naname-giri   [naname "diagonal"]   "slice diagonally"
    h. kaku-giri   [kaku "square"]   "cube, dice"
    i. hoso-giri   [hosoi "narrow"]   "cut into thin strips"
    j. mijin-giri   [mijin "bit"]   "mince"
    k. kushigata-giri   [kushi-gata "comb-shape"]   "cut into a comb shape (=a half moon shape)"

(18) W1=resulting shape by metaphorical reference

    a. wa-giri   [wa "ring"]   "cut into a round slice"
    b. hangetsu-giri   [hangetsu "half moon"]   "cut into a half moon shape"
    c. ichō-giri   [ichō "ginko"].   "cut into a quarter circle"
    d. ran-giri   [ran "riot"]   "cut into random shapes (of a similar size)"
    e. tanzaku-giri   [tanzaku "a strip of paper (for tanka and haiku)"]   "cut into thin rectangles"
    f. hyōshi-giri   [hyōshi "wooden clappers"]   "cut into thin rectangles (thicker than *tanzaku-giri* in (18e))"
    g. sen-giri   [sen "thousand"]   "cut into thin strips, julienne (slightly thinner than *hoso-giri* in (17i))"
    h. sainome-giri   [sainome "spots on dice"]   "cube, dice"

Many of the compounds in (17) are relatively interpreted according to the actual size of ingredients rather than in absolute terms. They usually cooccur with exact metric references like *5mm no usu-giri* "slice as thin as 5mm" to give a precise measurement. Naturally, some are applicable to a limited group of ingredients of similar shapes. For instance, *koguchi-giri* in (17c) is for long cylindrical ingredients like leeks and green onions (Nakamura 2011, 15). Similarly, *kushi-gata* "comb-shape" in *kushigata-giri* in (17k) refers to the shape of a traditional Japanese comb and applies to globe-shaped vegetables including tomatoes and onions (Ibid., 14). The first part of *zaku-giri* in (17d) and possibly that of *butsu-giri* in (17e) come from mimetics, *zakuQ* "the manner of chopping or gouging something roughly" and *butsuQ* "a dull sound made when a relatively thick, firm object is stabbed, chopped, or snaps once" (the definitions from Kakehi et al. 1996). *Zaku-giri* is typically used for roughly cutting leafy vegetables like cabbage and lettuce, whereas *butsu-giri* is seen regularly for fish and meat although leeks are not an unusual candidate for this cutting manner.

As for the compounds in (18), the metaphorical references of the first members are straightforward, but additional comments on some are in order. The first member *ran-* of *ran-giri* in (18d) is glossed as "riot," but it can serve as a prefix to mean a rough manner. As a compound of cutting, it describes a shape that does not have an orderly pattern as with the rest of the cutting modes in (18). In (18g) the numeral reference of *sen* in *sen-giri* amplifies plenty of thinly cut pieces resulting from this manner of cutting. The first members of (18e) and (18f) represent cultural references of historical origins that may not be familiar to every Japanese speaker today. *Tanzaku* in (18e) is a rectangular, often thick, piece of paper on which tanka and haiku poems were written. *Hyōshi* "wooden clapper" in (18f) is multi-purpose, ranging from a musical instrument for gagaku (imperial court music), a signal for the beginning of a kabuki play, to a warning sound for a fire alert.[12]

The terms in (17) and (18) together show quite a rich inventory of cutting vocabulary. V-V compounds and N-V compounds are widely instantiated in Japanese regardless of semantic fields. As such, these compound patterns and also compounding in general serve as a natural linguistic machinery to expand members of the cutting, and more broadly cooking, vocabulary as well. In addition, the semantic relationships between two (or more) members of a compound run a gamut that further increases creativity and productivity. On the one hand, cooking verbs and cutting verbs that have been discussed in this chapter certainly enrich our ability to verbally describe core essences and phases of food preparation. On the other, these terms have to be consciously learned along with the cultural and historical references encoded in many of the vocabulary items. As is the case with cooking verbs, cutting verbs in (17) and (18) are not always transparent to Japanese speakers at all ages. This is why we detect the kind of linguistic substitutions discussed above as well as instructional materials in various media that define or explain these cooking terms, rather than treating them as given. What is important to recognize, however, is that once learned, we can make the most of the cooking vocabulary that vibrantly exists in the fabric of Japanese culinary culture.

NOTES

1. In her 1969 article, Lehrer gives an extensive analysis of cooking verbs exclusively in English based on a similar componential approach.

2. Outside of the cooking field, *wakasu* can be collocated with *huro* "bath" for its direct object, as in *huro-o wakasu* "make/prepare bath." The basic concept of *wakasu*, i.e., heating the water to a boil, is preserved in the bath-making/preparing context even though the main purpose is not strictly bringing the bath water to the boiling point.

3. This characteristic of *yuderu* requiring water rather than other liquids does not need an additional specification since the primary component of [+Water] serves the purpose.

4. A *washoku* course is made up of dishes that represent eight general culinary methods. They are *wan* for soup, *ae-mono* made of ingredients dressed with a seasoned sauce, *ni-mono* for a dish cooked by the *niru* method, *yaki-mono* for a dish made in the *yaku* method, *mushi-mono* for a steamed dish (i.e., *musu*), *age-mono* for a deep-fried dish (i.e., *ageru*), *su-no-mono* for a vinegared dish, and *gohan-mono* for plain rice or a rice dish. The structure of a *washoku* course further confirms the prominence of *niru* over *yuderu*.

5. This feature is interpreted as a representative, rather than exhaustive, list of possible utensils for steaming as a cooking method.

6. I personally find *kome-o taku* "cook rice (grain)" very odd sounding, if acceptable at all, since I use *taku* exclusively with *gohan* as its direct object. However, when more detailed types of rice grain are collocated, the degree of acceptability seems to improve, as in *genmai/hakumai-o taku* "cook unpolished/polished rice (both grain forms)."

7. We may think of the secondary role of *murasu* as reflecting its critical but dispensable step in cooking. In cooking rice and brewing coffee or tea, the *murasu* phase could be skipped. It would still produce cooked rice and brewed coffee or tea although it may not achieve an ideal taste, flavor, texture, and the like. With other verbs, omitting the procedures named by them would negate the entire cooking processes, thus leading to no cooked ingredients or dishes as a result.

8. *Yaku* can be used as a creation verb, as in *kēki-o yaku* [cake-ACC cook] "bake a cake." In this case, however, it assumes the use of an oven and thus would be better classified as yet another variant of *yaku* (i.e., *yaku₃*). I exclude this use of *yaku* from our analysis since oven-baking, although increasingly adopted in recent decades, is not characteristic of Japanese cooking.

9. The distinction between *ageru* as the cooking verb to mean deep-frying and *ageru* as an aspectual verb to mark the completion of an action is clearly indicated by the orthography throughout this cookbook. The deep-frying sense of *ageru* is consistently written with the Chinese character as 揚げる but the aspectual sense is indicated in hiragana as X-あげる.

10. *Saka* in *saka-ni* corresponds to sake, but when compounded, it slightly changes the pronunciation of the second vowel.

11. We also discussed the example (53) in chapter 3 regarding the contrastive use of *saQ-to* and *sasaQ-to* collocating with *itameru* "stir-fry."

12. Additionally, the *kushi* of *kushigata* in (17k) means a women's comb that was used as a hair ornament in a historical context. Being made of ivory, tortoiseshell, or boxwood, *kushi* has a typical shape of half a moon.

Chapter Five

Metaphors

Our experience with eating food ranges from daily meals for dietary intake to leisurely dining-out, and yet, there are only a limited number of gustatory words that directly describe a taste, as those in (1) illustrate for Japanese.[1]

(1) oishii aji   "delicious taste"
    umai aji   "delicious taste"
    mazui aji   "unpalatable taste"
    amai aji   "sweet taste"
    suppai aji   "sour taste"
    nigai aji   "bitter taste"
    shoppai/shiokarai aji "salty taste"
    karai aji   "spicy taste"
    shibui aji   "astringent taste"

In his commentary on the language of restaurant guidebooks, Detake (1983, 68, my translation) cites (2) as an example of a restaurant introduction that "gives up on efforts to express the tastes." In angled brackets, relevant evaluative taste words are given in Japanese that correspond to the underlined (original) expressions.

(2) [dishes like] (salmon) sashimi, squid sashimi, soi (white fish) sashimi are delicious <*umai*>. In spring to summer, herring, crab, clam, . . . and corn are delicious <*oishii*>, nothing like what we can get around here. In fall to winter, offerings like mackerel, smelts, cod, skates, potatoes are good <*umai*>. In winter Ishikari Pot and Sanpei soup are good <*yoi*>.

As the English translations suggest, *umai*, *oishii*, and *yoi* are extremely generic and deficient in detailed explanations as to how they are "delicious" and "good" and why they are recommended. Such poverty of variety and creativity in verbal taste descriptions entirely misses the opportunity to communicate one's gustatory experiences convincingly to others.

The vagueness in (1) as well as the descriptive blandness and insufficient information in (2) largely have to do with the literal use of the words that pertain to food tastes. However, once we resort to non-literal and metaphorical words and phrases, the level of expressiveness exponentially increases. The adjectives in (3), all positive in meaning, are just starters.

(3) hukai aji   "deep taste"
    koi aji   "dense taste"
    marui aji   "round taste"
    akarui aji   "bright taste"
    karui aji   "light taste"
    sawayaka-na aji   "refreshing taste"
    shizuka-na aji   "quiet taste"

Similarly, metaphorical expressions make culinary descriptions more informative and rhetorically richer. In a dialogue with the cooking specialist Yoshiharu Doi, Kindaichi (2016, 404) quotes Doi's utterance in (4a), which piqued his interest. (4b) is Doi's follow-up comment in the dialogue. In both examples, Doi gives guidance on cooking tofu in language that personifies the ingredient. The bold-faced parts are instances of personification.

(4) a. …気持ち良さそうに浮いてきて、ゆらゆらしたところが食べごろです。

   … **kimochi yosa-sō-ni uite**-kite, yurayura-shita tokoro-ga tabe-goro-desu.

   "… (once the tofu) starts to **float, looking comfortable,** and begins to sway, that's the right time to eat it."

b. 強火でごんごん煮たら**豆腐が痛がっている**ように見えるんです。

   Tsuyobi-de gongon ni-tara **tōhu-ga itagat-te iru**-yō-ni omoeru-n-desu.

   "If you cook it vigorously over high heat, the tofu looks to me to **be in pain.**"

Somewhat comical, the metaphorized ingredient in (4) adds a fresh perspective to the food discourse even though the topic of the discussion, boiled tofu, is an extremely simple dish. Likewise, the adjectives in (5) modify the nature and extent of sweetness by analogizing the sweet taste with personal traits.

(5) shitsukoi amasa/amami   "persistent sweetness"
    jōhin-na amasa/amami   "elegant sweetness"
    yasashii amasa/amami   "gentle sweetness"
    tsutsumashii amasa/amami "modest sweetness"

Conversely, gustatory and culinary expressions can be used as metaphors for descriptions that do not pertain to foodways. The newspaper heading in (6) mentions the taste term *umami*, referring to the flavor of a food item or its degree. In this example, however, *umami* is applied to a condominium building.

(6) 築43年　「**うまみ**」なくなった？

Chiku 43-nen "**umami**" nakunatta?

"43 years since (the condominium) was first built – the '**flavor**' is gone?"

(Katada 2021)

The article reports that building management companies have been refusing to renew contracts in recent years. A suspected reason is expressed in (6): older buildings lose their *umami* "flavor"—i.e., their prime time—just as old food items that have long past their expiration dates do, and it would not be cost-effective to manage old properties considering additional expenditures on repairs and the like.

Another example of a food metaphor applied to non-food areas is found in compound terms with *niru* "cook in liquids" in chapter 4. Compounds with the intransitive counterpart of *niru*, i.e., *nieru*, are turned into metaphors to convey strong anger, as illustrated in (7).

(7) a. harawata-ga **nie**-kaeru/**nie**-kuri-kaeru
       "lit. Intestines are boiling"

   b. kanjō-ga **nie**-tagiru
       "lit. Emotions are boiling"

   c. hara-no soko-ga **nie**-tatsu
       "lit. The bottom of my stomach is boiling"

As cooking terms, *nie-kaeru*, *nie-kuri-kaeru*, *nie-tagiru*, and *nie-tatsu* all refer to a boiling point, some of which are more rigorous than others. Various degrees of boiling liquid are viewed parallel to angry states and their intensity in (7). Interesting to point out are the common references to digestive organs (*harawata* "intestines" and *hara* "stomach"), which represent a target location of angry feelings in a Japanese cultural context. Additionally, the compound, *ni-tsumeru* "boil down," was mentioned in chapter 4 as a term of a cooking method, and *ni-tsumeru* and its intransitive counterpart, *ni-tumaru* describe the cooking stage at which a seasoned liquid is cooked down after being absorbed by the ingredients. As a metaphor, *ni-tumaru* as in *giron-ga ni-tsumaru* [lit. discussions are boiling down] means approaching a conclusion or solution after a debate, signifying a positive outcome of a solution after undergoing a substantive discussion.

Metaphor expands and enriches the way in which our food experiences are communicated. At the same time and more broadly, they serve as an intriguing conduit that informs us of people's conceptual patterns in cultural and social contexts. This chapter discusses non-food expressions as metaphors for food and conversely, food expressions as metaphors for non-food, although more attention will be paid to the latter. We will witness the extent to which metaphors of and for food are deployed for descriptive and rhetorical enrichment. At the same time, we recognize important contributions that these metaphors make to linguistic investigations. To that end, I shall examine metaphor samples by focusing on their linguistic patterning and analytical implications.

1 METAPHORICAL EXTENSION FROM NON-FOOD TO FOOD

In studying metaphors in the language of food, Seto (2003, 2005) provides detailed resources for metaphors that analogize food tastes with objects or concepts that inherently do not belong to the food domain. Not only do Seto's volumes contain a great many examples of metaphors found in a wide range of sources, but they also put them in methodological contexts to shed light on analytical consequences that Japanese food metaphors have to the general study of metaphor. Due to the breadth and depth of their inquiries into the subject that extends beyond the purpose of the current investigation, I examine only a selective set of samples and their linguistic significance in this section. Two topics of linguistic relevance that I take up are synesthetic metaphor and conceptual metaphor.

Drawing from the Greek origin of *syn* "together" and *aesthesis* "perception," Ullmann (1962, 216) explains that synesthetic metaphors are "based on transpositions from one sense to another: from sound to sight, from touch to sound, etc." We can see examples of synesthetic metaphor in (3): *marui aji* "round taste," *akarui aji* "bright taste," and *shizukana aji* "quiet taste." The first two adjectives, *marui* "round" and *akarui* "bright," represent vision. By transposing from vision to taste, they elaborate on the type of taste. The third, *shizukana* "quiet," is an adjective of auditory sensation but again characterizes a food taste by crossing sense domains. Synesthetic metaphors as they are applied to food taste comes as no surprise given that the phrases like *gokan-de ajiwau* "taste with five senses" and *gokan-ni uttaeru* "appeal to five senses" are repeated almost like a maxim in the Japanese gustatory and culinary discourse. Whether participating in tasting or cooking activities, we are reminded that food is to be savored by invoking all the five senses.

The Nihon Cooking Academy, for one, puts out the well-known five essences of Japanese food or *washoku* at its homepage:[2] five cooking methods (raw, in-liquid cooking, frying, steaming, deep-frying), five tastes (sour, bitter, sweet, spicy, salty), five colors (white, black, yellow, red, blue/green), five types of appropriateness (temperature, ingredients, amount, technique, hospitality), and five senses (vision, hearing, smell, touch, taste). The maxim-like notion that stresses five senses is relevant not just to high-lineage food but also to home-cooking, as is evidenced by frequent reminders that cookbooks send to the reader. Kidosaki's (1987) hands-on cookbook that accompany many colored photos is typical of the message that emphasizes on calling all senses into play: "it is important 'to exercise five senses' whether a dish be Japanese, Western, or Chinese" (p. 5).[3] Synesthetic metaphors for food, thus, can readily be considered a natural representation of well accepted values entrenched in Japanese gustatory and culinary culture.

Examples of synesthetic metaphors that Seto (2003) compiled confirm that food tastes are characterized by the vocabulary of the four other senses. Particularly, transpositions from touch to taste and from vision to taste show more representations than other types of transpositions.[4] (8) presents selective samples from Seto's (2003, 70–71) list. My literal translations of the examples are intentional in order to highlight the meaning of the modifiers' original sense domain before synesthetic transpositions.

(8) a. touch → taste

omoi aji "heavy taste," karui aji "light taste," shita-o sasu aji "taste that pierces the tongue," togatta aji[5] "pointed taste," atatakai aji "warm taste," tsumetai aji "cold taste," kawaita aji "dry taste," shimeppoi aji "wet taste," nebari-no aru shokkan "sticky mouth feel," yawarakai shokkan "soft mouth feel," katai aji "hard taste," nameraka-na aji "smooth taste," arai aji "coarse taste," sugasugashii aji "refreshing taste"

b. vision → taste

maroyaka-na ajiwai "round (mellow) flavor," ō-aji "big taste," ko-aji "small taste," usu-aji "thin taste," koi aji "dark taste," aomi-gakatta aji "bluish taste," tōmei-na aji "transparent taste," nigotta aji "muddy taste," kurai aji "dark taste," heiban-na aji "flat taste," atsumi-no aru aji "thick taste," aji-no sō "layer of taste," kakushi-aji "hidden taste," aji-no hirogari "spread of taste," shizunda aji "sunk taste," hukuyoka-na umami "plump taste," boyaketa aji "fuzzy taste"

c. hearing → taste

urusai aji "noisy taste," (kokoro-ni) hibiku aji "taste that reverberates (to the heart)," aji-no yoin "resonance of taste," aji-onchi "taste tone-deaf," aji-no hāmonī "harmony of tastes," kiin-to suru aji "ringing (mimetic) taste," aji-no sasayaki "whisper of taste," aji-o kiku "listen to taste," kiki-zake "listening of sake [=sake tasting]"

d. smell → taste

kōbashii aji "aromatic taste," kusai aji "stinky taste," kōmi "aroma and taste," kaguwashii aji "aromatic taste," hōjun-na aji "mellow [smell] taste," tsun-to kuru aji "taste that hits the nose sharply (mimetic)," koge-aji "burned taste," nama-gusai aji "fishy taste"

The synesthetic metaphors for food taste in (8) are all well-attested, familiar expressions. The meanings should be largely transparent given the English counterparts, but further comments on a few may be helpful. The contrastive pair of *ō-aji* "big taste" and *ko-aji* "small taste" in (8b) describes a taste that does not have much flavor (i.e., bland taste) and a delicately-flavored taste, respectively. Also, in (8b), *aomi-gakatta aji* "bluish taste" is formed with a color term. As Komori (2003) discusses in detail, color terms that metaphorically characterize food tastes are not limited to blue but includes *shiroi* "white," *akai* "red," *kīroi* "yellow," as well as *azayaka-na iro* "bright color" (pp. 110–11).[6] Yamaguchi (2003) explains that these colors in general refer to those of ingredients and their typical tastes. For instance, white is associated with the light flavor of tofu, and red reminds us of the spiciness of red (hot) peppers. On the other hand, both Komori and Yamaguchi analyze that *aoi* "blue" serves as a metaphor for immaturity (an equivalent of the metaphorical use of *green* in English), and hence describes a taste associated with unripe food items.[7] The compound *aji-onchi* "taste tone-deaf" in (8c) is based on the term *onchi*, whose meaning ranges from the technical sense of tone deaf to a somewhat extended or broader sense of not having a good ear for music and being unable to sing on key. Analogized to the taste domain, *aji-onchi* refers to a person who has difficulty to recognize or appreciate particular or general flavors. These metaphorical descriptions across sense domains no doubt broaden the range of rhetorical means to speak to subjective food experiences with flexibility and creativity.

One of the contributions that the inquiries of synesthetic metaphors make to linguistics analysis has to do with the directionality of the transposition. Notable in this line of research is Williams (1976), who examined the diachronic development of English adjectives found in three reliable dictionaries, focusing on their metaphorization through synesthetic transfer. His survey shows that metaphorical transfer from one sense domain to another is unidirectional, and delimits synesthetic metaphors to certain types, disallowing others. The generalizations over permissible directions of metaphorical transfer are summarized in (9), along with his examples in English in parentheses.

(9) touch → taste (*sharp* taste), color (*dull* colors), sound (*soft* sounds)
taste → smell (*sour* smells), sound (*dulcet* music)
visually perceived dimension → color (*flat* color), sound (*deep* sounds)
color → sound (*bright* sounds)
sound → color (*quiet* colors)
smell → Ø

Applying the generalizations to Japanese, the examples in (8a), i.e., the transfer from touch to taste, are expected, whereas the remainder in (8) is not supposed to be permissible. From each of vision (both dimension and color), hearing (sound), and smell to taste represents a reverse direction of (9), and yet the transfer patterns are amply attested. Williams's study is based on English and admittedly may not be intended to extend to other languages. Furthermore, he reports on examples that illustrate the directions of transfer that are not predicted by (9) (e.g., *mellow* for taste to color, *loud* for sound to taste, *tart* for taste to touch) while confirming that 83 percent of his surveyed samples follow the expected patterns. That said, Japanese samples in (8) suggest that a crosslinguistic application of the unidirectional analysis of synesthetic metaphor as generalized in (9) faces some limitations.[8] It shows that the language in what may be a narrow area of food discourse can provide a fertile testing ground for hypotheses made in linguistic investigations.

Another area to which food metaphors (i.e., non-food expressions describing food tastes) have a linguistic contribution pertains to the notion of Conceptual Metaphor, which has been developed by Lakoff and Johnson (1980). Metaphor is non-literal speech in which a subject matter is spoken of in terms of another by analogy. Lakoff and Johnson's premise is that metaphors are pervasive "not just in language but in thought and action" (p. 3) and are extended to concepts. For instance, each of the expressions in (10), taken selectively from their samples (p. 4, emphasis original), contains a metaphor, but collectively, they mirror a more fundamental metaphor at the conceptual level. They are tied together by the conceptual metaphor of ARGUMENT IS WAR.

(10) a. Your claims are *indefensible*.
b. He *attacked every weak point* in my argument.
c. I *demolished* his argument.
d. I've never *won* an argument with him.
e. He *shot down* all of my arguments.

Similarly, the cooking terms in (11) are each used to express one's emotions, but they are mutually viewed to reflect the conceptual metaphor, EMOTION IS COOKING.

(11) a. His comments made me *boil*.
 b. His criticism *burned* me.
 c. Emotions *simmer* after bad loss to Jets.

Note that conceptual metaphors like ARGUMENT IS WAR and EMOTION IS COOKING single out a specific aspect of the target concept. These conceptual metaphors highlight negative facets of arguments and emotions in (10–11), but various other components of the targets may well be bases for other conceptual metaphors. Since conceptual metaphors reflect our language, thought, and actions, metaphorical concepts are "tied to our culture" (Lakoff and Johnson 1980, 22–24). It follows that the values underlying conceptual metaphors in one culture may not be universal, and as such, conceptual metaphors provide a significant window through which we can detect distinct beliefs and values that are embedded in specific sociocultural environments. Some of the examples of food metaphors in Japanese below, thus, may not uniformly sound coherent to speakers of other languages due to differences in those beliefs and values which one culture subscribes to but may not be shared by another.

As the title of Lakoff and Johnson (1980), *Metaphors We Live By*, suggests, metaphors are entrenched in our life, so much so that we may not consciously realize that we use them to the extent that we do. To illustrate it in the context of Japanese food metaphors, Tsujimoto (2003, 2005) analyzed a number of examples in terms of conceptual metaphors. I discuss three for illustration: (i) TASTE/FOOD IS LIVING BEING illustrated in (12–14), (ii) TASTE/FOOD IS HUMAN BEING in (15–17), and (iii) TASTE/FOOD IS MOVING OBJECT in (18–19).[9] These conceptual metaphors tend to be somewhat broad, but they set coherent grounds for linguistic expressions like the individual examples above.

(i) TASTE/FOOD IS LIVING BEING

(12) …シナモンの味と甘さが**喧嘩しないよう**にする…

 … shinamon-no aji-to amasa-ga **kenka-shinai-yō-ni** suru …

 "… so that the taste of cinnamon and the sweetness **won't fight** each other …" (Tsujimoto 2003, 167)

(13) …青首大根ではこの大トロの脂に完全に**負け**てしまう。

 … aokubi-daikon-de-wa kono ōtoro-no abura-ni kanzen-ni **makete-shimau**.

"... the Aokubi-daikon (radish) ends up completely **losing** to the fat of the fatty tuna." (Ibid., 169)

(14) ... アナゴ本来の味を**生か**したいと思ったんだ。

... anago honrai-no aji-o **ikashi**-tai-to omotta-n-da.

"... I thought I want to make the natural taste of a conger **live**." (Ibid., 173)

The first conceptual metaphor, TASTE/FOOD IS LIVING BEING, is the basis for considering food tastes to have the abilities to live, survive, and fight. In (12), a potential conflict between the two distinct tastes is viewed parallel to a physical fight or a quarrel that living beings are able to engage in. Conflicts between two living beings may end up with a winner and a loser, as in (13), in which the tuna is the winner whose fatty taste completely overpowers the radish. The conger in (14) is obviously a living being, but it is its taste that is treated as having a life. The context informs us that a chef maneuvers to maintain the natural taste and to bring it to the center stage.

(ii) TASTE/FOOD IS HUMAN BEING

(15) ... 一人前のパンになるんです。

... **ichininmae**-no pan-ni naru-n-desu.

"... [it will] become **independent** bread (after the baking process is completed)." (Ibid., 174)

(16) トカイ・アスーはとても**素直な**ワインと言えるのではないでしょうか。

Tokai asū-wa totemo **sunao-na** wain-to ieru-no-dewa nai-de-shō-ka.

"I wonder if you can say Tokaij Aszu is a **gentle/meek** wine." (Ibid., 176)

(17) やさしい味

yasashii aji

"**gentle** taste" (Ibid., 176)

The conceptual metaphor of TASTE/FOOD IS HUMAN BEING serves as a thread that holds the expressions in (15–17) together. A more narrowly captured concept than the TASTE/FOOD IS LIVING BEING metaphor, TASTE/FOOD IS HUMAN BEING highlights aspects of attributes by which humans are defined and looks at food through the lens of those attributes. *Ichininmae* in (15) is an expression to describe a young person establishing independence as a full-fledged adult. Tsujimoto (2003, 174) comments that the bread's developing its taste is spoken of in terms of a growing or maturing process of humans. The adjectives, *sunao-na* "gentle, meek" in (16) and *yasashii* "gentle" in (17), are descriptors for personalities and demeanors, which are applied to tastes of food items and beverages.

(iii) TASTE/FOOD IS MOVING OBJECT

(18) こうやって炒めると、濃い甘味がじんわりと出てきます。

Kō yatte itameru-to, koi amami-ga jinwari-to **dete-kimasu**.

"As I stir-fry it, rich sweetness gradually **comes out**."

(Tsujimoto 2005, 145)

(19) 肉の中まで味が入るんです。

Niku-no naka-made aji-ga **hairu-n-desu**.

"The taste **enters** the meat." (Ibid., 143)

This last conceptual metaphor considers food and taste parallel to moving objects that are expected to move with all directional orientations including coming in and out. Just as expected of what is capable of voluntary movements, sweetness emerges from the ingredient as it is being stir-fried in (18), while the broth enters into the meat in (19). The TASTE/FOOD IS MOVING OBJECT conceptual metaphor represents a particularly widespread way of thinking of culinary processes, and expressions that instantiate it, like those in (18–19), are well attested in food dialog especially in cooking instructions.

As is evidenced by the conceptual metaphors under (i) and (ii) above, food metaphors (and metaphors in other areas) seem to have a strong tendency to personify food items and tastes. That is, the conceptual metaphor of TASTE/FOOD IS HUMAN BEING is a conceptual basis of a number of expressions that have to do with foodways in general. To supplement Tsujimoto's examples in (15–17), I provide additional instances of such a personification strategy as a way of enriching food discourse. Consider (20–24), in which ingredients are analogized to humans and are portrayed to exhibit traits and behavior that characterize humans.

(20) …塩分とも仲良くつき合いたい。

…enbun-to-mo **nakayoku tsukiai**-tai.

"… we want to **be on good terms with** salt." (Watanabe 2015, 36)

(21) キャベツ、ウインナー巻き、牛すじ、…、多彩な**顔ぶれ**がずらり。

Kyabetsu, winnā-maki, gyūsuji, . . . , tasai-na **kaobure**-ga zurari.

"Cabbage, wrapped Vienna sausage, beef sinew, . . . , colorful **lineup**."
(Hiramatsu 2015, 38)

(22) …**くったりと疲れた**汁を吸い込み…

. . . **kuttari-to tsukareta** shiru-o suikomi . . .

". . . [porridge] sucking in the **totally exhausted** broth . . . ."
(Ako 2014, 94)

(23) …濃厚なデミグラスソースの香りに**背中を押され**、…

. . . nōkō-na demigurasu-sōsu-no kaori-ni **senaka-o osare**, . . .

". . . being **pushed in the back** by the aroma of the rich demiglace sauce . . ."
(Hiramatsu 2015, 202)

(24) …　白い湯気のなかからつるつるの**艶肌**が現れ、**風呂上りの眩し
さ**、甘い香りに悩殺された。

. . . shiroi yuge-no naka-kara tsurutsuru-no **tsuyahada**-ga araware, **huro-agari-no mabushisa**, amai-kaori-ni nōsatsu-sareta.

". . . smooth **shiny skins** appear from white steam, and [I] was captivated by **the glare after a bath** and the sweet aroma."　　　(Ibid., 228)

The context in which (20) appears is the dietary preference of reducing sodium intake, but *tsukiau* "socialize, be friends with" gives a more lenient stance toward salt by suggesting a reasonable amount, rather than totally avoiding it, just like humans wanting to hold a good relationship with others in the society. The adverb *nakayoku* "on good terms" further endorses cordial relationships on par with human interactions by way of moderate salt use. In (21) *kao* of *kaobure* literally means (human) face, and the compounded word *kaobure* collectively refers to the members of a group. There are many ingredients in the dish mentioned in (21) (e.g., cabbage, sausage, beef), and the "faces" of these ingredients together constitute the lineup, *kaobure*, while each makes its own contribution to the dish. In (22), just as we as humans become physically tired, the broth is described to have lost its original freshness and develops the appearance of fatigue. On the previous night, the broth was left over from a pot meal, and subsequently a porridge was made with the remaining broth in the pot. The leftover broth is tired-looking, after having used up all its energy for the vibrant flavor of the night before. The use of the mimetic word *kuttari-to* typically describes complete physical exhaustion, intensifies the extreme degree of fatigue, hinting that no flavor is left in the broth.

In (23), s*enaka-o osu* "lit. push one's back" itself is a metaphor of giving encouragement, but here used as a dynamic action figuratively carried out by the demiglace sauce. The aroma of the sauce is enticing enough to convince the writer to finish the dish despite being already full. Finally, (24) is about a meat bun called *bijin-buta-man* [beautiful.woman-pork-bun], which is the name of a meat bun likened to a beautiful woman. Following the analogy that the name reflects, the descriptions in (24) make references to what characterizes or stereotypes beautiful female figures. In this depiction, meat buns have just been steamed, which through the metaphor gives the image of a beautiful woman (or women) emerging from a steamy bath. The skin of a steamed bun is full of luster, resembling the smooth skin of a woman who has just taken a bath. The *tsuyahada* "shiny skin" is further intensified by the mimetic *tsurutsuru* for its exquisite smoothness. Compounded by the sweet smell, the glare after a bath is both sensual and sexual. The last verb *nōsatsu* "mesmerize," whose Chinese characters correspond to "brain-kill," can specifically mean a situation in which men come to be fascinated by attractive, beautiful women. The meat buns, just coming out of a steamer, have a multi-sensual appeal that one could not resist. This example reveals the cultural orientation of an aesthetic standard (or bias) for females. At the same time, we can ascertain the importance of inviting appearances, which is one of the facets that is expected of desirable food.

Metaphors are superbly effective in showcasing both positive and negative aspects of our experiences with food and in bringing them to a subjective level. Furthermore, the conceptual metaphor approach provides an analytical tool to generalize patterns of thinking into a coherent set, rather than randomly treating individual expressions one by one. In so doing, we have a glimpse at underlying cultural views that are accepted and followed in the society. The Japanese data and our discussion of them give credence to methodological validity to those analytical tools.

2 METAPHORICAL EXTENSION FROM FOOD TO NON-FOOD

The vocabulary and expressions pertinent to gustatory and culinary experiences serve as a rhetorically rich trope for non-food topics. This metaphorization path takes the reverse analogical direction of what we have discussed in the previous section. Synesthetic metaphor is one of the ways in which taste expressions are extended to non-food subjects. (25), selected from a more thorough list of Seto (2003, 70–71), presents the attested directions and their examples of synesthetic transfers.

(25) a. taste → smell

amai kaori "sweet aroma," oishii nioi "delicious smell," shibui kaori "astringent aroma," nigai kusai "bitter smelly"

b. taste → vision

amai iro "sweet color," amai hūkei "sweet scenery," shibui iro "astringent (refined) color," shoppai kao "salty face (frown)," nigai kōkei "bitter scene"

c. taste → hearing

amai koe "sweet voice," shibui oto "astringent (refined) sound," shoppai koe "salty (hoarse) voice"

d. taste → touching

amai hōyō "sweet embrace," tezawari-o ajiwau "taste (enjoy) the feel," pen-no kaki-aji "write-taste (the feel when writing) of a pen"

Regarding the generalizations in (9) that Williams (1976) draws over the directionality of synesthetic transfers, (25a) and (25c) are consistent with them whereas (25b) and (25d) are not. Along with Japanese examples in (8) that are counter to the predicted directions, widespread use of the expressions like those in (25b) and (25d) further attest to flexibility and productivity of synesthetic transfers in verbal metaphors.

This section focuses on another figurative mode of describing non-food in terms of food vocabulary by examining conceptual metaphors that take the pattern of X IS FOOD/COOKING, where X stands for concepts outside foodways. We then discuss a sociocultural implication of metaphor, i.e., that metaphor can reveal a set of social and cultural constructs with which the people may identify themselves. Following up on the social aspect of metaphor, the final subsection discusses the extent to which taste adjectives metaphorically expand their meanings beyond the food domain. It will be shown that the semantic extension of the base-line adjectives like *amai* "sweet" and *umai* "delicious" has interesting sociolinguistic implications.

2.1. Conceptual Metaphors

Diverse traits of food consumption and various phases of food preparation offer conceptual sources of analogical comparisons. I focus on conceptual metaphors of the following two patterns: X IS FOOD and X IS COOKING/

DINING, where X stands for topics outside foodways. Our first example of the X IS FOOD conceptual metaphor has to do with books and reading activities: BOOK/READING IS FOOD. This conceptual metaphor unifies aspects of reading books that are beneficial to us, just as food serves as a nutrient not only to our body but to our soul. (26–28) demonstrate the connection.

(26) 文字から**栄養**

moji-kara **eiyō**

"**nutrition** from letters" (Takii 2021, 85)

(27) a. 紙を**食わなければ**生きられないあなたに。

Kami-o **kuwa-nakereba** ikir-are-nai atana-ni.

"For you who cannot live **without eating** paper."

(Matsunaga 2021, 87)

b. 読書する＝**紙を食う**のが好きな人種

dokusho-suru = **kami-o kuu**-no-ga suki-na jinshu

"engage in reading = species who like to **eat paper**" (Ibid.)

(28) じつは読書は、自分で速さも時間も気の向くままに決められる、心の**スローフード**ではないだろうか。

Jitsu-wa dokusho-wa, jibun-de hayasa-mo jikan-mo ki-no muku-mama-ni kime-rareru, kokoro-no **surō hūdo**-de-wa nai-darō-ka.

"In fact, I wonder if reading is **slow food** for the mind for which we can decide the pace and the time depending on our mood."

(Numano 2020, 135)

The phrases in (26) and (27a) are the headings of a regular column of the magazine *Kurowassan*, in which new books are introduced by individuals from different professions. Each individual who writes for this column uses his/her own heading like (26) and (27a). It does not seem coincidental that two different individuals have opted to analogize books and reading with aspects of foodways. Instead, it gives credence to the conceptual metaphor BOOK IS FOOD as a representation of a general mode of thinking. In (26), which is written by a writer herself, the nourishing aspect of food is highlighted in the metaphor. Just as we take nutrients from the food we eat in order to live, books can be "feeding" sources of knowledge and information that fits the reader's purpose (e.g., guides to self-improvement, leisure, intellectual curiosity). (27a) is the heading chosen by another book recommender. Under the conceptual metaphor of BOOK IS FOOD, books are to be consumed, as the recommender further elaborates on the equation as in (27b). (27a), moreover, identifies the column not just for those who like to read books (*kami-o kuu hito* "those who eat paper") but for those who cannot survive without reading books (*kami-o kuwa-nakereba ikir-are-nai hito* "those who cannot live without eating paper"). So, the labeling of the column with the heading of (27a) gives a sense of urgency under which the books he introduces would be essential in filling the need.

In (28) reference to food is more specifically made to slow food, which is contrastive with fast-food. Like the phrases in (26) and (27a), the nutrition aspect of food is an underlying benefit that connects reading with food. However, the focus is more on the way that food is consumed. Unlike wolfing down a prepared fast-food meal in a short time without savoring its taste, the author suggests that we take our time in book reading and slow down as we encounter intriguing lines. Reading books when carried out in a relaxed manner and mood has beneficial effects on the mind and soul, as slowly consumed and digested foods are healthful to the body. Slow food, known as a movement, has a broader social meaning, but the context of (28) indicates that the author seems to be using the term more literally to mean dining at a leisurely pace.

Contrastive with generally perceived aspects of book-reading expressed in (26–27), metaphorical expressions in (29) are directed to a specific literary work in terms of food consumption.

(29) a. 江國さんの小説は**肉食**だ。**濃密な葡萄酒で煮込まれた肉**。それを**手摑みで食べる**。指の先までしっかり**舐める**。口の周りがべたべたしても構わない。そしてそれらはすぐに体の中に流れ始める。

Ekuni-san-no shōsetsu-wa **nikushoku**-da. **Nōmitsu-na budōshu-de nikom-are-ta niku**. Sore-o **tezukami-de taberu**. **Yubi-no saki-made shikkari nameru**. Kuchi-no mawari-ga betabeta shitemo kamawanai. Soshite sorera-wa sugu-ni karada-no naka-ni nagare-hajimeru.

"Ms. Ekuni's novel is **a meat dish. With meat that has been stewed in a rich wine. I eat it by hand. I lick my fingers thoroughly to the tips.** I don't care if it gets sticky around my mouth. And, it [=the meat] all starts flowing inside my body." (Mitsuno 2006, 228)

b. 私はこの短編集をどんどん**食べた**。もっともっとと思いながら、**一気に食べて**しまった。

Watashi-wa kono tanpenshū-o dondon **tabeta**. Motto motto-to omoi-nagara, **ikki-ni tabete**-shimatta.

"I rapidly **ate** this collection of short stories. Wanting more and more, I ended up **eating it all at once**." (Ibid., 232)

c. おかわりも三回した。... 三度目にはゆっくり**食べた**。

Okawari-mo sankai shita. ... Sandome-ni-wa yukkuri **tabeta**

"I even had a third **helping**. ... I slowly **ate** it third time."

(Ibid., 233)

The excerpts in (29) are from Momo Mitsuno's commentary on a collection of short stories by Kaori Ekuni. The collection as a whole and individual stories compiled in it are likened to food and the eating process, all presenting specific instances of the conceptual metaphor BOOK/READING IS FOOD. (29a) is particularly vivid in its equation of Ekuni's stories and their sense-arousing effects on Mitsuno with meat and meat-eating. The combination of meat cooked in a rich sauce and savoring every bit of it by hand until her fingers are licked clean captures the surprisingly wild and visceral experiences that have been brought out to Mitsuno. The impulsive reaction to the stories is further detailed in (29b) by her insatiable desire to read one story after the next without pause, just as we have a hard time resisting food with succulent flavors. In (29c), we learn that her voracious appetite for the stories kept her reading them three times. The conceptual metaphor consistently and continuously underlies (29c), as demonstrated by *okawari*, which is a dining term to mean "second helping, refill." The individual figurative expressions like those in (29) and a few more similar ones throughout the discourse of this commentary all point to BOOK/READING IS FOOD as a concept around which these instances logically cohere together.

Along a similar line, the pleasurable facet of food underlying BOOK/READING IS FOOD can be linked to enjoyable feelings that one might have after reading a specific story. It is common that books published in Japan are accompanied by a strip of paper called *obi* "sash" placed around the lower part of dust jackets for promotional purposes. We customarily see on *obi* appealing phrases about the book and the author that tempt potential readers. On the *obi* of Ito Ogawa's novel *Shokudō-katatsumuri* "Restaurant Snail," a caption says, *kokoro-ni oishii monogatari* [mind-to delicious story] "a story that is delicious to our mind." Using the conceptual linking BOOK/READING IS FOOD, the advertising phrase evokes the pleasure to our palate when we eat something delicious, and projects it onto similar emotional and psychological reactions to a pleasing and gratifying experience that Ogawa's story is promised to offer.[10]

A variety of art forms readily reflects the conceptual metaphor of the X IS FOOD pattern, in which the aspect of food is viewed as a source of nutrition in a similar vein to BOOK/READING IS FOOD. In addition to general book-reading in (26–28) and the particular literature instantiated in (29), music, play, gardening, and the like also serve as nourishing agents for our mind and life in general. (30) presents examples of connecting food with music and play.

(30) a. 今号は、音楽を愛し、**糧**にして生きてきた、ある人の物語から始まります。

Kongō-wa, ongaku-o aishi, **kate**-ni shite ikite-kita, aru hito-no monogatari-kara hajimarimasu.

"This issue starts with a story of someone who loves and **is fed by** music." (Kurashino Techosha 2021, 5)

b. 音や音楽は<u>心</u>に**栄養**を与えてくれて…

Oto-ya ongaku-wa <u>kokoro</u>-ni **eiyō**-o ataete-kurete …

"Sound and music give the <u>mind</u> **nutrition** …" (Takeda 2019)

c. 生の演劇は<u>心</u>の**糧**！

Nama-no engeki-wa <u>kokoro</u>-no **kate**!

"Live plays are **food** for the <u>mind</u>!"
(Gurōbaru-mama Kenkyūjo 2021)

As these examples demonstrate, food vocabulary like *kate* "food" in (30a, c) and *eiyō* "nutrition" in (30b), both in bold-faced, commonly cooccur with *kokoro* "mind" (underlined in (30b, c)).

Turning to the second pattern, X IS COOKING/DINING, life is a common theme that can be conceptually equated with the process aspect of foodways such as cooking and dining. Individual metaphors used in (31–32) instantiate the underlying conceptual metaphor LIFE IS COOKING/DINING. An excerpt from an essay on life in (31) points out that the course of one's life is a process of which one can be in charge, just like food flavors can be actively modified during cooking.

(31) 高い食材ではなくてもおいしいものができるのと同じように、自分がもっているものを活かすこと、そして自分だけのエッセンスを加えて**一味ちがう**ようにすると、人生が楽しくなる。

Takai shokuzai-de-wa nakutemo oishii mono-ga dekiru-no-to onaji-yō-ni, jibun-ga motte-iru mono-o ikasu koto, soshite jibun-dake-no essensu-o kuwaete **hitoaji chigau**-yō-ni suru-to, jinsei-ga tanoshiku naru.

"Just as we can make a delicious meal out of inexpensive ingredients, our lives become enjoyable once we make good use of what we have and make it **somewhat special** by adding our own essence."
(Umihara 2019, 115)

Before the passage of (31), the author asserts that her philosophical stance is "life is cooking." She elaborates on the view in (31), where she continues to use individual food metaphors. Relevant to this discourse is the term *essensu* "essence." Collocated with the verb *kuwaeru* "to add," it refers to an extract to enhance food flavors. In the metaphor for life, a food essence is equated to a personal trait that should be put to effective use for enrichment of the overall life prospect. The phrase *hitoaji chigau* "make somewhat special" consists of the food vocabulary *hitoaji* "one taste/flavor" and the verb *chigau* "to differ," and together it literally means "different by one flavor." When it is extended to advice on life, an individual quality, no matter how ordinary or how subtle it may seem, can benefit one's life, just as a touch of an extract can make a difference in cooking.

A message at a website on life guidance in (32) looks at human life as a dining experience of a full-course meal.

(32) a. 人生も、レストランの**フルコース料理**と同じです。
小学校、中学校、高校、大学、就職、結婚、出産……。
料理が1つずつ登場するように、人生でも、小さな課題が1つずつ現れます。

Jinsei-mo, resutoran-no **hurukōsu-ryōri**-to onaji desu.
Shōgakkō, chūgakkō, kōkō, daigaku, shūshoku, kekkon, shussan . . .
Ryōri-ga hitotsu-zutu tōjō-suru-yō-ni, jinsei-de-mo, chīsa-na kadai-ga hitotsu-zutsu arawaremasu.

"Life is the same as **a full-course meal** at a restaurant.
Elementary school, junior-high school, high school, college, job, marriage, childbirth . . .
Just as **dishes are served one by one**, also in life, small tasks emerge one by one."

b. 最後に登場するのは、**甘いデザート**です。
どんなデザートなのかは、人生最後になってからのお楽しみです。

Saigo-ni tōjō-suru-no-wa **amai dezāto** desu.
Donna dezāto-na-no-ka-wa, jinsei saigo-ni natte-kara-no otanoshimi-desu.

"Making an entrance last is **a sweet dessert**.
Finding out what kind of dessert it is will be the fun that you experience in the last phase of your life."   (Happy Lifestyle Corporation n.d.)

The passages in (32a) look at life in the long run, and various landmark events (e.g., schools, employment, marriage) in it are likened to different sequential dishes in a course meal. The message goes on to state in (32b) that the last event in life is yet unknown but something we look forward to. The anticipation parallels the excitement with which we wait for a dessert that ends the course meal with palatable pleasure.

Reflecting the conceptual equation FASHION IS COOKING/DINING, the analogy of fashion (or fashion coordination) with cooking showcases a creative process with which one can be engaged in these two areas. Not surprisingly, fashion magazines and particularly websites and social media sites offer rich resources for attesting to the connection, as discussed in Tsujimura (2018a). Examples include expressions like *kakushi-aji* [hide-taste] "lit. hidden flavor" and *jaketto-ni aji-tsuke* [jacket-to taste-attach] "lit. add flavors to a jacket." As a food vocabulary item, the former is a seasoning or the taste of a secret ingredient that brings out an unexpected flavor despite its often unrecognizable or unordinary existence. Extended to the fashion domain, it refers to a fashion idea or an item that is not immediately obvious but turns out to be effective on an overall appearance. The compound word *aji-tsuke* in the latter example simply means to add flavor(s). In the fashion context, an additional accessary (e.g., jewelry, scarf), playing a role as *aji* "taste, flavor," is suggested to improve on the coordination around a jacket. A similar example of *aji-tsuke* is shown in (33).

(33) シンプルなロングコートをヴィンテージバッグ&柄カーデで個性的に**味付け**！

Shinpuru-na rongu-kōto-o vintēji-baggu & gara-kāde-de koseiteki-ni **aji-tsuke!**

"In your own way, **add flavors** to a simple long coat with a vintage purse and a patterned cardigan!" (itSnap n.d.)

A purse and a cardigan serve as taste enhancers that elevate the modest design of the coat to a more unique outlook.

A subtle culinary step that gives a significant influence on overall results is further alluded to in (34).

(34) 今回は、ベーシックコーデに**ひとさじのスパイスを効かせる**「アラフォー世代が持っておきたいプラス1アイテム」をご紹介します。

Konkai-wa, bēshikku-kōde-ni **hitosaji-no supaisu-o kik-aseru** "arafō-sedai-ga motte-oki-tai purasu 1 aitemu"-o go-shōkai-shimasu.

"In this issue we introduce 'an additional item that women around 40 years old should have,' which **adds a spoonful of a spicy bite** to basic coordination." (CBK Magazine 2018)

Hitosaji in (34) is formed by *saji* "spoon" and the numeral *hito-* "one," together serving as a term for a kitchen measurement worth one spoonful. An add-on item of some kind will make a basic fashion outlook more eye-catching, parallel to the effect of modest condiments and seasoning in cooking, whether in terms of quality or quantity.

One of the principles that is valued in foodways is the peak season for a food item. Its importance in the Japanese gustatory and cooking scenes is evidenced by the unique word, *shun*, to refer to the season of the year for a specific food item to be savored. A metaphorical extension of this ideology to the fashion field is demonstrated in (35). The same website also includes the caption in (36), in which fashion coordination is analogized with cooking by the metaphorical use of *chōri* "cooking, preparation of food."

(35) 洋服にも旬がある。

Yōhuku-ni-mo **shun**-ga aru.

"There is **season** for clothing, too." (DRESS 2017)

(36) 少ないアイテムを自分らしく"**調理**"したい

Sukunai aitemu-o jibun-rashiku "**chōri**" shitai.

"You want to '**cook**' a few items to your liking." (Ibid.)

When a food item is in season, the price goes down and tempts us to buy more than we need. If we cannot use them up, the food becomes spoiled and wasted. The message of (35–36) is that even unworn clothes in a closet could miss out on the fashion trend and the "right time" to wear them. Consequently, more is not necessarily better. The take-home message is that you can bring fashionable originality out of a few resources.

The conceptual parallelism of makeup to cooking is very similar to that of fashion coordination to cooking in that all three domains are considered to involve processes that can showcase some creative ideas. The prevalence of the conceptual equation of makeup and cooking, summed up as MAKEUP IS COOKING, seems to be corroborated, for example, by an extensive use on social media of the term *kosume reshipi* "cosmetic recipe." *Kosume* is a clipped loanword of *kosumechikku* "cosmetic," and together with another loanword *reshipi* "recipe" it means a makeup tip. Similarly, the conceptual metaphor MAKEUP IS COOKING itself appears on a YouTube site (https://www.youtube.com/watch?v=Wd3jzJ6unK0): メイクアップは料理だ! "Makeup is cooking!" Makeup techniques are considered on par with culinary maneuvers that help enhance the overall outcome. Physical appearances resulting from tactful makeup techniques and the taste of a dish in cooking are two sides of the equation. (37–38) illustrate the analogy.

(37) 秋冬はネイビーメイクで**スパイス**を

Aki-huyu-wa neibī-mēku-de **supaisu**-o

"In fall and winter, add a **spice** by using navy-blue make-up"

(Arine 2020)

(38) このメイクは、**ダシを効かせた和食**に似ていますね。素材を生かして、**うす味**で充分、というような。

Kono mēku-wa, **dashi-o kik-aseta washoku**-ni nite-imasu-ne. Sozai-o ikashite, **usu-aji**-de jūbun, to iu-yōna.

"This make-up resembles **washoku (Japanese-style meal) that is rich with broth**. It's as if **light seasoning** is sufficient because the flavors of the ingredients are brought out." (Kurashino Techosha 2020, 72)

(37) speaks of eye-makeup that is centered around the navy-blue color. The use of the somewhat unordinary color (according to the context) is recommended to enliven the eye area. The role of the navy-blue color is likened to the seasoning that unexpectedly brightens the taste of the food.

The metaphor in (38) refers to washoku as well as culinary tenets and practices associated with it. The first sentence is a simile, marked by *nite-imasu* "be like, resemble," that asserts an analogical relation between makeup and washoku. In particular, the washoku in this analogy is the one that is built upon a deep-flavored broth, *dashi*. Compared with cooking ingredients in thick sauces, for instance, which add extrinsic tastes, washoku emphasizes preserving intrinsic flavors that ingredients characteristically have. To that end, a dense *dashi* (made of kelp, dried fish, fish flakes, and any combination of them) plays a vital role in bringing the inherent flavors to the fore while supplementing a foundational taste (umami) of its own. It does not seem to be an exaggeration that *dashi* is the heart of washoku. A consequence of a good *dashi* is spelled out in the second sentence in (38). If a dish is enriched with a solidly prepared *dashi*, the unique flavor of a main ingredient will present itself without adding strong seasoning. And, this is why *usu-aji* [thin-taste] "light seasoning" would be sufficient. Extended to the makeup context, *sozai* "ingredient" in this case is the model's face, and the intention is to bring out the facial features into prominence. The makeup advisor suggests that the model's facial features are well-defined enough for eye-makeup to be unnecessary, and that soft-colored lipstick complements her fair complexion. So, *usu-aji* "light seasoning" in the makeup setting stands for no eye-makeup and a quiet lip color. The unassuming degree of makeup is intended to foreground the natural qualities that the individual has. It should be remembered that metaphor is interpreted in cultural contexts. The example in (38) particularly speaks to the gustatory, culinary, and sensual values that pertain to washoku, representing part of a cultural practice that may not be shared by members of other cultures.[11]

2.2. Sexism

We have earlier examined metaphors that result from personification, like those in (12–17) and (20–24). They reflect conceptual metaphors like TASTE/FOOD IS LIVING BEING and TASTE/FOOD IS HUMAN BEING, which are attributed to coherent patterns in the conceptual system. The analogical relation in the opposite direction, i.e., objectification of humans as food, has been a topic of a larger discourse on gender issues in language. Hines (1999), for one, discusses the conceptual metaphor WOMAN AS DESSERT, which manifests degrees of prejudice against and sexism toward women. Her English examples range from general terms referring to women (e.g., cheesecake, cookie, (cherry) pie, tart), words that name specific female body parts (e.g., apples, cherries, watermelons), to action-oriented phrases (e.g., baking muffins "having sex with a woman," cut the cake "deflower a virgin," have a bun in the oven "be pregnant"). Emphasizing "the social role that metaphors play in transmitting coded messages," Hines argues that "metaphors are not merely a matter of conceptual systems but can also be a means of structuring our language—and our identity" (p. 146). It affirms that metaphor can constitute a conduit of not only cultural values but also people's attitudes pervasive in the society.

I illustrate how metaphor offers a lens through which we can glance at social beliefs that mirror a biased view of Japanese women, in particular, vis-à-vis their timing of marriage. Starting around the 1980s, the societal expectation that women should be married by the age 25 was expressed as *kurisumasu-kēki* "Christmas cake." The purported analogy is that women older than 25, having missed the ideal age for marriage, would have a difficulty with finding a mate, just as Christmas cakes are not needed and are viewed as a wasted commodity after Christmas Day. Over subsequent decades, the ideal age for marriage has risen to 31. Along with this transition, *kurisumasu-kēki* was replaced by *toshikoshi-soba* "New Year's Eve soba noodle," which is soba noodles that Japanese people traditionally eat on December 31. The reference to *toshikoshi-soba*, despite the delay in the ideal age, basically follows the same idea, maintaining the stance that there is the "right age" for women to find their husbands. Again, after that, they will be considered on par with unwanted (or even spoiled) food.

A yet more recent version, i.e., *osechi-ryōri*, seems to be available today. *Osechi-ryōri* is a traditional Japanese meal that is made at the end of the year in preparation for the New Year's three-day holiday for celebration. In both quality and quantity, the food is greater than a standard meal preparation, and consists of a variety of traditional and seasonal dishes along with special food items that are not served at the everyday dinner table at home. Since *osechi-ryōri* is consumed on January 1–3, these dates are converted to women's ages of 32–34, based on 25 (December 25) of *kurisumasu-kēki* and 31 (December 31) of *toshikoshi-soba*. The age range does not necessarily seem to identify a newly conceived marriable age, but in this metaphor women of 32–34 are thought to be a splendor with work and life experiences, drawing on the lavishness and nutrition that *osechi-ryōri* offers. From a slightly different perspective, *wain* "wine" seems to be an alternative word in this chain of food metaphor. Ideal timing for wine widely varies depending on the make, including the type of grape(s), year, and location, among other viticultural factors. The analogy of women with wine underscores unique individuality rather than setting an age-based cookie-cutter standard for all women.

Notwithstanding the apparent progression that these metaphors may suggest in the attitude toward Japanese women, it is important to recognize that they largely, if not exclusively, represent the view that capitalizes on a hegemonic society that places males above females. Even in the latter two terms discussed above (i.e., *osechi-ryōri* and *wain*), while seemingly better intended, women are still commodified and viewed to be consumed. Furthermore, they do not represent what women expect of themselves. Instead, they continue to reflect men's viewpoints and a traditional cultural norm that is shaped by them. It is further telling that we do not find male counterparts of these metaphors. Whatever stance one opts to take regarding the gender-biased metaphors described above, they do not exist in vacuum. Indeed, they are part of language that mirrors the beliefs, values, and attitudes with which the people identify themselves in social and cultural contexts.

2.3. Taste Adjectives

It has been shown earlier that the dearth of words that directly characterize food tastes can be compensated for by synesthetic metaphor, exemplified in (8), as a productive and rhetorically creative way to increase the range of expressiveness. That said, taste adjectives, though not many, exhibit instances of the reverse metaphorical direction and function to speak of non-food situations (Backhouse 1994; Muto 2001, 2002; Oda 2003; Yamazoe 2003). Among the words that directly describe food taste, the adjective *amai* "sweet" probably has more polysemous entries that are arguably tied together by metaphorical extension. Here I limit myself to some extended meanings that are not available to English *sweet* in order to point to crosslinguistic variation.

Aside from the function as synesthetic metaphor, *amai* describes (i) lack of rigor, (ii) careless and sloppy thoughts and actions lacking scruples, and (iii) insufficiency in mechanical function.[12] These three general groups are exemplified respectively in (39a), (39b), and (39c). Contrastive with what *amai* as a taste term denotes, the meanings in the metaphorical use of the adjective in (39) are all negative.

(39) a. {hyōka, saiten}-ga **amai**
{evaluation, grading}-NOM sweet

b. {handan, kangaekata, mamori}-ga **amai**
{judgment, view, defense}-NOM sweet

c. {doa-no neji, kuruma-no burēki, kamera-no pinto, naihu-no kireaji}-ga **amai**
{door screw, car break, camera focus, knife's sharpness}-NOM sweet

Lenient evaluations and grading may not always be regarded negatively, but *amai* in (37a) implies a less-than-ideal practice of assessment. The unfavorable nuance is based on expectations that assessors should maintain high standards. Judgments, the line of thinking, defense (e.g., in sporting events) in (39b) appear to follow the same vein as in (39a) because lack of rigor with which thoughts and actions are brought about is a common thread of both sets of examples. However, although the conceptualization path of *amai* to the general metaphorical sense in (39a) and (39b) may be treated on par, there is actually one area in which they do not pattern together.

The basic taste terms that are common in the Japanese foodways (*amai* "sweet," *karai* "spicy, salty," *nigai* "bitter," *shoppai/shiokarai* "salty," *shibui* "astringent," and *umami*) are not the type of descriptive words that find their semantic antonyms like *big-small, expensive-cheap,* and *hot-cold,* including relational opposites such as *parent-child, teacher-student,* and *employer-employee.* It is interesting to note, however, *amai* as a metaphor is paired with *karai* to form an antonymic relation.[13] Furthermore, *karai* can be used as *amai*'s antonym in (39a) but not in (39b). So, *saiten-ga karai* "grading is spicy [=strict]" is perfectly natural, having the opposite meaning of (39a): it describes someone who follows strict grading guidelines. In contrast, **kangaekata-ga karai* "*way of thinking is spicy [=with scruples]" as an opposite statement of (39b) is anomalous. It is not clear to me what gives rise to the difference in acceptability, but here we understand narrowly that *karai* has a metaphorically extended meaning in referring to the stringent manner applied to evaluation and grading. The metaphorical use of *amai* in (39c) speaks to a level of mechanical function that does not meet expected standards. So, the examples refer to looseness of door screws and car brakes, lack of camera focus, and dullness of blades, all failing to reach adequate benchmarks in the operational sense.

It seems relatively straightforward to connect the literal meaning of *amai* with positive aspects of non-foods in metaphorical extensions. Sweet tastes of foods generally give us pleasant feelings and temporary happiness, and these positive reactions are sustained in the metaphorical use of *amai*. Synesthetic metaphors demonstrate the pleasurable side of sensual appeals: *amai kaori* "sweet aroma," *amai iro* "sweet color," *amai koe* "sweet voice," and *amai hōyō* "sweet embrace." A similar conceptualization is maintained beyond the five senses, as is shown by expressions like *amai kioku* "sweet memory" and *amai shinkon-seikatsu* "sweet life of the newlywed." In contrast, it is more challenging to figure out how the sweet taste of *amai* connects to a negative concept that leads to sub-standard qualities.[14] Oda (2003) explains the connection as follows: "[s]weets bring pleasant sensations to us, make us relaxed, and lift the tension. They create a physically loose condition" (p. 196). So, the sweet taste is positively conceived to generate a physical looseness (i.e., relaxation), but physical looseness is evaluated as a negative quality when tightness is expected, like the objects mentioned in (39c). As for the metaphorical sense of *amai* in (39a–b), Oda analogizes the same looseness to mental and psychological aspects of human behavior (p. 198). Laxed rigor in evaluations and judgments in (39a–b), where strictness is considered of a higher value, amounts to a "loose condition" in a more abstract sense than (39c).

Incidentally, another instance of the negative (or less-than-desirable) connotation of *amai*, especially in contrast with *karai*, is exhibited in food discourse, in relation to gender stereotypes of Japanese men and women. As noted in endnote 13, *amai* and *karai* are adjectives to describe sake, and in this connection, there are compound words formed around them, *ama-tō* and *kara-tō*. They respectively refer to people who prefer sweets to alcohol and those who prefer alcohol to sweets. Related to the *ama-tō* vs. *kara-tō* opposition are believed stereotypes that women and children favor sweets (i.e., *ama-tō*) whereas men are assumed to prefer alcohol (i.e., *kara-tō*).[15] This dichotomy is a long-held societal view that reflects a historically male-hegemonic society. Holtzman (2018) unearths the actual sociocultural situation of how Japanese males believe and act concerning the *ama-tō* vs. *kara-tō* dichotomy and the associated gender stereotypes, especially masculinity. Given that not all men are *kara-tō*, the underlying question of his study is whether Japanese males who like to eat sweets could "problematize masculine identities" (p. 280). The interesting findings of Holtzman's research will be taken up in part II of this book, where the topic of gendering foods and gender stereotypes will be discussed. For now, though, I want to point out that the stereotypes that are rooted in the terms *ama-tō* and *kara-tō* are reminiscent of negative, or weakened, attributes to which the metaphorical use of *amai* in (39) alludes, especially in relation to the sense of masculinity underlying *kara-tō*.

Another taste adjective whose metaphorically extended meanings show linguistic relevance is *oishii*, a general term that describes a delicious taste.

Dictionaries that I have consulted agree that the meaning of good-tasting (in food) is metaphorically extended to the sense of personal convenience and benefit. For instance, in *oishii shigoto* "delicious job" and *oishii hanashi* "delicious proposition," *oishii* refers to appealing and tempting aspects of a job/position that may be too good to be true (e.g., unusually high pay for a little work).[16] (40) is an advertising phrase of a website that provides employment information.

(40) 楽して稼ぎたい！おいしいアルバイトは？

Raku-shite kasegi-tai! **Oishii** arubaito-wa?

"Do as little as possible and make money! How about **delicious** part-time jobs?" ("Mensetsu-ga Nai" 2020)

The type of part-time jobs about which this phrase speaks would bring money without hard work, i.e., the type that is too good to be true. It is relevant to note that the jobs mentioned in (40) do not imply food-related work but include whatever jobs are available in unspecified areas. As an advertising phrase, its intension is obviously to tempt web users (job-seekers in this case), although it is likely that web users will read the caption with an unspoken caveat in mind. The metaphorical sense of *oishii*, thus, could be nuanced with a cautionary undertone in similar contexts. *Oishii*, as a taste term, has a synonym, *umai* "delicious," and an antonym, *mazui* "unsavory." The metaphorical sense in *oishii shigoto* and *oishii hanashi* is maintained with *umai* (e.g., *umai hanashi* "a proposition too good to be true"). At the same time, the opposite meaning of "inconvenient, unfavorable" is obtained in *mazui* (e.g., *mazui koto-ni natta* "matters have turned inconvenient"). In addition to these two senses (i.e., good-tasting in food, convenience), *umai* has another sense that describes skillfulness, and its antonym *mazui* also carries over the parallelly negative meaning, i.e., unskillfulness and awkwardness. Examples include *umai ji* "nice handwriting" and *mazui purē* "poor play." Interestingly, however, *oishii* does not share this sense with *umai*. So, *oishii ji and *oishii purē are anomalous under the intended meanings of "nice handwriting" and "good play."

Muto (2002) discusses yet another sense of *oishii* that is increasingly common among younger generations of speakers. Building on the meaning of "convenient, beneficial," a new sense of *oishii* implies that, according to Muto, something is "desirable due to a deep sense of satisfaction one would receive from the special value that it has" (p. 31). This nuance is similar to the convenient/beneficial sense of *oishii* of *oishii hanashi* "delicious proposition" mentioned earlier, but Muto seems to suggest that the new usage is interpreted more positively in that it highlights acceptable values without cautionary undertones. Her examples are somewhat difficult to distinguish between these subtle differences, but to the extent that I can discern, (41–43), all from Muto (2003, 31), illustrate *oishii* under the more positive interpretation.[17]

(41) より美しい生活、より快適な生活、より**おいしい**生活を求めて、衣・食・住のすみずみにいたるまで徹底的にこだわるイタリアーノ。

Yori utsukushii seikatsu, yori kaiteki-na seikatsu, yori **oishii** seikatsu-o motomete, i・shoku・jū-no sumizumi-ni itaru-made tetteiteki-ni kodawaru itariāno.

"Italians, who are deeply concerned with all details about clothing, eating, and living, in search of a more beautiful, comfortable, and **delicious** life."

(42) 「力水」は高純度のミネラルを含んだ体にやさしいお水です。大切な体のために、体に**おいしい**「力水」をおすすめします。

"Chikaramizu"-wa kōjundo-no mineraru-o hukunda karada-ni yasashii omizu-desu. Taisetsu-na karada-no tameni, karada-ni **oishii** "Chikaramizu"-o osusume-shimasu.

"'Chikaramizu' contains highly pure minerals and is gentle to your body. For your important body, we recommend 'Chikaramizu' that is **delicious** to your body."

(43) ショーン・コネリーがボンドを演じた頃の作品に親しんでいる人なら、**おいしい**ギャグがてんこ盛り。

Shōn konerī-ga bondo-o enjita koro-no sakuhin-ni shitashinde-iru hito-nara, **oishii** gyagu-ga tenko-mori.

"For those who are familiar with the films around the time Sean Connery played Bond, there are a lot of **delicious** gags (in it)."

Muto comments that *oishii* in these examples characterizes the "pleasant and desirable" aspect of life. Particularly underscored by *oishii* are a sense of satisfaction in (41), special values that the water offers in (42), and attributes residing in "rare values" of film productions in (43). In contrast, the positive value beyond personal convenience is missing with *umai*, as is demonstrated by the anomalous examples like *umai arubaito "delicious part-time job" and *umai seikatsu "delicious life." Muto explains that these metaphorically extended meanings are due to the sense of satisfaction that we experience when we eat tasty food, while at the same time the satisfaction can be transformed negatively into a guilty pleasure (p. 33). The increasing prevalence of the positive nuance of *oishii* underlying in examples like (41–43) testifies to the dynamic nature of language that is subject to change.

3 VISUAL METAPHORS

Metaphors reveal our conceptual patterns, but sources in analogy are not limited to concepts. Metaphors can be visually grounded and their instances based on food are abundantly found. One of the most direct illustrations may be names of food products through visual resemblance. For instance, *monburan* "Mont Blanc" is the name of the famous mountain in Switzerland, but it is also the Japanese name of a cake with rich chestnut cream. Pureed chestnut cream is squeezed out spirally on top of a small cup-sized sponge cake, and its resulting shape is reminiscent of the snow-covered Mont Blanc. Also, the compounded name of the Chinese-style dessert *annin-dōhu* consists of *tōhu* "tofu"[18] because the almond-flavored gelatin that is cut into squares in this dessert looks just like (savory) tofu even though it is not made of tofu.

Of further interest is that food-based visual metaphors have been crafted into a secret language whose use is transparent only to a restricted group of speakers. Yonekawa's (1998) examples below illustrate such a process of assigning new meanings to existing words. They were used primarily by the youth in the 1970s and 1980s but did not survive for a long time. Nevertheless, the new metaphorical senses underlying these examples are all based on the physical appearance of the food items.

(44) atama-ga   **kyabetsu/nattō**
head-NOM   cabbage/fermented.soybeans
"I'm confused."

(45) mimi-ga   **gyōza**
ears-NOM   pot.stickers
"I don't want to hear it."

(46) kuchi-ga   **shūmai**
mouth-NOM   steamed.dumpling
"I don't want to say anything."

(47) kinniku-ga   **bāmukūhen**
muscle-NOM   baumkuchen
"well defined muscles"

In order to understand (44), we need to imagine a cabbage that is cut vertically, or stirred fermented soybeans in natto from which sticky threads run. Both visual images evoke complicated and chaotic cognitive or mental states. The shape of a pot sticker in (45) specifically refers to the pleated side of a dumpling. It resembles an ear when it is folded forward. The folded ear makes it hard to hear, and through that connection, a folded ear symbolizes refusal of listening. In (46) another type of Chinese dumpling, *shūmai*, which is popular in Japan along with pot stickers, also indicates unwillingness to communicate although this time oral communication. The dumpling looks like pursed lips, which are construed as a sign of reluctant speech. *Bāmukūhen* in (47) is a German cake whose Japanese adaptations have been very successful to date. One form of this cake is cylindrical with a rippled outer surface, which reminds us of well-defined, bulging muscles. English equivalents include "six-pack abs" and "washboard abs."

In addition to these visual metaphors, Yonekawa discusses so-called *yasai-go* "vegetable language" (including occasional references to non-vegetable food items) that was prevalent in the 1980s particularly among college-age speakers. As the examples in (48) demonstrate, in the phrase of *hanashi-ga* X "story is X" where X is filled with a name of a common vegetable, students can use these expressions as secret language and language play, upon commenting on professors' lectures or speaking ill of peers, for instance.

(48) hanashi-ga _____
 story-NOM

   a. pīman   "green pepper"   → no significant content
   b. kyūri   "cucumber"   → long
   c. serori   "celery"   → logical
   d. tomato   "tomato"   → lie
   e. paseri   "parsley"   → delicate and witty
   f. dojō   "loach"   → vague, elusive

A physical attribute of each food item is intended to characterize the nature of a class lecture or conversations with peers. For example, in (48a) the inside of a green pepper is largely a vacuum, not filled with much to eat, so a lecture is viewed to offer very little of value. Outer appearances of the vegetables are direct bases for (48b, e): compared to those available in the US, Japanese cucumbers are long; and the parsley in (48e) refers to the curly type rather than flat-leaf.

In addition to physical appearances, (48c, d, f) call for related idioms built around the food items in order to "de-code" the messages. Celery has a lot of strings or fibers, an equivalent of *suji* in Japanese. An idiom pertinent to (48c) is *suji-ga tōru* [string-NOM go.through], which figuratively means that something is logical or rational. Tomatoes referred to in (48d) are red ones, and the color is the basis of the idiom *makka-na uso* [very.red lie] "downright lies." Lectures metaphorically characterized as tomatoes are not factually well grounded. Loaches are slippery and it is hard to hold them. The idiom related to the slippery and slimy touch of loaches is *tsukami-dokoro-ga nai* [hold-spot-NOM there.isn't]. The phrase literally means that there is no grip, and it is metaphorically interpreted that something is vague, fuzzy, and elusive. The use of food items in (44–48) exemplifies a secret language in which language serves not only to verbally connect to others within a socially definable group of speakers but as a special code by which the group members playfully communicate.[19]

In this chapter we have witnessed that metaphors offer a rhetorically effective and colorful mechanism to enrich the expressive power in the language of food. They are particularly useful in compensating for the dearth of vocabulary that directly describes a wide range of attributes relevant to food and foodways. Conversely, the language of food appears as metaphors in communicating about aspects of life outside of food experiences—perhaps more prevalently than we may realize, attesting to the depth at which the concept of food is embedded in our culture and society.

NOTES

1. Backhouse (1994) further treats *ama-zuppai* "sweet-sour," *ama-karai* "sweet-pungent," and *horo-nigai* "pleasantly bitter" as members of "non-basic" taste terms. The first two are compounds of two individual taste adjectives in (1) (i.e., *amai* "sweet" and *suppai* "sour") while in *horo-nigai*, *nigai* "bitter" is prefixed by *horo-* to add the meaning of "slightly." Even with these compounded and prefixed words, the list of words that directly describe tastes is not long. For Korean, Rhee and Koo (2017) discuss in detail the systematic mechanisms that the language employs in describing food tastes.

2. http://www.nihon-chouri.ac.jp/glossary/gohou/.

3. Ai Kidosaki is among the most popular and influential cookbook writers in 20th century Japan, especially around the time when women started to join the country's workforce while at the same time meeting expectations to tend to household tasks.

4. In her series of work Hayakawa (2003, 2007, 2013) illustrates the prevalence of texture expressions in describing food tastes. (Also see Hayakawa et al. [1997] and Hayakawa et al. [2005] on the same topic.) As is discussed in chapter 3 of the current book, mimetic words that characterize texture are frequently employed for descriptions of tastes and cooking processes. Putting them together, the touch sense plays an important role in giving particulars in gustatory and culinary communication.

5. *Togatta* "pointed" seems to me to be better classified under vision.

6. Komori (2003, 110–11) explains that *shiroi aji* "white taste" describes (cooked) white rice, lotus loots, and tofu; and *kīroi aji* "yellow taste" is used to refer to the tastes of spoiled eggs, custard (pudding), wilted vegetables, and curry.

7. Although Komori and Yamaguchi both treat *aoi* "blue" based on the metaphorical sense of immaturity, at least Komori's examples are more in line with his analysis of *shiroi* "white" and *akai* "red" that the color terms reflect the appearance of ingredients. Relevant examples illustrating this connection are *soramame-mitai-na aoi aji* "blue taste like broad beans" and *aoi aji* that is used to describe the taste of *edamame* "soybeans."

8. Notwithstanding some differences in methodology and research goal, Lehrer (1978) argues that the directions that would be disallowed by (9) are indeed represented in her English data. Whether internal to English or across languages, the unidirectionality of metaphorical transfer through synesthesia cannot be sustained as strictly as William's study concludes.

9. In (12–19) the emphasis is original, and translations are my own.

10. In addition to these aspects of books and reading analogized to food and food consumption, the process of book writing can be viewed analogous to that of food preparation, as the following example demonstrates ("Book" 2022, 84): (i) 残り物を工夫して**料理した**のが私の小説 **nokorimono**-o kuhū-shite **ryōri-shita**-no-ga watashi-no shōsetsu "my novel, as a result of trying to figure out how to **cook leftovers**."

11. The reverse analogy of MAKEUP IS COOKING, i.e., COOKING IS MAKEUP, is instantiated by the use of the cosmetic term *usu-geshō* "[lit. thin-makeup] light makeup" applied to a stage of food preparation by the cooking specialist, Yukiko Kawatsu. In Hasegawa (2021, 16), Kawatsu serves as a culinary advisor and suggests dusting chicken breast with cornstarch before cooking it in a liquid. Referring to the technique as the metaphor *usu-geshō*, Kawatsu explains the term, "this *usu-geshō* prevents the chicken flesh from toughening." Adding a very thin layer of cornstarch powder is likened to using light makeup.

12. Muto (2001) and Oda (2003) categorize metaphorical meanings of *amai* into more narrowly defined groups than these three.

13. The only taste field in which *amai-karai* opposition holds is sake, roughly corresponding to sweet-dry in describing tastes of wine.

14. The negative concept associated with *amai* "sweet" in Japanese seems to be a sharp diversion from English *sweet*, which is exhaustively interpreted to describe positive values.

15. I advisedly say the *ama-tō* vs. *kara-tō* opposition is associated with "believed" stereotypes, taking into consideration Holtzman's (2018) research findings that the stereotypical views are changing as younger generations of males do not hold them to the degree that has been previously thought.

16. Despite the consistent listing across dictionaries, I do not use *oishii* myself to mean personal convenience or benefit and thus find *oishii shigoto* and *oishii hanashi* odd-sounding. In my own speech, *umai hanasi* is far better than *oishii hanashi* although *umai shigoto* does not sound natural to my ears.

17. Muto notes that she found these examples in internet sources, but I have been unable to find their working online sites.

18. The phonological process of Rendaku (sequential voicing) changes the initial consonant of tofu [t] to [d] in the compound of *annin-dōhu*.

19. Yonekawa (2007) discusses a wide variety of examples that illustrate secret language and euphemism in speaking of food items among prisoners, Buddhist priests in a historical context, and other socially defined groups. For discussion, see Tsujimura (2022b).

Part II

LANGUAGE OF FOOD IN SOCIETY

Chapter Six

Recipes and Cookbooks

Individual recipes and their compilation in the form of cookbooks can be regarded as a linguistic register just as restaurant menus are in Zwicky and Zwicky's (1980) analysis. Finegan (1994) defines register as "[l]anguage varieties that are characteristic of particular situations of use" (p. 366). He explains that three important elements that determine a situation of use are setting, purpose, and participants (p. 392). Applied to recipes and cookbooks, the setting would be cooking in a kitchen; the purpose would be providing instructions for meal preparation; and the participants would be individuals who have created recipes and are giving them out as well as those who receive the information and instructions. As Zwicky and Zwicky discuss in the context of restaurant menus, a linguistic register has a specific style with a format. The recipe format shows slight variation depending on the author but generally consists of the following components: title, headnote, ingredients list, instructions, servings (yield) line, note, and variation (Whitman and Simon 1993).

Given the instructive orientation of the purpose within a relatively defined format, recipes and cookbooks are regarded as a discourse of objective statements. On the other hand, cooking instructions are transmitted through language in social interaction (Cotter 1997). Accordingly, they mirror sociocultural values and practices (or the author's interpretations of them) as an important background shared by the participants. This is succinctly summarized by Cotter (1997, 52): "[t]he way language is used in the context of recipe discourse shapes our interpretation of many aspects of the cookbook, not only concerning things culinary but also how we view a particular community and its values." Recipes and cookbooks, thus, provide a window through which we can learn the social and cultural environments at the time and dynamic transitions over time, as many other scholars have discussed their significant implications (e.g., Fisher 1968; Cotter 1997; Neuhaus 2003; Lakoff 2006; Higashiyotsuyanagi 2010; Yuen 2014).

Despite the stylistic appearance of objectively-stated directives, cooking instructions also reveal a great deal of subjectivity, as Cotter indicates. It is common that some parts of recipes, especially headnotes in which the author's personal views and anecdotes appear, are subjectively written, making the general outlook of the cooking discourse individualized and sometimes personal. It means that subjectivity in recipes and cookbooks reflects a sense of the participants' individual and group identity based on diverse social contexts. In fact, food is considered to have a strong association with our identity, as the common cliché "We are what we eat" alludes to. It comes as no surprise, then, that the relationship between food and identity construct has been examined in a variety of scholarly works (e.g., Bourdieu 1984; Fischler 1988; Ochs et al. 1996; Lakoff 2006; German 2011; Koike 2014; Yuen 2014; Tsujimura 2018b). Lakoff (2006), for example, discusses that the knowledge of food in different contexts of communication, both spoken and written, can be regarded as markers of identity since "culinary preferences and sophistication contribute significantly to our sense of ourselves" (p. 165). Distinguishing from commonly discussed identity canons like gender, race, ethnicity, and sexual orientation ("major identity"), Lakoff argues that taste centering around food consumption and preparation constitutes a "minor identity," as does more broadly conceived taste (e.g., tastes in music, fashion, and the like parallel to the sense of taste in Bourdieu [1984]). Identity is viewed both on an individual basis and through group membership, and the construction of one is mutually relevant to that of the other (p. 144). She recognizes that cuisine brings an influence on the language we use, ranging from vocabulary to discourse, and illustrates that in connecting to their patrons for food preparation, recipes (and menus) serve as an identity construct. So, the language of food exhibited in cookery writings offers an interesting forum to discuss how identity is constructed and manifested within the specific linguistic register.

Keeping in mind a larger theme of individual and group identity, this chapter examines social meaning that Japanese cookbooks display by observing the ways in which the language of cookery instructions, both form and use, contributes to transmitting the social meaning. In so doing I pay closer attention to language use for communication than in part I, although the formal aspect of language is palpably relevant. Due to their written format and the unidirectional instructive content, the food discourse in cookbooks is monologic in that there is no turn-taking typical of oral conversation. I will argue, however, that authors adopt a variety of linguistic and rhetorical tools as a vehicle for virtual interpersonal communication that gives the audience the "feel" of dialogic interaction. This is consistent with Cotter's afore-mentioned idea about the nature of social interaction that the language of recipes exhibits. The linguistic system that is encoded in cookbooks further demonstrates the ways in which linguistic forms and discourse elements in the virtual interactive communication serve as a medium to link to a broader social identity of the author and the reader (i.e., the participants) (Ochs 2002).

As a conceptual foundation, I use the term "identity" as it is broadly defined by Bucholtz and Hall (2005, 586): "[i]dentity is the social positioning of self and other." My examination and discussion of identity to follow are framed within recent gender-related sociolinguistic literature as well as approaches in cross- and inter-disciplinary food studies proposed primarily for issues concerning gender and food. As diverse as the disciplinary areas may seem, their perspectives are united on dynamic, rather than static and monolithic, views of constructing identity in social contexts, as in, for example, Butler (1990), Cameron (1997, 2008), Kiesling (1997), Connell (2000), Eckert (2000, 2012), Ochs (2002), Bucholtz and Hall (2005), Julier and Lindenfeld (2005), Sobal (2005), and Meyerhoff and Ehrlich (2019). These works shed light on the emergent, performative, relational, and intersectional nature of identity, coalescing around the principal tenet that identity is not an introspective sense of self that is reduced to a singular axis or criterion, but instead it discursively emerges from social interaction.

Approaching from a sociocultural linguistics perspective, Bucholtz and Hall (2005) essentialize an analytical framework for the study of identity into five principles. One of them, in relation to indexicality (Silverstein 1976), is relevant to the current chapter: "identities may be linguistically indexed through labels, implicatures, stances, styles, or linguistic structures and systems" (p. 585). It will be shown how language-specific linguistic mechanisms can be deployed for indexing identity of the author, ultimately putting cookery discourse in a broader context of social meaning that is relevant to both the author and the audience. The indexical relation between linguistic forms and social identity is not necessarily direct or overt (Ochs 1992, 2002). The context in which social interactions take place coupled with cultural and social values that serve as its background contribute to discerning social meaning on which construction of identity is dependent. Consideration of diverse types of social contexts, as Ochs (2002, 109) elaborates, is valid for recognizing the path to the formation of identity: "[t]he contextual dimension of social identity comprises a range of social personae, including, for example, social roles, statuses, and relationships, as well as community, institutional, ethnic, socioeconomic, gender, and other group identities."

Led by these conceptual guides, this chapter focuses its primary aim on presenting a case study to demonstrate how identity is constructed and indexed in Japanese cookbook writing. To that end I single out cooking expert

Katsuyo Kobayashi (1937–2014) for a narrow but localized examination. Kobayashi stands out as a notable figure in the culinary genre of Japanese home cooking during the last quarter of the 20th century. Her recipe writing demonstrates plentiful examples of unique linguistic choices that have significant implications to the construction of her identity. The overall picture of her linguistic practice, inclusive of the lexical, morphological, and stylistic characteristics, points to a substantial departure from normative styles and formats that are typical of Japanese cookbooks as a linguistic register. I argue that Kobayashi's distinctive linguistic practice indexes her identity through linguistic mechanisms and her social stances. Her linguistic choices and cookery discourse help us understand the social meaning that is injected in her written communication about and beyond her culinary profession. An examination of Kobayashi's cookery writing as a linguistic register does not simply demonstrate that recipes offer a helpful guide to food preparation, but that they further serve as an effective platform for interpersonal communication from which the author's multiple personae emerge.

As a broader background of the case study, I shall begin by a general survey of selective cookbooks written from 1927 to 2011, focusing on linguistic features that are relevant to my analysis of Kobayashi's cookbooks.[1] The survey is intended to give witness to the transition in recipe format over time as well as to the range of normative styles and contents that have been standardized for recipes today.

1 GENERAL BACKGROUND OF RECIPE WRITING

In chapter 3 (section 4) I reported on my survey of 21 cookbooks to discuss the use of mimetics. My linguistic observations in this section are drawn mainly from the 11 cookbooks by female authors (i.e., those that are indicated by "F" in table 3.1). Additionally, I include in my discussion the two books published in the 1920s (i.e., Nihon Hōsō Kyōkai Kantoshibu 1927, 1928) because they are targeted toward female audiences even though their authorship (and thus the authors' gender) is not identified in the publications. These 13 cookbooks represent each decade from the 1920s to the 2010s except for the 1930s. My primary interest for linguistic observations centers on variation in linguistic and communication style and how it has transitioned over the time period under survey.[2]

Recipes for practical purposes in a domestic setting were commonly found in women's magazines at the beginning of the 20th century (Murakami 1995; Ohashi 1997; Higashiyotsuyanagi 2010).[3] Ohashi (1997) explains that early cookbooks and cooking articles, especially those written by culinary professionals, lacked details like precise amounts and measurements, suggesting that cooking-related information was not totally transparent to many of the participants. Starting in 1925, cooking instructions on radio broadcasts, in contrast, provided ample specifics and thus ameliorated the shortcoming that early written forms of recipes faced. Examples of such radio broadcasting include "Ryōri Kondate" and "Katei Kōza" in 1925, "Hujin Kōza" in 1926, and "Katei Daigaku Kōza" in 1927 (Murase 2009). Cookbooks *Shiki-no Ryōri* "Cooking for Four Seasons" and *Hibi-no Ryōri* "Everyday Cooking" were published based on radio programs aired from January 1926 to January 1927 for the former and from February 1927 to January 1928 for the latter. Each recipe in these compilations is minimally structured into title, ingredients list, and prose-style instructions that include comments on food items and cooking processes.

There are two observations of note regarding these two cookbooks that are relevant to our later discussion. First, the sentences in the instruction section tend to be very long, connecting one activity to another by coordination. An example is shown in (1), which is the very first sentence of the instruction prose for *yudōhu* "tofu in hot water" in *Shiki-no Ryōri* (p. 3). The purpose of this exposition is to show the length of a single sentence filled with numerous verbs that denote culinary actions. Verbs of cooking actions are underlined both in the original and in the English translation.

> (1) これは、はっきり分量は申し上げませんでも、大抵豆腐一丁若しくは豆腐二丁を三人前として<u>出し</u>、昆布を鍋の底だけに<u>切り</u>、砂を拂ひ<u>落し</u>、水を<u>加へ</u>、豆腐はざっと<u>沸騰する</u>のを度とし、鍋からすぐに<u>取ります</u>ならばそのままで、又格別お行儀よく、一人毎にお椀に<u>とります</u>なれば、お寒い時分はこのお椀をお湯で<u>洗って</u>、<u>温めて置く</u>ことをお忘れにならないやうに願ひます。
>
> "I won't tell you the exact amount, but it generally <u>serves</u> 1~2-cho for three people; <u>cut</u> kelp to place at the bottom of a pot; <u>remove</u> sand; <u>add</u> water; quickly <u>boil</u> the tofu; leave it as is if you plan to <u>serve</u> it in the pot; but if you would rather properly <u>serve</u> it in individual bowls, please do not forget to <u>rinse</u> the bowls with hot water and <u>keep</u> them warm in the cold season."

The dish is known to be simple, but there are nine actions, indicated by underlined verbs, all within a single sentence. The sole sentence includes not only the instructions of relevant steps to be taken to make the tofu dish but cautionary notes on serving. Taking the prose style, the instructions are not separated by numbers (or bullets) that would help organize the process in a chronological order, as recipes in later days adopt. We see the continuing use of this type of prose style until the 1980s although the use of numbering for individual steps appears in some of the recipes in Sawasaki (1941), Egawa

(1957), and H. Tatsumi (1960). Individual sentences remain long in Sawasaki's cookbook and somewhat in Egawa's, but gradually, each instructive sentence becomes shorter and more concise. To show a contrastive look, I give in (2) Kurihara's (1992, 66) instruction for *kuzudōhu* "tofu with kuzu starch." Attention should be paid to the brevity of each instruction and the numerical organization.

(2)　① 豆腐はざるなどに入れ、10分ほどおいて軽く水きりをしておく。
　　② ねぎは5cm長さの縦二〜四つ割りに。
　　③ しいたけは2cm幅のそぎ切りにする。
　　④ 耐熱容器に①の豆腐を一口大にくずして入れ、ねぎ、しいたけを入れたら、たれをかける。ラップでおおって、電子レンジに約6分かけ、上下を返して、さらに2分かける。好みでご飯にかけ、七味か山椒をふって食べる。

"① Put the tofu in a colander and the like, and lightly drain the water for about 10 minutes.
② Vertically cut the scallions into 2~4 5cm-long pieces.
③ Sliver the shitake mushrooms into 2cm-wide pieces.
④ In a heat-resistant plate put the tofu in ①, broken into bite-size pieces, add the scallions and mushrooms, and pour the sauce over them. Microwave the wrapped plate for about 6 minutes, mix the ingredients, and microwave it for additional 2 minutes. If you prefer, pour it [=the tofu mixture] over rice, and sprinkle Shichimi pepper mix or Sansho pepper before eating."

The cooking procedure is divided into numbered steps, each of which is stated in much simpler and shorter sentences. The use of sequential numbers is efficient in organizing the cooking procedure. It is particularly convenient to refer to previous steps, as the fourth step demonstrates. The format in (2) has become the standard in the instruction section of recipes and cookbooks available today.

The second observation has to do with sentence final forms. In written Japanese, when a sentence ends with a verb, it takes either the *-masu* or *-ru* form, as in *tabe-masu* "eat-masu" or *tabe-ru* "eat-ru." When a predicative noun is at the end of a sentence, it appears in the *-desu* or *-da* form, like *sushi-desu* or *sushi-da*, both meaning "it is sushi." Regardless of the *desu/masu* or *da/ru* ending, the content of a sentence is the same. The cooking instructions of the 1927 and 1928 cookbooks are written in the *desu/masu* style.[4] The single instructive sentence in (1), for instance, ends in the *-masu* form (*negai-masu* "I ask"). In general, some components of a recipe, such as headnote and note, are personal in content, and it is common to see the *desu/masu* style throughout my samples. Instructions, in contrast, are more objectively stated, and this is in fact the section of a recipe where the authors are divided in their choice of the two styles. Focusing on the language used in instructions, the authors of the cookbooks published up to the 1980s in my samples all adopt the *desu/masu* style whereas the cookbooks in and after the 1990s take the *da/ru* style.[5] Furthermore, as I have noted above, the more contemporary cookbooks divide cooking steps of the instruction section into shorter and numbered or bulleted sentences, just like (2). As far as cooking instructions (i.e., as a recipe component) are concerned, recipes in cookbooks, magazines, and social media today overwhelmingly follow this pattern.[6]

Traditionally, the difference between *desu/masu* and *da/ru* has been prescriptively and simplistically reduced to the contrast in formality and politeness, namely, the *desu/masu* form being more formal and polite than the *da/ru* form. Yet, the distinction has been reevaluated to deepen our understanding of the forms by looking at their use in broader contexts, both linguistic and non-linguistic (e.g., Cook 1997, 1998, 2008; Maynard 1991, 1993, 2008; Jones and Ono 2008). In discussing various styles in written Japanese, Maynard (2008) provides the following base-line characteristics of *desu/masu* and *da/ru*. The former is "chosen in the writing with a tone of addressing to the audience," while the latter is for "general broad audience" and is "often used when the writer takes on the descriptive mode" (p. 99). Presumably due to the addressing tone of *desu/masu* vs. the descriptive mode of *da/ru* that Maynard refers to, *desu/masu* sounds comparatively softer and more approachable in written discourse on various topics including recipes. Cook (1997, 1998, 2008) investigates the *desu/masu* form in oral conversation from a perspective of indexicality and claims that the form has "multiple situational meanings" that vary depending on social contexts. In Cook (1998), which examines how interlocutors mix these two styles within a single person's speech, she argues that the *desu/masu* form "indexes speaker-focused self-presentation in a context in which the speaker is on public display and/or shows a social persona" (p. 94). Cook's claim converges with Maynard's characterization mentioned above. That is, applied to the recipe context, the cookbook author's virtual voice in the *desu/masu* style may evoke a social setting where she acts as an instructor speaking in front of her live audience. In contrast, the *da/ru* style creates an affective distance between the participants, which makes the cooking instruction sound more descriptive and less intimate.

It is worth pointing out that photos showing completed dishes or some important steps for which visual depictions are helpful appear as early as Egawa's (1957) cookbook. At first, photos are black-and-white, but colored ones are included in H. Tatsumi (1960). It seems to be an established standard nowadays that photos accompany virtually each recipe at least in cookbooks that are strictly for providing cooking instructions (as opposed to so-called "cookbooks to read" like Okuzono 2012).

In addition to the two linguistic observations above, the recipes in my sample of 11 cookbooks exhibit evidence of increase in informativeness and individuality over the period of nearly nine decades. I should underscore, furthermore, that the increase in informativeness and individuality has been aided by linguistic tools, including orthographical ones. Headnotes and notes of recipes are sections that are suitable for detailing the ingredients, the cooking process, the output, as well as other messages that the authors intend to convey to their readers. They are likely places in which the authors can speak about personal stories regarding the dish. As brief as they may be, titles (i.e., recipe names) can also be crafted in a personalized manner to provide information about the dish far more than just baseline knowledge of primary ingredients and cooking methods. Recipe names, thus, can be an informative source for discerning the individual persona of the authors.

As Tsujimura (2018b) demonstrates, earlier recipe names take minimally structured schemata that advise the reader what is to be cooked and how. Typically, they take the noun-phrase form of X-*no* Y, where X is a primary ingredient, -*no* is the Genitive case marker, and Y refers to a method or manner of cooking. Also common is the compound form of X-Y, in which either X or Y names a primary ingredient and the other a (general) cooking style. For instance, the two earliest cookbooks in my survey include *buri-no yamakake* "yellowtail topped with grated yam," as an example of the first form, and *yu-dōhu* "tofu in hot water" and *nanakusa-gayu* "rice porridge with seven plants" instantiating the compound format. The first example informs us that the main ingredient is *buri* "yellowtail" and it is served with grated yam poured over, which is indicated by *yamakake*. The compound examples exhibit two opposite orders between a primary ingredient and the manner or style of cooking. In *yu-dōhu* the main ingredient, *tōfu* (phonetically changed to *dōhu* as a result of compounding), is the second member of the compound and *yu* "hot water" suggests its cooking and serving style. Contrastively in *nanakusa-gayu*, the first member of the compound, *nanakusa* "seven plants," refers to the ingredients that showcase the dish, and *kayu* (again, phonetically changed as *gayu* in the compound) "rice porridge" tells us about the general style or even genre of food. These two linguistic forms are sufficiently informative. Although most of the recipe names in the earlier cookbooks appear in these patterns, the cookbooks that follow them also use the same format as standard patterns and default templates for recipe names.

For the latter half of the 20th century and moving onto the turn of the century, recipe names have gradually expanded their scope both in content and form. As a result, they exhibit an increasing degree of informativeness and personal involvement in the naming process. First, mimetics have started to appear in recipe names. As I reported on in chapter 3, the use of mimetics in the language of cooking instructions shows individual variation, but many of the cookbook authors in my survey started to make an interesting and sometimes innovative use of mimetics in recipe names. Since mimetics directly appeal to our senses, they add sensual descriptions of the dishes to the basic information about the primary ingredients and/or cooking techniques. Examples of recipe names in (3) basically follow the form of X-*no* Y while those in (4) are compounds. Of the five senses to which mimetics in recipe names appeal, descriptions of texture are most frequently referred to although visual features are also effectively depicted, as in (3b) and (4a). In the examples below, mimetics are in boldface.

(3) a. kyabetsu-no   shin-no   **huwahuwa**
       cabbage-GEN   core-GEN   fluffy<mimetic>
       "fluffy cabbage core"   (Egawa 1957)

   b. aburaage-no   **peQtanko**-ni
      deep-fried.tofu-GEN   flat<mimetic>-cooked
      "deep-fried tofu cooked until flat"   (Kidosaki 1987)

(4) a. **purupuru**-konnyaku
       wobbly<mimetic>-konjak
       "wobbly konjak"   (Tatsumi 1978)

   b. **saQpari**-poteto-salada
      light<mimetic>-potato-salad
      "light potato salad"   (Kidosaki 1987)

   c. **shakishaki**   wahū-sarada
      crisp<mimetic>   Japanese.style-salad
      "crisp Japanese-style salad"   (Kurihara 1992)

The mimetic words in (3a), (4b), and (4c) evoke the mouth feel upon or after eating the dishes, although *huwahuwa* in (3a) may additionally speak to the soft, fluffy appearance. In (3a), given the generally hard texture of a cabbage core, the mimetic implies a tender and hearty feel in the mouth resulting from a long(er) cooking time. In cookbooks and recipes available today, *huwahuwa* has increased its frequency even more, and we see compounded food names like *huwahuwa-tamago* [eggs], *huwahuwa-hanbāgu* [hamburger steak], and *huwahuwa-pankēki* [pancakes] as generic food terms.[7] In a general context *peQtanko* in (3b) may give a negative connotation leading to lack of volume. However, *peQtanko* in this recipe name evokes an image that deep-fried tofu, which is dry and crisp before cooking, is to be heated in the seasoned liquid for some time to yield a moist and flavorful result even though its shape becomes flat.

The main ingredient in (4a), *konnyaku*, does not have a strong flavor by itself, but the blandness is made up for by the *purupuru* texture that has some resistance in appearance and in the mouth. This recipe name gives an appetizing outlook to what would otherwise seem to be of a bland taste. Similarly, *shakishaki* in (4c) highlights the crispiness as an attraction for which one's attention is drawn to a seemingly ordinary vegetable salad. In (4b) *poteto-sarada* "potato salad" is commonly a rich dish perhaps due to mayonnaise, but the mimetic *saQpari* details its lighter taste and refreshing after-taste.

In the set of cookbooks under examination, examples like (3) and (4) appear only sparsely in those published between the 1950s and the 1980s, but we see more instances in later publications including Kurihara (1992), Kobayashi (1995), and Okada (2007). The mimetics in these recipe names can provide details about the dishes beyond primary ingredients and cooking methods or styles in the succinct and subjective way where their prosaic counterparts would not be as successful. It is of further note that Okada (2007), the most recent of the data set, includes emphatic mimetic forms like those in (5), which are far more common in spoken Japanese.

(5) a. **moQchimochi**   kaisen   chijimi
    chewy   seafood   Chijimi
    "chewy seafood Chijimi [savory Korean pancake]"

b. **puriQpuri**   ebi-chiri-don
    springy   shrimp-spicy-rice.bowl
    "spicy springy shrimp in a rice bowl"

The two mimetics in (5) are emphatic forms of *mochimochi* and *puripuri*, and underscore the chewiness of the pancakes and the plump texture of the shrimp that the recipes are expected to highlight. Since emphatic forms of mimetics tend to be used more frequently in informal speaking, the mimetic words in (5) do not just detail the recipes but their casual speaking style gives the reader the impression that the author is directly addressing her in a relaxed and friendly manner. In this light, cookbooks are considered more than manual-like texts for "how-to" in cooking, but are additionally able to provide a venue for the authors to reach out actively to their readers for personable communication. Under this situation, emphatic mimetic words, as are instantiated in (5), can be considered to index informality.

Enhanced informativeness of recipes and apparent proximity between the authors and their readers in recipe names are achieved in other ways. In (6), instead of the base-line compound of the form X<ingredient>-Y<cooking method/style>, utensils used for serving and cooking enter into compounding relations.

(6) a. sara-udon
     plate-udon
     "udon served on a plate" (Kobayashi 1995)

   b. huraipan-sukiyaki
      frying.pan-sukiyaki
      "sukiyaki in a frying pan" (Okada 2007)

Udon noodles are commonly associated with bowls as a serving-ware. An underlying assumption is that udon is cooked and served in a broth. In (6a) the juxtaposition of *udon* with a (flat) plate in the compound leads us to anticipate that the recipe does not involve a broth, but instead udon is likely to be stir-fried. It is perfectly acceptable to use compounds like *itame-udon* "stir-fried udon" or *yaki-udon* "pan-fried udon," which indicate the cooking method more directly. Although (6a) does not necessarily fit the standard mold of compounded recipe names, it nevertheless appeals to the reader by the novelty of the naming pattern. The recipe name is effective in piquing the reader's curiosity and attention. In a similar vein, the association of a frying pan with sukiyaki in (6b) is not commonplace since it is usually cooked and served in a deeper pan. However, not every household has a pan specific for sukiyaki, whereas a frying pan is a far more typical kitchen utensil that the average household is likely to have. So, a frying pan is a welcome replacement for the specialty equipment. These compounds introduce a linguistic pattern that incorporates a new type of information in recipe names.

As short as they are, recipe names can be made personal to establish proximity to participants in culinary communication. We have already discussed one instance of that with the emphatic mimetic forms in (5). Personalization is clearly a trend that is observed with the headnotes and notes sections of the more recent cookbooks in my examination, but it is also detectible in recipe names. The examples in (7) are enigmatic and need detailed explanation as to what type of dish is expected and how underlying stories are related to the names. On the surface, they may seem to lack informativeness. Yet, there is no denying that they are eye-catching and likely to draw the reader's attention enough to urge her to continue reading the rest of the recipe.

(7) a. nasu-no   wasure-ni
       eggplant-GEN   forget-cook
       "long-cooked eggplant"   (Tatsumi 1960)

   b. manpuku-ika
      full.stomach-squid
      "stuffed squid"   (Kobayashi 1980)

c. natsu-no   omoide-no   owan
   summer-GEN   memory-GEN   soup.bowl
   "summer memory soup"   (Kidosaki 1987)

d. takana   chāhan-no   bōshi-nokke
   leaf.mustard   fried.rice-GEN   hat-placing
   "leaf mustard fried rice topped with a hat [egg]"   (Kurihara 1992)

In (7a) we know the recipe has to do with eggplants but have no clue about *wasure-ni*. The reader would have to read the author's headnotes, where she explains with humor that the eggplants are to be cooked so long that we would forget about them. Equally humorous is (7b), which serves as a shorthand of (literally) stuffed squids. The first compound member, *manpuku* "full stomach," describes people who have eaten more than enough. The recipe name tactfully portrays the primary ingredient literally and figuratively. Although poetically phrased, (7c) is quite distant from standard recipe names in that it does not even inform us of a main ingredient. The reference to *owan* "bowl" is the sole clue for a soupy dish. The author's comments clarify that the recipe brings her back to a pleasant memory of a summer resort, free of heat and humidity. Once the story behind the name is revealed, the recipe is shared with the reader along with the nostalgic feeling that the soup dish reminds the author of. As such, this recipe name is not simply a label but a trigger for the cookbook author to share a personal story with her reader on matters that coalesce around food and cooking. Note, at the same time, that the author's socioeconomic class can be discerned through the reference to the time spent at a summer resort.

The recipe name in (7d) is also personalized to tell the reader about a simple but creative style of serving. We ascertain from the first part of the name, *takana chāhan*, that the recipe is fried rice with leaf mustard. Fried rice is a very versatile dish whose ingredients besides cooked rice can be modified according to what is available at the time of cooking. The author, however, learned from her own experience that even plain fried rice with ordinary ingredients in it strikes her children as a big treat once an omelet (thinly made in this case) is placed on top of the fried rice. The whole dish is personified as a person (fried rice) wearing a hat (omelet), and omelet topping became a style of dish in her family. In her 1992 cookbook, Kurihara also has a recipe that is named *hōrensō-to moyashi-no bōshi-nokke* "spinach and bean sprouts topped with a hat [egg]," to which the omelet placing is applied, and speaks of her children who routinely refer to the cooking/serving style as *bōshi* "hat." The recipe name in (7d), further elaborated on in headnotes, suggests an ingenious tip for a cooking and serving idea, but it also provides a venue where the reader gets to know about the author and her family life. Through the additional narrative regarding the family story around *bōshi-nokke*, we are able to witness Kurihara's role as mother.

Since the 1920s, linguistic forms of recipe names have been diversified. In addition to the noun phrase of the X-*no* Y form and compounds, we start to see the use of relative clauses like (8a) and (8b), phrasing borrowed from a foreign language as in (8c), and elided sentences like (8d) and (8e). Some of these recipe names also exemplify cryptic contents that are built upon personal anecdotes.

(8) a. kaori-no   yoi   yaki-miso
       aroma-GEN   good   roast-miso
       "roasted miso with nice aroma"   (Egawa 1957)

   b. waga   michi-o   iku   wantan
      my   way-ACC   go   wonton
      "wonton that goes its own way"   (Kobayashi 1980)

   c. paeria   a ra   kamakura
      paella   à la   Kamakura
      "paella in Kamakura"   (Tatsumi 1978)

   d. tabetara   harumaki
      upon.eating   spring.roll
      "[you realize they are] spring rolls upon eating" (Kidosaki 1987)

   e. shihan-no   namuru-de   kantan   bibinba
      on.market-GEN   namul-with   easy   bibimbap
      "easy bibimbap with namul that is available in a store" (Okada 2007)

In (8a) and (8b) the recipes are for *yaki-miso* "roasted miso" and *wantan* "wonton," respectively. They are further specified by the clausal modifiers (i.e., relative clauses) *kaori-no yoi* "[that] has a nice flavor" and comically sounding *waga michi-o iku* "[that] goes its own way." Not only does (8b) take on a new linguistic form for a recipe name but its mysterious naming draws special attention. We understand that wontons are made with some filling into the shape of dumplings, but the author cuts the cooking time by putting each of the wonton skins and the filling directly into a soup without forming customary dumplings. She cleverly uses the proverbial phrase *waga michi-o iku* "going my way" to describe such a cooking process. The personification of the ingredients adds extra humor, too, as if each ingredient insists on its own way rather than getting together into a dumpling.

In (8c) the French phrasing *à la* is combined with Japanese words. The French loanword *aramōdo* "à la mode" cooccurs with other loanwords in menus and recipes (e.g., *purin aramōdo* "custard topped with ice cream"), but (8c) is different in that it juxtaposes the French phrase *à la* and the

Japanese place word, Kamakura. The reference to Kamakura has to do with the fact that the dish has more rice than what is expected of a Spanish paella. Kamakura playing a role as representing Japanese food is quite a stretch, and the association of paella with the French phrase is puzzling. Nevertheless, the inventiveness behind the naming cannot be denied in both its form and content, especially given that the cookbook was printed in the 1970s.

Linguistically, (8d) and (8e) are best analyzed as full sentences that have been shortened or elided. A potential basic sentence for (8d) would be *tabetara harumaki-datta* "when I ate it, (I realized that) it was a spring roll." Since *tabetara* is the provisional form of *taberu* "eat," it signals a complex sentence in which *tabetara* serves as a subordinate clause. In terms of the recipe content, just like (8b), all the ingredients that are expected for spring rolls are listed in the recipe, but they are not assembled into the customary form of spring rolls. That is, there is no filling or wrapping according to the instruction. As for (8e), a possible base sentence would be *shihan-no namuru-de kantan(-ni) bibinba(-o tsukurō)* "(Let's make) easy bibimbap with store-bought namul." The phrase *namuru-de* "namul-with" would be *namuru-de-no* "namul-with-GEN" in order for it to be in the customary noun phrase format of recipe names. The absence of the Genitive marker, *-no*, suggests that the name in (8e) takes a sentential pattern. However, since it ends with a noun, *bibinba*, rather than a verb, it is best to consider that the verbal element is elided. Despite the partial omission, the recipe name is fully transparent in its content.

The examples in (8) show that the inventory of formats of recipe names and types of information contained in them has been expanded, so that recipes are more flexibly and creatively labeled. Where they may seem to lack sufficient information about cooking itself, the personal storytelling that appears within the recipe makes up for it. Taking into consideration the degree of interest and curiosity that these recipe names invite, individuality observed with the naming practice is a surplus from the viewpoint of interpersonal communication. Furthermore, as Jackson and Meah (2019) argue, humor plays an important role as lubricant in food-related interactions, illuminating its socially relational aspect. Given that the nature of humor used in our examples is benign and friendly, the humorous naming helps create an informal interactive space within the register that typically maintains a neutral, objective instructive tone.

Finally, the presence of the internet and social media has contributed to the change in appearance of recipe names. The use of symbols and emojis, in particular, has been routinely seen in recent recipe and cookbook writing.8 Okada (2007), for one, is a compilation of recipes based on her blog posting, and contains a number of recipe names that incorporate symbols, Romanized scripts, and English words. The recipe names in (9) are given in Japanese to make the orthographical effects clear.

(9) a. 簡単＊和風ツナスパゲティー
　　　kantan * wahū　　　　tsuna　　　spagetī
　　　easy Japanese.style　　tuna　　　spaghetti
　　　"easy * Japanese-style tuna spaghetti"

　　b. 鶏つくねDON
　　　tori　　　　tsukune　　　　　　don
　　　chicken　　chicken.meatball　　rice.bowl
　　　"rice bowl topped with chicken meatballs"

　　c. 10 minutes ティラミス
　　　10 minutes tiramisu
　　　"10-minute Tiramisu"

The asterisk in (9a) is placed not for necessity but for attention-grabbing effects. The recipe name is perfectly informative. (9b) need not be written partially in Romanized letters. Yet, the inclusion of DON certainly makes one wonder if there is any novelty associated with the recipe. Similarly, in (9c), the English form *10 minutes*, put side by side with the loanword katakana word for tiramisu, is not essential by the informativeness canon. The use of an English phrase and a loanword caters toward younger audiences who are accustomed to globalization of cuisine and culture in general.

Zwicky and Zwicky (1980) discuss restaurant menus as an instance of linguistic register. Recipes exhibit much to share with menus in purposes, strategies, and linguistic characteristics that they point out. Among them, I consider informativeness, advertising, and brevity to be aspects that are also applicable to recipe naming, as I have alluded to in my analysis of the survey above.9 Throughout the period of the study, recipe names take the basic principle that reflects informativeness and brevity as their standard goals. However, we have observed a great deal of diversification in form and content since the time of the cookbooks in the 1920s. Such transitions over time are attributed, at least indirectly, to advertising considerations. Efforts to that end have resulted in personalization or individualization of recipe names, which is often achieved at the apparent expense of informativeness and brevity. Striking a balance among informativeness, advertising, and brevity is not always successful, but all in all, we see a trend that cookbooks in recent years devise more recipe names that catch consumers' attention. Since recipe names are the face of recipes, any small difference that breaks mundane patterns is beneficial to making recipes more conspicuous and inviting. Nevertheless, I argue that these authors' attempts to attract the reader's curiosity are not always motivated by marketing purposes. As I have remarked above, the personalized form and content, in which a sense of humor is often injected, can be understood to help create a relaxed setting for social interaction between the authors and their readers.

2 RECIPES AND IDENTITY—THE CASE OF KATSUYO KOBAYASHI

As one of the most influential *ryōri-kenkyūka* "cooking experts," Katsuyo Kobayashi (1937–2014) is viewed to have revolutionized Japanese home-cooking in the 1980s (Ako 2013, 2015). Out of over 200 books (both cookbooks and essays) that she published, her 1980 cookbook particularly provides a rich linguistic and sociocultural source for investigating how cookbooks serve as a communication channel that transmits more than culinary information. It is known that Kobayashi has made immense contributions to the culinary world in Japan in that her recipes have essentially changed the ways in which home cooking is conceptualized. Beyond that, however, I shall argue that her marked linguistic choices in her cookbooks have significant implications to building her own identity as a professional woman and also to sharing that identity with her audiences. Compared to headnotes and other types of notes contained in recipes, cooking instructions are a priori impersonal, their function being compilation of "rules" of cooking that are to be followed.[10] However, the language that Kobayashi uses in cooking instructions demonstrates that they exceed the function as a set of rules in the same manner that recipe names have diversified their form and content as discussed above.

This section first describes Kobayashi's linguistic choices that exhibit a substantial departure from normative recipe styles. Her linguistic practice, then, will be examined vis-à-vis her collective stances in the culinary dimension as well as in the sociocultural context. Putting them together, her distinctive linguistic practice is best understood to be in a mutual feeding relation with her sociocultural stances, and that they jointly index her identity that she aspires to share with her audience.

2.1. Non-Standard Linguistic Practice

2.1.1. Mimetics

Table 3.2, which tallies mimetics used in the cooking instruction section of the cookbooks in my survey, shows that Kobayashi's 1980 cookbook stands as the second highest next to Kidosaki's 1987 cookbook in frequent mimetic use, both in token and type per recipe.¹¹ However, a closer look at the range of her mimetic expressions informs us of two interesting characteristics that are not shared with other recipe writers: (i) emphatic mimetic forms, and (ii) mimetics that are not specific for cooking instructions. These two features commonly surface in conjunction in her recipe writing practice.

As table 3.3 illustrates, many of the frequently used mimetics by cookbook authors take the morphological form of reduplication (CVCV-CVCV, e.g., *hitahita, kotokoto*) and forms that contain or end with a geminate consonant (CVQCV-*ri*, e.g., *saQpari*; CVQ-*to*, e.g., *saQto*). Existing or conventionalized mimetics can often be emphasized or intensified (or exaggerated) by the lengthening of a vowel or a consonant (i.e., geminate), as the parings of *torori* vs. *toro̱ori* (for creaminess) and *kochikochi* vs. *koQchikochi* (for hardness) indicate. An inserted syllable(s) can also add an emphatic force, as is shown by the contrast between *saQ-to* and *sa̱saQ-to* (or even *sa̱sa̱saQ-to*). These emphatic forms are particularly common in speech where the lengthening of a consonant or a vowel may be extended even more for an exclamatory purpose. Kobayashi routinely uses these types of emphatic mimetic forms in the cooking instruction section of her cookbook(s). Examples include *toro̱o-to* (not *toroQ-to*), *toro̱ori* (not *torori*), *kyuu̱Q-to* (not *kyuQ-to*), and *zuu̱Q-to* (not *zuQ-to*) for vowel lengthening; *zakuQzakuQ-to* (not *zakuzaku-to*), *gasaQgasaQ-to* (not *gasagasa-to*), and *paraparaQ-to* (not *parapara-to*) for consonant lengthening/insertion; and *za̱zaQ-to* (not *zaQ-to*) for an inserted syllable. In each of these examples, the mimetic in parentheses represents a basic non-emphatic form.

Note that contemporary recipes of the 21st century incline to use more emphatic mimetic forms. The tendency is noticeable especially in cookbooks that have originated from blog postings, such as Aita (2006) and Okada (2007). For instance, Aita uses *toroori* (for *torori*), in which the vowel lengthening is indicated by a tilde (トロ～リ), and *sasasaQ-to* (for *saQ-to*). Okada also has mimetics like *puriQpuri* (for *puripuri*), *saQsaQ-to* (for *saQ-to*), *jiiQkuri* (for *jiQkuri*), *guguQ-to* (for *guQ-to*), and *kooNgari* (for *koNgari*; written with a tilde as こ～んがり). Notwithstanding the similarities in form, the recurrent appearance of these informal, speech-oriented, and somewhat dramatic sounding words in Kobayashi's recipes is unconventional but original, taking into consideration the time of their publications, i.e., the last quarter of the 20th century.

Mimetics that fall under the characteristic (ii), the use of mimetics not specific to cooking instructions, include *baaQ-to*, *gushuQ-to*, *gaaQ-to*, *goshigoshi*, *gushagusha*, *dobadoba*, and *paQpaQ-to*, among others. These mimetics are not frequently used by recipe writers in elaborating on cooking procedures. Table 3.3 clearly suggests their absences. Unlike many of the cooking-related mimetic expressions we discussed in chapter 3, they describe manners of actions for broader references, and as such they appear in diverse types of discourse beyond the culinary domain. For example, *baaQ-to, gaaQ-to*, and *uwaQ-to* refer to the rigorous and rapid manner of action with a large quantity; *paQpaQ-to* describes the manner of quick action; *kyuQkyuQ* is common for the manner of tightening or pressing something firmly; *gushagusha* refers to the state in which something becomes shapeless, and similarly, *gushuQ-to* evokes the image of something squashed; *dobadoba* depicts the manner in which a large quantity (of liquid) flows forcefully; and *dobon-to* mimics a sound made by a heavy object falling into water. So, Kobayashi broadens the repertoire of mimetics in her cookbooks showing a great deal of freedom beyond the genre of cooking.

It is noteworthy that many of these mimetics have the nuance of rigorous, forceful, and often rough and manly manner of action. Furthermore, the mimetics listed just above largely start with voiced consonants, e.g., [b, d, g]. These instances of Kobayashi's mimetic choice are reminiscent of the sound symbolism that voiced consonants display, particularly in comparison with their voiceless counterparts, as was discussed in chapter 3 in connection with Hamano's (1998) observations and other research that supports them. The semantic features that these voiced consonants symbolize include heaviness, large size, coarseness, and thickness (Hamano 1998). The dynamic and almost masculine image that is associated with these mimetic words is counter to what is expected to be stereotypical female manners that might be equated with elegance and gentleness. In this respect, Kobayashi's mimetic choice betrays the audience, so to speak. Instead of expected connotations of a conventional feminine demeanor, we see more mannish language by a female cooking expert. Note, however, that Kobayashi avoids the seemingly unfitting tone that these mimetics may typically (and stereotypically) have, and instead turns them into a humorous force that is caused by their unanticipated use in cooking instructions. As (10–13) illustrate, this point is suggested by the contexts in which *baaQ-to, gaaQ-to, goshigoshi*, and *dobadoba* are used in her language of cooking instructions.

(10) 引き上げる直前に、いったん火を**バァッと**強くして、...

Hikiageru chokuzen-ni, ittan hi-o **baaQ-to** tsuyoku-shite, ...

"Right before taking [the chicken] out, turn the heat **very** high once, ..." (p. 28)

(11) あとはふたを取り、**ガァーッと**いためて終り。

Ato-wa huta-o tori, **gaaQ-to** itamete owari.

"All you need to do then is remove the lid and **quickly** stir-fry." (p. 18)

(12) じゃがいもは皮を**ゴシゴシ**きれいに洗い、…

Jagaimo-wa kawa-o **goshigoshi** kirei-ni arai, . . .

"**Scrub [hard]** the potato skin clean, . . ." (p. 24)

(13) …トンカツソースを**ドバドバ**と入れ、またいためます。

. . . tonkatsu sōsu-o **dobadoba-to** ire, mata itamemasu.

". . . add **much of** the cutlet sauce, stir-fry [the noodles] again." (p. 42)

The instructions in (10–13) can easily do without the mimetic words since the remainder of each sentence makes the content sufficiently clear. However, just like emphatic forms discussed earlier, the inclusion of these mimetics that have forceful and intense nuances raises the level of exaggeration, which in turn produces the effect of making simple cooking actions rather dramatic and hence comical and lively. For instance, (11) simply gives an instruction for a quick action of stir-frying leafy greens as the final cooking stage, but *gaaQ-to* could evoke images that involve powerful actions on something large or heavy. The remoteness of such images from the actual light-weight vegetable is the source of the humor underlying the use of the mimetic word. Similarly, *dobadoba* in (13) sounds as if a large amount of sauce gushes out to season yakisoba. The amount that *dobadoba* implies would result in stir-fried noodles floating in a pool of thick sauce. In this instruction, Kobayashi could not have meant that literally a large quantity of sauce is called for, as it is evident from the ingredients list, which states the amount of the sauce is *tekiryō* "a suitable amount" or "to taste" as a recipe term. The creative gap between *dobadoba* and *tekiryō* is transparent to the reader, and so too is Kobayashi's intended humous exaggeration.

Kobayashi's use of the mimetic vocabulary like those in (10–13) and similar ones have undertones of rigor, forcefulness, roughness, and the like, which may be associated more readily with manly mannerism than with feminine demeanor, viewed from a stereotypical perspective. I contend that these mimetic choices of hers are interpreted not just as rhetorical and linguistic hyperbole that draws a humorous reception, but they have significant implications to the way she communicates with her audiences, who consist of working women. In addressing them through the language of cooking instructions, the "manly" mimetics can embody boldness in overcoming the fear of challenging the unknown and making mistakes. For instance, the sudden increase in the temperature of the oil for frying chicken in (10) may create a somewhat nervous moment for some, but the reference to *baaQ-to* plays a role as an encouragement for not being timid. The potatoes in (12) are to be roasted with their skins, and a little harshness of *goshigoshi* in scrubbing the dirt off is a reassuring guidance. A bit of rough action, rather than a gentle rinse, would meet the practical purpose of cleansing the potatoes more efficiently and quickly. Also, in (13), the unspecified amount of the sauce on the ingredients list is understood to be "no need to be sparing; if you like the tonkatsu sauce, use as much as you like" (tonkatsu sauce can be likened to ketchup or mayonnaise in American cuisine).

Deliberately or not, Kobayashi presents her carefree, bold, unflinching, and often daring disposition with humor, and expresses her belief that cooking is carried out with pleasure but not with fear or nervousness. She is fully aware from her own experiences how disappointing it is to fail in cooking and baking. Her own unsuccessful stories strongly motivated her to introduce manageable and enjoyable cooking processes that are easily accessible (Kobayashi 1980, 92). Her selection of mimetics provides a linguistic apparatus that aids her in communicating to the reader these philosophical stances on home cooking. The type of mimetics for which Kobayashi opts, exemplified by (10–13), is not repeated by other recipe writers, both past and present, which puts her in a unique position as a "linguistic outlier" in a very constructive sense.[12]

It is interesting to observe that Kobayashi's attitude toward cooking as it is reflected by her distinctive language use, especially when addressing women, is reminiscent of the American cooking icon Julia Child (1912–2004). Like Kobayashi's case, Child's actions and their underlying philosophy in cooking scenes can be epitomized for boldness, audacity, and even a touch of roughness in the same sense that we have been discussing Kobayashi. For example, in a video that documents a cooking show she broadcasted on TV, Child tries to demonstrate how to flip apparently mushy potatoes in a pan.[13] She starts by saying, "when you flip anything, you really, you have to have a courage of your convictions, particularly when it's sort of loose mass like this." Somewhat nervously looking, she tries to flip it but failed to do so, and the "loose mass" scatters around the burner. She continues: "Well, that didn't go very well. See, well, when I flipped it, I didn't have the courage to do it the way I should've," as she collects some of the mass with her bare hand and a spatula and puts it back to the pan, pressing it down to the remainder of the potato. She finally adds, "Who is going to see? But, the only way you learn how to flip things is just flip them." Child's message in this scene to her viewers is undoubtedly that we should not be afraid of making mistakes because we can only learn from our own errors. Her cooking philosophy and its practical delivery with humor are remarkably similar to Kobayashi's attitude toward home cooking.[14, 15]

2.1.2. Prosaic Vocabulary Items

Kobayashi's pattern of breaking the normative boundary in the language of cooking instructions extends to prosaic (i.e., non-mimetic) vocabulary. To begin, the strategy of emphasis by means of vowel lengthening is applied to prosaic words. Examples, indicated phonetically, include *usuuku* (vs. *usuku*) "thinly," *yooku* (vs. *yoku*) "well," *maaruku* (vs. *maruku*) "round," *sukooshi* (vs. *sukoshi*) "a little," *sugooi* (vs. *sugoi*) "very," and *kitanaai* (vs. *kitanai*) "dirty." Reduplication is another strategy for emphasis or intensification. The adverb *yoku*, in addition to *yooku*, appears in its reduplicated form *yokuyoku* as in *yokuyoku mazeawasemasu* "mix very well." The noun *dama* "lump" is commonly used as in *dama-ni naranai-yōni* "so that it won't be lumpy" for making a white sauce, for instance, but Kobayashi's reduplicated variation is *damadama-ni narazu* "without forming lumps." Likewise, in explaining how itchy peeling raw taro potatoes makes your hands feel, she expresses *kayukayu-ni natte* instead of the more common *kayuku natte* "become itchy," where *kayu* is based on the adjective *kayui* "itchy." There is no specific reason that these examples must have lengthened vowels or reduplicated syllables, as their counterparts without the linguistic deviations are the standard in the same context. Indeed, they are rarely seen in printed forms.[16] Yet, it seems undeniable that one would recognize Kobayashi's zeal, commensurate with the emphatic linguistic forms, in getting relevant points across. In addition, it is further evident that Kobayashi's instructional language contains contracted forms, which are characteristic of spoken Japanese and again are not expected in recipe writing. For instance, *tabechau* is shortened from *tabete-shimau* "end up eating," *ii-n-desu* from *ii-no-desu* "it's fine," and *kizanda-n-o* from *kizanda-no-o* "what has been chopped."

The *desu/masu* form is maintained as the overall style of the instruction language of Kobayashi's cookbook, and as was mentioned in section 1 of this chapter, the *desu/masu* style (in writing) gives "a tone of addressing to the audience" and indexes "presentation of self." The occasional switch to the spoken mode that is signaled by the emphatic and contracted expressions discussed above, however, is not in conflict with the public persona that is indexed by the *desu/masu* form, since multiple indexical values can cooccur under shifting contexts (Cook 1998). Incorporating casual elements, the overall perspective of Kobayashi's recipe narrative, instead, changes its footing and foregrounds informality in delivering cooking instructions. As a result, her act of communication sounds more spontaneous, lively, and in person with such shifts in style.

2.1.3. Elements in the Sentence-Final Position

Following up on the matter with the styles, there are other ways in which the *desu/masu* style in writing can be made more informal. Some cookbooks maintain the same style throughout the sections that constitute each recipe, but it is more customary that the style varies depending on the section (e.g., headnotes, cooking instructions, notes). Speaking strictly of the cooking instructions section, once the *desu/masu* or *da/ru* form is chosen, it is rare to shift it to the other. Although the instructions in Kobayashi's 1980 cookbook keep the *desu/masu* style, they exhibit bits of linguistic diversions that encode informality, still within the overall *desu/masu* style.

First, where nominal and adjectival predicates with *desu* or verbs with *masu* are expected to show up at the end of sentences, her cooking instructions also include sentences that end with mimetic forms without completing the sentences by the anticipated *desu* and *masu* marking. Examples include the following, which gives the sense of deviation from the formal way of completing utterances.

(14) a. 皿にとってから塩を<u>パッパ</u>。

  Sara-ni totte-kara shio-o <u>paQpa</u>. (paQpa "(sprinkling) quickly")

  "Transfer it to a dish and sprinkle the salt." (p. 41)

  b. きゅうりは、… 食べやすい大きさに<u>ポキポキ</u>。

  Kyūri-wa, . . . tabe-yasui ōkisa-ni <u>pokipoki</u>. (pokipoki "snap")

  "Break the cucumbers into the size that is easy to eat." (p. 17)

Mimetics like those in (14) are, in isolation, unable to designate the part of speech categories (e.g., verb, noun). These sentences are, thus, best interpreted as having collocated verbs in the *masu* form elided although the omission of expected verbs does not hinder the interpretation of the intended messages. For example, *paQpa* in (14a) is likely to be shortened from *paQpa-to kake-masu* "sprinkle (a small amount of the salt) in the *paQpa* (quick) manner." Similarly, *pokipoki* in (14b) is interpreted on par with *pokipoki ori-masu* "break the cucumbers in the *pokipoki* (snapping) manner." It is common to encounter these sentences in informal writing and casually spoken utterances as well as headlines of newspapers and magazines and advertisements where brevity is required. However, as instructional language like that of the recipe register, elliptical statements are not a pervasive standard. The sentence-final mimetic without its completing with the verbal element serves to switch the rhetorically directive-sounding tenor of the cooking instruction section to a bit more casual, colloquial, and friendly tone, although still within the written mode.

To a similar end, some of Kobayashi's instruction sentences end with nouns without the expected style marker *desu*. The following are representative examples.

(15) a. …竹ぐしをじゃがいもに刺して、すっと通れば焼けた<u>しるし</u>。

    . . . takegushi-o jagaimo-ni sashite, suQto tōreba yaketa <u>shirushi</u>.

"If you can stick a bamboo skewer into the potato without resistance, it indicates the potato is cooked." (p. 87)

b. 揚げすぎるくらいに揚げたほうが香ばしくっていい<u>味</u>。

Age-sugiru kurai-ni ageta hō-ga kōbashikutte ii <u>aji</u>.

"The chicken will have a good, appetizing taste if it is virtually over-fried." (p. 28)

Standard equivalents of these sentences would add *desu* to the end: *shirushi-desu* for (15a) and *aji-desu* for (15b). Without the *desu* ending, the instruction sentences in (15) again sound less formal, while at the same time tinted with spontaneous mild excitement.

The equal impact is also detected with verbs, as in (16), and phrases that end in postpositions and function (as opposed to content) words, as in (17).

(16) a. 最後に白いいりごまを<u>ふって</u>。

Saigo-ni shiroi irigoma-o <u>hutte</u>.

"Sprinkle toasted sesame seeds over (the green peppers) at the end." (p. 26)

b. 余分なパン粉ははたき<u>落として</u>。

Yobun-na panko-wa hataki-<u>otoshite</u>.

"Pat off excess breadcrumbs." (p. 22)

(17) a. ジャーパチパチというけど、あわてずそのまま<u>に</u>。

Jaapachipachi-to iu-kedo, awatezu sono-mama-<u>ni</u>.

"It makes the 'jaapachipachi' sound, but stay calm and leave it as is." (p. 28)

b. ペーパータオルかふきんで鶏の汁気をおさえてから、そろりと鍋<u>へ</u>。

pēpā-taoru-ka hukin-de tori-no shiruke-o osaete-kara, sorori-to nabe-<u>e</u>.

"After removing the liquid of the chicken with a paper towel or cloth, slowly put it into the pot." (p. 28)

c. あとは弱火で40分くらい、コトコト煮る<u>だけ</u>。

Ato-wa yowabi-de 40-pun-kurai, kotokoto niru-<u>dake</u>.

"After that, you only need to cook in a slow heat for about 40 minutes." (p. 29)

In (16), instead of the expected *masu*-forms like *hurimasu* "sprinkle" and *(hataki-)otoshimasu*, the verbs appear in the gerundive forms, *hutte* in (16a) and *(hataki-)otoshite* in (16b). Regarding (17), *-ni* in (17a) and *-e* in (17b) are postpositions, while *-dake* in (17c) is a function word that means "only." In the *desu/masu* style, these sentences are elliptical. For instance, in their more complete equivalents, we would see the underlined parts to be followed by *shite-okimasu* "leave (it as is)" for (17a), *iremasu* "put (it in)" or *utsushimasu* "move (it)" for (17b), and simply the style marker *desu* for (17c).

Finally, the clearest case of Kobayashi's cooking instructions being proximate to the spoken form is shown by the use of sentence-final particles. These particles index the illocutionary force of utterances and have various pragmatic and sociolinguistic functions (Hasegawa 2015; Iwasaki 2002; Tsujimura 2014). Sentence-final particles do not change the referential meaning of a sentence but "impart some additional hint of the speaker's attitude toward what he is saying—doubt, conviction, caution, inquiry, confirmation or request for confirmation, recollection, etc." (Martin 1987, 914). Furthermore, the particles *no* and *ne* serve to index the speaker's "affective stance" (e.g., rapport, intimacy) (Cook, 1990, 1992, 1998). The particle *ne* in (18a) and the sequence of two particles *ka* (question) and *na* in (18b) exemplify such sentence final particles that are typical of speaking. Additionally, in (19), the particles *yo* (assertion) and *na* are elongated for emphasis, which are transcribed with the combination of two orthographical modes, i.e., hiragana and katakana syllabaries.

(18) a. …のんびりしているとネバネバになってしまうから手早く<u>ね</u>。

　　　　…nonbiri shite-iru-to nebaneba-ni natte-shimau-kara tebayaku-<u>ne</u>.

　　　　"… if you take your time, it will become sticky, so [wash] it quickly." (p. 65)

　　b. 30分、それ以上<u>かな</u>。

　　　　30-pun, sore ijō-<u>ka</u>-<u>na</u>.

　　　　"[Continue on] for 30 minutes, perhaps a little longer?" (p. 28)

(19) a. つやっとしてとろっとして、ご飯に合います<u>よオ</u>。

　　　　TsuyaQ-to shite toroQ-to shite, gohan-ni aimasu-<u>yō</u>.

　　　　"Shiny and thick, it [=teriyaki fish] will go great with rice!" (p. 21)

　　b. あればきくらげも入れたい<u>なア</u>。

　　　　Areba kikurage-mo iretai-<u>nā</u>.

　　　　"If available, it will be great to add tree ears to it [=udon]!" (p. 44)

The pragmatic function of *ne* in (18a) fits the role to "soften requests" in Martin's (1987, 916) explanation as well as to creation of rapport in Cook's afore-mentioned analysis of the particle. The recipe calls for a quick action, indicated by *tebayaku* "quickly," but the addition of *ne* makes the directive sounds gentler and empathetic. The juxtaposition of the two particles in (18b), *ka-na*, instantiates Martin's description, "a softer way to ask a question. It is also used when talking to yourself—with others invited to eavesdrop . . ." (p. 934). Kobayashi first estimates the cooking time to be 30 minutes, but then wonders if possibly an additional time may be likely. This somewhat tentative, instinctive, soliloquy-like utterance is shared with her audience thanks to *ka-na* at the end.

As for (19), Iwasaki (2002, 282) explains that the particle *yo* "enables the speaker to present information presumed not to be available to the addressee"; and according to Martin (1987, 916), *na* "soften[s] a statement and invite[s] confirmation on the part of the hearer: 'don't you think, n'est-ce pas?'" The vowel lengthening of the particles in (19), indicated in boldface, highlights the extra tip for a serving plan in (19a), and Kobayashi's hope for an even better cooking outcome with an additional ingredient in (19b). It is of further interest that the elongated vowels are orthographically represented in the katakana syllabary, likely adding a visual effect to the somewhat theatrical emphasis and casualness. Through the combination of the phonetic and orthographical effects, Kobayashi's excitement delivered with an increased degree of colloquialism surfaces, resonating louder to the reader as if Kobayashi is speaking in person. The occurrences of these speech-oriented particles confirm that the language of her cookbook is not just a collection of one-way cooking instructions. Instead, it further suggests that Kobayashi welcomes an active culinary dialogue as part of dynamic social interaction.[17]

2.1.4. *Humorous Contents*

We have thus far documented linguistic choices that Kobayashi makes in her cookbook writing, many of which suggest that she has a good sense of humor. It comes as no surprise, then, that the contents of her instructions and descriptions witness a great deal of funny and witty ideas. This, too, is what separates her from other recipe writers. One cannot help smiling (or even laughing) upon reading the comments like (20–23) below.

First, the underlined phrasing in (20) is obviously an amplification of the manner of the cooking action.

(20) a. 別の鍋にたっぷりの湯を沸かし塩を<u>ほうり込んで</u>、…

Betsu-no nabe-ni taQpuri-no yu-o wakashi shio-o <u>hōrikonde</u>, . . .

"Boil plenty of water in another pot and <u>throw in</u> the salt, . . ." (p. 29)

b. ゆでたスパゲッティに大急ぎで具を加え、…

Yudeta supagetti-ni ōisogi-de gu-o kuwae . . .

"Add the ingredients to the cooked spaghetti in a great hurry . . ." (p. 81)

The verb *hōrikonde* in (20a) (the gerund of *hōrikomu* "throw in") is a compound in which the first member *hōru* literally means to throw something, usually in a rough or forceful fashion. Although the amount of salt to be added is not given in the ingredients list of the recipe, *hōrikonde* evokes the image that a large amount of salt should be thrown in the boiling water with force. The phrasing resembles the manner in which we hurriedly toss scattered clothes into the closet of the messy house upon receiving an unexpected visitor. It is also similar to the mimetics in (10–13), which have the tone of a carefree attitude that is not afraid of making mistakes. In (20b), if taken literally, the word *ōisogi*, in which *ō-* has an intensifying function, also overplays the degree of utmost immediacy. It is easily recognizable to any reader that the cooking process in each context of (20) does not call for the level of intensity that the word literally means. As I pointed out earlier, the contrast between the fictional descriptions and the real situations is unexpected of recipes, giving rise to humorous reactions.

The comical effect of the two examples in (21) additionally lessens potential stress that novice readers might feel.

(21) a. あとはほかの用でもたしながら、時々玉じゃくしで油をすくって鶏にかけてあげます。

Ato-wa hoka-no yō-demo tashi-nagara, tokidoki tamajakushi-de abura-o sukutte tori-ni kakete-agemasu.

"After that, ladle out the oil and pour it over the chicken every now and then, while doing other things." (p. 28)

b. あとは弱火で40分くらいコトコト煮るだけ。知らん顔しててもできてます。

Ato-wa yowabi-de 40-pun-kurai kotokoto niru-dake. Shirankao shitete-mo dekitemasu.

"The rest is to cook it slowly at a low heat for about 40 minutes. It will be done even if you pretend to pay no attention to it." (p. 29)

The recipe that embeds (21a) is for deep-frying a whole chicken. A short caption that prefaces the recipe says, "Does this look easy?" Despite this apparently daunting introduction, Kobayashi makes the process simpler and manageable. The underlined part in (21a) is perfectly dispensable, but the intentional inclusion of "you can do this while doing your (other) business at the same time" certainly eases nervous minds. *Yō-o tasu* independently means "do your business" or "run errands." So, by humoring that simultaneous multi-tasking is allowed, Kobayashi hints that pouring the frying oil over the whole chicken does not need the reader's exclusive and constant attention. (21b) is the last (simmering) stage of a creamy stew. Just like (21a), the underlined comment is unnecessary. The noun *shirankao* means to pretend not to notice or to look as if you are indifferent. In this context, it sounds like treating the stew as an independent living being with a mind of its own, while at the same time, sending a practical instruction that no further cooking task is needed. In both instances of (21), the presence of such auxiliary comments that hardly seem to pertain to cooking itself makes the message entertaining and enchanting. The fact that these ad-on notes strike us as funny rather than superfluous and irksome is presumably owing to her knack in word choice that flawlessly fits each context.

Embedded in Kobayashi's recipe-writing are engaging topics, outside of cooking in popular culture, that are presumed to be familiar to the reader. (22) is such an example that refers to the American drama, Columbo, whose dubbed version was aired in Japan at the time.

(22) 刑事コロンボ好みじゃないかしらん。

Keiji koronbo-gonomi-janai-kashiran.

"It's to Detective Columbo's liking, isn't it?" (p. 15)

This brief note appears immediately before a list of instructions for *pirikara sūpu mekishikohū* "Mexican-Style Spicy Soup." Detective Columbo is known to eat chili every day, so Kobayashi lightheartedly adds a comment that he would enjoy the recipe. The reference to the beloved detective in a familiar TV drama relates the character's daily diet routine to the recipe, raising the culinary dialogue to the level of popular culture as part of social and personal life.[18]

Ranging from formal linguistic markers to incorporation of humor and popular cultural topics in recipe narratives, the linguistic mechanisms that she so adeptly uses effectively index the presence of an informal social context in which such a dialogue is embraced. At the same time, through the affective stance toward the audience encoded in her linguistic choices, Kobayashi positions herself not in a one-way conduit of cooking instructions but as an excited and animated facilitator of practical tips in a camaraderie relationship with the audience.

2.1.5 Regional Dialect

Appearance of regional dialect in recipes, beyond a sporadic use of isolated expressions, is very rare, if it occurs at all. Kobayashi's cookbook is atypical in that light. Born and raised in Osaka, Kobayashi stayed there for about the first three decades of her life before moving to the eastern region. The Osaka dialect is distinctively different from the dialect spoken in Tokyo, as is detected by difference in the pitch patterns, vocabulary, and grammar. Regardless of the genre of writing, the standard dialect is the norm in written texts, and the use of local dialect would be marked for its specific occurrence. It is, thus, not expected to see cookbooks whose instructional sentences are written in a regional dialect; and this aspect particularly distinguishes Kobayashi's 1980 cookbook from others certainly in her contemporaries and even to this day. Her instructional sentences show ample examples of incorporating the dialect, as illustrating samples demonstrate below. Her 1980 cookbook consists of five parts. One of them (part II) is entitled *waga hurusato-wa ōsaka nariki* "My Home Was Osaka" and features recipes that she grew up with. She reminisces about pleasant food memories that have driven her to include the recipes in that part of the book. Writing in the regional dialect is, thus, motivated by the theme and her proud identity.[19] That said, the use of the Osaka dialect is novel given that the primary purpose of the book is to offer cooking instructions framed in the particular linguistic register of recipe. The incorporation of the dialect evidently adds another instance to the list of her linguistic diversions from the conventional pattern of recipe writing.

The first two examples, (23a) and (23b), appear in brief comments immediately before the procedural instructions, whereas the rest are part of the instructions themselves. In (23a) and (23b), the underlined endings characteristically mark the Osaka dialect. Their standard counterparts would be without *nanda* in (23a) and *nen* in (23b). The underlined parts of the remaining examples also characterize the Osaka dialect, and the corresponding standard equivalents are given to the right of the arrow.

(23)   a. ... たいして変わりはありません<u>なんだ</u>。

   ... taishite kawari-wa arimasen-<u>nanda</u>.

   "... there is no big difference." (p. 22)

   b. ... 大阪では、熱々を、卵つけながら食べます<u>ねん</u>。

   ... ōsaka-de-wa, atsuatsu-o, tamago tsuke-nagara tabemasu-<u>nen</u>.

   "... in Osaka, we eat it very hot, dipping it in beaten eggs." (p. 42)

c. <u>よう</u>ほぐれます → yoku

   <u>Yō</u> hoguremasu.

   "It (=noodles) becomes well separated." (p. 42)

d. ... なんにもついて<u>こなんだら</u>焼けてます。 → konakat-tara

   ... nannimo tsuite <u>konan-dara</u> yaketemasu.

   "if it comes out clear, it suggests it's cooked." (p. 43)

e. ... 粉がつおをふると<u>よろし</u>。 → yorosii(desu)/ii(desu)

   ... kona-gatsuo-o huruto <u>yoroshi</u>.

   "... sprinkling powdered bonito is advised." (p. 43)

f. <u>やわらこう</u>なった粕を ... → yawarakaku

   <u>Yawarakō</u> natta kasu-o ...

   "Softened sake lees ..." (p. 44)

g. あらの塩味が<u>ほどよう</u>ついてる<u>はずやけど</u>... → hodoyoku, hazu-da-kedo

   Ara-no shioaji-ga <u>hodoyō</u> tsuiteru <u>hazu-ya-kedo</u>

   "It should have a sufficient salty taste, but ..." (p. 44)

The Osaka dialect is one of the dialects that is familiar to Japanese speakers, and the range of the variation demonstrated in (23) would be intelligible enough for the readers. The dialect connects her with her upbringing, and the gastronomic tastes that she developed growing up in that region have surely inspired her recipes. By revealing her personal background, the use of the Osaka dialect signifies the personal and personable nature of her cooking instructions. Her dialect use suggests that she is comfortable with her own skin, and at the same time, it indicates her bold and witty stance to make such a considerably different language choice as a cookbook writer.

To summarize, this section has illustrated Kobayashi's linguistic practice that is uncommon in recipe writing, which amply substantiates that Kobayashi wields language in a remarkably ingenious manner. Individually and collectively, the traits that the samples demonstrate are out of the norm, putting her in a unique position as a cookbook writer. Her linguistic practice stands out in writing the most fundamental, obligatory, and usually impersonal part of a cookbook that is allocated to step-by-step directives for food preparation. That said, most of the specific types of unconventional choices of language that Kobayashi demonstrated in her recipe writing should not be viewed as anomalies since other cookbook writers exhibit some samples of them although their number is not large, especially before 1980. For example, Kidosaki's 1987 cookbook shows instances of mimetics in emphatic forms. The more contemporary and younger authors like Okada (2007), Aita (2006), and Kokubun and Kentaro (2009), who have the experience of media appearance in blogs and TV programs, use extensive colloquialism, particularly in their comments section, including noun- and particle-ending sentences as well as creative use of mimetics and other vocabulary items. Still, it is indisputable that Kobayashi was at the forefront in her linguistic innovation and that she was ahead of her time in this respect. On the other hand, the use of local dialect is perhaps particular to Kobayashi. So, it is the extent and variety of the non-traditional language use, unexpected in the genre of recipe writing, that makes Kobayashi's linguistic practice worthy of study.

2.2. Identity-Building and Identity-Sharing

Beyond the analysis of the formal and functional aspects of the language in her recipes, contextualizing Kobayashi's language use leads us to better understand her stances on broader concerns that underlie her linguistic practice and its potential social meaning. The stances that she took as a working woman and as a professional cook (as opposed to a chef) are important building blocks for discerning her identity that comes to light in her cookbook(s). A multi-dimensional interpretation of her unconventional language use that I wish to advance here resides in the social, cultural, and political climate of Japan during the last quarter of the 20th century when she was most active as one of the professional "cooking experts" (*ryōri-kenkyūka*).[20] I view that the out-of-the-norm linguistic choices that she made index her professional and social identity, at the same time serving as an effective means to share the identity with the readers. Underlying her professional success is her strong social stance promoting women's advancement in the society and her principle that ostensibly complicated dishes can be simplified both in time and in process without compromising taste. That is, her viewpoints have a consequential relation to the sociocultural situation at the time in Japan.

Thriving through the time of the high economic growth (1954–1975) and surviving the *oiru shokku* "oil crisis" in the 1970s, Japan entered into its economic peak in the so-called "bubble" period of 1986–1991, until its burst in 1991–1993. Notably, the Equal Employment Opportunity Law was enacted in 1986, which was propelled by the stable economic wealth, setting an important political and socioeconomic stage for the emerging presence of working women. From the viewpoint of food supply and food consumption, the long-established *hōshokujidai*, an era of plentiful food, has been enjoyed by the people, in stark contrast with the war and post-war time when food shortages were one of the nation's grave concerns.

Kobayashi's 1980 cookbook emerged in this socioeconomic setting, and together with subsequent cookbook publications, came to be regarded as the bible of home cooking (Ako 2013, 2015). A working mother of two children herself, Kobayashi understood the challenge that working women face because cooking for the family was still a household duty that women, almost exclusively, were expected to carry out. The male hegemony in the cooking sphere is suggested by the old saying, 男子厨房に入らず "men should not be in the kitchen," which was still a prevalent idea in the Showa era (1926–1989). Some of the principles of home cooking Kobayashi advocated in her cookbooks (and at other public venues) include: (i) no other genre of cooking is more important than home cooking, (ii) seemingly cumbersome or elaborate dishes can be perfected without compromising the taste by simplifying the procedure (which saves cooking time), and (iii) recipes she provides are simply a rough estimate, and ingredients and amounts should be freely adjusted to the taste of the reader and her family (Kobayashi 1980, 92–93). Although she devises various processes to shorten the total cooking time, it is always the taste that is taken into the foremost consideration. In a lecture she gave in 1997, she commented on a current trend of dishes that are "not flavorless but not delicious, either," and distinguished between what to eat and how to eat. To her, the concern with how to eat food amounts to how to cook the food, which leads to the ultimate goal toward good (food) taste (Kobayashi 1997a, 37–38).

Her recipes for speed cooking grounded on uncompromised taste routinely introduce techniques and processes that break long-held Japanese culinary tradition, often the type of instructions that are opposite of what has been the norm at the time and even to this day. For example, deep-frying assumes heating plenty of oil enough to submerge ingredients, but Kobayashi advocates the use of much less oil that covers just half the ingredients. She explains that the reduced amount of oil allows the moisture of the ingredients to escape freely (from their top part), resulting in an ideal crispiness. In addition, the use of less oil cuts down on the initial time of heating it and eventually on the overall cooking time. Furthermore, storing and recycling left-over oil for future use is more manageable if we have to handle far less than a panful of oil (Kobayashi 1987, 2003). The reduced amount for deep-frying has increasingly been common in recent recipes of the 21st century, but Kobayashi was already sowing a novel idea in the 1980s leading to the new wave of cooking methods.[21]

A similar attitude applies to the stance that Kobayashi takes on precooked food items (Kobayashi 2014b). In Japan sales of precooked, store-bought food have long been a very familiar scene at supermarkets and the basements of department stores, commonly called *depa-chika* "basement of department store." These conveniently prepared food packages were, at least in the past, thought to be particularly suitable for working single men, but a number of women, whether they are working women or homemakers, have been their regular consumers. As widely popular as they are nowadays, they have long been considered next to home-made, from-scratch food. As recently as 2020, reflecting the traditional view that cooking for family is women's responsibility, there were extremely contentious exchanges over a Twitter message by a woman. This dispute has come to be known as the "potato salad debate." Shopping with her young son, the woman was holding a package of prepared potato salad for purchase when an older man passed by her, spitting harshly that she should make her own potato salad at home. Underlying his comment is the thought that potato salad, an epitome of home cooking, is a simple enough dish that any woman can and should make her own at home. Although the ensuing heated debates suggest an encouraging change in women's status in the society today, the man's sentiment was more openly shared by many people, including women, still in the late 20th century.

Even long before the incident that led to the recent potato salad debate, Kobayashi challenged such a societal canon and enthusiastically endorsed incorporation of precooked foods in everybody's dinner plan (Kobayashi 2015[22]). She rationalizes that single women and homemakers are no different from men and have days that they are too tired to cook. Not only does she justify serving store-bought meals at home but she also suggests adjusting their flavors to the liking of family members. Interestingly, she further asserts that browsing around vendors of precooked foods has given her new ideas for cooking for her family and hence expanded her culinary repertoire. As these comments represent, her messages to her audience are always forward-looking, promoting women's curiosity and joy of "studying" prepared foods that are lined up in supermarkets and *depa-chika*. The culinary stances that she took, many of which may appear audacious given the social atmosphere at the time, are in a perfect alignment with Kobayashi's linguistic practice that departs from conventional writing for the genre.

Kobayashi took an equally firm stance regarding women's social and cultural advancement, as is evident from her public lectures, interviews, and essays (Kinoshima 1996; Kobayashi 1991, 1997a, 1997b, 2003, 2015). She positioned herself in the sociocultural setting where working women with family are steadfastly progressing, while acknowledging that women's status was still low in comparison with men in the late 1990s.[23] In her 1997 lecture (Kobayashi 1997a), she gave the audience an example that TV casters would ask her what she thinks about the rising cost of eggs, but they would not solicit her opinions on other topics including politics and the world situation like military affairs, because to them she was merely a person who cooks (p. 43). She claimed: "[a]lthough I'm a cooking expert, I don't just devote myself to cooking. Nor do I simply answer questions about cooking. I constantly look at the society and contemplate how women could transcend. I want to walk on the same path with those women" (p. 39, my translation).[24] She passionately encouraged women to hold onto their jobs, so that their children would follow the footsteps that they took and regard their mothers as role models. It is irrefutable that Kobayashi values home cooking and that women play a very important role in family life, but she also promotes that cooking should be shared by men. To her, doing everything for the family and pampering men and children would deprive them of the opportunity to foster an independent mind. Such a social stance Kobayashi took as a working woman and as a professional home cook resulted from her own search for a new identity, free of the traditional label that equates home cooking with *ryōsaikenbo* "good mother, good wife" (Kinoshima 1996).

Kobayashi's cookbooks are reflective of her culinary philosophy, which is an amalgamation of a view toward home cooking and a consideration toward a busy working woman who cooks after work. They stand firmly on her sociocultural stances regarding women's status in the society and at home. These stances constitute a strong basis for shaping her identity in a discursive fashion. Being outside of the box, culinarily as well as linguistically, Kobayashi's cooking ideology and practical advice that comport with it are significant in social and cultural contexts. The ideology—both professional and personal—underlying her cooking instructions coupled with the style of language she chooses in communicating with (rather than merely speaking to) her audience feed into her unparalleled identity that has social meaning to herself and to her audience. The uncommon linguistic choices she makes have jointly become her "style" of recipe writing where styles are best captured as "part of a *system of distinction*, in which a style contrasts with other possible styles, and the social meaning signified by the style contrasts with other social meanings" (Irvine 2001, 22, emphasis original). I have illustrated Kobayashi's linguistic choices that stand out particularly in the recipe register, as is highlighted by her distinctive selection of vocabulary and pragmatic markers, employment of humor, and the use of the Osaka dialect. These mechanisms available in the language have helped her form her own communication style and aided her in mirroring her viewpoints in multiple sociocultural dimensions especially gender-relevant ones.

I have pointed out that Kobayashi's linguistic choices coalesce to her efforts to create an informal and casual tone although recipes as a linguistic register customarily maintains an objective and impersonal voice in their delivery of cooking instructions. Informality in utterances has its so-called "reactional" function that the speaker selects in consideration of his/her interlocutor(s), for instance, as in-group communication (Coupland 2001; Eckert 2000). In her case, though, Kobayashi's linguistic maneuvering has broader social implications. She actively and voluntarily generates a multiplicity of personae that stand for her culinary, social, cultural, and political views, i.e. what Eckert (2000) describes as "performances of personae." The use of the Osaka dialect is also consistent with this picture in that she is being herself, comfortable with her own skin and audacious about being non-traditional in the way of cooking and in giving cooking instructions. With the utmost focus on her audience and in the relaxed and at-ease manner of delivery of culinary directives, unpretentiousness brings her and her readers closer. Kobayashi's linguistic practice as is demonstrated in her recipe writing critically contributes to the emergent process of constructing her identity. Her language of recipes, made more direct, vivid, and personal by the collective linguistic style she creates, further helps Kobayashi to interact effectively with the readers who are likely to share her social conditions and viewpoints. The audiences who appreciate her linguistic style (i.e., language choices) and the identity discursively constructed in the cookbook discourse understand the deep social message conveyed in her cookbooks. They view Kobayashi as a paragon of the progressive woman who thrives to strike a balance between her role in the workplace and at home. As a natural consequence, Kobayashi's popularity and influence, deeply rooted in strong moral and practical appeals to working women and women in general, lasted virtually unparalleled for 25 years.[25]

NOTES

1. My examination focuses on Kobayashi's writing, but the observations I make in this chapter apply to her oral communication as well. Her involvement in the public cooking sphere, in fact, started with her appearance on a TV show in the 1960s, and in subsequent decades she was actively sought after in the media. In particular, NHK's *Kyō-no Ryōri* "Today's Cooking" is a daily TV cooking program on which she was a regular face.

2. The number of cookbooks representing each decade is admittedly small for the historical examinations of how the language and style of cookbooks have shifted over time. The purpose of this section, however, is to give a general overview of cookbook writing as a background for the next section, rather than a comprehensive historical survey.

3. Higashiyotsuyanagi (2010) particularly gives an interesting historical overview on the emergence of early cookbooks for home cooking at the beginning of the 20th century, putting it in the context of the social, economic, and political milieu of the time.

4. Additionally, the style of the instructions in these cookbooks is extremely polite by contemporary standards. This may reflect that the cookbooks were written versions of oral radio broadcasting.

5. Interestingly, the observation regarding these style differences does not apply to the cookbooks written by and for men that are included in the survey reported on in chapter 3. Among those cookbooks, the ratio between the *da/ru* and *desu/masu* styles is three to five, but the division does not correspond to any systematic chronological pattern, leaving the choice largely up to the individuals.

6. As far as the the *desu/masu* vs. *da/ru* style contrast is concerned, the only exception that I am aware of is recipes that are included in the magazine *Kurashi-no Techō* and its recipe supplements published by the Kurashi-no Techosha. Step-by-step instructions in the recipes of these publications are written consistently in the *desu/masu* style to this day.

7. Another mimetic word that has come to be widely used as part of a compound is *saQto* "quickly." Among the cookbooks in my survey, Kurihara (1992) contains the example *saQto-ni*, where the second member is a derived form of the verb *niru* "cook in liquid." It has been extended to another cooking term, *itameru* "stir-fry," to generate *saQto-itame*. Both *saQto-ni* "quick cooking in liquid" and *saQto-itame* "quick stir-frying" frequently appear in recipe names today (e.g., *kyabetsu-no saQto-ni* "quick cooking (in seasoned liquid) of cabbage," *yasai-no saQto-itame* "quick stir-fry of vegetables").

8. Creative ways of incorporating a variety of symbols, both in recipe names and in headnotes, are regularly seen especially in online recipe cites and social media. See Tsujimura (2018b) for additional examples and discussion.

9. Other relevant facets that Zwicky and Zwicky (1980) consider includes connoisseurship and play with language. Although the cookbooks on which I have reported in this chapter do not include clear examples of connoisseurship, thanks to increasing popularity of international cuisines and a deluge of food-related loanwords, the naming of many recipes in the 21st century takes into consideration the reader/user's (also not to mention the author's) sophisticated culinary knowledge. As for play with language, (7b), (7d), and (8b) exemplify such a linguistic tactic.

10. Gopnik (2010) refers to the technical aspect of recipes and cookbooks as "the grammatical turn: the idea that what the cookbook should supply is the rules, the deep structure—a fixed, underlying grammar that enables you to *use* all the recipes you find" (p. 269, emphasis original). He comments that a sequence of detailed instructions of how to slice with a knife like *You still press down, just with a little more precision, and cut into thick or thin slices of fairly uniform size* "feels masculine in tone" (p. 271). Cooking instructions in Japanese cookbooks in general share the same type of impersonal tone, as is often the case with instructional sentences outside of the culinary field as well (e.g., how to assemble furniture, how to use tools), but different styles marked by specific endings available in Japanese can alleviate the neutral tone.

11. A similar tendency is detected in her other cookbooks (e.g., 1995, 2011) as well.

12. Baba's (2003) study shows that the use of mimetics in spoken Japanese positively correlates with emotive intensity determinants like subjectivity and

involvement, which increase the level of emotivity in discourse. Although using the written form, Kobayashi's extensive employment of mimetics can be viewed to help deepen her engagement in communicating with her audience, thereby generating psychological closeness among the participants.

13. The YouTube source is https://www.youtube.com/watch?v=k6s6rVAkFrE. It is dated February 12, 2015, but the date of the original broadcasting is not included in it.

14. Kobayashi traveled to the States several times in her life. One of those occasions, in the late 1980s, she stayed in Santa Barbara for 2 months, leaving her family in Japan, to take classes in an adult education program. According to Nakahara (2017), Kobayashi, although her English language skills were marginal, introduced herself as "Julia Child of Japan." It is not clear from Nakahara (2017) and from Kobayashi (1991), in which she talks about the experience in California, to what extent she knew about Julia Child. None of Kobayashi's writings that I reviewed include information related to the American culinary icon.

15. Parasecoli (2017) observes that Julia Child's success comes from masculinity, which allows for making mistakes and making a mess. In Kobayashi's case, the masculine features that Parasecoli refers to are further indicated by her use of "manly" mimetics we discussed above.

16. Of the linguistic strategies for emphasis, reduplication of prosaic expressions may give an impression of sounding childish. Nevertheless, examples are attested, although sparsely, in modern cookbooks including *yawayawa* (vs. *yawarakai* "soft, tender"), *momimomi* (vs. *momu* "massage"), and *surisuri* (vs. *suru* "rub") (Okuzono 2012). They tend to be found in supplementary notes of various kinds rather than in the cooking instructions themselves.

17. The characteristics regarding the way that instructional sentences end in Kobayashi's 1980 book are rarely observed in any of the cookbooks that I surveyed except for those written in the 21st century by younger authors who have experience in blog-sites (e.g., Okada 2007; Aita 2006). Kurihara (1992) shows examples of sentences that end with the gerundive form of verbs (like those in (16)) and with postpositions (like those in (17)), but the pattern of use is not as extensive as Kobayashi. Given that Kobayashi's 1980 cookbook exhibits ample examples of these characteristics and also that her subsequent cookbooks take the same pattern, it suggests that the linguistic choices she made in the 1980 publication have been her standard linguistic practice. Incidentally, the observations made about mimetics are also sustained throughout her later cookbooks.

18. Kobayashi's sense of humor is mirrored in recipe names as well. Of the examples we have discussed earlier, (7b) and (8b) instantiate her playful naming pattern. Additionally, *namakemono shichū* "lazy person's stew" (implying an easier process), *kankan raisu* "can-can rice" (referring to the use of canned foods), *shomin-no ebi-chāhan* "shrimp stir-fried rice for the common people" (reflecting the use of a less expensive ingredient), and many more witty recipe names are found throughout Kobayashi's cookbooks (e.g., Kobayashi 1980, 1995, 2007, 2011).

19. Outside of part II of the cookbook, there is at least one instance of the dialectal use, *o-imo-san* "(sweet) potato." In the western region of Japan, some food items are

called with the suffix *-san*, as in *o-kayu-san* "porridge," *o-mame-san* "beans," and *o-age-san* (for *atsuage*) "deep-fried tofu."

20. The term "cooking experts" as a translation of *ryōri-kenkyūka* (lit. cooking researcher) is an equivalent of "cook" in contrast with "chef" as the terms were used in Ferguson (2014).

21. Additional examples of her unorthodox cooking methods are easy to find. Nakahara (2017) explains that Kobayashi's recipe for *nikujaga* "meat and potato" calls for water instead of the standard *dashi*, the stock that is basic to Japanese-style cooking. Obviously, the substitution of water for dashi rids the need to make the stock. Her method of making dashi is also an instance of breaking the norm, but her reasons are always consistent with her philosophy of speed cooking without compromising flavorful taste (Kobayashi 2003).

22. Kobayashi (2015) was postmortemly published. According to a note at the end of the book, Kobayashi's then assistant Akiko Honda undertook a reproduction of Kobayashi's 1996 version published by Dainihon Tosho, and included her (=Honda's) own commentaries in the text, reminiscing about the days she worked with Kobayashi. Additional recipes in Kobayashi Katsuyo Kitchen Studio (2008) are also added to the 2015 version.

23. Kobayashi's advocacy for gender equality is not inconsistent with her strong conviction for cooking for her family. The relation between the two has also been discussed in Western contexts (e.g., Hollows 2003; Tunc 2018).

24. In Kobayashi (2015, 241), one of her assistants, Akiko Honda, recalls that Kobayashi frequently repeated, "those who are engaged in food should always be attentive to politics."

25. Harumi Kurihara (1947–), one of the leading *ryōri-kenkyūka* "cooking experts," is sometimes compared with Kobayashi among her contemporaries (e.g., Ako 2013, 2015; Kubo 2020). Kurihara solidified her fame after her 1992 bestseller cookbook, *Gochisōsama-ga Kikitakute* "I Want to Hear Thank You [for the meal]," and has been popular particularly among homemakers.

Chapter Seven

Construction of Gendered Images in Foodways

Association of gender with food and foodways is a topic that has been observed and discussed within a culture and across cultures from viewpoints of scholars in diverse disciplines (e.g., Lupton 1996; Sobal 2005; Wilk and Hintulian 2005; Chen 2012; Counihan 2012; Hamada 2017; Holtzman 2018). Examples of gendered food items that are commonly mentioned include meat and beer for men, and chocolate, salad, and yogurt for women. Gendered food items do not exist in a vacuum; they are closely tied to gender stereotypes entrenched in our daily activities around food. To give an anecdotal story, a former student of mine worked at a restaurant where she waited on a couple who always ordered the same dishes: the woman a hamburger and the man a salad. However, my student repeatedly switched the orders when she brought them to their table. She told me how difficult it was for her to defy the preconceived association between food and gender. It illustrates that in her mind, meat and salad are firmly gendered with men and women, respectively, without much room for perforation of the boundary.

In the dimension of consumerism, gender indexing is effectively used as a practical strategy that takes advantage of consumers' stereotype perceptions of products rigidly aligned with femininity or masculinity. This is amply attested in TV advertisements including Arby's and Burger King commercials. A series of Arby's TV commercials, for example, all end with "We have the meats," affirmed by a man with a deep voice.[1] The way that he avers ample meat in Arby's sandwiches and the low pitch of the voice that delivers the message project an image of a "manly man." Interestingly, when the boundary for gendering is, or needs to be, crossed, the food item might be termed differently to create a new image, like "brogurt" for a protein-rich yogurt marketed for men (Merwin 2013).

For another illustration of gendered food and stereotyped images, Chen (2012) discusses an intersection of gendering and racializing of meat and rice in the historical background of the California Gold Rush that started in the mid 19th century. Rice was one of the food items that represented Chinese immigrants at the time. The propaganda that favors white Americans and oppresses Chinese immigrants assumes the association of meat with "material abundance, power, and masculinity," and that of rice with "scarcity, weakness, and femininity" (p. 434). In this example, meat and rice carry social values, creating a boundary that distinguishes "us" from "others." Thus, food items can be aligned with a variety of identity canons such as gender, race, and socio-economic class, and their perceived images serve as convenient indexing tools for diverse social purposes.[2]

Gendering is observed with aspects of cooking as well. Cooking methods that use direct heat and those that require little preparation, such as grilling and barbecuing, as well as outdoor cooking in general are connected to men. Women have been typified to be fastidious about precise measuring. In a larger, social context, professional chefs are overwhelmingly men, whereas home cooking is considered women's responsibility. On the one hand, women's home cooking is taken for granted, men who cook at home, on the other, are celebrated as an exemplar of liberal or egalitarian views (cf. Sobal 2005, 2017; Szabo 2014a; Szabo and Koch 2017; Leer 2019). Notwithstanding a great deal of stereotyping involved in gendering of this sort, the divisions have been interpreted to stem from gender roles and gender norms in a hegemonic society. The traditional gender roles in the home kitchen are reflected even in cookbooks for children. In describing one of the pictorial illustrations in *Jolly Times Cookbook* published in 1934, Kugler (2018) notes, ". . . the artwork in 'Jolly Times Cookbook' depicts girls creating most of the dishes while the boys watch." It indicates that children from early on are exposed to the fixed idea of gendered roles in the domestic setting. The dichotomy of men's role as bread winners and women's role as home makers that is pervasive in a hegemonic society, thus, underlies and corelates with many gendered patterns in foodways.

As odd sounding as it may seem, tableware can be a target of gendering. Takei (2000) discusses that rice bowls (*meoto-jawan* "married.couple-bowl"), chopsticks (*meoto-bashi* "married.couple-chopsticks"), and teacups (the type without a handle for green tea) in Japan are paired for married couples and come in contrastive sizes and lengths. They are regarded as suitable gifts for newlywed couples. The larger (bowls) or longer (chopsticks) ware is for husbands, and the smaller or shorter one is for wives. These paired tableware items are also colored according to the gender. For example, brighter colors like red for wives, and darker colors like black and blue for husbands. Takei explains that since rice bowls, chopsticks, and teacups are held by hands, the contrast in size and length takes physical differences into practical consideration. Nevertheless, she suggests, the image of male hegemony is unescapable as part of traditional ideology regarding gender that has been reinforced by the Japanese society and culture.

In the late 2000s the word *sōshokukei-danshi* [grass.eating-men] "herbivore men" emerged in the Japanese society to describe the new type of men who do not fit the traditional image of masculinity, i.e., those who are gentler and less aggressive (Kroo 2018). Contrastive with it is *nikushokukei-joshi* [meat.eating-women] "carnivore women." The words *sōshokukei* and *nikushokukei* refer to common gender associations with grass (vegetables) and meat as criteria for femininity and masculinity, respectively. In the recent context, however, switching these descriptors for opposite gender assignments mirrors new characterizations and images of masculinity emerging in the society. Traditional masculinity has been epitomized by salaryman, a man who works diligently as the breadwinner of his family. In light of predispositions to food choices, men have been thought to prefer alcohol to sweets whereas women and children are considered to favor sweets. However, one of the food-related traits of the new *sōshokukei-danshi* is liking of sweets, which they do not hide, and distancing from alcohol. Thus, the term refers to a seemingly "emasculated" form of masculinity (Holtzman 2018).

Louisa Lim's reporting on "herbivore boys" on National Public Radio (NPR), broadcasted on November 25, 2009, sheds an interesting light to the shifting sense of masculinity held by these so-called herbivore men. They contrast with their fathers' salaryman generation, who symbolizes the economically prosperous society of the 1980s. These salarymen fathers glorified macho masculinity that is notably symbolized by alcohol consumption.[3] The report reveals that even though in reality men like and eat sweets just as women do, it is the cultural values that revolve around gendered food that constructed the traditional form of masculinity. And, the people, both men and women, have long responded to them with social expectations that accord with them. Thus, the emergence of *sōshokukei-danshi*, or perhaps better put, the emerging concept of *sōshokukei-danshi* and public discussions over it mean shifting perspectives of individual values that construct a new face of masculinity, rather than a representation of an "emasculated" form of masculinity. In addition, not only the way food becomes gendered but language representations of gendered food, such as *sōshokukei-danshi* and *nikushokukei-joshi*, reveal transformed characterizations of men and women and the society's ideological expectations of them. The contrast between men in the salaryman generation and *sōshokukei-danshi* in the 21st century indicates that social expectations and cultural values undergo transitions over time, and so does gender identity.

This chapter aims at exploring images of gendered foodways in the context of Japanese language and society. I intend to examine the ways and contexts in which gender and masculinity are shadowed in Japanese food discourse, as they are represented by food and food writing. More specifically, I will first survey how coffee has been promoted in the commercial market and to what extent images of masculinity play a role in the process. Coffee was introduced to Japan as early as the 17th century. Its circulation in the public has gone through different stages in Japanese history, but the gender images associated with its taste have also evolved over time. I will examine the transformation of the images that are represented in the language of advertisements particularly through the lens of gendered sweet-bitter dichotomy known as the pairing of *amatō* and *karatō*.

As another case study, I will look at cookbooks for men and comic books whose storylines are built around cooking men. There are quite a few comic books with food and cooking themes distributed in Japan, but the ones I examine in this chapter contain recipes that are similar in content to cookbooks in the more standard format. These cookbooks, broadly conceived, shed an interesting light to various conceptual paths to constructing masculinity. I will examine how social and cultural changes in gender roles and subsequently in images of masculinity are mirrored in cookbooks catered toward, and written by, men. While making a brief note on the linguistic indexing of gender where relevant, my textual analysis will primarily focus on aspects and contexts of communication, including what is communicated, how, and why.

Continuing to be couched in the conceptual framework for identity to which I have subscribed in chapter 6, my examinations of gender matters concerning cookery discourse in this chapter assume a performative view of gender. This approach is advocated by Butler (1990) and has been applied to analyzing language and communication data. As is echoed by the sociolinguistic literature such as works by Cameron (1997, 2008), Kiesling (1997), Bucholtz and Hall (2005), and Meyerhoff and Ehrlich (2019), among others, the performative view expects masculinity to emerge in different and often unorthodox ways through communicative acts, as summarized by Cameron (1997, 50): "[p]eople do perform gender differently in different contexts, and do sometimes behave in ways we would normally associate with the 'other' gender." As a consequence, femininity and masculinity are enacted in plural ways according to the social contexts. Upon considering the study of gender and the study of food and cooking, the performative view is consistent with a model of masculinity which endorses multiple modes of masculinities that are "situationally enacted" (Sobal 2005) by individuals through social interactions, as opposed to a view that statically essentializes masculinity to a set of social norms that are expected of men. Situated in these conceptual frameworks, discussions in this chapter focus on the two contexts in which images of masculinity are projected.

My inquiry revolves around linguistic aspects—language and discourse—of advertisements for coffee on the one hand and cookbooks and comic books with recipes on the other. These types of sources are popular artifacts created by authors, editors, and publishers for commercial profit, and as such, one may claim that they do not directly or necessarily depict actual (and quantifiable) views, attitudes, and behavior of the people in the society at the intersection of food and gender. The goal of this chapter, however, is not so much about how masculinities are constructed around food and cooking in Japanese society as how the language of advertisements and the language and discourse in cookery books represent perceived or perceivable images of masculinities that pertain to food and foodwork. Studying gender and American cookbooks over time, Neuhaus (2003, 2) observes: "[c]ookbooks echoed a national debate about women's social roles in general and represented particular kinds of food and cooking as gendered." She recognizes significant scholarly contributions that cookbooks make, and further states: "[p]opular texts warrant close examination because they enable us to reconstruct the norms, visual images, and received truths that encased and thus could not help but influence daily lives" (pp. 3–4). Similarly, coffee advertisements to be discussed below share much of these contributions that cookbooks make. In this regard, Barthes's (2013, 27) reflections of the role that advertisements play is helpful: "[t]here is no question that advertising provides only a projected image of reality; but the sociology of mass communication has become increasingly inclined to think that large-scale advertising, even though technically the work of a particular group, reflects the collective psychology much more than it shapes it." Advertisements sometimes follow and sometimes inject gender norms that were or will be widespread in the society.

In the Japanese context, Yuen's (2014) examinations and discussions of a TV program hosted by two men and their cookbook based on the show serve as an apt example that illustrates the relevance of these media forms contributing much to analyzing gender and social norms that give rise to alternative ways of viewing them. I examine the same cookbook in Yuen's article at the end of section 2 of this chapter. Aoyama (2003, 2008, 2010) analyzes gender, masculinity, and food as they are portrayed in Japanese literature and comic books. In these studies, she illustrates that the narrative on food and cooking informs us of the social structure, class, gender roles, and the like. So, explorations of advertisements, cookbooks, and comic books on cooking in this chapter will be an addition to the existing body of literature that deals with the topic of food and society, presenting interesting observations and conclusions. Furthermore, as a type of communication conduits, advertisements and cookery writing can offer a glimpse at, or insight into, the implications that food and foodwork may have to the ways that the society perceives gender identities. It is with this implicit reasoning that I discuss images of masculinities projected in food and gender narratives, drawing from the two contexts, coffee advertisements and men's cookbooks.

1 GENDERED IMAGES OF COFFEE

The taste of coffee is typically characterized as bitter in Japan, and the bitterness of coffee plays a central role in gendering the beverage with men. I will discuss the bitter taste in its pairing with sweetness, but in order to situate bitter taste in the discourse on the intersection between gender and gendered food, it is helpful to give a brief background of gendered taste flavors in relation to gender dichotomy. The association is best illustrated by the terms *amatō* and *karatō*.

1.1. The Notion of *Amatō* and *Karatō*

As I mentioned in chapter 5 (section 2), the terms *ama-tō* "(lit.) sweet-sect" and *kara-tō* "(lit.) spicy-sect" refer respectively to those who have a sweet tooth and those who have the liking of alcohol. *Kara* of *kara-tō* is the base part of the adjective *karai* "spicy (also salty)," which basically amounts to strong, pungent tastes that branch out to spicy, salty, and sour tastes as well as alcohol, according to Kopii (1992). In gender alignment, women and children are considered *amatō* and men *karatō*. Furthermore, the two words are not meant to overlap but are strictly divided. The gendered associations are, thus, not interpreted to cross, and the gender ideology has come to be part of the social and cultural norm that has been entrenched in the society for a long time.[4,5] Stereotypical representations of the association between sweet taste (typically confection) and women are ubiquitously seen in commercial advertisements.

To illustrate, during the 1960s–1970s in Japan, sweetness together with creaminess is presented in Meiji Seika's chocolate advertisements as a trait of female liking and femaleness. The bar of chocolate under the name of *Hi Milk Chocolate* was marketed with catch phrases like *redī-no chokorēto* "chocolate for ladies," *miruku-ga tappuri* "full of cream," and *onna-no-ko-dake-no chokorēto* "chocolate only for girls." The chocolate bar that is companioned with *Hi Milk Chocolate* is *Black Chocolate*, catered toward male consumers. It features a less sweet taste with a tint of bitterness, which characterizes purported men's taste choice. Note that bitterness is placed in *karatō* in the gendering norm of the sweet (*amatō*) vs. alcohol (*karatō*) polar opposition. A series of catch phrases suggests that bitter taste shadows manliness. Exemplary phrases that align the bitter taste and masculinity include *amasa-o koroshita otoko-no chokorēto* "men's chocolate with killed [=reduced] sweetness," *dansei-muki-no ii chokorēto* "nice chocolate for men," *horo-nigai shigeki* "slightly bitter stimulus," *nigami-bashitta atarashii aji* "a new, manly taste," and *nigami-bashitta ii chokorēto* "nice manly chocolate." The word *nigami-bashitta* in the last two examples is a compound consisting of *nigami*, which is the noun form of *nigai* "bitter," but the compound itself does not refer to the food taste of bitterness. Instead, it uniquely characterizes a man who has a sober, refined face—an element that defines virility. So, even without specific references to *otoko* "man" or *dansei* "man," the catch phrases *nigami-bashitta atarashii aji* "a new, manly taste" and *nigami-bashitta ii chokorēto* "nice manly chocolate" strongly insinuate a masculine image of the product. The gendered tastes, totally aligned with the concepts of *amatō* and *karatō*, are further reinforced by appealing to visual effects of color indexing of gender. The wrapper of *Hi Milk Chocolate* is red whereas that of *Black Chocolate* is black. This certainly comports with the pattern of gender coding by color as it is applied to Japanese tableware mentioned earlier. The masculinity that *Black Chocolate* projects through the multi-modal appeals (taste and vision senses) is highlighted by another catch phrase, *kuro isshoku-de tsutsumikonda chokorēto* "chocolate wrapped only in black."

The bitter taste in these chocolate advertisements is primarily used in the polar opposition to sweetness, but the bitterness of beer products provides a direct connection between food taste and males. *Nigami* "bitterness" is characteristic of beer, and the effort of its promotion is readily detectable in the product name *Shihuku-no Nigami* "blissful bitterness" by Sapporo Beer. It should be remembered that beer, as an alcoholic beverage, exemplifies a drink choice of *karatō* to which men belong according to the social norm. So, ranging from the genuinely bitter taste of beer to the comparatively less sweet taste of *Black Chocolate*, the term *nigami*, <u>in reality</u>, covers a wide gamut of tastes. On the other hand, the word has an undeniably priming tone that associates with masculinity and therefore serves as a convenient marketing tool. Its derivational connection with *nigami-bashitta* "manly (in characterizing a man's face)," as explained above, thus helps establish *nigami* as a key word that linguistically indexes a manly man's image.

The *amatō* vs. *karatō* dichotomy has been deeply rooted in the Japanese diet culture with significant social implications. However, just as the aforementioned NPR report by Louisa Lim reveals, Holtzman (2018) uncovers updated reactions to the normative ideology that younger generations of Japanese hold in today's society. Parallel to the transformations illustrated by the emergence of the *sōshokukei-danshi* [grass.eating-men] "herbivore men" mentioned earlier, Holtzman studies how the *amatō* vs. *karatō* distinction as a social and cultural concept and their purported stereotypical gender identity reside in people's beliefs and behaviors. In real life there are indeed men who opt for sweets and men who cannot drink alcohol, falling out of the stereotypical opposition, even among the age cohort of salarymen who thrived through the economic peak of the 1980s. Such perceived emasculated form of masculine identity sometimes drives them to being closet sweet-tooths. In contrast, younger generations of men who are regarded as *sōshokukei-danshi* [grass. eating-men] "herbivore men" are more open than their parents' generation in not denying their preference of confections. Nevertheless, the challenge that these younger men face is the public perception that their masculinity is weakened because of the stance they openly take about preferring sweets. Holtzman is interested in how the sweets-loving men negotiate their own attitude toward sweets and the stereotypical view that *amatō* men are identified with weakened masculinity. Responses to his real time interviews are met with "ambiguous" and "uncertain" sentiments. Some men adamantly reject the stereotypes, to the extent that they even deny their existence. But simultaneously, the same men are anxious as to how their stance would look like in the public eye. Holtzman also reports on men who do not find anything odd about men liking sweets or the public perception of it as being out of the norm. His examination of sweets-loving Japanese men points to an intriguing way of situating gender and food in the construction of culture, as he concludes below.

> The point is not whether the Japanese (albeit shifting) stereotype that sweets lovers are more effeminate *really* is true, or even if this stereotype is *really* deeply felt or even has wide purchase. Rather, it is the fact that there are many ways that it is both true and not true; it can simultaneously be both deeply felt, lived, experienced and fraught at the same time that it is dismissed as a trifling inanity. There is, then, much to consider here, not only about the relationship of gender and eating but the ways in which cultural systems—culinary or otherwise—are constructed and lived. (p. 292, emphasis original)

Interestingly, the concepts of *amatō* and *karatō*, the stereotypical gender identities attached to them or indexed by them, and the way in which the Japanese people view them and behave around them are all integral elements to be considered in looking at how coffee has been marketed in the Japanese society over time.

1.2. The Bitterness of Coffee

Although coffee was introduced to Japan as early as the 17th century by Dutch traders, it was more actively spread in the late 19th century especially through the establishment of cafés (Kamo 1999; Tanaka 2017). One of the first such cafés includes Café Paulista located in Tokyo. Café Paulista marketed coffee under the catch phrase, "black as a demon, sweet as love, and hot as hell"[6] (Kuga 2007; Takai 2014). The reference to the "sweet" taste obviously means added sugar, and the practice of serving coffee with sugar seems to have been adopted from the beginning of coffee consumption in Japan. Generally, coffee advertisements did not single out the bitter taste of coffee as its stand-out attribute. Tanaka (2017, 112) notes that the bitterness of coffee in the early days was particularly strong, and many people drank it with much sugar.

While coffee at cafés originally attracted the upper-class and literary intellectuals, the industry attempted to make it widely available to the larger population. In this effort, women's magazines played an important role to broaden the circulation of coffee especially through home consumption. Kuga (2008, 2009, 2010) details the process of marketing coffee in advertisements and relevant articles that appeared in women's magazines for the first 40 years of the 20th century. One of the three major women's magazines at the time was *Shuhu-no Tomo* "Housewives' Friend," which catered toward general female audiences and gained popularity. The magazine's motto was "for family happiness and improvement of women's status" (Kuga 2008, 21). Advertisements of (brewed) coffee advanced the connection between women's elegance and drinking coffee, while at the same time instructing women to brew coffee for domestic consumption. MJB Coffee regularly posted one-page advertisements in the *Shuhu-no Tomo* magazine. The adverts printed in the late 1920s, for instance, accompany illustrations of ladies, some in kimono and others in Western clothing, with stylishly coiffed hair. The captions vary depending on the magazine issue, but the pages always include the uniform characterization of the coffee as having a refreshing aroma and rich taste. Another women's magazine, *Hujingahō* "Women's Pictorial," has advertisements for Brazilian coffee.[7] Of the magazine's advertisements, those that appeared in the 1930s show photographs of a pair or a group of ladies in the background. The women were dressed fashionably in Japanese or Western attire and depicted as having a leisurely conversation over coffee served in a cup with a saucer. As Kuga (2007) aptly points out, these coffee ads in the women's magazines consistently generate and ingrain the image in their reader's mind that strongly links together women, elegance, and coffee.[8]

As for home consumption, coffee was newly introduced to the Japanese food scene, where green tea had been the primary and habitual choice of the nation's non-alcoholic beverage. So, how to brew it was a serious practical question if people wanted to drink it at home, rather than (or in addition to) ordering it at cafés. Coffee companies recognized the need to teach housewives how to brew coffee at home in order to widen the consumer market. In surveying a progressive women's magazine, *Hujin-Sekai* "Women's World" (1906–1933), Kuga (2010) examines articles that deal with broad topics about coffee. Some of them are instructions for brewing hot and cold coffee for domestic purposes. Based on the articles she found on coffee, drinking coffee with sugar was indeed the norm.

The brief sketch of how coffee was marketed in the early 20th century suggests several points. First, the narrative introducing and promoting coffee consumption does not associate coffee as a drink or its bitter taste with a particular gender. Also, coffee does not enter the context of the *amatō* and *karatō* opposition. It seems that coffee is not considered a gendered beverage from either marketing or consumer perspectives. Second, sugar is described as a standard and assumed accompaniment to coffee, regardless of who drinks it. Here again, sugar as a condiment for coffee is not regarded in terms of a gendered preference. Third, at least coffee advertisements in some of the well circulated women's magazines at the time generate an image that elegant women drink coffee or an image that the coffee drinking behavior is elegant. Either image is well situated in the progressively Westernizing society of prewar Japan. Nevertheless, the situation of coffee-drinking women that is tied with the projected image of feminine elegance in adverts does not seem to have fully developed into a social perception strong enough to associate coffee with women or femininity.

A gendered image of coffee was constructed for the marketing of canned coffee, in which masculinity was manifested. Starting in the 1970s, canned coffee was targeted for men. In particular, "heavy users"—consumers who drink canned coffee multiple times a day—are men in their late 20s to 30s, salarymen, as well as truck drivers and construction workers (Takai 2014). As for its taste, it is widespread knowledge that canned coffee is generally very sweet, although there have been brands that feature less or no added sugar in more recent years (Yamazaki 1993; Takai 2014). The packaging of *Pokka Coffee* distinguishes between the regular and café au lait flavors by colors, brown-black for the former and red for the latter (Yamazaki 1993). The milk-rich version in a red can is suggestive of female liking, as it is reminiscent of the color coding of the Meiji chocolate bar, *Hi Milk*, discussed earlier. Definitive language used to promote canned no-sugar coffee clearly indicates that less or no sugar is unmistakably a liking of men. Yamazaki (1993, 51) inserts a newspaper advertisement of a canned coffee by the Pokka Corporation that he preserved. The new Pokka product was introduced to the market in the 1980s under the name *Pokka Mr. Coffee*, suggesting exclusively male propriety. The caption says "[we, men] have graduated from coffee that is only sweet." The phrase of "graduating" from sweet taste also induces a sense of the fully mature adult. Distancing from the overly sweet taste, canned coffee with no added sugar has picked up its distribution. It is typically marketed in black labels as the color virtually indexes men's consumption of these products. In addition, the masculine image of the no-sugar canned coffee is reinforced by TV commercials that use male actors and singers. For instance, UCC announced in a 2016 news release that a famous singer, Keisuke Kuwata, will appear in a commercial for *UCC BLACK Mutō* "UCC Black no sugar" under the concept "Men's Black."[9]

The number of canned and bottled coffee is large. That Ikeda (2013) reports on a taste test of 14 coffee products with no added sugar suggests that canned and bottled black coffee is widely distributed. The report has a caption that starts with *otoko-wa damatte burakku!* [men-TOP silently black], which roughly translates as "men silently drink coffee black." This elliptical phrase models after the Sapporo Beer commercial, which ran between the 1950s and 1980s with a renowned actor, Toshio Mihune. Mihune frequently appeared in samurai movies directed by Akira Kurosawa and is considered to embody masculinity. So, Mihune's profile of manly man drinking beer is superimposed on the masculine image of a man drinking black coffee. A series of TV commercials for black coffee follow the same phrasing of *otoko-wa damatte X*, [men-TOP silently X] "Men silently X." So, this parallelism serves to treat both beer and black coffee as masculine drinks. Furthermore, the reference to *damatte* "silently" is associated with another culturally held masculine value of not talking much while at the same time, totally distancing men from women who are characterized as liking to talk.

The generated masculine image of black coffee applies to bottled coffee as well. An online site that primarily introduces new *shōchū* (strong spirits) features a bottled coffee by Marumiya Coffee in Kumamoto.[10] The commentator quotes the owner's (i.e., the coffee producer's) description of the coffee's prominent taste that is enriched by a locally known natural salt. This bottled coffee does contain a small amount of sugar. The brief announcement ends with the comment that consumers will be satisfied with this product, which he calls *otoko-no naka-no otoko-no kōhī* "manly man's coffee." This is not a social media posting by Marumiya Coffee itself, but the commentator is indeed promoting the masculine image that the bottled coffee is purported to have, namely, the gendered taste of bitterness rather than sweetness.

In addition, the product name presents a linguistic and orthographic ingenuity in terms of the masculinity that the bottled coffee intends to exude. The online announcement reports that the name of the coffee product is *nigamibashitta otoko-no kōhī* にがみばしった男の珈琲, but a small photo of it, which is placed at the upper righthand corner, reveals that a punctuation mark is placed in the first part of the name, *nigamibashitta*, as in (1).

(1) にがみば・しった ［男の珈琲］
nigamiba・shitta [otoko-no kōhī]

Recall that earlier we briefly discussed the phrase *nigamibashitta* in relation to the catch phrases like *nigami-bashitta atarashii aji* "a new, manly taste" and *nigami-bashitta ii chokorēto* "nice manly chocolate," which are used in marketing dark chocolate bars for men. Although *nigami* independently means bitterness (as in taste), *nigamibashitta* is a descriptor specific to a solemn and refined face of a virile man, and as such it symbolizes unambiguous masculinity. The name of the coffee product in (1), thus, would be interpreted as "coffee for a manly man" if no punctuation were placed between *nigami* and *bashitta*. Cleverness resides in the linguistic characteristic of the Kumamoto dialect in which the punctuation plays an important role in this product name. The orthographical separation of *nigamiba* from *shitta* prompts the interpretation that *shitta* is a verb to mean "know." In this local dialect, furthermore, *-ba* after the noun *nigami* functions as a marker for direct object, corresponding to *-o* in the standard dialect. Putting all parts together, then, *nigamiba shitta* means "know bitterness," and ultimately the name of the coffee is "coffee for a man who knows bitterness." This interpretation is appreciated even more in the context of the *amatō* vs. *karatō* dichotomy. Someone who "knows bitterness" in this context is regarded as a coffee connoisseur who has deep knowledge of and appreciation for the bitter taste and pungent flavor. Thus, the word *nigami* in the name contributes to the language play around an attributive taste of coffee, which is consistent with what *karatō* is believed to represent. Together, the rhetoric centering on the coffee product constructs an image of ruggedly handsome men who are knowledgeable coffee connoisseurs. Its intension is to capture male consumers' attention especially in the local (i.e., Kumamoto) context. It is intriguing to see advertisers make remarkably creative use of a wide range of linguistic knowledge in constructing masculine images as a strategic tool to communicate with a target audience.

The effort to impose masculinity—sometimes hyper-masculinity—on canned and bottled coffee since the latter half of the 20th century to date is palpable even in the limited instances of advertisements discussed above. Notably, the rhetorical strategy does not directly capitalize on the bitter taste of coffee itself as a favorable and ideal tenet to relate to male identity. Instead, it relies on the opposite concept, namely, departure from or suppression of sweetness, as a commercialized icon of masculinity. The name of the bottled coffee, n*igamibashitta otoko-no kōhī* in (1), contains the word *nigami* "bitterness," yet it is in the presence of the dual interpretations, embedded in the unique linguistic and orthographic context, that makes the naming effectively eye-catching. Crucially, these rhetorical representations of masculine images with which coffee adverts attempt to appeal to male consumers are grounded on the conceptual dichotomy of *amatō* vs. *karatō*. Then, taking Holtzman's (2018) conclusion into consideration, masculine image and identity that are constructed around gendered coffee products portrays how deeply the *amatō* vs. *karatō* concept and their embodying stereotypes are entrenched in the fabric of society as a cultural pattern of their dietary life.

2 HOME COOKING AND COOKING MEN

Home cooking has been viewed as women's domestic responsibility in many cultures. In that context, men who cook at home for their families provide an interesting topic to examine concerning gender roles and masculinity. Indeed, there have been multidisciplinary studies that investigate men who are willingly engaged in home cooking, as articles in Szabo and Koch (2017), for instance, attest to. The Japanese proverb, *danshi chūbō-ni hairazu* (男子厨房に入らず) "men should not be in the kitchen," reflects a traditional view that was held in the society of male hegemony for a long time. That said, just as we observe with the societal transitions suggested by the afore-mentioned term *sōshokukei-danshi* [grass.eating-men] "herbivore men," the perspectives of home cooking, both by males and by females, have been changing in Japan. In this section, I will examine how such shifting views toward "men's cooking" are mirrored in cookbooks for men that are written by men. In my examination, I also include comic books that contain recipes, since they share with standard cookbooks one of the goals of cookery writing, namely, communicating with the reader through cooking instructions and related matters that pertain to food and foodwork.

2.1. Three Waves of Men's Cooking

It is helpful to see a chronological overview that summarizes the social and economic landscape of Japan during the last quarter of the 20th century, since it provides background in which men's views toward home cooking transformed. Murakami (2000) considers primarily three stages during the last 30 years of the 20th century. The changing sociocultural and economic circumstances motivated men to cook at home for diverse reasons. It is true that despite the old proverb mentioned above, there were indeed men who (like to) cook in domestic environments, but the traditional norm and negative public perceptions around it generate the idea that it is a shameful thing for men to cook in the home kitchen.

A new trend starts to appear in the 1970s that promotes men's cooking. One forefront propagator was Katsuhiko Nakamura's 1975 book *Danshi Chūbō-ni Haire—Onna-no Daidokoro-o Kokuhatsu-suru!!* "Men should be in the kitchen [lit. Men, enter the kitchen]—Denounce women's kitchen!!" (published by Kobunsha). The first part of the title, *danshi chūbō-ni haire* "enter the kitchen," is a twist of the old proverb, changing the negative *hairazu* "not enter" to the affirmative *haire* "enter," encouraging men to cook at home. However, the tone is not that of advocating gender equality in domestic chores.[11] The second half of the title along with the double exclamation marks, *Onna-no Daidokoro-o Kokuhatsu-suru!!* "denounce women's kitchen!!," does not merely defy the concept that the kitchen is a domestic space for women. It also sounds as if it purports the superiority of men's cooking. As Murakami explains, "men's cooking" in this context is more in line with "Sunday cooking" and "cooking as hobby" than cooking as daily responsibility, to which women were still assigned at the time. This idea of cooking by men parallels to "leisurely entertainment, culinary artistry, or performance" (Szabo 2014a, 229) and "self-oriented leisure" (Szabo 2014b, 18). The contrast between men's cooking and women's cooking during this wave also corresponds with Bourdieu's references to the "tastes of luxury (or freedom)" and "tastes of necessity" (Bourdieu 1984, 177), which illuminate reasons and circumstances of home cooking that men and women are each engaged with. The first wave of the new trend-setter in the 1970s sends men willingly to the (non-professional) kitchen, but the idea about domestic cooking and gender roles does not cross far beyond the hegemonic boundary that the proverb *danshi chūbō-ni hairazu* "men should not be in the kitchen" firmly draws.

Murakami recognizes that the second wave of cooking men started to appear in the 1980s. Motivated by practical needs for self-help and independence, these men cook their own daily meals. Many of them are single men, elderly widowers, and married men who are relocated to local branches, living apart from their families. According to Murakami, access to convenience stores and ready-made food coupled with common appliances like refrigerators and microwaves made it easier than before for single men and relocated married men to take care of their daily meals. As expedient as they are, though, store-bought meals begin to pall if one must rely on them day after day, and concerns for a balanced diet eventually arise. In addition, Murakami explains, younger men may find genuine pleasure in cooking as cooking for oneself sets in as a daily routine.

As for elderly men, they are the generation of men who grew up deeply embedded in the philosophy of *danshi chūbō-ni hairazu* "men should not be in the kitchen," and thus had very little or no experience of cooking. Yet, their wives' illnesses and deaths may leave them home alone. As the aging population of Japan increases, men's inability to cook is no longer a personal problem but a social issue that has a variety of adverse consequences. It is in this environment that practical cookbooks, cooking shows on TV, and cooking schools started to emerge and drew men's serious attention. Unlike the first wave, the level of cooking is kept introductory since the primary goal is to receive basic, hands-on instructions that are easy to follow and build one's confidence. So, the type of defiance to women's home cooking that underlies the first wave of men's cooking is not the sentiment found among the cooking men and their facilitators in the second wave. In the continuously aging society today, this trend is still active as is evidenced by the number of men's cooking groups, *danshi chūbō-ni hairō-kai* (or *dan-chū-kai* for short) mentioned in endnote 11. These group gatherings have been organized throughout Japan today.

Finally, the third wave is characterized by men who cook as part of shared domestic responsibilities with their wives, similar to what Szabo (2014a) refers to as "joint family project." The number of these men started to increase in the 1990s. They are called *shuhu* (主夫) "house husband" as a new term, paired with the homophonous *shuhu* (主婦) "house wife," although it does not mean that they are stay-at-home husbands. With the enactment of the Equal Employment Opportunity Law in 1986 as a social and economic springboard, a growing number of women started to work just like their husbands. The men described in the first wave can and do cook, but importantly they do not do so as a daily routine. As Murakami points out, cooking for the family after coming back from work every day can be time consuming and labor intensive. At the same time, figuring out the menu each day is quite a burden. Cleaning up after meals is also part of the domestic duty. Recognizing fairness in sharing household responsibilities with their working partners, the cooking men in the third wave willingly participate in domestic chores. Notwithstanding the new trend that is founded on an egalitarian view of gender roles in domestic duties, however, Murakami notes (at the time of her writing in 2000) that the time men and women spend in household activities is still unevenly distributed. Equal division of domestic labor is an attitude that motivates the third wave cooking men, but only 30% of male students in a college survey consider the equality in domestic work to be an ideal. A compounding reason as to why equal gender roles in the domestic environment may not be sustainable, Murakami adds, has to do with the reality that there are women who cannot cook.[12]

Murakami does not cover the 21st century, but at the turn of a new century, the national discourse around *sōshokukei-danshi* and similar concepts coupled with their social and domestic implications point to the current situation that considers gender equality more constructively. Today, family no longer entails marriage or a heterosexual couple, and the number of men and women who opt to stay unmarried has been rising. An ideological shift in gender roles, thus, is necessitated by these changes in the social fabric. At the same time, it offers alternative ways to think about cooking by men and cooking by women from new angles.

2.2. Images of Cooking Men

I shall turn to four types of cookery writing in which different images of cooking men are projected. The cookbooks by men and comic books of the men's cooking theme that I examine were published after the very end of the 20th century. The images depicted in these sources reflect overlapping characteristics of the trends pertinent to the concepts and practices of cooking men surveyed just above. So, the four types into which I classify my samples capture cooking men differently from one another, but each type does not exclusively correspond to the conceptual basis for men's cooking that can be attributed to a specific transitional stage observed in the Japanese society of the 20th and 21st centuries. It is demonstrated that constructed images of cooking men in these samples are often multi-faceted.

Cooking men in the first wave, as discussed above, are skillful and proud cooks. They view that cooking is a hobby that they are willingly engaged in. Their version of cooking is different from, and to their mind even superior to, women's daily home cooking, which they consider tedious and unexciting. Cookbooks that are written under a similar premise frequently use the phrase *otoko-no ryōri* (男の料理) "men's cooking" and its equivalent in the titles (e.g., Shimizu 1975; Chiseisha 1990; Nishikawa 1996; Nishi 2007). It immediately begs the question of what is meant by *otoko-no ryōri* and what sense of masculinity underlies it.

Shoji (1984, 7), for example, essentializes men's cooking to "four 'no' laws": no ingenuity, not taking time, no advanced technique, and not minding style or manner.[13] In the prose-style recipe for roast beef, which calls for flambéing a chunk of meat, he comments that the flame makes him feel brave, and announces, "this IS men's cooking!" (p. 90). Applications of direct heat have been considered a gendered cooking method in other cultures as well (e.g., Wilk and Hintulian 2005). Furthermore, Tamamura (1999, 143–45) refers to anthropological observations that men's and women's cooking manners are contrasted as being uncivilized/primitive vs. cultured/refined.[14] Arising from these remarks may be the contrast between nature and culture, in a similar manner that Lévi-Strauss (2013) considers roasting and the unelaborated to represent nature while boiling and the elaborated to exemplify culture.

These two aspects—nature and the unelaborated—constitute a connecting theme of the cookbooks that overtly publicize *otoko-no ryōri* "men's cooking" and are reflected not only in recipe choices (both ingredients and cooking methods) but in presentation styles. To illustrate, Chiseisha's (1990) *Otoko-no Ryōri: Yasei-ni Kaeru* "Men's Cooking: Return to Wild Nature" is a recipe compilation contributed by professional chefs and public figures including celebrities and writers who are supposed to be skillful in cooking. They are cooking men who correspond, in concept, to those in the first wave discussed above. The recipes feature meats, wild game, and fish. Both the title and photo presentations in the book explicitly point to the nature-and-the-unelaborated theme. For instance, the beginning of the instructions for beef jerky shows a photo which consists of a large lump of raw, red meat as the primary ingredient and beef jerky as the resulting form. I should hasten to add that beef jerky speaks clearly to rarity as a choice of recipe and confirms that the type of cooking represents "culinary artistry," "cooking as hobby," or "tastes of luxury." Another recipe gives step-by-step instructions for cooking whole fish in an outdoor setting. Both fish and side dishes of assorted potatoes are cooked in foil over direct heat. The potatoes are unpeeled and are either cooked whole or cut into large pieces. Furthermore, the instruction depicts how to eat the whole fish by removing the skin by hand. The choice of ingredients, the manner of cooking and serving, and the visual presentations of each aspect of cooking procedures are well aligned with the "wild nature" theme of the book.

Furthermore, some other photographic inserts are surprisingly grotesque. Two recipes, one for roasting a whole pig and another for sautéed rabbit with mushroom sauce, are prefaced by large photos showing a pig and a wild rabbit that have just been slaughtered. In the case of the rabbit recipe, the same picture also depicts a couple of live ones in the cage. Side by side, they are lined up with another photo of how cooked dishes look like, as if they were the "before" and "after" pictures. These photographic exposures of what will be cooked and eaten are connected to the masculine image of hunting. Considering the choice of ingredients and the feast-like occasions for which the recipes are intended, "men's cooking" here is apparently tailored toward a narrow group of men with wealth and high social class. As rare as this type of vivid visual presentations appears in cookbooks, however, if evoking images of strong physical manhood is the attained goal that the cookbook aims to communicate through the visual apparatus, it seems to be a bit too hyperbolic and unappetizing. In contrast, the language of the recipe texts maintains the standard neutral (as opposed to men's or women's) style without linguistically indexing the male gender (e.g., by sentence-final particles or vocabulary choice).

Another conceptual characterization of *otoko-no ryōri* is simplicity in the cooking process, as mentioned in Shoji's "four 'no' laws." Adding to that is a fearless, confident manner in carrying them out.[15] Nishi (2007), for instance, contains much vocabulary that refers to those traits. The attitude underlying the title is reminiscent of cooking men in the first wave: *Otoko-no Reshipi—Daitan. Gōkai. Shinpuru. Onna-mo Tsukuritakunaru Otokomae-no Ryōri* "Men's Recipes—Bold. Magnificent. Simple. Handsome Men's Cooking that Women Also Want to Try." The last part of the subtitle suggests that the recipes introduced in Nishi's cookbook offer a renewed sense of cooking, which separates "handsome men's cooking" from ordinary everyday cooking that women take on. The words like *daitan* "bold, fearless," *gōkai* "magnificent, enthralling," *shinpuru* "simple," and *dainamikku* "dynamic" are cues with which this cookbook attempts to appeal to the reader's masculinity. They recur repeatedly throughout the cookbook, but a close look at the contexts of the vocabulary use reveals that their reference to masculinity is not always explicit.

We first examine those cue words that suggest masculinity (i.e., *daitan* "bold, fearless," *gōkai* "magnificent, enthralling," *shinpuru* "simple," *dainamikku* "dynamic") in relatively clear contexts. They include those in (2–4). Individual vocabulary items of the key words and others that suggest manly images are bold-faced.

(2) 数ある調理法の中でも、<u>際立って**豪快**かつ**男らしい**印象を与える「焼く」という行為</u>

Kazu aru chōrihō-no naka-de-mo, <u>kiwadatte **gōkai** katsu **otoko-rashii** inshō-o ataeru "yaku"-to iu kōi</u>

"of many cooking methods, the action of *yaku* [roast, fry, broil] gives <u>the impression of notable **magnificence** and **manliness**</u>" (p. 21)

(3) 割り箸を口に刺し込み、えらをフックにして一気にひねり、はらわたを抜き出す。包丁いらず、これぞ**男**のテクニック。

Waribashi-o kuchi-ni sashikomi, era-o hukku-ni shite ikki-ni hineri, harawata-o nukidasu. Hōchō irazu, korezo **otoko**-no tekunikku.

"Stick a chopstick into the mouth [of mackerel]; hook the gill and twist it at once; and remove the guts. No knife is needed, this IS **men's technique**." (p. 26)

(4) オーブンから取り出した瞬間、歓声が上がることは間違いなし。<u>手で骨を持ち、**豪快**にむしゃぶりつく</u>のがうまい。

Ōbun-kara toridashita shunkan, kansei-ga agaru koto-wa machigai nashi. <u>Te-de hone-o mochi, **gōkai**-ni mushaburitsuku</u>-no-ga umai.

"Getting cheer is guaranteed as soon as [the spare rib] is taken out of the oven. It tastes good when you <u>hold the bones by hand and **grandly** devour it</u>." (p. 30)

I discussed the cooking method of *yaku₁* and *yaku₂* in chapter 4. Nishi's cookbook has a section for recipes centering around the *yaku* method, which mostly refers to *yaku₂* ([-Water] [-Fat] [+Direct heat] [+Gridiron]). (2–4) appear in that section and the cooking method featured in it include direct heat, corresponding to grilling and torching, although oven-roasting is mentioned in (4). The use of direct heat has been gendered with men, and the general introduction to recipes with the *yaku₂* method in (2) states that the *yaku₂* action stands out as magnificent and manly. (3) is a portion of the instructions for grilled salted mackerel. The instruction of removing the fish guts suggests the use of hands, rather than utensils like a knife, and a presumed degree of physical strength resulting from twisting (*hineru*) the fish and pulling the guts out (*nuki-dasu*). Recall that the use of hands is adopted in the grilled fish recipe in Chiseisha (1990) discussed earlier. Thus, the underlined phrase in (3), *otoko-no tekunikku* "men's technique," is equated with the manner of preparation that demonstrates physical strength. (4) is a recipe for oven-roasted pork spare ribs. The suggested manner of eating the roasted ribs by hand evokes a masculine image of consuming boned meat without using utensils. In particular, the underlined verb, *mushaburitsuku*, calls up a scene in which a wild animal wolfs down its prey, rather than elegantly tasting it bit by bit with silverware. Besides (2–4), a similar tone is repeated with the word *daitan* "bold, fearless." For example, roasting half an American eggplant, whose size is larger than Japanese counterparts, and the use of a large bowl (rather than a small individual cup) for making steamed savory custard are labeled as being *daitan*.[16]

We have mentioned earlier that meat and salad are often contrastively gendered with males and females, respectively. It is worth noting that Nishi's cookbook has a section on salad, which is prefaced by a note that includes the lines in (5) (p. 10).

(5) 「サラダ」といえば、まず、生野菜にドレッシングをかけた、こじんまりとした料理像を思い浮かべるのではないだろうか。だけど、<u>もっとボリュームが欲しい、食った！という満足感を得たい、そんな**男のためのサラダ**を紹介</u>。でき上がりはもちろん、あえて、たたいて、炒めて作る、**パワフル**な工程も醍醐味だ。

"Sarada"-to ieba, mazu, nama-yasai-ni doresshingu-o kaketa, kojinmari-to shita ryōrizō-o omoi-ukaberu-no-de-wa nai darō-ka. Dakedo, <u>motto boryūmu-ga hoshii, kutta!-to iu manzokukan-o etai, sonna **otoko-no**</u>

tame-no sarada-o shōkai. Dekiagari-wa mochiron, aete, tataite, itamete tsukuru, **pawahuru**-na kōtei-mo daigomi-da.

"Speaking of 'salad,' what immediately comes to our mind is probably a compact dish of raw vegetables with dressing over it. But, <u>I introduce salads for men who want more volume, a sense of satisfaction, 'I'm full!'</u> The finish is a delight, but so too are **powerful** processes ranging from mixing, hitting, to stir-frying."

The second sentence in (5), underlined, defines *otoko-no tame-no sarada* "salad for men" in terms of a large quantity enough to give men a sense of satisfaction. The boldfaced word *pawahuru* "powerful" in the last sentence describes the cooking methods to be used for the salad dishes in the section. They consist of mixing, hitting, and stir-frying, which are meant to be contrastive with the simplicity (and unsatisfaction) of dressed raw vegetables. Yet, it is not clear why these methods stand for powerfulness and manliness. Cookbooks for and by women are no different in making use of these actions. Hitting may imply the use of force but cookbooks are indiscriminate of gender for the hitting action. For instance, *tataku* "to hit" is customary for some cucumber salads and for smashing garlic cloves.

One of the "must-have" salad recipes in the same section of Nishi's cookbook is "whole cabbage with garlic oil." The recipe yields four servings of a quartered raw cabbage, and is to be served with microwaved bacon and hot garlic olive oil. Its finished picture occupies half a page of the recipe, appearing with the word *dainamikku* "dynamic" on the side. The headnote under the recipe name includes an additional description, as in (6) (p. 17).

(6) 余計な手間は必要なし！
すべての工程が**ダイナミック**、これぞ**男の料理**。ジュッとオイルをかけたら、あ つあつをすぐにいただこう。

Yokei-na tema-wa hitsuyō nashi!
Subete-no kōtei-ga **dainamikku**, korezo **otoko-no ryōri**. JuQ-to oiru-o kake-tara, atsuatsu-o sugu-ni itadakō.

"There is no unnecessary process!
Every process is **dynamic**. This IS **men's cooking**. Let's eat it hot after pouring sizzling oil."

The instructions consist of cutting a raw cabbage into four and heating bacon and olive oil in a microwave. It is certainly simple, yet it begs the question as to why the process is considered "dynamic." It makes us wonder if the use of a whole cabbage head generates a sense of dynamicity, but the serving of a quarter of it per person does not strike one as fitting to the word. Nor does it make a man sated with a sense of satisfaction. Similarly, the emphatic declaration of "men's cooking," boldfaced in (6), remains as a slogan that does not contribute a substantive message beyond an image-generating rhetorical tool.

A different narrative of masculinity, as is displayed in (7), gives a new image of cooking men, not as "manly man" but as "family man."

(7) 家族のために男が腕をふるった日は、家族がとびっきりの笑顔になる日。どんなコミュニケーションよりも、思いのこもった惣菜一品が心を動かすこともある。照れくささや、日頃の忙しさに甘えてしまい、なかなか直接伝えられない思いを込めて、今週末は台所に立ってみるというのはいかがだろうか。

"A man's family becomes all smiles when he shows his cooking skills for them. One everyday dish that you make with love could sometimes move them more than words. You might have been using shyness [that men feel toward cooking] and your busy daily schedule as an excuse, but how about cooking this weekend with love and affection that you have not been able to convey directly to your family?" (p. 90)

The men's shyness toward cooking mentioned in (7) largely stems from the traditional gender role that is represented by *danshi chūbō-ni hairazu* "men should not be in the kitchen," and subsequent stereotypical perceptions imbued in the society that cooking men's masculinity is weakened. It is in fact reminiscent of the embarrassment that men, who are expected to be *karatō*, often feel in giving in to sweets. A departure from the social pressure in favor of a more intimate involvement in family life defines a new image of masculinity as a family man. Given the publication date of the cookbook, 2007, it is not surprising to see the family man's image projected here since the third wave cooking men already emerged by the turn of the century. Although the cooking men assumed in this passage are not presented as firm believers of an egalitarian view, the stance taken in (7) seems to indicate a way that these men may negotiate with the conflicting masculine images created by the manly adjectives (e.g., *daitan* "bold, fearless," *gōkai* "magnificent, enthralling," *shinpuru* "simple," *dainamikku* "dynamic") in the earlier examples.

The bold-magnificent-simple locution reverberates throughout Nishi's cookbook, but it is not always consistently and explicitly used to characterize or identify men's cooking or men's recipes. The structure and content of the recipes do not define "man's cooking," although larger sizes and a few cooking and eating actions are described as such. In that regard, the manly locution is benign and, despite the insinuation in the title, does not share the attitude of the first wave cooking men, i.e., that men's cooking is superior to women's. Oddly enough, furthermore, the instructions of the recipes are written in the *desu/masu* style. Recall our discussion in chapter 6 that most recipes of cookbooks adopt the *ru/da* style, and that generally, the *desu/masu* style in writing bears a softer tone that sounds more approachable to the audience. The *desu/masu* style in Nishi's recipes, then, gives a gentler image that contrasts with the undertone of the bold-magnificent-simple expressions. All these being considered, the deluge of the manly adjectives may be better interpreted as heartfelt encouragements for those men in solidarity who can and like to cook but feel shy or unsure about it. In fact, as we discussed in chapter 6, this is parallel to what we have observed in Katsuyo Kobayashi's use of mimetics that have masculine nuance, and the masculinity behind Julia Child's success.

The next type of cookbook I now examine are those written for men who want to learn how to cook by necessity. This group of cookbooks is widely written by both men and women. The targeted audience is the second wave cooking men, who are single men, older divorcée or widower, and relocated married men. The style and tone of the language used in these cookbooks is gentle, not intimidating, and gives the reader the sense of "I'm with you." These cookbooks for self-help often have their origin in a small gathering of men, where an instructor is invited to provide hands-on cooking lessons. *Oyaji-no Te-Ryōri—Otoko-no Ryōri-Kyōshitsu* "Dad's Homecooking—Cooking Class for Men" (2004), for instance, takes a similar history. Shōnan-supaisu (2007) reports that a group under the name the Cooking Class for Men was launched five years before the cookbook's publication. A group of women originally complained about their retired husbands. They noted that despite many places at which the retired men can be active, they ended up following their wives every time they go out. Also, finding it irksome to make three meals for their husbands, the wives suggested to their husbands to participate in cooking lessons. A female instructor led the class, and a small group grew to 15 members. For the husbands, the lessons provided a good way of simultaneously socializing and learning something new. Furthermore, thanks to their participation in the cooking lessons, they seem to become more aware of household matters, and some can now prepare easy meals when their wives are away. These practicum sessions have led to the 2004 cookbook.

Driven by a similar motivation, Deguchi (2002) is a compilation of the recipes that are used in his cooking class. As a veteran cooking instructor, Deguchi observes that men's interest in cooking had greatly changed during the past ten years prior to the book's publication. Before, male students opted to learn how to create lavish meals with expensive ingredients (i.e., "tastes of luxury"), but their interest has shifted to the type of ordinary meals that they eat at home every day (i.e., "tastes of necessity"). He notes that more men have been realizing the importance of three daily meals.

Deguchi's cookbook is very accessible to beginners and explains the very basics carefully and in detail. For example, the first few pages are spent on instructions of how to hold a knife and how to cut ingredients, while at the same time giving suggestions on standing postures that make cutting actions easy on the body. Also, rinsing the rice is so commonplace that it is rare to see cookbooks going over its how-to, but Deguchi gives thorough instructions for this fundamental step of cooking rice: "[b]ring the rice toward you, and wash it by pressing it against your palm. Repeat it, with the sound jaQ-jaQ" (p. 16). The use of an onomatopoeic word (e.g., *jaQ-jaQ*) evokes an auditory image as if it were the sound to remember as part of the process. There is no rhetorical sign that suggests manliness in this cookbook, like those in Nishi's cookbook discussed above. That said, (8) is probably the only male-oriented expression that is directed to male audience.

(8) いかにも「しっかり**飯を食つた**」という満足感がいい、丼物3品

Ikanimo "shikkari **meshi**-o **kutta**"-to iu manzokukan-ga ii, donburimono 3-pin

"3 donburi dishes that surely give you the satisfaction of 'I'm really full.'" (p. 22)

The boldfaced words, *meshi* and *kutta* in *meshi-o kutta* [meal-ACC ate] "I ate a meal," likely index men's speech: *meshi* for *gohan* "meal" and *kutta* for *tabeta* "ate," the latter variant of each being the gender neutral form. In addition to these gender-indexing vocabulary items, *donburimono* "donburi dishes" contains much rice in a bowl larger than a standard rice bowl, and as such, it is assumed to be a type of dish that men opt for. Note that the verb *kutta* as well as the reference to larger quantity appear in Nishi's cookbook, as discussed in relation to (5), where they contribute to creating a masculine image of men's cooking. Beyond the instances of men's speech in (8), the content and the language of Deguchi's cookbook do not form a gender-specific trope or discourse. Instead, the genuinely pedagogical tone is consistent with the goal to support male beginners in learning basic skills of cooking and gaining confidence in the home kitchen, while simultaneously appreciating the importance of home cooking.

Some of the self-help cookbooks specifically address divorces at an advanced age and wives' illnesses and deaths as practical problems that necessitate men's independence in domestic responsibilities including cooking. For example, Tokuoka (2009) and Kamebuchi and Doi (2010) are explicit about these issues as understandable reasons for becoming full-fledged cooking men. Authorship of male professional chefs, as in these two cookbooks, is a helpful asset to responding to the social shift that has significant implications to the gender role in domestic environments. They give novice men not only cooking instructions but opportunities to become aware of the pleasure of cooking. Tokuoka is a professional chef who specializes in Japanese cuisine. In the preface, recognizing an increasing rate of divorces at an older age, he speculates that men are bound by the stereotypical idea that they are expected to play the bread-earning role as their sole responsibility, thereby failing to strike a balance in their domestic partnership. He also affirms the joy of creating dishes that mirror individual personality. Men whom Tokuoka has in mind as the target audience of the book would wake to the reality they face, want to cook in order to share domestic responsibilities with their wives, and find it not an irksome burden but a pleasure of entertainment that is formed by their own culinary creation. The recipes in the book do not necessarily seem to be suitable for novice learners, and give an impression that they assume some prior knowledge and experience in cooking.[17] On the other hand, the instructions are very detailed and precise, and they are reiterated as summaries. The instructions are accompanied by photos that illustrate cooking steps that are narrowly broken down. There is no specific male-indexing or male-oriented vocabulary in the cookbook. It is notable, in fact, that the entire recipes are written in the *desu/masu* style throughout the book. As mentioned earlier, this written style softens the instructional tone, and is helpful in creating a warm narrative atmosphere, almost as if Tokuoka were watching out for the audience as a caring instructor.

The sense of a support system between a male instructor and a male audience is an effective advantage in Kamebuchi and Doi (2010). This cookbook is a collaboration of a DJ (Kamebuchi) and a professional cook with training in Western cuisine (Doi). Doi is a strong advocate for home cooking directed not just to men but to a broader audience of both genders. The format of this cookbook contains extensive dialogues between Kamebuchi, as a cooking man in training, and Doi, as his instructor. Kamebuchi begins with his motivations to learn how to cook, reasons that are by now familiar to those men at a retirement age or older. He wonders what would happen if his wife died and realizes that it is time for him to start learning to cook. Although he is not yet an apt cook, he has been envious of men who are, and enthusiastically wants to become one. Doi is a facilitator of conceptual and practical bases of home cooking. Notably, Doi tells Kamebuchi that he (Doi) will guide him (Kamebuchi) to the fundamentals of home cooking, but that wives have been cooking for a long time and are "professional" in the sphere of home cooking. Keeping that in mind, Doi, in his gentle and comical way, warns Kamebuchi not to expect to do better than them. Respect for women's home cooking and humbleness with which men approach learning to cook are the opposite of the superiority and defiance underlying the image of men who cook as hobby common to cooking men in the first wave.

The Kamebuchi and Doi cookbook consists of lively and often humorous conversations between the two men. Doi gives hands-on instructions and general commentaries, starting with thorough handwashing. Kamebuchi responds to them with comical remarks on Doi's directives. The exchange of the two is very animated and funny, and the language used is casual. The cooking processes are visually aided by many photos depicting them. Altogether, the book is 200-pages long including recipes for 26 dishes, but only 15 pages are allocated to the actual recipes. The remainder is detailed elaboration of each recipe. The number of actual recipes is indeed small, but foregrounded is the dialogue between the two men, in which ingredients, processes, and some scientific information are closely delineated in concrete terms that are easy to follow.

The comprehensible context seems to benefit, at least in part, from the use of frequent mimetics. It may be recalled that I included another cookbook of Doi's, Doi (2014), in the survey of mimetics reported in chapter 3. As table 3.2 shows, out of eight cookbooks written by male authors, Doi's use of mimetics stands at the top in the type count and the second in the token count. In Kamebuchi and Doi's cookbook, too, mimetic expressions are actively used to increase the level of depictions. For instance, *huQkura* and *huwaQ-to* appear in recipes for egg dishes to enrich the soft and fluffy texture, *zaQzaQ-to* and *zaaQ-to* refer to the sounds that rice makes when washing and rinsing it, and *sukaQ-to* for fish evokes the image of a sharp blade slicing the flesh of the fish without any resistance. Doi recognizes the effectiveness of mimetics in cooking, and claims that food textures and their associated sounds are linked to the tastes of food (Kindaichi 2016). So, in this cookbook, mimetics are effectively deployed to have the reader aware of five senses in cooking.

Following up on the reliance of senses, Doi's commentary section of Kamebuchi and Doi (2010) takes an interesting stance on men's sensual reactions not only to home cooking but to life in general. Remarking on Kamebuchi's excitement about a salad dish, Doi states the following (my translation).

(9) 亀渕さんはさすが感性の人、美意識が高い。できあがったサラダの美しさに、食べる前から大喜びされている。日本の男性には少ないタイプである。しかし、おいしさは、常に見た目の美しさに現れる。美しさを感じる心は、料理上手への道であり、料理づくりをずいぶん楽しいものにしてくれる。日本の男子も遅ればせながら、日常にある美しさに目覚めていただきたい。

"As expected, Mr. Kamebuchi is a man of sensitivity; he has a high aesthetic sense. He is jubilated at the beauty of the salad even before he tastes it. We rarely see this type of men in Japan. But, good taste always emerges from the beautiful appearance. The mind that captures beauty paves a path to a good cook and gives cooking a lot of fun. I hope that Japanese men, even belatedly, would wake up to the beauty that commonly surrounds us." (p. 49)

The reference to aesthetics in cooking may come from his training as a professional chef, which is represented overwhelmingly by men. In the area of home cooking, however, his comments suggest a familiar view that beautiful food presentations are not something men pay attention to. He promotes men's awareness to an aesthetic sense and sensitivity to it in home cooking and broadly in life.

Doi further addresses the connection between the taste and the appearance of food regarding the cooking method of *yaku*, specifically *yaku$_2$*. As we noted a few times thus far, the *yaku$_2$* method uses direct fire and does not require elaborate preparation. As such, it is gendered in alignment with males. Yet, Doi explains that "in fact, it is difficult to perfect it and to produce a beautiful and tasty dish. Simple but actually deep, this process should be of interest to many men" (p. 156). Building upon simplicity and open fire that stereotype men's cooking, the traits of an emerging image of cooking men that Doi alludes to are inquisitiveness and a challenging attitude. This image is indeed replicated as a kind of antidote that aging men after retirement recognize. Speaking of his experience with participating in a men's cooking group, Mr. Eikichi Okumura, who was born in 1930, explains in Kobayashi (2001) that besides cooking, he has been taking up learning about social work to foster his curiosity. Challenging new things, of which he finds cooking the best example, allow him to be in an "attacking mode," and now he even wants to tackle a bit more complicated cooking. So, the attitude of aggressively pursuing new knowledge and experience in Doi's and Okumura's comments serves as a ground for a form of mature masculinity.

Kamebuchi and Doi's cookbook presents an intriguing mixture. It is in a genuine camaraderie with men who hope to learn practical how-to in cooking. The content, the user-friendly language, and repeated information together achieve the goal of providing a helpful guide to novice cooking men who are in (or entering) the "golden age." But at the same time, cooking instructions and commentaries are more broadly contextualized for cultivating qualities that have not immediately been identified with men. Such an image of masculinity crucially emerges from a serious interaction with the axis of age. It is constructed based on a renewed sense of independence and a search for a new challenge to which aging men in an aging society are forced to have.

The third type of cookbook is conceptualized based on an egalitarian view of gender roles to which cooking men subscribe. The ultimate image of ideal man framed in such a context is portrayed in the comic book *Kukkingu Papa* "Cooking Dad." It started in 1985 as a series in a comic magazine for young men and still continues to date, now as individual comic books. It is important to keep in mind that the year 1985 coincides with the passing of the Equal Employment Opportunity Law. The main character is Ichimi Araiwa, a salaryman with a large muscular physique and a gentle mind, who likes to cook and is good at it. His wife, Nijiko, works for a newspaper company and is passionate about her work. Cooking is not her forte, and she relies on Ichimi for the kitchen duties including making the family members' lunch. Ichimi and Nijiko share other domestic responsibilities, ranging from the laundry to child care (e.g., changing diapers, feeding the baby girl in the middle of the night). They have a son, Makoto, and a daughter, Miyuki. An individual volume has about ten episodes, each of which contains a recipe that is featured in the story. That Ichimi is an apt cook was a secret at the beginning. The secrecy reflects that husbands who cook well were still not a wide-spread phenomenon in the mid 1980s. This "closeted" cooking man finally came out in 1996 (Minami 2013).

An episode (episode #221, Ueyama 1991) highlights Ichimi's stance of men's cooking very distinctly. In Makoto's home-economics class at the elementary school, the students learn how to make fried eggs. Mitsugu, an active, mischievous boy in the class, enthusiastically starts the process with unnecessary roughness. He cracks the eggs into a bowl so hard that the yolks break; he splashes the oil upon putting the eggs into a pan; and he scrapes the fried but already broken eggs roughly enough to turn the whole thing into a mess. He declares that he does not like home-economics. Makoto, in a stark contrast, makes the best fried eggs in class. Asked by his classmates why he is so good in cooking, Makoto responds that his father is a great cook and frequently shows him how. This remark generates total puzzlement among his classmates, and leads to a scene where Ichimi invites them to his house and gives cooking demonstrations. Impressed by Ichimi's skills and elated by the uncharted taste of the deep-fried eggs he prepared for them, one child asks him why Ichimi cooks even though he is a man. His response is, "I like it, you know. You've grown by eating a variety of things, right? When you are hungry and lethargic, food gives you energy, right? You become happy when you eat something really, really delicious, right?" (p. 161) and to each question, the children answer affirmatively. Ichimi, then, concludes, "in other words, cooking means giving pep and pleasure as a gift for the person who eats the meal. I love doing that. So, man or woman, it doesn't matter" (p. 162). The kids are all fascinated by his reason, but particularly Mitsugu, finding Ichimi cool, renews his interest in cooking. Ichimi's explanation perforates the gender boundary set for home cooking and gives it a new definition. This particular scene defies the stance of *danshi chūbō-ni hairazu* "men should not be in the kitchen" and the perception and stereotype of cooking men prevalent in the hegemonic society. Moreover, the scene creates an opportune moment that a parent teaches the next generation that one cooks not because of the assumed gender role but because of the happiness and pleasure that it brings to people. Openly expressing these ideas without any sense of shame or embarrassment and putting them in action by cooking constitute a new image of masculinity.

The equal gender roles in the domestic setting portrayed in *Kukkingu Papa* show an interesting aspect that is related to men's sensitivity, especially awareness of common beauty that Doi talks about in (9). In episode #218 (Ueyama 1991), Nijiko is in her 6-month childcare leave from her work. To relieve her from the care of the newly born daughter Miyuki, Ichimi offers Nijiko a few hours of "free time" on Sunday. While she goes out for diversion, Ichimi steps outside with Miyuki in his arms. In a garden he finds beautiful flowers, and speaks to his newly born daughter, in all smiles: *ha—na. Kireida-nā, Miyuki* "flo—wer. They are beautiful, aren't they, Miyuki?" (p. 107). Appreciating the beauty of simple garden flowers is perceived feminine but sharing the moment with his baby daughter and pronouncing the word "flo-wer" to her embodies the sensitivity to the common beauty around us. These seemingly effeminate displays of behavior by Ichimi do not at all entail a weakened version of masculinity. Instead, it projects an image of a man who has a mature appreciation for sensual reactions, which is also relevant to cooking as Doi says in (9).

Ichimi's masculinity is represented by his being a diligent and responsible salaryman who is a good boss to his subordinates and does his job well. I mentioned earlier that he is portrayed as a man of strong build. These images of masculinity are further supplemented by his language use that indexes a male speaker. Gender differences in Japanese are exhibited in personal pronouns and sentence-final particles, and serve as a convenient linguistic tool to typecast characters in, for example, literature, comic books, TV dramas, and movies (Kinsui 2003, 2007). Ichimi's men's speech is observed commonly with sentence-final particles, and examples are found in dialogue lines, like those in (10). The linguistic marking also appears in the commentary part of recipes (equivalent to headnotes), as in (11). The examples are all from Ueyama (1991).

(10) a. [to a young man in his neighborhood] ああ、いつでもいい<u>ぜ</u>

ā, itsu-de-mo ii-<u>ze</u>

"yea, any time (is good)" (p. 65)

b. [to himself] <u>めし</u>は炊けてる<u>なっ</u>

<u>meshi</u>-wa taketeru-<u>naQ</u>

"rice has been cooked" (p. 32)

c. [to his wife] 果汁をやってん<u>のか</u>

   kajū-o yatte-n-<u>no-ka</u>

   "are you giving her fruit juice?" (p. 121)

(11) a. お好みで調節して<u>くれ</u>

   o-konomi-de chōsetsu-shite-<u>kure</u>

   "please make an adjustment as you like" (p. 16)

   b. 超簡単だ<u>ぞ</u>っ

   chō-kantan-da-<u>zo</u>Q

   "it's really easy" (p. 96)

   c. うまい<u>ぞ</u>

   <u>umai-zo</u>

   "it's tasty" (p. 159)

   d. ケガする<u>なよ</u>！！

   kega-suru-<u>na-yo</u>!!

   "don't get injured!!" (p. 49)

In (10) the underlined elements at the end of the utterances mark assertion, confirmation, and question, and identify them as stereotypical male speech. Furthermore, the noun *meshi* "rice" in (10b) is of male-orientation, as we discussed in relation to (8). The examples in (11) are from the comments that Ichimi gives in recipes directed to the reader. The sentence final particle *-zo* in (11b) and (11c) are for an emphatic assertion, *-kure* in (11a) is for a request, and *-na-yo* in (11d) is for a warning not to do something. The adjective *umai* "delicious" in (11c) indexes male speech as a taste term (as opposed to the other meaning of "skillful"). So, the patterned use of these linguistic tools gives Ichimi the male identity.

Kukkingu Papa demonstrates a variety of versions of masculinity in a variety of dimensions. Regarding construction of masculine images relevant to men's cooking, the traditional gender roles normalized by *danshi chūbō-ni hairazu* "men should not be in the kitchen" are deconstructed and reconstructed into a version that comports with the social changes that call for men's equal participation in household responsibilities. Home cooking and other household duties are portrayed virtually gender neutral since domestic responsibilities are viewed not based on gender demarcation but on individual disposition and the nature of partnership. This is a version of domestic masculinity. At the same time, masculinity is enacted elsewhere through the linguistic mechanism that indexes the gender identity of Ichimi as the speaker addressing the reader. And, all these are presented together with the visual depiction of his manly physical appearance.

The last set of cookbooks I shall examine reflect social changes in the 21st century that include the emergence of the *sōshokukei-danshi* generation and shifting ideologies relevant to home cooking. We begin with the cookbook *Danshi-gohan-no Hon* "Book for Men's Cooking" (Kokubun and Kentaro 2009) (henceforth, *Danshi-gohan*). It is written by a musician and TV personality, Taichi Kokubun (born 1974), and Kentaro (born 1972), who is a graphic designer turned professional cook. Kentaro is Katsuyo Kobayashi's son and his interest in cooking and professional career are undeniably influenced by his mother. The book resulted from the namesake TV cooking show that started to air in 2008 and continues to date.[18] The recipes compiled in the book version come from those covered on the TV shows between 2008 and 2009. Subsequent volumes have been published, totaling nine volumes as of 2019. Mirroring the TV setting, the cookbook contains a number of dialogues between the two authors (many from the broadcasting) including stories behind the scenes as well as introductions and recommendations for kitchen utensils. The recipes are for familiar and popular home cooked items like curry, hamburger steaks, and pot stickers, but creative, modified versions of those common dishes and those for a small gathering are also covered. The detailed and easy-to-follow instructions are interspersed with Kentaro's additionally helpful tips that elaborate on the directives. The supplementary comments further provide reasons for a given cooking process so that the reader understands why as well as how. The servings of each recipe range from 2, 2 to 3, to 4 people. The smaller serving size suggests that family is not necessarily an assumed setting. Kokubun and Kentaro were single until 2010 and 2015, respectively.

With respect to the title of the cookbook, the reference to *danshi* "men" in contrast with *otoko* "men" is important to the authors and is significant to the discussion of masculinity, as Yuen (2014) explores the point in detail. In the preface, Kokubun claims, cited in (12), that their cookbook is not about *otoko-gohan* [men-meal] but about *danshi-gohan* [men-meal]. Both *danshi* and *otoko* literally mean "man, men," but they are specifically distinguished in the authors' mind.

(12) この本は、「男子ごはん」であって「男ごはん」ではありません。僕とケンタロウさんに、それほどの男っぽさはありません。だから、ふんどし一丁で料理もしませんし、日本海の荒波の前で料理を作ったり、漁にも出ません。もちろん、できあがり前に和太鼓も叩きません。普通のパンツを履き、くだらない話をしなが

ら料理を作り、穏やかな波の前で舌鼓を打つ。それが「男子ごはん」です。

"This book is 'danshi cooking,' not 'otoko cooking.' Kentaro and I do not have much of such manliness. So, we don't cook in just loincloths; nor do we cook facing the rough Sea of Japan or go fishing in the sea. Of course, we don't hit a Japanese drum as we finish cooking. We wear ordinary pants, cook while talking trivial, and enjoy the meal in front of calm ripples. That's 'danshi cooking.'" (p. 002)

To them "*otoko* cooking" is embodied by strong, physical images of men who daringly cook despite undesirable or adversative environment and circumstances. The references to loincloths and a Japanese drum stage dramatic scenes that are not associated with women. And the apparently banal and effeminate presentations and circumstances of "*danshi* cooking" are immaterial to them. Instead, "*danshi* cooking" is characterized in terms of the satisfaction and pleasure of solidarity that are experienced upon cooking and savoring simple dishes together. Also significant is that "*danshi* cooking" makes notable reference to the entire prospect in which mutual cooking and dining are experienced, with an emphasis on the value of the entire course of the events. I take it that commensality among participating men is essentialized in "*danshi* cooking." Given the premise underlying (12), I surmise that *Danshi-gohan* speaks to men who are likely single and are in their 20s and 30s with respect to age.

It is worth noting that *Danshi-gohan* is not the first cookbook to use the word *danshi* in cooking discourse. For instance, the traditional ideology, *danshi chūbō-ni hairazu* "men should not be in the kitchen," indeed has the word *danshi* in it. Also, Tokuoka's cookbook that we have discussed earlier has *danshi* in its title, *Danshi-no Daidokoro* "Men's Kitchen." Recall that in Doi's remarks about men's sensitivity in (9) cited from Kamebuchi and Doi (2010), *danshi* is used where "Japanese men" are referred to in the last sentence. The words *danshi* and *otoko* both mean "man, men," but the former additionally has a narrower sense of "boy, boys." Although the instances of *danshi* in connection with men's cooking mentioned just above do not make specific nuances of the word beyond a generic reference to men, *Danshi-gohan* obviously makes a distinction between the two, as defined in (12), by distancing from the macho masculinity image that *otoko-gohan* "otoko-cooking" may have.

Yuen (2014) examines cooking men in postwar Japan, particularly exploring how masculinity is portrayed in mass media. One of the sources she uses for her textual analysis is *Danshi-gohan*. Although her study is based on *Danshi-gohan*, both the original TV shows and the cookbook, as well as other

236   Chapter Seven

media sources, the observations she makes, cited in (13–14) below, are helpful to understand how *danshi* cooking and the term *danshi* in the cookbook *Danshi-gohan* should be situated in a larger discourse of masculinity.

(13) "... I argue that the proliferation of this specific form of *danshi* cooking—that is, **the simultaneous distancing from both men's adventurous cooking and women's home cooking, which forms the core characteristic of *danshi* cooking**—and the very reference to these male cooks as '*danshi*' instead of as '*otoko*' (men), arises from the socio-economic condition of post-bubble Japan, and may be indicative of larger changes to notions of masculinity in Japanese society." (p. 223, emphasis added)

(14) "In short, notions of domesticity often associated with women's cooking have been removed from the *danshi* cooking discourse. Although the *danshi* cook in the home kitchen and make simple, mundane meals, **cooking for these men is portrayed as anything but their duty and responsibility**." (Ibid., emphasis added)

To put Yuen's claims in our terms, *danshi* cooking is not "cooking as hobby" or "self-oriented leisure" that cooking men under the new wave of the 1970s were engaged in, as instantiated by Nishikawa (1996) and Nishi (2007), for instance. Nor is it "everyday cooking" for the family that is assigned to wives under the traditional ideology of *danshi chūbō-ni hairazu* "men should not be in the kitchen." Yuen also summarizes that the meals that the *danshi* make "belong to neither categories of 'manly meals nor mom's home cooking'" (p. 221). Limiting my observations to the cookbook version for now, I agree with Yuen's assessment that the new image of masculinity projected in *Danshi-gohan* mirrors the socioeconomic landscape of late 20th and early 21st century Japan. On the other hand, a further look at the language and discourse of the cookbook brings forth alternative interpretations of what *danshi* cooking stands for.

First, in some recipes, captions and head comments make specific reference to *danshi* and *danshi gohan* "*danshi* cooking" that indicates manliness in the same sense as *otoko* in the cookbooks examined thus far. Examples include those in (15–17).

(15) これぞ**男子ごはん**！がっつりウマイ、中華の炒め物と<u>家庭</u>でもパラパラに仕上げられる本格派チャーハン

Korezo **danshi-gohan**! GaQtsuri umai, chūka-no itamemono-to <u>katei</u>-de-mo parapara-ni shiager-are-ru honkakuha chāhan

"This is an ultimate **danshi cooking/meal**! Really tasty Chinese stir-fry and genuine fried-rice that you can perfect its non-sticky version <u>at home</u>" (pp. 056–057)

(16) お供のごはん物には、これぞ**男子的**なメニュー、ねぎチャーハン！

Otomo-no gohan-mono-ni-wa, korezo **danshi-teki**-na menyū, negi-chāhan!

"As a rice dish on the side, leek/scallion fried-rice, an ultimate **danshi-like** menu!" (p. 056)

(17) これぞ、**男子流**。<u>豪快</u>で<u>簡単</u>、<u>激ウマ</u>メニュー

Korezo, **danshi-ryū**. <u>Gōkai</u>-de <u>kantan</u>, <u>geki-uma</u> menyū

"This is indeed **danshi-style**. <u>Magnificent</u> and <u>simple</u>, <u>super-delicious</u> menu" (pp. 024–025)

The words that consist of *danshi*—*danshi-gohan* "men-cooking/meal" in (15), *danshi-teki* "characteristic of men" in (16), and *danshi-ryū* "of men's style" in (17)—uniformly describe rice dishes. (15) and (16) are comments on fried-rice with Japanese leeks that accompanies the main dish of stir-fried pork. (17) is the caption for pork ginger donburi, i.e., pork ginger served on a bed of rice in a bowl. Both rice dishes are served in larger quantities than the standard size of a bowl for rice, which, along with the presence of meat, characterize *danshi*. It should be remembered that the association of donburi rice with men was made in Deguchi's (2002) recipe, discussed in (8). The larger quantity was also highlighted in relation to men's satisfaction that Nishi's (2007) salad recipe talks about, as in (5). Furthermore, the first underlined words in (17), *gōkai* "magnificent," is one of the crucial vocabulary items that Nishi frequently uses to evoke an image of strong manliness in men's cooking. The simplicity indicated by the second underlined word *kantan* "simple" in (17) is also named as a feature of men's cooking (Shoji 1984). The prefix *geki-* "super, extraordinary" to modify *uma* (a clipped form of *umai* "delicious") in *geki-uma* in the same line dramatizes an enticing result of the recipe. So, *danshi* in (15–17) is no different from *otoko* in its reference to a masculine image.

This is further evidenced by the exchange between Kokubun and Kentaro, shown in (18), about the scrumptious smell coming from the pork ginger in connection with (17).

(18) 「**男**には絶対人気あると思いますよ！」；「**男**ばっかり集まってくる」

"**Otoko**-ni-wa zettai ninki aru-to omoimasu-yo!"; "**Otoko**-bakkari atsumatte kuru"

"I think it is definitely popular among **men** (*otoko*)!"; "Only **men** (*otoko*) will crowd" (p. 024)

In this dialogue, both authors use *otoko*, rather than *danshi*. They agree that the mouthwatering smell will no doubt lure men. So, *danshi* and *otoko* in (15–18) make no difference, and they equally point to an image of masculinity that is evoked by the amount of food they consume and preference to calorie-rich food items including meat (and the combination of the two). Although this image of masculinity does not point to the aspect of "adventurous cooking" per se that Yuen mentions in (13), it nevertheless overlaps with the characterizations of men's cooking that are observed with the cookery materials we discussed earlier. In that respect, *danshi* cooking in *Danshi-gohan* has more to share with versions of men's cooking that come before it than Yuen's observation seems to suggest.

As for the departure from women's (or mom's) home cooking in (13) and the absent sense of home cooking as domestic duties or responsibility, mom's home cooking and home cooking as a domestic task that a family member (or members) takes up are indeed nuanced as an important background that is an indispensable aspect to *danshi* cooking. For instance, there are recurrent associations of the recipes with taste of home (家庭の味) and staples (定番) of Kentaro's family (e.g., potato croquette, meat and potatoes, hamburger steak, macaroni au gratin). These are the dishes that the authors grew up with, and their tastes constitute nostalgic and comforting reminders of mom's home cooking. In the recipe for *niku-jaga* "meat and potatoes (cooked in a broth of soy sauce and sugar)," widely considered to epitomize home cooking and taste of home, the headnote claims that it is a soul food for everybody and is one of the therapeutic, healing dishes (癒し系料理). Furthermore, the caption for this recipe urges the reader to make it with his partner: カップルで作ってほしい！ (p. 058) "[We] want couples to make this [together]!" The suggestion alludes to a partnership in the cooking task.

Participation in cooking is not limited to adult partners but is inclusive of children. The recipe for three kinds of bread dishes for lunch and the recipe for crab pilaf appear with the notes in (19) and (20), respectively.

(19)　…　大人も子供も"作ること"を楽しめる三品

"... three dishes which both adults and children can enjoy 'making'" (p. 029)

(20)　とにかく簡単に作れるので、急な来客時や子供と一緒に作る料理にオススメです。

"It is indeed very easy, so we recommend it in case of unexpected visitors and cooking with your children." (p. 100)

(19) makes it clear that children's involvement in the cooking process is viewed as a pleasure that home cooking can offer them. The crab "pilaf"

that (20) speaks of does not actually involve the standard stir-frying process but simply mixing rice with the other ingredients. Given that simplicity, the recipe is suitable for showing children an easy how-to in the home kitchen. So, although home cooking is not presented in terms of a domestic responsibility that is assigned to a specific gender, it is the authors' premise that home cooking is a type of skill which all family members should be responsible for and simultaneously take pleasure in.

I have given my alternative interpretations to Yuen's conclusions cited in (13–14): that is, that the nuanced sense of mom's home cooking and cooking as a household chore that belongs to any family member is intrinsically communicated in *Danshi-gohan*. In addition to the rhetorical bases that lead to my interpretations, Kentaro's personal background is instrumental to setting the general undertone of *danshi* cooking that is injected in the cookbook. As mentioned earlier, Kentaro is a son of Katsuyo Kobayashi, who, as I discussed in chapter 6, played a vital role in home cooking in the last quarter of the 20th century. Through her series of cookbooks, essays, and public events, she supported women's independence and equal sharing of domestic responsibilities. Kentaro and his older sister, as small children and then young adults, grew up watching their mother segue from work to household responsibilities in the 1980s and 1990s. This is also the time that women started to seek employments outside home. In her essay, Kobayashi (2014b) states that her children do dishes and are not bound by the idea that kitchen work belongs to their mother. She admits that kitchen work can be completed quickly if she does it all by herself. But she explains that she did not want Kentaro to grow into a husband who does not help his working wife or who does not sense when his wife needs help. Kobayashi further rationalizes that it is more effective to give children some kitchen tasks (e.g., setting the table, coming up with the menu, cooking preparation) as their responsibilities rather than having them give their mothers a helping hand. Holding children responsible for such work would cultivate a voluntary motivation to engage in various tasks in the home kitchen. Besides these conceptual matters regarding gender roles, it is evident from the recipes in *Danshi-gohan* that Kentaro follows his mother's motto, namely, easy-but-delicious home meals that do not take time for preparation. As mentioned above, some of Kobayashi's recipes and techniques are repeated in *Danshi-gohan* as staples of the Kobayashi family and the like.

Viewed from these perspectives, Yuen's conclusion that "cooking for these men is portrayed as anything but their duty and responsibility" in (14) seems only apparent. Together with the comments on family participation discussed around (19–20), cooking as "duty and responsibility" is reconceptualized as one of domestic tasks that any family members (individually or together) freely take up rather than as an onus assigned to one person or one gender.

Taking into consideration the family environment in which Kentaro was raised and his viewpoints centering around home cooking and gender roles, the stance that he takes vis-à-vis home cooking and men's role in domestic responsibilities is a natural consequence of personal upbringing and the social milieu during his early years.

The spirit of *danshi* cooking, essentialized to male bonding around home-cooked meals, is a central theme of Otokuni's (2017, 2018a, 2018b, 2019, 2020) comic book series, *Kōkokugaisha, Danshiryō-no Okazu-kun* "Okazu at Male-only Dorm of Advertising Company" (henceforth *Okazu-kun*). Just like *Danshi-gohan*, cooking for and eating with others as an event is depicted in each story line as a valuable experience that young men enjoy. *Okazu-kun* has been published in seven volumes between 2017 and 2021. Each volume consists of half a dozen episodes, and at the end of an episode, its featured recipes are attached. Additionally, ingredients and cooking processes (of usually the main dishes) appear as part of cooking scenes of an episode.

Stories are told around four single salarymen in their 20s and 30s who live in the male-only dormitory of Minato Advertising Company where they work. Kazu Nishio (24 years old), Keisuke Higashira (25), Tadashi Nangō (28), and Ippei Kita (33) are the four men, who have been the company's employees for two years. They belong to different divisions of the company but occasionally interact with each other at work. Although the building is called dorm, they each have a separate apartment in it. In their verbal interactions, Nishio and Higashira, as junior members by age, use the polite speech style when speaking to the other two, marked by the *desu/masu* ending. Kita is the oldest of the four and speaks to the rest in the casual speaking style. Nangō carries a formal demeanor and converses in the *desu/masu* style whoever he speaks to.

On every Friday evening, they cook assigned dishes and dine together at Nishio's apartment. Nishio is responsible for a main dish, Higashira a soup, Nangō a side dish, and Kita rice. On a few occasions, Nangō also makes dessert items. Kita is the least prone to cooking, and hence assigned to making rice (usually taking advantage of a rice cooker), but when occasions arise, he can make more elaborate dishes including risotto and pasta. Most scenes indicate that Nishio and Higashira cook together at Nishio's kitchen since their apartments are adjacent to each other and the four gather in Nishio's apartment. Their cooking scenes are described in detail, either as dialogues between these two or as side notes, and Nishio often gives Higashira cooking tips and reasons for certain cooking steps. The menus consist largely of dishes that are common in everyday home cooking (e.g., stir-fried meat and vegetables, curry, meat and potatoes) and are kept simple since they cook after work. However, slightly elaborate dishes are occasionally presented

Cooking instructions, both in an episode and a summary at the end, are detailed with verbal descriptions and visual illustrations. Typical of comic books, mimetic expressions (many being onomatopoeia) are ubiquitous, which increases depictive force. The manner of cooking actions and measurements, for instance, explained in terms of mimetic words (e.g., *zaQku-zaQku* for rough cutting, *koNmori* for heaping amount, *juu* for sizzling), make the recipes easy to follow for the reader. Nishio is the most skillful and knowledgeable cook among the four men but does not hesitate to use instant and packaged condiments and canned foods, thereby reducing cooking time.

Once they sit down to eat, they extensively exchange their appreciative comments on the meal, not just uttering *oishii* and *umai* "delicious." They complement each other's dishes by remarking taste, texture, fitting combinations of ingredients, and also nostalgic feelings they reminisce. What happened at work is talked about on occasion during cooking and eating, but at the center is always the meal that they each prepare and share with others. These food-related comments are not of the pretentious or technical sort but indicative of sincere joy of eating simple home-cooked meals and sharing congenial experiences together. Canned beer is usually consumed with the dinner, but the atmosphere is nothing like the one that represents drinking culture of salaryman, in which alcohol takes a center stage and venues are outside home. Furthermore, they all enjoy eating sweets. The cleaning after the meal is shared by all, rather than holding a single person or junior members responsible for the duty. All in all, what stands out from these aspects of *Okazu-kun* setting and storylines is a significant weight on commensal pleasures.

Ochs and Shohet (2006) discuss the important role of commensality in communication and social relationships. They claim that "[u]niversally, commensality is central to defining and sustaining the family as a social unit" (p. 37), and consider mealtimes to "constitute universal occasions for members not only to engage in the activities of feeding and eating but also to forge relationships that reinforce or modify the social order" (p. 36). Commensality refers to the act of eating meals together in a social group, but in *Okazu-kun*, their commensal pleasures do not involve takeout meals or eating out. Crucially, each person's active contribution through voluntary cooking engagements at home kitchen every Friday plays an important role in generating joy and comfort in their commensal experience. Words of acknowledgment and appreciation for the pleasure that brings to the four men are reverberated multiple times throughout the episodes. In one scene where the four cannot be together due to their work schedule, Kita and Nangō exhibit the wholehearted exchange in (21).

(21) 南郷： 金曜日なのに4人じゃないなんて変な感じですよね…
    北： はは　確かに！　ここ数年のルーティンだもんな！いつの間にか… 当たり前になってたんだなぁ…
    南郷： 来週の金曜日が今から待ち遠しいですね
    北： だねぇ

    Nangō: It's Friday, but not being four of us is very odd.
    Kita: Yea, that's true! It's been a routine for a few years. Without realizing it, we have taken it for granted.
    Nangō: I am already looking forward to next Friday.
    Kita: Yea.   (Otokuni 2018a, 122–23)

Virtually the same dialogue exchange is repeated between Nishio and Higashira in a later episode.

The social interaction through commensality depicted in *Okazu-kun* can be situated in the evolving images of masculinity especially in relation to the concept of *sōshokukei-danshi* "herbivore men." The commensal arrangement in *Okazu-kun* serves as an exciting yet comforting coda of the working week that revolves around home cooking and mealtime conversation. In the setting that creates a sense of virtual family, the four men establish a localized social unit for a new form of male bonding, parallel to male bonding in viewing sports. Tierney (2016) discusses the commensality in the Sumo wrestling world in Japan and describes the relationships among wrestlers as strictly hierarchical. In sharp contrast, the comradery relationship that the four men in *Okazu-kun* fosters is totally horizontal and is deeply cherished by all. Furthermore, in the context of the ideology regarding *amatō* vs. *karatō* and the associated social norm expected of salarymen, the commensality setting in *Okazu-kun* can be viewed as an alternative to the drinking-man's culture and comports well with the concept of the herbivore men.

Regarding the emasculated image of *amatō* men, the four characters in *Okazu-kun* find a natural place for sweets in their commensal pleasures. Although not frequently, their Friday dinner menus include home-made dessert items. In an episode Kita feels dejected by a failed romance, so much so that he forgets to bring rice. Nangō makes as a dessert a chocolate cake (*gatō shokora*) with a shape of a heart drawn on it to cheer him up. When Nangō leaves his seat to fetch the cake, Kita responds by saying (22).

(22) えー　デザート？！　楽しみだな

    "Wow, dessert?! Looking forward to"   (Otokuni 2017, 96)

On the one hand, Kita drinks more beer than others at dinner, but on the other, he does not hide his excitement of a dessert for the meal. Given the *amatō* vs. *karatō* dichotomy, not only enjoying the tastes of the sweets but making their own home-made desserts is counter to the image of men; it is contrary to the traditional sociocultural expectation that men, as *karatō* by default, are expected to shy away from sweets.

In another episode, Nangō makes a different dessert item, a pie with the filling of pumpkin and bean paste. Nishio's and Higashira's reactions in (23) illustrate that tastes of sweets transcend the matter of gender stereotypes.

(23) 西:　　　　　おいしい！　和菓子と洋菓子の真ん中やー！
　　　東良:　　　　パイとお茶に癒される〜
　　　Nishio:　　　Yum! It's between Japanese sweets and western sweets!
　　　Higashira:　 The pie and [roasted] tea are so therapeutic
　　　　　　　　　　　　　　　　　　　　　　　　　　(Otokuni 2018a, 87)

Nishio is excited and impressed by the pie while Higashira considers the dessert therapeutic. Enjoying both sweets and alcohol, the four men certainly cross the *amatō-karatō* boundary. Impervious to the traditional ideology associated with the dichotomy, however, we see no internal struggle or negotiation to justify food choices they make.

The four men in *Okazu-kun* further present an interesting picture regarding their preferences for canned coffee (Otokuni 2019, 2020). Recall that we discussed how unsweetened black canned coffee is marketed. Of particular relevance to the construction of the underlying masculine image for advertising purposes is the reduced or no sugar content that agrees with the *karatō* norm and the black packaging label. Not confined by the gendered taste, the four men's canned coffee preferences cannot be more diverse: Nishio regularly drinks a few cans of unsweetened black coffee a day; Higashira exclusively opts for café-au-lait and never drinks black coffee; Kita generally has the one with reduced sugar although he claims that he also drinks black and café-au-lait; and Nangō varies depending on his mood of the day, including jasmin tea (Otokuni 2019, 156; Otokuni 2020, 163). So, here, too, these male characters do not fit the stereotypical image of masculinity that canned coffee advertisements have generated.

Neutralization of gender is also detectable in the way that the four men face an economic problem—a situation parallel to family budgeting. Each man contributes 2000 yen per month to their weekly Friday dinner. However, the costs of ingredients rise due to inflation, and one week, they find only 500 yen left in their budget. Nishio comes up with the idea of creating three dishes (main, side, and soup) out of a single daikon radish along with only a few inexpensive ingredients. Recognizing that different parts of daikon yield slightly dissimilar tastes, Nishio, Higashira, and Nangō devise a menu of three dishes within 500 yen. Moreover, they prepare the three daikon dishes by using three different cooking techniques, i.e., *yaku* "pan fry," *niru* "cook in broth," and *orosu* "grate," thereby escaping from banality. Upon eating, they comment that the variety in cooking method gives a single ingredient great versatility in taste. The issue with managing food expenses without compromising the quality of meals in this episode is analogous to the problem-solving situations in the domestic context. These are the situations that women encounter as part of their domestic responsibilities when women's cooking is equated with daily cooking for family, as was the case in the early 20th century. Interestingly, the young single men in *Okazu-kun* are portrayed as responsible household managers who balance the budget without lowering expectations for their home meals. In this regard, they are indeed taking the whole aspect of home cooking with a sense of responsibility, unlike Yuen's (2014) characterization of herbivore men's cooking as stated earlier in (14). All things considered, then, these men's cooking practice is in close proximity to "women's home cooking" rather than distancing from it, further providing an alternative interpretation of Yuen observation in (13).

Like *Danshi-gohan*, *Okazu-kun* locates cooking men in a domestic setting which neutralizes the strict gender dichotomy in a hegemonic society, even when other aspects of social hegemony simultaneously exist, such as the use of speech styles appropriate for seniority. What is essentialized in the portrayal of these men, instead, are commensality and accompanying comradery dialogue around it. By commensality, though, I mean to include the preparatory stage of the meals that they share as an indispensable element of the socially meaningful relationship. An image of masculinity constructed here is male bonding similar to the one in sports events. However, the version of male bonding in *Okazu-kun*, as it is also replicated in *Danshi-gohan*, does not consider physical strength to be a basis of male identity. Rather, the thread that connects these cooking men is the nourish-and-nurture quality inherent to cooking and eating, and they find pleasure in doing these things with others, forming a localized social unit for their identity. What they do in their home kitchens on Friday evening, in its essence, is not much different from domestic duties that are stereotypically gendered with women, but those domestic responsibilities are fulfilled in *Okazu-kun* by men in solidarity.

In this section I have examined cookbooks for men and comic books that portray cooking men in order to ascertain how images of masculinity are constructed and casted. All materials that have been given textual analysis were published after the very end of the 20th century. In none of these books, do we find an exclusive image that is tied to the social changes that motivated or necessitated men's cooking. We instead see multiple, sometimes conflicting, images of gender roles and identities projected and performed in cooking discourse. This is precisely what we expect to see given that masculinity is constructed by interactions of various social and cultural canons, and also given how social transitions intricately intersect with patterns of cultural systems. Of the sources analyzed, *Kukkingu Papa* and *Okazu-kun* are undeniably fiction with imaginary role players. As such, my examination is not intended to mirror directly how masculinity of cooking men are constructed in the Japanese society today. Nevertheless, I view that projected images entertained in these comic books incorporate some elements of the national discourse suggestive of and pertinent to gender roles, gender identity, and social norms. To that extent, comic books can be a source of value to scholarly investigations that look into the intriguing relationship between food and gender.

NOTES

1. The Burger King commercial for a Texas Double Whopper is based on the gendering of meat with men. The ad song is a take on Helen Reddy's "I Am Woman." The lyrics of the song and the video are full of phrases and scenes that are intended to disparage commodities including food (e.g., quiche, tofu, family van) that are gendered with women. (https://www.luerzersarchive.com/en/magazine/commercial-detail/burger-king-36371.html.)

2. In a broader sense, this is an example of what Parasecoli (2022) calls "gastro-nativism," which he defines as "the ideological use of food in politics to advance ideas about who belongs to a community and who doesn't."

3. The original report on the radio and its written script are available at https://www.npr.org/templates/story/story.php?storyId=120696816.

4. In analyzing *amatō* and *karatō* in their religious connection, Kopii (1992) explains that *amatō* is tied not only to women and children but to those who are ill, and in contrast, *karatō* gives rise to the image of sake-drinking samurai. Based on aspects of religious rituals (e.g., voting offerings), she analyzes that *amatō* is consistent with Buddhism while *karatō* aligns well with Shintoism.

5. Considering the association of alcohol with men, it is interesting to see an advertisement for a beer product (Sakura Bīru) appearing in an early women's magazine. In the July 1926 issue of *Hujin-no Tomo* "Ladies' Friend," which was a magazine for the general female audience, a caption says that the beer is appropriate for "regular consumption by modest wives" and promotes "blood flow for bright appearance."

6. Takai (2014) explains that the catch phrase was taken from the words by the diplomat Charles-Maurice de Talleyrand-Périgord in the French Revolution but was arranged by Café Paulista for advertisement. Takai translates the original French version into Japanese, which means in English: "[g]ood coffee is dark as a devil, hot as hell, pure as an angel, and sweet as love" (pp. 50–51).

7. Kuga (2008) comments that *Hujingahō*, first published in 1905, targeted upper-class women, but its circulation was far smaller than that of *Shuhu-no Tomo*.

8. Fleming (2021) discusses a significant role that women played in (instant) coffee culture in 1960s Britain through examinations of coffee advertisements.

246   Chapter Seven

According to her, women who drink (instant) coffee are portrayed in advertisements as "glamorous," parallel to the image in the Japanese adverts. Fleming points out, however, that coffee-drinking women in the 60s UK are also depicted with sexual connotations—the link that is missing in the Japanese context.

9. https://www.ucc.co.jp/company/news/2016/rel160413.html.

10. http://www.imo.ne.jp/shop2/meijingai/topics/topics.cgi.

11. Murakami notes that influenced by Nakamura's leadership, a men's cooking group was launched in 1977 under the name of *danshi chūbō-ni hairō-kai* "group of let's-enter-the-kitchen." Based on an online search, I have found that several similar groups have started not only in Tokyo but in regional locations since then (http://www2s.biglobe.ne.jp/~chuchan/01/01_1.htm). However, some of these groups seem to enjoy cooking together, sometimes learning from female instructors, without the aggressive, challenging tone that is evident in the title of Nakamura's book. Participants in these cooking groups seem to be relatively old (e.g., retirees) and are motivated to learn cooking so that they can take care of their own meals. As far as their reasons to (want to) cook and their perspective toward men's cooking are concerned, then, it is more appropriate to categorize these men under the second wave of cooking men both on conceptual and practical grounds.

12. Ako (2013) discusses that women who were born after the 1960s form a generation of women who are not confident, or interested, in cooking. Ako explains that these women grew up in the middle of the country's high economic growth, having more access to ready-made meals and opportunities to eating out than previous generations of women. In the rich economic environment that brought significant implications to family life, they further forfeited occasions to be in the home kitchen with their mothers to help them and learn how to cook from them.

13. The author, Sadao Shoji, is a comic writer and essayist. Shoji (1984) is written in the style of an essay but chronicles, with much humor and illustrations, the process in which he and his friends venture on a couple of dozen menu items.

14. This characterization should not be understood as the stance that Tamamura takes in his book, which is intended as a self-help guide for beginner audiences. He advocates men's independence and self-support in the kitchen and provides beginners hands-on advice on preparing daily meals at home.

15. Recall that in chapter 6, I described the language that Katsuyo Kobayashi uses in her recipes as bearing a masculine air. The nuance of the language is analyzed as her way of encouraging the reader not to be afraid of making mistakes.

16. The words suggestive of masculinity that appear in the title of Nishi (2007) are not isolated to his cookbook. For example, in the cookbook *Otoko-no Ryōri-wa Dōgu-to Waza-ni Oku-no Te-ga Aru* (Hōmuraihu Seminā 1999), which seems to be predominantly "cooking as hobby" as its underlying concept, we witness a number of references to men that appear in the phrase of *otoko-no X* "men's X" (e.g., *otoko-no sakana-ryōri* "men's fish dishes," *otoko-naradewa-no shokuzai* "ingredients particular to men") as well as words like *yūkan* "heroic," *yūsō* "brave," and *daitan* "bold, fearless," in referring to various aspects of cooking and actions. In relation to the use of direct fire as a gendered technique, it also contains theatrical expressions like

moeru otoko-no akai honō "red flame of burning men" in speaking of the burning fire when bonito is broiled in an open fire with straw (p. 72).

17. For example, the cooking method known as *uragoshi* is mentioned without further explanations although it does not seem to be a technique that is familiar to everybody, especially beginners. *Uragoshi* is used, for instance, to mash cooked potatoes by pressing them against a sieve. The mashed potato passes through the fine mesh of the sieve.

18. Due to a motorcycle accident in 2012 that disabled Kentaro, he has since been replaced by Shinpei Kurihara.

References

Abarca, Meredith E. 2004. "Authentic or Not, It's Original." *Food and Foodways* 12 (1): 1–25.
Abe, Naomi. 2020. "Watashi-no Shigoto #5—Bentōya Tenshu Sakiyama Mitsuyo-san" [My Job #5—Box Lunch Shop Owner, Ms. Mitsuyo Sakiyama]. *Kurashi-no Techo* 5: 91–93.
Agawa, Sawako. 2012. *Musume-no Aji—Nokoru-wa Shokuyoku* 3 [Daughter's Taste—Remaining Is Appetite 3]. Tokyo: Magajinhausu.
Aita, Koji. 2006. *Kō-chan-no Kantan Ryōri Reshipi* [Ko-chan's Recipes for Easy Cooking]. Tokyo: Takarajimasha.
Akita, Kimi. 2009. "A Grammar of Sound-Symbolic Words in Japanese: Theoretical Approaches to Iconic and Lexical Properties of Mimetics." PhD diss., Kobe University.
Ako, Mari. 2013. *Shōwa-no Yōshoku Heisei-no Kafe-Meshi* [Western Food in Showa and Café-Meals in Heisei]. Tokyo: Chikuma Shobo.
———. 2014. *Shōwa-Sodachi-no Oishii Kioku* [Showaite's Delicious Memory]. Tokyo: Chikuma Shobo.
———. 2015. *Kobayashi Katsuyo to Kurihara Harumi: Ryōri-kenkyūka to Sono Jidai* [Katsuyo Kobayashi and Harumi Kurihara: Cooking Experts and Their Era]. Tokyo: Shinchosha.
Allison, Ralph I., and Kenneth P. Uhl. 1964. "Influence of Beer Brand Identification on Taste Perception." *Journal of Marketing Research* 1 (3): 36–39.
"Amakarai Okazu." 2014. *Kurashi-no Techo* 72: 18–29.
Aoyama, Tomoko. 2003. "The Cooking Man in Modern Japanese Literature." In *Asian Masculinity: The Meaning and Practice of Manhood in China and Japan*, edited by Kam Louie and Morris Low, 155–76. London: Routledge Curzon.
———. 2008. *Reading Food in Modern Japanese Literature*. Honolulu: University of Hawaii Press.
———. 2010. "Food and Gender in the Manga of Yoshinaga Fumi." *Center for Comparative Japanese Studies Annual Bulletin* 6: 153–61.

Arine. 2020. "Aki Huyu-wa Neibī-Meiku-de Supaisu-o" [Add a Spice with Navy-Makeup in Autumn and Winter]. Posted June 3, 2020. https://arine.jp/articles/17394.

Armstrong, Robert Plant. 1971. *The Affecting Presence: An Essay in Humanistic Anthropology*. Urbana: University of Illinois Press.

———. 1975. *Wellspring: On the Myth and Source of Culture*. Berkeley: University of California Press.

Baba, Junko. 2003. "Pragmatic Function of Japanese Mimetics in the Spoken Discourse of Varying Emotive Intensity Levels." *Journal of Pragmatics* 35: 1861–89.

Backhouse, A. E. 1994. *The Lexical Field of Taste: A Semantic Study of Japanese Taste Terms*. Cambridge: Cambridge University Press.

Barthes, Roland. 2013. "Toward a Psychosociology of Contemporary Food Consumption." In *Food and Culture: A Reader*, Third Edition, edited by Carole Counihan and Penny Van Esterik, 23–30. New York: Routledge. [Originally published as: Barthes, Roland. 1961. "Vers une Psycho-Sociologie de L'alimentation Modern." *Annales: Économies, Société, Civilisations* 5: 977–86.]

"Book." 2022. *Kurowassan* 1065: 84.

Bourdieu, Pierre. 1984. *Distinction: A Social Critique of the Judgment of Taste*. Translated by Richard Nice. Cambridge, MA: Harvard University Press.

Bucholtz, Mary, and Kira Hall. 2005. "Identity and Interaction: A Sociocultural Linguistic Approach. *Discourse Studies* 7: 585–614.

Butler, Judith. 1990. *Gender Trouble: Feminism and the Subversion of Identity*. New York: Routledge.

Cameron, Deborah. 1997. "Performing Gender Identity: Young Men's Talk and the Construction of Heterosexual Masculinity." In *Language and Masculinity*, edited by Sally Johnson and Ulrike Hanna Meinhof, 47–64. Oxford: Blackwell Publishers.

———. 2008. "Theoretical Issue for the Study of Gender and Spoken Interaction. In *Gender and Spoken Interaction*, edited by Pia Pichler and Eva Eppler, 1–17. Basingstoke, UK: Palgrave Macmillan.

CatchCappuccino. 2009. "Nikaidō Shuzō." Posted September 29, 2009. http://catchcopy1.blog101.fc2.com/?tag=食品.

CBK Magazine. 2018. "'Tōshindai Fasshon'-ni Hitosaji-no Supaisu-o" [Add a Spoonful of Spice to "Life-Size Fashion"]. Posted May 20, 2018. https://magazine.cubki.jp/articles/70152206.html.

Chen, Yong. 2012. "Food, Race, and Ethnicity." In *The Oxford Handbook of Food History*, edited by Jeffrey M. Pilcher. 428–43. Oxford: Oxford University Press.

Chiba, Michiko. 1996. "Takenoko-to Shin-Kyabetsu-no Itameni" [Sauté-Simmering of Bamboo Shoots and New Cabbage]. *Orenjipeji net*. Posted April 2, 1996. https://www.orangepage.net/recipes/detail_114279.

Chin, Ken'ichi. 2008. "Mābōdōhu." *Gurunabireshipi*, YouTube video, January 10, 2008. https://www.youtube.com/watch?v=limiFRJzpvM.

Chiseisha, ed. 1990. *Otoko-no Ryōri: Yasei-ni Kaeru* [Men's Cooking: Return to Wild Nature]. Tokyo: Shogakkan.

Connell, R. W. 2000. *The Men and the Boys*. Berkeley: University of California Press.

Cook, Haruko Minegishi. 1990. "An Indexical Account of the Japanese Sentence-Final Particle *no*." *Discourse Processes* 13: 401–39.
———. 1992. "Meanings of Non-Referential Indexes: A Case Study of the Japanese Sentence-Final Particle ne." *Text* 12: 507–39.
———. 1997 "The Role of the Japanese *Masu* Form in Caregiver-Child Conversation." *Journal of Pragmatics* 28: 695–718.
———. 1998. "Situational Meanings of Japanese Social Deixis: The Mixed Use of the *Masu* and Plain Forms." *Journal of Linguistic Anthropology* 8 (1): 87–110.
———. 2008. "Style Shifts in Japanese Academic Consultations." In *Style Shifting in Japanese*, edited by Kimberly Jones and Tsuyoshi Ono, 9–38. Amsterdam: John Benjamins Publishing Company.
———. 2012. "Language Socialization and Stance-Taking Practices." In *The Handbook of Language Socialization*, edited by Alessandro Duranti, Elinor Ochs, and Bambi B. Schieffelin, 296–321. Malden, MA: Wiley-Blackwell.
Cotter, Colleen. 1997. "Claiming a Piece of the Pie: How the Language of the Recipes Defines Community." In *Recipes for Reading: Community Cookbooks, Stories, Histories*, edited by Anne L. Bower, 51–71. Amherst: University of Massachusetts Press.
Counihan, Carole. 2012. "Gendering Food." In *The Oxford Handbook of Food History*, edited by Jeffrey M. Pilcher, 99–116. Oxford: Oxford University Press.
Coupland, Nikolas. 2001. "Language, Situation, and the Relational Self: Theorizing Dialect-Style in Sociolinguistics." In *Style and Sociolinguistic Variation*, edited by Penelope Eckert and John Rickford, 185–210. Cambridge: Cambridge University Press.
Dan, Kazuo. 1975. *Dan-ryū Kukkingu* [Dan-Style Cooking]. Tokyo: Chuko Bunko.
Deguchi, Kazumi. 2002. *Otoko-no Ryōri-Kyōshitsu* [Cooking Class for Men]. Tokyo: Shunhosha.
Detake, Hisao. 1983. "Ryōriten Gaidobukku-ni Miru Aji-no Hyōgen" [Taste Expressions in Restaurant Guidebooks]. *Gengo Seikatsu* 382: 66–69.
Diffloth, Gérard. 1972. "Notes on Expressive Meaning." *Chicago Linguistic Society* 8: 440–47.
Dingemanse, Mark. 2011. "Ideophones and the Aesthetics of Everyday Language in a West-African Society." *The Senses and Society* 6 (1): 77–85.
DiVirgilio, Didi. 2010. "The Emergence of the Cookbook and the Evolution of Cooking Terminology in Imperial Russia." In *Food and Language*, edited by Richard Hosking, 94–104. London: Prospect Books.
Doi, Masaru. 1969. *Wahū Kyō-no Ryōri* [Today's Japanese-style Cooking]. Tokyo: Nippon Hoso Shuppan Kyokai.
Doi, Yoshiharu. 2014. *Doi Yoshiharu-no Natsukashi-Gohan* [Yoshiharu Doi's Nostalgic Meals]. Tokyo: NHK Shuppan.
DRESS. 2017. "Ryōri-to Fasshon-wa Nite-iru. Sukunai Aitemu-o Jibun-rashiku 'Chōri' Shitai" [Cooking and Fashion Are Similar. You Want to "Cook" a Few Items to Your Liking]. Posted June 15, 2017. https://p-dress.jp/articles/4093.
Eckert, Penelope. 2000. *Linguistic Variation as Social Practice: The Linguistic Construction of Identity in Belten High*. Oxford: Blackwell.

———. 2012. "Three Waves of Variation Study: The Emergence of Meaning in the Study of Sociolinguistic Variation." *Annual Review of Anthropology* 41: 87–100.

Egawa, Tomi. 1957. *Watashitachi-no Okazu* [Our Dishes]. Tokyo: Shibata Shoten.

Elder, Ryan S., and Aradhna Krishna. 2010. "The Effects of Advertising Copy on Sensory Thoughts and Perceived Taste." *Journal of Consumer Research* 36 (5): 748–56.

Feld, Steven. 1988. "Aesthetics as Iconicity of Style, or 'Lift-up-over Sounding': Getting into the Kaluli Groove." *Yearbook for Traditional Music* 20: 74–113.

Ferguson, Priscilla Parkhurst. 2014. *Word of Mouth: What We Talk about When We Talk about Food*. Berkeley: University of California Press.

Finegan, Edward. 1994. *Language: Its Structure and Use*, Second Edition. Fort Worth: Harcourt Brace & Company.

Fischler, Claude. 1988. "Food, Self and Identity." *Social Science Information* 27 (2): 275–92.

Fisher, M.F.K. 1968. *With Bold Knife and Fork*. New York: Smithmark.

Fleming, Isabel. 2021. "Youth, Consumerism and Domesticity: Drinking Instant Coffee in 1960s Britain." Undergraduate thesis, Oxford University.

Fukutome, Nami. 2014. "Chōri-ni Okeru Huttō-o Arawasu Yōgo, Hyōgen" [The Vocabulary and Expressions of Boiling in Cooking]. *Nihon Chori Kagaku Kaishi* 47 (5): 239–46.

Gerhardt, Cornelia, Maximiliane Frobenius, and Susanne Ley, ed. 2013. *Culinary Linguistics: The Chef's Special*. Amsterdam: John Benjamins Publishing Company.

German, Kathleen M. 2011. "Memory, Identity, and Resistance: Recipes from the Women on Theresienstadt." In *Food as Communication / Communication as Food*, edited by Janet M. Cramer, Carlnita P. Greene, and Lynn M. Walters, 137–54. New York: Peter Lang.

Goodman, Nelson. 1976. *Languages of Art: An Approach to a Theory of Symbols*. Indianapolis: Hackett Publishing Company.

Gopnik, Alan. 2010. "What's the Recipe?: Our Hunger for Cookbooks." In *Best Food Writing 2010*, edited by Holly Hughes, 264–75. Cambridge, MA: Da Capo Press. (The original appeared in *The New Yorker*, November 23, 2009.)

Gurōbaru-mama Kenkyūjo. 2021. "Nama-no Engeki-wa Kokoro-no Kate! Koronaka-de Hajimatta 'Shiatā-Deribarī'" [Live Plays Are Food for Mind! "Theater-Delivery" Beginning in Corona Pandemic]. GetNavi web. Posted April 12, 2021. https://getnavi.jp/world/587773/.

Halloran, Vivian. 2014. An Introduction to the Exhibit Pamphlet—Book Bites: Texts that Influenced and Reflected How America Eats. Lilly Library. Indiana University.

Hamada, Iori. 2017. "Transnational Domestic Masculinity: Japanese Men's Home Cooking in Australia." In *Food, Masculinities, and Home: Interdisciplinary Perspectives*, edited by Michelle Szabo and Shelley Koch, 75–91. London: Bloomsbury.

Hamano, Shoko. 1986. "The Sound-Symbolic System of Japanese." PhD diss., University of Florida.

———. 1998. *The Sound-Symbolic System of Japanese*. Stanford, CA: CSLI.

Happy Lifestyle Corporation. n.d. "'Jinsei-to-wa Nani-ka'-o Kangaeru 30-no Kotoba" [30 Expressions that Make You Think "What Is Life"]. Happy Lifestyle. Retrieved December 15, 2021. https://happylifestyle.com/11911.

Harada, Aya. 2012. "Reshipi-no Buntai-ni Kansuru Kenkyū" [An Investigation of the Style of Recipes]. *Kokubun* 117: 51–61.

Hasegawa, Mio. 2021. "Tamago, Tori, Tōhu" [Eggs, Chicken, Tofu]. *Kurowassan* 1052: 12–19.

Hasegawa, Yoko. 2015. *Japanese: A Linguistic Introduction*. Cambridge: Cambridge University Press.

Haspelmath, Martin. 2001. "Lexical Borrowing: Concepts and Issues." In *Language Typology and Language Universals*, edited by Martin Haspelmath, Ekkehard Koenig, and Wulf Oesterreicher, 35–54. Berlin: Mouton de Gruyter.

Hatanaka, Mieko. 2020. "Nihonjin-no Shoku-Seikatsu-o Sarani Tayōka-shita Esunikku-Hūdo" [Ethnic Food that Further Diversified Japanese Food Culture]. *Vesta* 118: 4–9.

Hayakawa, Fumiyo. 2003. "Tabemono-no Tekusuchā-to Gengo-Hyōgen" [Food Texture and Linguistic Expressions]. *Shokuseikatsu* 97 (9): 40–45.

———. 2007. "Giongo, Gitaigo-ga Hōhu-na Shokkan Hyōgen" [Mouth Feel Expressions Rich with Mimetics]. *Vesta* 65: 44–45.

———. 2013. "Nihongo-no Tekusuchā-Hyōgen-to Taishō Shokumotsumei-ni Tsuite" [On Texture Expressions and Their Corresponding Food Names in Japanese]. *Shokuhin to Yooki* 54 (9): 566–71.

Hayakawa, Fumiyo, Keiko Hatae, and Atsuko Shimada. 1997. "Ankēto-ni Yoru 'Aburakkosa'-no Tokuchōzuke" [Characterization of 'Oiliness' through Questionnaires]. *Nihon Kaseigakkaishi* 48 (1): 19–28.

Hayakawa, Fumiyo, Kana Ioku, Sayuri Akuzawa, Masayoshi Saito, Katsuyoshi Nishinari, Yoshimasa Yamano, and Kaory Kohyama. 2005. "Nihongo Tekusuchā-Yōgo-no Shūshū" [Collection of Japanese Texture Terms]. *Nippon Shokuhin Kagaku Kogaku Kaishi* 52 (8): 337–46.

Higashi, Michio. 2016. "Amerika-no Shoku-wa Sekai-no Sore-to-wa Mattaku Betsumono-rashii" [American Food Seems to Be Totally Different from the World's Food]. *Vesta* 103: 52–56.

Higashiyotsuyanagi, Shoko. 2010. "The History of Domestic Cookbooks in Modern Japan." In *Japanese Foodways, Past and Present*, edited by Eric C. Rath and Stephanie Assmann, 129–44. Champaign, IL: University of Illinois Press.

Hines, Caitlin. 1999. "Rebaking the Pie. The WOMAN AS DESSERT Metaphor." In *Reinventing Identities: The Gendered Self in Discourse*, edited by Mary Bucholtz, A. C. Liang, and Laurel A. Sutton, 145–62. Oxford: Oxford University Press.

Hinton, Leanne, Johanna Nichols, and John J. Ohala. 1994. "Introduction: Sound-Symbolic Processes." In *Sound Symbolism*, edited by Leanne Hinton, Johanna Nichols, and John J. Ohala, 1–12. Cambridge: Cambridge University Press.

Hiramatsu, Yoko. 2015. *Aji-na Menyū* [Tasteful Menus]. Tokyo: Gentosha.

Hobbis, Stephanie Ketterer. 2017. "'The Comic and the Rule' in Pastagate: Food, Humor and the Politics of Language in Quebec." *Food, Culture & Society* 20 (4): 709–27.

Hoegg, JoAndrea, and Joseph W. Alba. 2007. "More than Meets the Tongue." *Journal of Consumer Research* 33 (4): 490–98.

Hollows, Joanne. 2003. "Feeling Like a Domestic Goddess: Postfeminism and Cooking." *European Journal of Cultural Studies* 6 (2): 179–202.

Holtzman, Jon. 2018. "The Weakness of Sweetness: Masculinity and Confectionary in Japan." *Food, Culture & Society* 21 (3): 280–95.

Hōmuraihu Seminā, ed. 1999. *Otoko-no Ryōri-wa Dōgu-to Waza-ni Oku-no Te-ga Aru* [Men's Cooking Has Secrets in Utensils and Techniques]. Tokyo: Seishun Shuppan.

Hosking, Richard, ed. 2010. *Food and Language*. Blackawton: Prospect Books.

Hoyer, Wayne D., and Steven P. Brown. 1990. "Effects of Brand Awareness on Choice for a Common, Repeat-Purchase Product." *Journal of Consumer Research* 17 (2): 141–48.

Ichise, Etsuko. 2014. "Hakusai-no Boryūmu Okazu" [Filling Meals with Napa Cabbage]. *Kyono Ryori Biginazu* 11: 8–20.

Ikawa, Noriaki. 1991. "Shokukankaku-o Arawasu Gokan-no Kīwādo" [Keywords for the Five Senses on the Expression of Sense in Food]. *Meijidaigaku Nogyobu Kenkyu Hokoku* 91: 1–16.

Ikeda, Takayuki, ed. 2013. *Gutto Kuru Kōhī* [Gulping Coffee]. Tokyo: Tokuma Shoten.

Irvine, Judith. 2001. "Style as Distinctiveness: The Culture and Ideology of Linguistic Differentiation." In *Stylistic Variation in Language*, edited by Penelope Eckert and John Rickford, 21–43. Cambridge: Cambridge University Press.

Irwin, Mark. 2011. *Loanwords in Japanese*. Amsterdam: John Benjamins Publishing Company.

———. 2016. "The Morphology of English Loanwords." In *Handbook of Japanese Lexicon and Word Formation*, edited by Taro Kageyama and Hideki Kishimoto, 161–97. Boston: Walter de Gruyter Inc.

Ishizawa, Kiyomi. 2004. *Yasai Tappuri Oishii Okazu* [Delicious Dishes Rich with Vegetables]. Tokyo: Oizumi Shoten.

itSnap. n.d. "Shinpuru-na Rongu-Kōto-o Vintēji-Baggu&Gara-Kāde-de Koseiteki-ni Ajitsuke" [Season a Simple Long Coat with a Vintage Purse and a Patterned Cardigan]. Retrieved October 2, 2021. https://itsnap.jp/coordinate/8142.

Iwasaki, Shoichi. 2002. *Japanese*. Amsterdam: John Benjamins Publishing Company.

Izawa, Yumiko. 2015. "Buta-renkon" [Pork-lotus Roots]. *Minna-no Kyō-no Ryōri* [Today's Cooking for Everyone]. October 13, 2015. https://www.kyounoryouri.jp/recipe/20972_豚れんこん.html.

Jackson, Peter, and Angela Meah. 2019. "Taking Humor Seriously in Contemporary Food Research." *Food, Culture & Society* 22 (3): 262–79.

Jo, Jiro. 2021. "Shehu-no Reshipichō" [Chef's Recipe]. *Kurashiru*, YouTube video, April 27, 2021. https://www.youtube.com/watch?v=p873luVd6bE.

Jones, Kimberly, and Tsuyoshi Ono. 2008. "The Messy Reality of Style Shifting." In *Style Shifting in Japanese*, edited by Kimberly Jones and Tsuyoshi Ono, 9–38. Amsterdam: John Benjamins Publishing Company.

Julier, Alice, and Laura Lindenfeld. 2005. "Mapping Men onto the Menu: Masculinities and Food." *Food & Foodways* 13 (1): 1–16.

Jurafsky, Dan. 2014. *The Language of Food: A Linguist Reads the Menu*. New York: W. W. Norton & Company.

Kaishiden. 2013. "Tenkaippin-no 'Kossari'-tte Itsunomanika Ofisharu Menyū-ni Natte-ta-no-ne" ["Kossari" at Tenkaippin Has Become an Official Menu Item]. Posted October 3, 2013. https://bloggingfrom.tv/wp/2013/10/03/11431.

Kakehi, Hisao. 1989. "Mikaku: Kikizake-no Kotoba" [Language of Sake Tasting]. *Gengo* 18 (11): 54–59.

Kakehi, Hisao, and Ikuhiro Tamori, ed. 1993. *Onomatopia: Gion · Gitaigo no Rakuen* [Onomatopoeia: Paradise of Phonomimes and Phemomimes]. Tokyo: Keiso Shobo.

Kakehi, Hisao, Ikuhiro Tamori, and Lawrence Schourup. 1996. *Dictionary of Iconic Expressions in Japanese*. Berlin: Mouton de Gruyter.

Kamebuchi, Akinobu, and Yoshiharu Doi. 2010. *Otoko-no Ryōri Nyūmonjuku—Ikutsu-ni Natte-mo Hajime-rareru* [Men's Introductory Cooking School—You Can Start at Any Age]. Tokyo: Gakken Paburisshingu.

Kamo, Akihiro. 1999. "Kōhī: Hukuyoka-na Kaori-to Kokoro Nagomasu Aji-no Sekai" [The World of Rich Flavor and Taste that Relaxes Mind." *Rekishi-to Tabi* 26 (11): 250–53.

Kanagawa Minami Iryō Seikyō Zushi Shinryōjo Gurūpu Shōnan Supaisu, ed. 2004. *Oyaji-no Te-Ryōri—Otoko-no Ryōri-Kyōshitsu* [Dad's Home-Cooking—Cooking Class for Men]. Tokyo: Ikkosha.

Kariya, Tetsu. 1991. *Oishinbo Tanteikyoku* [Oishinbo Detective Office]. Tokyo: Kadokawa Bunko.

Katada, Takaya. 2021. "Manshon 'Kanri Kyohi' Zōka Zendai-Mimon-no Hazu-ga Kanrigaisha-no Jijō-wa" [Increasing "Management Refusal" of Condominiums—It Should Be Unheard of—Situations with Building Maintenance Companies]. *Asahi Shinbun Digital*, September 7, 2021. https://digital.asahi.com/articles/ASP965W76P91ULEI002.html.

Kato, Keiko, ed. 2019. *Doi Yoshiharu-no Sōzai-no Reshipi* [Recipes for Meals by Yoshiharu Doi]. Tokyo: TV Asahi.

Kawabata, Akiko, and Shoko Huchinoue, ed. 2006. *Oishisa-no Hyōgen Jiten* [Dictionary of Expressions of Good Taste]. Tokyo: Tokyodo Shuppan.

Kidosaki, Ai. 1986. *Suteki-na Kidosaki Ai-no Osusume Ryōri* [Lovely Ai Kidosaki's Suggested Meals]. Tokyo: Gurahusha.

———. 1987. *Isogashii Hito-no Oishii Osōzai* [Delicious Dishes for Busy People]. Tokyo: Kairyusha.

Kiesling, Scott Fabius. 1997. "Power and the Language of Men." In *Language and Masculinity*, edited by Sally Johnson and Ulrike Hanna Meinhof, 66–85. Oxford: Blackwell Publishers.

Kijima, Ryuta. 2021. "Kijima Ryūta-no Ouchigohan: Toromi Yudedori" [Ryuta Kijima's In-House Meal: Tender Boiled Chicken]. *Asahi Shinbun Digital*, YouTube video, April 4, 2021. https://digital.asahi.com/articles/ASP413D14P30DIFI001.html?iref=pc_ss_date_article.

Kikkoman. n.d. "Kindan-no . . . Dashibata TKG" [Forbidden . . . TKG with Dashi and Butter]. https://www.kikkoman.co.jp/homecook/search/recipe/00007126/index.html.

Kindaichi, Hideho. 2016. "Tatsujin-ni Kiku 'Shin・Nihongo-no Ryūgi'" [Ask Professionals—"New: Styles of Japanese Language"] (Interview with Doi Yoshiharu). *Bungeishunju* 94 (1): 404–11.

Kinoshima, Terumi. 1996. "Gendai-no Shōzō—Kobayashi Katsuyo" [Modern Portrait—Katsuyo Kobayashi]. *Asahi Shinbun Weekly AERA* 48: 55–60.

Kinsui, Satoshi. 2003. *Bācharu Nihongo Yakuwarigo-no Nazo* [Mysteries of Role Language, the Virtual Japanese]. Tokyo: Iwanami Shoten.

———, ed. 2007. *Yakuwarigo Kenkyū-no Chihei* [The Horizon of Research on Role Language]. Tokyo: Kurosio Shuppan.

Kita, Sotaro. 1997. "Two-Dimensional Semantic Analysis of Japanese Mimetics." *Linguistics* 35: 370–415.

Klink, Richard R. 2000. "Creating Brand Names with Meaning: The Use of Sound Symbolism." *Marketing Letters* 11 (1): 5–20.

———. 2001. "Creating Meaningful New Brand Names: A Study of Semantics and Sound Symbolism." *Journal of Marketing: Theory and Practice* 9: 27–34.

Kobayashi, Katsuyo. 1980. *Kobayashi Katsuyo-no Rakuraku Kukkingu* [Katsuyo Kobayashi's Easy Cooking]. Tokyo: Bunka Shuppankyoku.

———. 1987. *Kobayashi Katsuyo-no Teryōri-Jōzu-no Kurashi-Memo* [Katsuyo Kobayashi's Life Notes for Good Home Cooking]. Tokyo: Mikasa Shobo.

———. 1991. *Sate, Kōhī-ni Shimasen-ka?* [Well, How About Some Coffee?]. Tokyo: Daiwa Shobo.

———. 1995. *Kobayashi Katsuyo-no Zakkubaran-ni Omotenashi* [Katsuyo Kobayashi's Carefree Entertainment]. Tokyo: Nippon Hoso Shuppan Kyokai.

———. 1997a. "Kobayashi Katsuyo—Kōen 'Shizen-ga Oshieru Watashi-no Ryōri'" [Katsuyo Kobayashi—Lecture: Cooking that the Nature Teaches Me]. *Seikatsu Kenkyu* 28: 29–44.

———. 1997b. *Kobayashi Katsuyo-no Kicchin-Techō* [Katsuyo Kobayashi's Kitchen Notebook]. Tokyo: Mikasa Shobo.

———. 2001. *Otoko-no Oi-jitaku Meshi-jitaku* [Men's Preparation for Aging and Meals]. Tokyo: Kairyusha.

———. 2003. *Jissen Ryōri-no Heso!* [Practical Cooking Core]. Tokyo: Bungei Shunju.

———. 2007. *Kobayashi Katsuyo-no Mainichi Okazu* [Katsuyo Kobayashi's Everyday Meals]. Tokyo: Kodansha.

———. 2008. *Kobayashi Katsuyo-no At-to Iu Ma-no Okazu* [Katsuyo Kobayashi's Quick Meals]. Tokyo: Daiwa Shobo.

———. 2011. *Kobayashi Katsuyo-no "Haha-Okazu"—Kiso-no Washoku* [Katsuyo Kobayashi's 'Mom's Dishes'—Basic Japanese-style Meals]. Tokyo: Kodansha.

———. 2014a. *Kobayashi Katsuyo-no Oishii-ga Ichiban!* [Katsuyo Kobayashi—Delicious Is the Best!]. Tokyo: Daiwa Shobo.

———. 2014b. *Hataraku Josei-no Kicchin-Raihu* [Working Women's Kitchen Life]. Tokyo: Daiwa Shobo.

———. 2015. *Onaka-ga Suku Hanashi* [Stories that Make You Hungry]. Tokyo: Kawade Shobo Shinsha.
Kobayashi Katsuyo Kitchen Studio. 2008. *Kobayashi Katsuyo-no At-to Iu Ma-no Okazu* [Katsuyo Kobayashi's Quick Meals]. Tokyo: Daiwa Shobo.
Koike, Chisato. 2014. "Food Experiences and Categorization in Japanese Talk-in-Interaction." In *Language and Food: Verbal and Nonverbal Experiences*, edited by Polly Szatrowski, 159–83. Amsterdam: John Benjamins Publishing Company.
Kokubun, Taichi, and Kentaro. 2009. *Taichi x Kentarō Danshi-Gohan-no Hon* [Taichi x Kentaro Book for Men's Cooking]. Tokyo: M.Co.
Komori, Michihiko. 2003. "Motto Gokan-de Ajiwau" [Tasting More with Five Senses]. In *Kotoba-wa Aji-o Koeru* [Language Transcends Taste], edited by Ken'ichi Seto, 79–116. Tokyo: Kaimeisha.
Kopii, Jaanu. 1992. "Karatō-no Kami-to Amatō-no Hotoke" [Spice-Loving God and Sweet-Loving Buddha]. In *Matsuri-e-no Manazashi* [A Look into Rites], edited by Tsuneya Wakimoto and Kei'ichi Yanagawa, 37–49. Tokyo: Tokyo Daigaku Shuppankai.
Krishna, Aradhna. 2010. "An Introduction to Sensory Marketing." In *Sensory Marketing: Research on the Sensuality of Products*, edited by Aradhna Krishna, 1–13. New York: Routledge.
Krishna, Aradhna, and Ryan S. Elder. 2010. "The Gist of Gustation: An Exploration of Taste, Food, and Consumption." In *Sensory Marketing: Research on the Sensuality of Products*, edited by Aradhna Krishna, 281–301. New York: Routledge.
Kroo, Judit. 2018. "Gentle Masculinity in East Asia: 'Herbivore Men' and Interlocutor Constructed Language." *Journal of Asian Pacific Communication* 28 (2): 251–80.
Kubo, Akinori, 2020. *"Katei-Ryōri"-to Iu Senjō. Kurashi-wa Dezain Dekiru-ka?* [Battlefield Called Home-Cooking. Can Life Be Designed?]. Chiba: Kotonisha.
Kubozono, Haruo. 1995. *Go-Keisei to On'in-Kōzō* [Word Formation and Phonological Structure]. Tokyo: Kurosio.
———. 2015. "Loanword Phonology." In *Handbook of Japanese Phonetics and Phonology*, edited by Haruo Kubozono, 313–61. Boston: Walter de Gruyter Inc.
Kuga, Mutsuko. 2007. "Kōhī-no Hukyū-Katei-ni Okeru Rekishi-teki Purosesu 1" [Historical Steps of Popularization Process of Coffee 1]. *Kōhī Bunka Kenkyū* 14: 33–44.
———. 2008. "Kōhī-no Hukyū-Katei-ni Okeru Rekishi-teki Purosesu 2" [Historical Steps of Popularization Process of Coffee 2]. *Kōhī Bunka Kenkyū* 15: 20–34.
———. 2009. "Kōhī-no Hukyū-Katei-ni Okeru Rekishi-teki Purosesu 3" [Historical Steps of Popularization Process of Coffee 3]. *Kōhī Bunka Kenkyū* 16: 19–35
———. 2010. "Kōhī-no Hukyū-Katei-ni Okeru Rekishi-teki Purosesu 4" [Historical Steps of Popularization Process of Coffee 4]. *Kōhī Bunka Kenkyū* 17: 60–74.
Kugler, Carol. 2018. "When Kids Are Cooks." *The Herald Times* D1, August 29, 2018. Bloomington, IN.
Kumagai, Gakuji, Ryoko Uno, and Kazuko Shinohara. 2022. "The Sound-Symbolic Effects of Consonants on Food Texture: An Experimental Study of Snack Names

in Japanese." In *The Language of Food in Japanese: Cognitive Perspectives and Beyond*, edited by Kiyoko Toratani, 80–110. Amsterdam: John Benjamins Publishing Company.

Kurashino Techosha. 2020. "40-sai-kara-no, Jiyū-ni-naru Meiku" [Makeup in Your Own Way for over 40]. *Kurashi-no Techo* 5: 70–77.

———. 2021. Introduction. *Kurashi-no Techo* 12: 5.

Kurashiru. 2020. "Shioaji TGK" [Salty-Flavored TGK]. Posted January 17, 2020. https://news.line.me/issue/oa-kurashiru-news/8bb2a2039fad.

Kurihara, Harumi. 1992. *Gochisōsama-ga Kikitakute* [I Want to Hear Thank You (for the Meal)]. Tokyo: Bunka Shuppankyoku.

Kusaba, Michiko, ed. 2017. *"Ato Ippin"-ga Sugu Kimaru! Yasai-no Okazu 365* [Easy Decision for "One More Dish"! Vegetable Dishes 365]. Tokyo: NHK Shuppan.

Labov, William. 1972. *Language in the Inner City: Studies in the Black English Vernacular*. Philadelphia: University of Pennsylvania Press.

Lakoff, George, and Mark Johnson. 1980. *Metaphors We Live By*. Chicago: The University of Chicago Press.

Lakoff, Robin. 2006. "Identity à la Carte: You Are What You Eat." In *Discourse and Identity*, edited by Anna de Fina, Deborah Schiffrin, and Michael Bamberg, 142–65. Cambridge: Cambridge University Press.

Leer, Jonatan. 2019. "New Nordic Men: Cooking, Masculinity and Nordicness in René Redzepi's *Noma* and Claus Meyer's *Almanak*." *Food, Culture & Society* 22 (3): 316–33.

Lehrer, Adrienne. 1969. "Semantic Cuisine." *Journal of Linguistics* 5 (1): 39–55.

———. 1972. "Cooking Vocabularies and the Culinary Triangle of Lévi-Strauss." *Anthropological Linguistics* 14 (5): 155–71.

———. 1978. "Structures of the Lexicon and Transfer of Meaning." *Lingua* 45: 95–123.

Levin, Beth. 1993. *English Verb Classes and Alternations: A Preliminary Investigation*. Chicago: The University of Chicago Press.

Levin, Irwin P. 1987. "Associative Effects of Information Framing." *Bulletin of the Psychonomic Society* 25 (2): 85–86.

Levin, Irwin P., and Gary J. Gaeth. 1988. "How Consumers Are Affected by the Framing of Attribute Information Before and After Consuming the Product." *Journal of Consumer Research* 15 (3): 374–78.

Levin, Irwin P., Richard D. Johnson, Craig P. Russo, and Patricia J. Deldin. 1985. "Framing Effects in Judgment Tasks with Varying Amounts of Information." *Organizational Behavior and Human Decision Processes* 36: 362–77.

Lévi-Strauss, Claude. 2013. "The Culinary Triangle." In *Food and Culture: A Reader*, Third Edition, edited by Carole Counihan and Penny Van Esterik, 40–47. New York: Routledge. [Originally published in 1965 as "Le Triangle Culinaire." *L'Arc* 25: 19–29.]

Lodge, David. 1990. "Narration with Words." In *Images and Understanding: Thoughts about Images, Ideas about Understanding*, edited by Horace Barlow, Colin Blakemore, and Miranda Weston-Smith, 141–53. Cambridge: Cambridge University Press.

Lovins, Julie. 1975. *Loanwords and the Phonological Structure of Japanese*. Bloomington: Indiana University Linguistics Club.

Lupton, Deborah. 1996. *Food, the Body and the Self*. London: Sage Publications.

Mamadays. 2020. "Jūshī Kara'age" [Juicy Fried Chicken]. YouTube, February 2, 2020. https://www.youtube.com/watch?v=rJVsn4lfUyU.

Martin, Samuel. 1987. *Reference Grammar of Japanese*. Rutland: Charles E. Tuttle Company.

Matsunaga, Tenma. 2021. "Kami-o Kuwanakereba Ikirarenai Anata-ni" [For You Who Cannot Live Without Eating Paper]. *Kurowassan* 1049: 87.

Matsushita, Kazuhiko. 2021. "Minami-Shinshū-to Mikawa, 'Shio-no Michi'-ga Musunda 'Karamisoage' Kaihatsu" [Southern Shinshu and Mikawa, Development of "Karamisoage" Tied by "Roads of Salt"]. *Asahi Shinbun Digital*, July 28, 2021. https://digital.asahi.com/articles/ASP7W7V3KP78UOOB00X.html?iref=pc_ss_date_article.

Maurer, Daphne, Thanujeni Pathman, and Catherine J. Mondloc. 2006. "The Shape of Boubas: Sound–Shape Correspondences in Toddlers and Adults." *Developmental Science* 9 (3): 316–22.

Maynard, Senko K. 1991. "Pragmatics of Discourse Modality: A Case of Da and Desu/Masu Forms in Japanese." *Journal of Pragmatics* 15: 551–82.

———. 1993. *Discourse Modality: Subjectivity, Emotion and Voice in the Japanese Language*. Amsterdam: John Benjamins Publishing Company.

———. 2008. "Playing with Multiple Voices: Emotivity and Creativity in Japanese Style Mixture." In *Style Shifting in Japanese*, edited by Kimberly Jones and Tsuyoshi Ono, 91–129. Amsterdam: John Benjamins Publishing Company.

"Mensetsu-ga Nai!-kara Kiraku-ni Sugu Dekiru." 2020. Posted May 1, 2020. https://www.premamurthy.net/raku.html.

Merwin, Hugh, 2013. "Brogurt, or Greek 'Yogurt for Men,' Is a Real Thing." Grub Street. Posted on February 25, 2013. https://www.grubstreet.com/2013/02/powerful-yogurt-greek-yogurt-for-men.html.

Meyerhoff, Miriam, and Susan Ehrlich. 2019. "Language, Gender, and Sexuality." *Annual Review of Linguistics* 5: 455–75.

Minami, Nobunaga. 2013. *Manga-no Shokutaku* [Dining Table in Comic Books]. Tokyo: NTT Shuppan.

Mitsuno, Momo. 2006. "Commentary." In *Gōkyū-suru Junbi-wa Dekiteita* [I Was Ready to Wail], a novel by Kaori Ekuni, 228–33. Tokyo: Shinchosha.

Moriguchi, Takeshi. 2015. "Shokuhin-Sangyō ni Okeru Kankaku-Māketingu no Jūyōsei" [The Importance of Sensual Marketing in Food Industry]. *Ashita-no Shokuhin-Sangyo* 12: 3–4.

Murai, Gensai. 2005. *Shokudōraku* 1–2 [Epicureanism 1–2]. Tokyo: Iwanami Bunko.

Murakami, Akiko. 1995. *Taishō・Shōwa-shoki-no Kateiryōri-no Hon* [Cookbook for Home-cooking at the Beginning of Taisho-Showa]. Tokyo: Suna Shobo.

Murakami, Motoko. 2000. "'Otoko-to Ryōri'-o Onna-no Gawa-kara Miruto" [Looking at 'Men and Cooking' from a Women's Perspective]. In *Shoku-to Jendā* [Diet and Gender], edited by Emiko Takei, 128–51. Tokyo: Domesu-Shuppan.

Murakami, Ryu. 1998. *Murakami Ryū Ryōri-Shōsetsushū* [Ryu Murakami Cooking Novels]. Tokyo: Kodansha.

Murase, Keiko. 2009. "Rajio-no Ryōribangumi-to Shuhu-no Imēji" [Cooking Programs on Radio and Images of Housewives]. *Vesta* 76: 44–49.

Muto, Ayaka. 2001. "Mikaku Keiyōshi 'Amai' to 'Karai' no Tagi Kōzō" [Polysemous Structure of Taste Adjectives "Sweet" and "Spicy"]. *Nihongo Kyoiku* 110: 42–51.

———. 2002. "'Oishii' no Atarashii Imi to Yōhō—'Umai' 'Mazui' to Hikaku-shite" [New Meanings and Usages of "Oishii"—In Comparison with "Umai" and "Mazui"]. *Nihongo Kyoiku* 112: 25–34.

———. 2003. "Aji-Kotoba-no Giongo, Gitaigo" [Phonomimes and Phenomimes of Taste Terms]. In *Kotoba-wa Aji-o Koeru: Oishii Hyōgen-no Tankyū* [Language Transcends Taste: Exploration of Delicious Expressions], edited by Ken'ichi Seto, 241–300. Tokyo: Kaimeisha.

Nagao, Tomoko. 2021. "Sozai-no Deaimono #169: Tamago + Kēru" [Meeting with Ingredients #169: Eggs + Kale]. *Kurowassan* 1043: 71.

Nakahara, Ippo. 2017. *Watashi-ga Shindemo Reshipi-wa Nokoru. Kobayashi Katsuyo-den* [Recipes Will Stay Even After I Die. A Biography of Katsuyo Kobayashi]. Tokyo: Bungei Shunju.

Nakamura, Hisako, ed. 2011. *Mō Mayowanai! Reshipi-no Kotoba* [No Longer Get Lost! The Vocabulary of Recipes]. Tokyo: Orenji Peeji.

Nakamura, Katsuhiko. 1975. *Danshi Chūbō-ni Haire—Onna-no Daidokoro-o Kokuhatsu-suru!!* [Men Should Be in the Kitchen—Denounce Women's Kitchen!!]. Tokyo: Kobunsha.

Nasu, Akio. 2002. "Nihongo Onomatope no Gokeisei to Inritu-Kōzō" [Word Formation and Prosodic Structure of Japanese Onomatopoeia]. PhD diss., Tsukuba University.

Neuhaus, Jessamyn. 2003. *Manly Meals and Mom's Home Cooking: Cookbooks and Gender in Modern America*. Baltimore: Johns Hopkins University Press.

Ngo, Mary Kim, Reeva Misra, and Charles Spence. 2011. "Assessing the Shapes and Speech Sounds that People Associate with Chocolate Samples Varying in Cocoa Content." *Food Quality and Preference* 22: 567–72.

Nihon Hōsō Kyōkai Kantoshibu, ed. 1927. *Shiki-no Ryōri: Rajio Hōsō* [Cooking for Four Seasons: Radio Broadcasting]. Tokyo: Nihon Rajio Kyokai.

———, ed. 1928. *Hibi-no Ryōri: Rajio Hōsō* [Everyday Cooking: Radio Broadcasting]. Tokyo: Nihon Hoso Kyokai Kantoshibu.

Nikkei Resutoran, ed. 2014. *Oishii Mise-wa Menyūbukku-ga Umai* [Delicious Restaurants Make Good Menus]. Tokyo: Nikkei BP Marketing.

Nishi, Jun'ichiro. 2007. *Otoko-no Reshipi* [Men's Recipes]. Tokyo: Gurahusha.

Nishikawa, Osamu. 1996. *Motsu Madness: Otoko-no Ryōri—Naizō* [Entrails Madness: Men's Cooking—The Internal Organs]. Tokyo: Magajinhausu.

Noda, Mari. 2014. "It's Delicious! How Japanese Speakers Describe Food at a Social Event." In *Language and Food: Verbal and Nonverbal Experiences*, edited by Polly Szatrowski, 79–102. Amsterdam: John Benjamins Publishing Company.

Numano, Mitsuyoshi. 2020. "Kokoro-ni Surōhūdo-o" [Give Slow Food to Mind]. *Kurashi-no Techo* 8: 135.

Ochs, Elinor. 1992. "Indexing Gender." In *Rethinking Context: Language as an Interactive Phenomenon*, edited by Alessandro Duranti and Charles Goodwin, 335–58. Cambridge: Cambridge University Press.

———. 2002. "Becoming a Speaker of Culture." In *Language Acquisition and Language Socialization: Ecological Perspectives*, edited by Claire J. Kramsch, 99–120. London: Continuum.

Ochs, Elinor, Clotilde Pontecorvo, and Alessandra Fasulo. 1996. "Socializing Taste." *Ethnos* 61 (1–2): 7–46.

Ochs, Elinor, and Merav Shohet. 2006. "The Cultural Structuring of Mealtime Socialization." *New Directions for Child and Adolescent Development* 111: 35–49.

Oda, Nozomi. 2003. "Amakute Suīto" [Sweet and Sweet]. In *Kotoba-wa Aji-o Koeru: Oishii Hyōgen-no Tankyū* [Language Transcends Taste: Exploration of Delicious Expressions], edited by Ken'ichi Seto, 186–214. Tokyo: Kaimeisha.

Ohala, John J. 1994. "The Frequency Code Underlies the Sound-Symbolic Use of Voice Pitch." In *Sound Symbolism*, edited by Leanne Hinton, Johanna Nichols, and John J. Ohala, 325–47. Cambridge: Cambridge University Press.

Ohashi, Kyoko. 1997. "Rajio-Hōsō-to Ryōri—Taishō 14-nen~Shōwa 9-nen" [Radio Broadcasting and Cooking—Taisho 14 ~ Showa 9]. *Gakuen* 691: 86–95.

Ohashi, Masahusa. 2010. *"Oishii" Kankaku-to Kotoba: Shokkan-no Sedai* [The Sense of "Delicious" and Language: Generation of Mouth-Feel]. Tokyo: B.M.FT.

———. 2015. *Sizzle Word: Shizuru Wādo no Genzai* [Sizzle Word Today]. Tokyo: B.M.FT.

———. 2016. "Shizuru-Wādo-wa 'Mocchiri' 'Huwahuwa' 'Torōri'" [Sizzle Words Are "Mocchiri" "Huwahuwa" and "Toroori"]. In *Huwatoro: Sizzle Word "Oishii" Kotoba-no Tsukaikata* [Huwatoro: Sizzle Word—How to Use "Delicious" Words], edited by B.M.FT Kotoba Rabo, 228–47. Tokyo: B.M.FT.

Okada, Shiori. 2007. *Tsukutte Agetai Kare-Gohan* [Cooking for Him]. Tokyo: Takarajimasha.

"Okome Henshin Gūzen Geru-ka Itami-nikusa-mo Shokuhinsōgōken" [Rice Transformation Accidentally Gelled and Hard to Damage Food Research Institute]. 2015. *Asahi Shinbun* 5, August 14, 2015.

Okubo, Naoki. 2019. "(Oagariyasu) Tabi-no En-no Aji Karada-ni Shimi-Wataru" [(Bon Appetit) The Taste of Fate in Travelling Penetrates the Body]. *Asahi Shinbun Digital*, December 16, 2019. https://digital.asahi.com/articles/ASMD56D1NMD5PLZB010.html?iref=pc_ss_date_article.

Okuzono, Toshiko. 2012. *Okuzono Toshiko-no Yomu Reshipi* [Recipes to Read by Toshiko Okuzono]. Tokyo: Sankei Shinbun Shupan.

Ono, Masahiro, ed. 2007. *Nihongo Onomatope Jiten* [Japanese Onomatopoeia Dictionary]. Tokyo: Shogakkan.

Ota, Yasuhiro. 2000. "Tekusuchā Kankaku-no Hyōgen" [Expressions of the Sense of Texture]. *Nihon Kanno Hyoka Gakkaishi* 4 (1): 21–27.

Otake, Takashi. 2015. "Mora and Mora-Timing." In *Handbook of Japanese Phonetics and Phonology*, edited by Haruo Kubozono, 493–523. Boston: Walter de Gruyter Inc.

Otokuni. 2017. *Kōkokugaisha, Danshiryō-no Okazu-kun* [Okazu at Male-only Dorm of Advertising Company]. Tokyo: Ribure.

———. 2018a. *Kōkokugaisha, Danshiryō-no Okazu-kun* 2 [Okazu at Male-only Dorm of Advertising Company 2]. Tokyo: Ribure.

———. 2018b. *Kōkokugaisha, Danshiryō-no Okazu-kun* 3 [Okazu at Male-only Dorm of Advertising Company 3]. Tokyo: Ribure.

———. 2019. *Kōkokugaisha, Danshiryō-no Okazu-kun* 4 [Okazu at Male-only Dorm of Advertising Company 4]. Tokyo: Ribure.

———. 2020. *Kōkokugaisha, Danshiryō-no Okazu-kun* 5 [Okazu at Male-only Dorm of Advertising Company 5]. Tokyo: Ribure.

Otsubo, Heiji. 1989. *Giseigo-no Kenkyū* [Studies of Onomatopoeia]. Tokyo: Meiji Shoten.

Panasonic. n.d. "Mikisā・Jūsā" [Mixer, Juicer]. Advertisement. Retrieved February 15, 2022. https://panasonic.jp/juice/.

Parasecoli, Fabio. 2017. "Honey, Where's the Stew? Performances of Masculine Domesticity in American Comedy Film." Paper presented at the Annual Conference of the Association for the Study of Food and Society. June 15, 2017. Occidental University, Los Angeles.

———. 2022. "Gastronativism: Food, Identity, Politics." Paper presented at the Annual Conference of the Association for the Study of Food and Society. May 18–21, 2022. Athens, GA. [The book under the same title is scheduled to be published in July 2022, by Columbia University Press.]

Pilcher, Jeffrey. 2012. *Planet Taco: A Global History of Mexican Food*. New York: Oxford University Press.

Portnoy, Sarah. 2015. "Authenticity of Cuisines." In *The SAGE Encyclopedia of Food Issues*, edited by Ken Albala. Thousand Oaks: SAGE Publications. DOI: http://dx.doi.org/10.4135/9781483346304.n35

———. 2017. "Good Food and the Problematic Search for Authenticity." KCET. Posted November 6, 2017. https://www.kcet.org/shows/the-migrant-kitchen/good-food-and-the-problematic-search-for-authenticity.

Rhee, Seongha, and Hyun Jung Koo. 2017. "Multifaceted Gustation: Systematicity and Productivity of Taste Terms in Korean." *Terminology* 23 (1): 38–64.

Riley, Kathleen C., and Amy L. Paugh. 2019. *Food and Language: Discourses and Foodways across Cultures*. New York: Routledge.

Rozin, Paul, and Julia M. Hormes. 2010. "Psychology and Sensory Marketing, with a Focus on Food." In *Sensory Marketing: Research on the Sensuality of Products*, edited by Aradhna Krishna, 303–21. New York: Routledge.

Ryoyukai, ed. 1937. *Guntai Chōrihō* [Army Cookbook]. Tokyo: Ryoyukai.

Sakamoto, Maki, and Junji Watanabe. 2016. "Cross-Modal Associations between Sounds and Drink Tastes/Textures: A Study with Spontaneous Production of Sound-Symbolic Words." *Chemical Senses* 41 (3): 197–203.

Sakamoto, Mitsuru. 2002. "Dō Suru? Gairaigo-no Hyōki-to Hatsuon" [How Should Loanwords Be Transcribed and Pronounced?]. *Hoso Kenkyu-to Chosa* 52 (10): 50–71.

Samarin, William. 1970. "Inventory and Choice in Expressive Language." *Word* 26: 153–67.

sanono230. 2021. "Takenoko-to Konnyaku-no Irini" [Bamboo Shoots and Konnyaku in Seasoned Broth]. Cookpad. Posted April 14, 2021. https://cookpad.com/recipe/6735300.

Sawasaki, Umeko. 1941. *Kateiryōri Kiso-hen* [Home Cooking—Basics]. Tokyo: Hujinnotomosha.

Schourup, Lawrence. 1993. "Nihongo-no Kakikotoba/Hanashikotoba-ni Okeru Onomatope-no Bunpu-ni Tsuite" [On the Distribution of Onomatopoeia in Written and Spoken Japanese]. In *Onomatopia: Gion/Gitaigo-no Rakuen* [Onomatopoeia: Paradise of Phonomimes and Phenomimes], edited by Hisao Kakehi and Ikuhiro Tamori, 77–100. Tokyo: Keisosha.

Seto, Ken'ichi, ed. 2003. *Kotoba-wa Aji-o Koeru* [Language Transcends Taste]. Tokyo: Kaimeisha.

———, ed. 2005. *Ajikotoba-no Sekai* [The World of Taste Vocabulary]. Tokyo: Kaimeisha.

Shibatani, Masayoshi. 1990. *The Languages of Japan*. Cambridge: Cambridge University Press.

Shimada, Masaharu, and Akiko Nagano. 2017. "Use of English Prepositions as Japanese Predicates: A Challenge to NLP." *Proceedings of the 23rd Annual Conference of the Association for Natural Language Processing*, 294–97.

———. 2018. "Japanese Recipe Names with Prepositions." Paper presented at the Conference on the Language of Japanese Food. York University, Toronto.

Shimizu, Kei'ichi. 1975. *Otoko-no Ryōri—Onna Muyō-no Te-Ryōri Nyūmonsho* [Men's Cooking—A Guide to Home Cooking that Needs No Women]. Tokyo: Asahi Sonorama.

Shinohara, Kazuko, Ryoko Uno, Fumiyuki Kobayashi, and Sachiko Odake. 2017. "Sound Symbolism of Food Texture: Cross-Linguistic Differences in Hardness." *ICLC-14 Book of Abstracts*: 456.

Shiota, Maruo. 1997. *Shinshi-no Daidokoro* [Gentlemen's Kitchen]. Tokyo: Gurahusha.

Shoji, Sadao. 1984. *Shōji-kun-no "Ryōri Daisuki!"* [Shoji's "I Love Cooking!"]. Tokyo: Shinchosha.

Shōnan-supaisu. 2007. "Isoiso Dekakeru Otoko-no Ryōri-Kyōshitsu. Sore-wa Tsuma-tachi-no Kaiwa-kara Hajimatta" [Cooking Class for Men Who Joyously Go Out. It Started with Conversations Among Wives]. *Josei-no Hiroba* 336: 26–29.

Silverstein, Michael. 1976. "Shifters, Linguistic Categories, and Cultural Description." In *Meaning in Anthropology*, edited by Keith H. Basso and Henry A. Selby, 11–56. Albuquerque: University of New Mexico Press.

Simner, Julia, and Jamie Ward. 2006. "The Taste of Words on the Tip of the Tongue." *Nature* 444: 438.

Smith, Jennifer. 2006. "Loan Phonology Is Not All Perception: Evidence from Japanese Loan Doublets." In *Japanese/Korean Linguistics* 14, edited by Timothy J. Vance and Kimberly Jones, 63–74. Stanford: CSLI Publications.

Sobal, Jeffery. 2005. "Men, Meat, and Marriage: Models of Masculinity." *Food & Foodways* 13 (1): 135–58.

———. 2017. "Men's Foodwork in Food Systems: Social Representations of Masculinities and Cooking at Home." In *Food, Masculinities, and Home: Interdisciplinary Perspectives*, edited by Michelle Szabo and Shelley Koch, 126–44. London: Bloomsbury.

Strauss, Susan. 2005. "The Linguistic Aestheticization of Food: A Cross-Cultural Look at Food Commercials in Japan, Korea, and the United States." *Journal of Pragmatics* 37: 1427–55.

Strauss, Susan, Heesun Chang, and Yumi Matsumoto. 2018. "Genre and the Cultural Realms of Taste in Japanese, Korean, and U.S. Online Recipes." In *Pragmatics of Japanese: Perspectives on Grammar, Interaction and Culture*, edited by Mutsuko Endo Hudson, Yoshiko Matsumoto, and Junko Mori, 220–43. Amsterdam: John Benjamins Publishing Company.

Sugiyama, Kaoru. 2016. "'Oishii' Shokkan to Hyōka" ["Delicious" Mouth Feel and Evaluation]. *Japanese Journal of Sensory Evaluation* 20 (2): 132–34.

Suter, Rebecca, Caroline Miller, Timothy Gill, and John Coveney. 2020. "The Bitter and the Sweet: A Cultural Comparison of Non-Alcoholic Beverage Consumption in Japan and Australia." *Food, Culture & Society* 23 (3): 334–46.

Szabo, Michelle. 2014a. "'I'm a Real Catch': The Blurring of Alternative and Hegemonic Masculinities in Men's Talk about Home Cooking." *Women's Studies International Forum* 44: 228–35.

———. 2014b. "Men Nurturing through Food: Challenging Gender Dichotomies around Domestic Cooking." *Journal of Gender Studies* 23 (1): 18–31.

Szabo, Michelle, and Shelley Koch. 2017. "Introduction." In *Food, Masculinities, and Home: Interdisciplinary Perspectives*, edited by Michelle Szabo and Shelley Koch, 1–28. London: Bloomsbury.

Szatrowski, Polly, ed. 2014. *Language and Food: Verbal and Nonverbal Experiences*. Amsterdam: John Benjamins Publishing Company.

Takahashi, Midori. 2012. *Watashi-no Sukina Ryōri-no Hon* [My Favorite Books on Cooking]. Tokyo: Shinchosha.

Takai, Naoyuki. 2014. *Kafe-to Nihonjin* [Café and Japanese]. Tokyo: Kodansha.

Takamine, Hideko. 2012. *Daidokoro-no Ōkesutora* [Orchestra in the Kitchen]. Tokyo: Shinchosha.

Takeda, Kyoko. 2019. "Kongetsu-no Myūjin—Myūjishan Fujii Fumiya" [This Month's Sound-Playing Person—Musician Fumiya Fujii]. Yamaha. Posted June 3, 2019. https://jp.yamaha.com/sp/myujin/monthly_myujin/fumiyafujii.

Takei, Emiko. 2000. "Shoku-ni Arawareru Jendā—Kawariyuku Kōzō-to Sono Yukue" [Gender in Foodways—Changing Structure and Its Path]. In *Shoku-to Jendā* [Foodways and Gender], edited by Emiko Takei, 205–32. Tokyo: Domesu Shuppan.

Takii, Asayo. 2021. "Moji-kara Eiyō" [Nutrition from Letters]. *Kurowassan* 1052: 85.

Tamamura, Toyo'o. 1999. *Menzu Kukkingu Nyūmon* [Introduction to Men's Cooking]. Tokyo: Chuokoron Shinsha.

Tamori, Ikuhiro. 1993. "Jo-ni Kaete" [In Place of Preface]. In *Onomatopia: Gion/ Gitaigo-no Rakuen* [Onomatopoeia: Paradise of Phonomimes and Phenomimes], edited by Hisao Kakehi and Ikuhiro Tamori, i–vii. Tokyo: Keisosha.

———. 2002. *Onomatope Gion・Gitaigo-o Tanoshimu* [Joy of Onomatopoeia]. Tokyo: Iwanami Shoten.

Tamori, Ikuhiro, and Lawrence Schourup. 1999. *Onomatope* [Onomatopoeia]. Tokyo: Kurosio.

Tanaka, Kei'ichi. 2017. *Kōbe-to Kōhī: Minato-kara Hajimaru Monogatari* [Kobe and Coffee: A Story that Begins at a Harbor]. Kobe: Kobe Shinbun Sogo Shuppan Senta.

Tatsumi, Hamako. 1960. *Teshio-ni Kaketa Watashi-no Ryōri* [My Cooking with Love]. Tokyo: Hujinnotomosha.

Tatsumi, Yoshiko. 1978. *Yuzuriuketa Haha-no Aji* [Mom's Taste I Inherited]. Tokyo: Hujinnotomosha.

Thomason, Sarah. 2001. *Language Contact: An Introduction*. Washington, DC: Georgetown University Press.

Tierney, R. Kenji. 2016. "Consuming Sumo Wrestlers: Taste, Commensality, and Authenticity in Japanese Food." *Food, Culture & Society*: 19 (4): 637–53.

Tokuoka, Kunio. 2009. *Danshi-no Daidokoro* [Men's Kitchen]. Tokyo: Bajiriko Kabushikigaisha.

Toratani, Kiyoko, ed. 2022. *The Language of Food in Japanese: Cognitive Perspectives and Beyond*. Amsterdam: John Benjamins Publishing Company.

Tsujimoto, Tomoko. 2003. "Ajikotoba-no Kakushi-Aji" [Hidden Taste of Taste Vocabulary]. In *Kotoba-wa Aji-o Koeru* [Language Transcends Taste], edited by Ken'ichi Seto, 156–83. Tokyo: Kaimeisha.

———. 2005. "Hiyu-de Ajiwau" [Tasting by Metaphor]. In *Ajikotoba-no Sekai* [The World of Taste Vocabulary], edited by Ken'ichi Seto, 137–61. Tokyo: Kaimeisha.

Tsujimura, Natsuko. 2014. *An Introduction to Japanese Linguistics*. Third Edition. Malden, MA: Wiley Blackwell.

———. 2018a. "From Tasty Adjective to Succulent Metaphor: What the Language of Food Reveals." *Japanese/Korean Linguistics* 25: 309–26.

———. 2018b. "Recipe Names as a Gateway to Interpersonal Communication." *Names: A Journal of Onomastics* 66 (4): 233–45.

———. 2022a. *Expressing Silence: Where Language and Culture Meet in Japanese*. Lanham: Lexington Books.

———. 2022b. "The Language of Food in Japanese Through a Linguistic Lens." In *The Language of Food in Japanese: Cognitive Perspectives and Beyond*, edited by Kiyoko Toratani, 27–52. Amsterdam: John Benjamins Publishing Company.

———. Forthcoming. "Cooking Verbs and the Cultural Conceptualization of Cooking Processes in Japanese." In *Cultural Linguistics, Ideologies and Critical Discourse Studies*, edited by Monika Reif and Frank Polzenhagen. Amsterdam: John Benjamins Publishing Company.

Tsujimura, Natsuko, and Stuart Davis. 2009. "Dragon Ash and the Reinterpretation of Hip Hop: On the Notion of Rhyme in Japanese Hip Hop." In *Global Linguistic Flows: Hip Hop Cultures, Youth Identities, and the Politics of Language*, edited by H. Samy Alim, Awad Ibrahim, and Alastair Pennycook, 179–93. New York: Routledge.

Tunc, Tanfer Emin. 2018. "Domestic Sensualism: Laurie Colwin's Food Writing." *Food, Culture & Society* 21 (2): 128–43.

Ueyama, Tochi. 1991. *Kukkingu Papa 22* [Cooking Dad 22]. Tokyo: Kodansha.

Ullmann, Stephen. 1962. *Semantics. An Introduction to the Science of Meaning*. New York: Barnes & Noble.

Umihara, Junko. 2019. *Kokoro-no Shinkokyū* [Deep Breath for Mind]. Tokyo: Hujinnotomosha.

Uno, Ryoko, Fumiyuki Kobayashi, Kazuko Shinohara, and Sachiko Odake. 2022. "Analysis of the Use of Japanese Mimetics in the Eating and Imagined Eating of Rice Crackers." In *The Language of Food in Japanese: Cognitive Perspectives and Beyond*, edited by Kiyoko Toratani, 56–77. Amsterdam: John Benjamins Publishing Company.

Voelts, F. K. Erhard, and Christa Kilian-Hatz. 2001. "Introduction." In *Ideophones*, edited by F. K. Erhard Voelts and Christa Kilian-Hatz, 1–8. Amsterdam: John Benjamins Publishing Company.

Vos, Frits. 1963. "Dutch Influences on the Japanese Language." *Lingua* 12: 341–88.

Wansink, Brian, Sea Bum Park, Steven Sonka, and Michelle Morganosky. 2000. "How Soy Labeling Influences Preference and Taste." *International Food and Agribusiness Management Review* 3: 85–94.

Wansink, Brian, Koert van Ittersum, and James E. Painter. 2005. "How Descriptive Food Names Bias Sensory Perceptions in Restaurants." *Food Quality and Preference* 16: 393–400.

Ward, Jamie, and Julia Simner. 2003. "Lexical-Gustatory Synaesthesia: Linguistic and Conceptual Factors." *Cognition* 89: 237–61.

Watanabe, Nanao. 2015. "Kyūjussai-no Ryōrikenkyūka, Suzuki Tokiko-san—Oaji-no Hikizan-wa Dekimasen, Te-to Shita-de 'Ii Kagen'-o Oboete" [90-Year-Old Cooking Specialist, Ms. Tokiko Suzuki—Tastes Cannot Be Subtracted, Please Get the Sense of 'the Right Balance' by Your Hands and Tongue]. *Kurowassan* 911: 36–39.

Whitman, Joan, and Dolores Simon. 1993. *Recipes into Type: A Handbook for Cookbook Writers and Editors*. New York: Harper Collins Publishers.

Wilk, Richard, and Persephone Hintulian. 2005. "Cooking on Their Own: Cuisines of Manly Men." *Food and Foodways* 13 (1): 159–68.

Williams, Joseph. 1976. "Synaesthetic Adjectives: A Possible Law of Semantic Change." *Language* 52 (2): 461–78.

Yamaguchi, Haruhiko. 2003. "Sarani Gokan-de Ajiwau" [Tasting with Five Senses Even Further]. In *Kotoba-wa Aji-o Koeru* [Language Transcends Taste], edited by Ken'ichi Seto, 120–53. Tokyo: Kaimeisha.

Yamaguchi, Sei'ichiro. 2017. "Sutaba Shinsaku 'Sheikun Appuru Grīn Tī' Kasutamaizu-ya Karorī" [New Item by Starbucks "Shaken Apple Green Tea" Customize and Calorie]. Y. Coffee and Sweets. Posted March 21, 2017. https://yamaguchi-coffee.com/starbucks-sheiken-apple-green-tea/.

Yamazaki, Mikio. 1993. *Kan-Kōhī Hūkeiron* [Prospects of Canned Coffee]. Tokyo: Yosensha.

Yamazoe, Shugo. 2003. "Nigakute Bitā" [Bitter and Bitter]. In *Kotoba-wa Aji-o Koeru* [Language Transcends Taste], edited by Ken'ichi Seto, 215–38. Tokyo: Kaimeisha.

Yonekawa, Akihiko. 1998. *Wakamonogo-o Kagaku-suru* [A Scientific Study of Youth Language]. Tokyo: Meiji Shoin

———. 2007. "Zokugo, Ingo-wa Naze Umaretaka" [Why Was Slang/Secret Language Created]. *Vesta* 65: 25–27.

Yorkson, Eric, and Geeta Menon. 2004. "A Sound Idea: Phonetic Effects of Brand Names on Consumer Judgments." *Journal of Consumer Research* 31: 43–51.

Yuen, Shu Min. 2014. "From Men to 'Boys'—The Cooking Danshi in Japanese Mass Media." *Women's Studies International Forum* 44: 220–27.

Yuzuki, Asako. 2013. *Amakara Karutetto* [Salty-Sweet Quartet]. Tokyo: Bungei Shunju.

Zwicky, Ann, and Arnold Zwicky. 1980. "America's National Dish: The Style of Restaurant Menus." *American Speech* 55: 87–92.

Zwicky, Arnold. 1976. "Well, This Rock and Roll Has Got to Stop. Junior's Head Is Hard as a Rock." *Chicago Linguistic Society* 12: 676–97.

Index

aburakkoi ("oily, greasy"), 49
aburu ("grill"), [-Water] [-Fat] cooking verb, 102, 114–15, 116
acclimatization, glocalization and, 11
adaptations: linguistic, 11–12; loanword, 14–29; sound-based, 14, 15
adjectives, 23, 138–39; modifiers, 16, 48; pairs, 5; taste, 134, 155–59, 162n1, 163n16, 163nn12–14; tasty, 39–40
adoption, linguistic, 4, 11–12
advertisements: alcohol, 215, 245n5; *amatō, karatō* and chocolate, 210–11; coffee, 209–10, 213–17, 245n8; with gender and food, 205, 209–11, 213–17, 245n8; mimetics and, 41–42
affecto-imagistic dimension, mimetics, 44–45, 52, 91
age, 57, 90–91
ageru, aspectual sense of, 131n9
ageru ("deep-fry, French fry"), [-Water] [+Fat] cooking verb, 102, 107, 110, 111, 112, 114
Aita, Koji, 28, 183, 196
Akita, Kimi, 43, 73
Ako, Mari, 246n12
alcohol: beer, 12, 40, 42, 205, 211, 215, 241, 245n5; masculinity and, 207; non-alcoholic beverage, 21, 95n8, 213; sake, 53, 76–79, 105, 119, 138, 157, 163n13, 245n4. *See also amatō* vs. *karatō*
Alka-Seltzer, 69
Allison, Ralph I., 40
amai, taste adjective, 155–57, 163nn12–14
amatō (sweet) vs. *karatō* (alcohol): Buddhism and, 245n4; dichotomy, 157, 163n15, 208, 210–12, 214, 216–17, 242–43
analytical dimension, prosaic words, 44–45
anime, 21–22
Aoyama, Tomoko, 209
apples, 1–3, 16, 22, 26
appropriateness, five types of, 137
argument is war metaphor, 139, 140
Armstrong, Robert Plant, 95n4
aruku ("walk"), 70
Asahi Digital, 63–64
assonance, 93–94
auditory borrowing, 19–20
Australia, non-alcoholic beverages, 95n8
authenticity, 11, 20, 34, 35n1

Baba, Junko, 201n12
Backhouse, A. E., 162n1

Barthes, Roland, 209
"basement of department store" (*depachika*), 198
BBK (Bunkachō Bunkabu Kokugoka), 30
beer, 12, 40, 42, 205, 211, 215, 241, 245n5
bitterness: of coffee, 210, 212–17; men with *karatō* and, 210–11
BMFT Kotobarabo language lab, 55–56
bodily sensation outside oral cavity, mimetics, 66
body parts: "Hand Salad with Yogurt-Lemon Dressing," 2–3, 7n1; sexism, 3, 95n10, 154
"boil" (*yuderu*), 102, 105–7, 109, 110, 126–27, 130n3
"boil" (*gotogoto*) cooking, 89
"boil down" (*ni-tsumeru*), 136
"boil [water]" (*wakasu*), 102, 104, 110, 130n2
Bon Appetite website, 7n1
"Book for Men's Cooking" (*Danshi-gohan-no Hon*) (Kokubun and Kentaro), 234–36, 237–38
book/reading is food metaphor, 146–48, 163n10
borrowing language, 4, 11, 14
bottled coffee, 215–17
Bourdieu, Pierre, 29, 218
brand labels, taste and, 40
brewing: coffee, 17, 110, 130n7, 213–14; tea, 23, 110, 130n7
Brown, Steven P., 40
"bubble" economy period (1986–1991), 196
Bucholtz, Mary, 169, 208
Buddhism, 163n19, 245n4
"(be) bumpy" (*wulthwung pwulthwung*), 52
Bunkachō Bunkabu Kokugoka (BBK), 30
burdock roots, 64, 96n15
Butler, Judith, 169, 208

Café Paulista, Tokyo, 213, 245n6
cafeteria menus, 39–40
California Gold Rush, 206
Cameron, Deborah, 169, 208
Canada, Pastagate, 30, 32
canned coffee, 214–15, 216, 243
carnivore women (*nikushokukei-joshi*), 207
"char" (*kogasu*), 102, 116
Chen, Yong, 206
"chewy" (*mochimochi*), 56, 57
Child, Julia (1912–2004), 186, 202nn14–15, 226
childish undertone, of mimetics, 63, 64
children, 178, 197, 199, 231; *amatō* and, 210, 245n4; cookbooks for, 206; cooking with, 238–39; "ice cream for kids," 48; sweets and, 157, 207, 210
Chin (Chef), 73, 74
Chinese immigrants, 206
Chiseisha, 221, 223
chocolate advertisements, 210–11
chokchok, "(be) moist with dew, (be) slightly damp," 52
chō-kurīmī! on tama pote-sara "super-creamy! potato salad topped with an egg [fried, sunny-side up]," 37n13
clauses: recipe names and relative, 179; *tabetara* as subordinate, 180
clipping, loanwords, 17–18, 21, 22
Coco's Restaurant, loanwords on menu, 32–33, 34, 37n19, 37n20
coda consonants, 17, 43
coda nasal sound, 15, 35n2, 94n3
coffee: brewing, 17, 110, 130n7, 213–14; packaging of, 214, 243
coffee, gendered images of: advertisements, 209–10, 213–17, 245n8; *amatō* and *karatō*, 208, 210–12; bitterness, 210, 212–17; bottled, 215–17; brewing, 213–14; canned, 214–15, 216, 243; with magazines for women, 213–14; without sugar, 214–15; sweetened with sugar, 213, 214

cognitive mode of meaning, 44–45
colors: five, 137; gender and, 206, 211, 214, 215; taste and, 41, 138, 162n7
Columbo (fictional character), 193
"comb-shape" (*kushi-gata*), 128, 129, 131n12
comics, cookbooks, 230–34, 240–45
compound forms, recipe names: personalization, 177–79; utensils for serving and cooking, 176–77; of X-Y, 174, 175, 176
compounding: *age-ni*, 122, 123; *age-yaki*, 120; cutting verbs, 127–30; *iri-ageru*, 121–22; *iri-ni*, 121; *itame-ni*, 122, 123; *mushi-ni*, 119–20; *mushi-yaki*, 119–20; *mushi-yude*, 120; *ni-*, 123, 125; *ni-komu*, 123–24; N(oun)-V(erb), 124; periphrastic extensions, 118–25; W1 and W2 relationship, 118–19; W1 before W2 relationship, 122; W1-*ni*, 118; W1-*yaki*, 118; words, 17, 18, 20, 22, 80; *yaku*, 124–25
compound terms: anger conveyed with *niru*, 135; with *ni-tsumeru* signifying positive outcome, 136
conceptual metaphors, 5, 136, 139–42, 144, 145–54
Connell, R. W., 169
consonants: clusters, 15–16; coda, 17, 43; geminate, 15, 35n2, 43, 94n2; sound symbolism and, 87–88, 89–91
Cook, Haruko Minegishi, 173, 190–91
"cook" (*ryōri-suru*), 100, 102
cookbooks: for children, 206; comics, 230–34, 240–45; *Jolly Times Cookbook*, 206; men and types of, 220–45; *otoko-no ryōri*, 220–26; photographs in, 96n18, 173–74, 221, 229; radio broadcasts and, 171, 201n4; self-help, 226–30; setting, purpose and participants, 167; *sōshokukei-danshi* generation, 234–45; with women and social roles, 209; writing, 200n2. *See also* home cooking, men and; recipe writing
cookbook survey, of mimetics, 80, 84, 86, 89–90, 95n13; authors and publication dates, *82*; gender and, 81, 91; most frequently used, 84, *85*, 85–86, 183; token and type counts, 82, *83*, 84, 182, 229
cooking: with children, 238–39; emotion is cooking metaphor, 140; fashion is cooking/dining metaphor, 151–52; life is cooking/dining metaphor, 149–51; makeup is cooking metaphor, 152–54, 163n11; Nihon Cooking Academy, 137
cooking actions: core concepts, 99–100; cutting verbs, 127–30; humor and, 191–93; instructions, 74–76; in numbered steps, 172–73; verbs in prose style, 171–72
Cooking Class for Men group, 226, 246n11
"Cooking Dad" (*Kukkingu Papa*) (Ueyama), 230–34, 245
"cooking experts" (*ryōri-kenkyūka*), 182, 196, 203n20, 203n25
"Cooking for Four Seasons" (*Shiki-no Ryōri*), 171
cooking instructions: hand movements, 75–76; ingredient amount and size, 76–78; ingredients size and shape, 78; language and, 167; liquid amount, 77–78; mimetics, 69–80; mimetics not specific for, 183–84; motions and actions, 74–76; processes, 78–79; subjectivity with, 168; times, 72–74; useful tips, 79–80; with verbal descriptions, 241. *See also* recipe writing
cooking is makeup metaphor, 163n11
cooking methods: five, 137; gender, food and, 206
cooking sphere, gender and, 197

cooking utensils, 11, 107, 109, 112, 124, 176–77
cooking verbs: English, 5; with liquid or solid ingredient, 100; Russian, 5
cooking verbs, lexicalization and semantic components: "boil" componentialized, 100; classification of English cooking words, 100, *101*, 102; classification of Japanese cooking words, 102, *103*, 104, 109, 118, 127; cooking actions and core concepts, 99–100; culinary triangle, 98; rice cooking in two stages, 108–9; summary of semantic components for Japanese cooking words, 116, *117*, 118, 123; [-Water], 102, 116; [-Water] [-Fat], 102, 114–16, 121, 223; [-Water] [+Fat], 102, 110–14; [+Water] [-Fat], 102, 103–10, 119
"cook in liquid." See *niru*
Cookpad.com, 14, 23, 35n4, 36n11, 37n16
"cook [rice]" (*taku*), 97, 102, 105, 107, 108, 109, 110
"cook rice [grain]" (*kome-o taku*), 108, 130n6
Cotter, Colleen, 96n17, 167–69
"crisp" (*sakusaku*), 56
"[be] crunchy, crispy" (*pasak pasak*), 52
"cubed dehydrated tofu" (*korokoro-kōya*), 46, 47
"culinary linguistics," 3, 4
culinary traditions, innovations, 197–98, 203n21
culinary triangle, 98
culture: food, language and, 1–7; humor and popular, 193; nature and, 220–21; rice, 18, 55; women and advancements, 198–200
curries, 19–20, 32, 162n6, 234
cutting verbs, 130n1; compounding, 127–30; manner of cutting or resulting shape, 128, 129–30; resulting shape by metaphorical reference, 128, 129, 130

CVCVN, 51, 73
CVCVQ, 44, 51, 61, 65, 72

Dainihon Tosho, 203n22
Danshi Chūbō-ni Haire ("Men should be in the kitchen") (Nakamura), 218
Danshi-gohan-no Hon ("Book for Men's Cooking") (Kokubun and Kentaro), 234–36, 237–38
Danshi-no Daidokoro ("Men's Kitchen") (Tokuoka), 235
da/ru style: *desu/masu* vs., 173, 201n6, 226; recipe writing, 172, 173, 201nn5–6
dashi ("stock"), 27, 68, 71, 105, 122, 153, 203n21
de, use of, 28–29
deep-fry: *ageru*, 102, 107, 110, 111, 112, 114, 131n9; oil amounts, 203n21
"deep-frying with brown color, crisp texture" (*koNgari*), 69
Deguchi, Kazumi, 226–27, 237
deliciousness in food, mimetics, 55–57, 67, 80, 90–92
depa-chika ("basement of department store"), 198
desu/masu style, recipe writing, 172, 201n5; *da/ru* vs., 173, 201n6, 226; elements in sentence-final position, 187–90; men, home cooking and, 226; prosaic vocabulary items, 187
Detake, Hisao, 133
Diffloth, Gérard, 44, 45
Dingemanse, Mark, 53
Doi, Yoshiharu, 84, 88–89, 127, 134, 227–30, 232, 235
donor language, 11–12, 16, 19–24, 30, 34, 35n4
donuts, 13–14, 17, 18
dryness-wetness, touch and, 54
Dutch, as donor language, 12, 21

"eat" (*tabetara*), 179, 180
ebi-hurai ("fried shrimp"), 17, 22, 36n8

ebi-katsu ("shrimp cutlet"), 36n8
Eckert, Penelope, 169, 200
economy, "bubble" period, 196
Egawa, Tomi, 96n18, 171–72, 173
Ehrlich, Susan, 169, 208
Ekuni, Kaori, 147, 148
elasticity, touch and, 54
Elder, Ryan S., 94n1
emojis, 180
emotion is cooking metaphor, 140
emphatic mimetic forms: recipe names, 176; recipes and identity, 183; regional dialect and, 196
English, 5, 12, 14, 15, 88
epenthesis, vowel, 15, 17
Equal Employment Opportunity Law, 196, 219, 231
era of plentiful food (*hōshokujidai*), 196–97
"ethnic food," 21
"Everyday Cooking" (*Hibi-no Ryōri*), 171
expressions, food-related, 3, 54

fashion is cooking/dining metaphor, 151–52
fast-food, 147
fat, use of, 102. *See also* cooking verbs, lexicalization and semantic components
Feld, Steven, 45, 95n4
femininity, 205–8, 214
Ferguson, Priscilla Parkhurst, 203n20
fiction, written food discourse, 64–66
Finegan, Edward, 167
Fleming, Isabel, 245n8
food: book/reading is food metaphor, 146–48, 163n10; era of plentiful, 196–97; "ethnic," 21; fast-, 147; globalization and glocalization of, 4; identity and, 29, 168; Italian, 37n20; language, culture and, 1–7; loanwords of, 4; metaphorical extension from food to non-, 144–59; metaphorical extension from non-food to, 136–44; Mexican, 35n1; mimetics and deliciousness in, 55–57, 67, 80, 90–92; non-food items, 3, 5; politics and, 203n24, 245n2; precooked items, 197–98; professionals and written food discourse, 60–62; slow, 146, 147; spoken discourses, 58–60; taste/food is human being metaphor, 141–42, 154; taste/food is living being metaphor, 140–41, 154; taste/food is moving object metaphor, 140, 142; texture, 49, 55–63, 96n22; touch and mimetics related to, 53–56; written discourses, 60–62. *See also* gender, food and; menus
food packaging, 5, 20, 241; from "basement of department store," 198; coffee, 214, 243; glass drink bottles, 19; mimetics, 66–68
food preparation, vocabulary of: cutting verbs, 127–30; lexicalization and semantic components of cooking verbs, 98–118; periphrastic extensions, 118–27
food-related expressions, 3, 54
foodways, "authenticity" in, 35n1
foreign vocabulary category, NINJAL survey, 12
French, 12, 13, 28–29, 30
Frequency Code, 86–87
"fried shrimp" (*ebi-hurai*), 17, 22, 36n8
Frish, Frequency Code, 87
Frosh, Frequency Code, 87
fruit juice with natural black vinegar (*sarasara-su*), 46, 48
fry. *See* deep-fry
Fukutome, Nami, 126

Gaeth, Gary J., 40
gastronativism, 245n2
GBS poteto, 27, 28
geminate consonant, 15, 35n2, 43, 94n2
gender: color and, 206, 211, 214, 215; cookbook survey of mimetics and,

81, 91; cooking sphere and, 197; division of labor, 219; equality, 196, 203n23, 218, 220, 230–34; roles, 206, 218, 232; taste and, 57
gender, food and: advertisements, 205, 209–11, 213–17, 245n8; *amatō* vs. *karatō* dichotomy, 208, 210–12, 214, 216–17, 242–43, 245n4; coffee and, 208, 210–17, 243, 245n8; cooking methods, 206; herbivore men, 207, 211–12, 217, 234–45; home cooking and cooking men, 217–45; home kitchen, 206; masculinity and, 205–9, 211–12, 214–17, 242, 244; meat, 205, 206, 245n1; meat and rice, 206; meat and salad, 205; neutralization, 243; tableware, 206–7; women with, 206, 207, 209–10, 213–14
German, 12, 89
Ghana, 53
gijōgo 擬情語 (psychomimes), 43–44
giseigo 擬声語/*giongo* 擬音語 (phonomimes), 43
gitaigo 擬態語 (phenomimes), 43–44
gizagiza-potato (potato chips), 45, 47
globalization: glocalization and, 4, 11; loanword perception and culinary, 29–35
glocalization, 4, 11, 18
Gochisōsama-ga Kikitakute ("I Want to Hear Thank You [for the meal]") (Kurihara, H.), 203n25
Gold, Jonathan, 35n1
Goodman, Nelson, 95n4
Google, 34
Gopnik, Alan, 201n10
gotogoto ("boil") cooking, 89
"the grammatical turn," 201n10
"greasy, oily" (*aburakkoi*), 49
"green-tea" (*gurīn-tī*), 22–23, 55
"grill" (*aburu*), 102, 114–15, 116
gungun-sōsēji (processed sausage), 46, 48
gurīn-tī ("green-tea"), 22–23, 55
guzuguzu, 61

Hall, Kira, 169, 208
Halloran, Vivian, 96n18
Hamano, Shoko, 51–52, 87, 91, 184
hand movements, cooking instructions, 75–76
"Hand Salad with Yogurt-Lemon Dressing," 2–3, 7n1
Harada, Aya, 84, 86
hardness-softness, touch and, 54
Hasegawa, Mio, 163n11
Haspelmath, Martin, 11, 13
Hayakawa, Fumiyo, 49, 55, 92–93, 95nn5–6, 162n4
headnotes, recipe writing and personalization, 174, 177–79
hearing: food-related mimetics and, 54, 55; to taste, 138; taste to, 145
heat. *See* cooking verbs, lexicalization and semantic components
herbivore men (*sōshokukei-danshi*), 207, 211–12, 217, 234–45
Hibi-no Ryōri ("Everyday Cooking"), 171
Higashi, Michio, 61–62
Higashiyotsuyanagi, Shoko, 200n3
Hines, Caitlin, 154
Hip Hop lyrics, 94
Hobbis, Stephanie Ketterer, 30
Hōchi Newspaper, 35n4
hokuhoku ("warm and flaky"), 56
hokuhoku-masshupoteto (potato salad), 46, 47
Holtzman, Jon, 157, 163n15, 211–12, 217
home cooking: principles, 197; women and, 236, 238–39, 246n12
home cooking, men and: cookbook types, 220–45; *Kukkingu Papa* comic book, 230–34, 245; as leisure activity, 218, 220; *otoko-no ryōri*, 220–26; as practical activity, 218–19; recipes in *desu/masu* style, 226; self-help and as necessity, 226–30; as shared domestic duty, 219; *sōshokukei-danshi* generation, 234–45; three waves of, 217–20

home kitchen, gender, food and, 206
Hōmuraihu Seminā, 246n16
Honda, Akiko, 203n22, 203n24
Hormes, Julia M., 94n1
hōshokujidai (era of plentiful food), 196–97
"The Housewife's Friend" (*Shuhu no Tomo*) magazine, 84, 213, 245n7
Hoyer, Wayne D., 40
Huchinoue, Shoko, 1–2
Hujingahō ("Women's Pictorial") (magazine), 213, 245n7
"Hujin Kōza" (radio broadcast), 171
Hujin Kurabu ("The Women's Club") (magazine), 96n19
Hujin-no Tomo ("Ladies' Friend") (magazine), 96n19, 245n5
Hujin-Sekai ("Women's World") (magazine), 214
hukasu ("steam"), [+Water] [-Fat] cooking verb, 102, 107–8, 110
humor: popular culture, 193; recipe names and, 178, 179, 180, 182, 202n18; recipe writing with identity and, 191–93
"hurt" (*itamu*), 70–71
hybrid vocabulary category, NINJAL survey, 12

"I Am Woman," 245n1
ice cream, 17, 18, 22, 46, 48, 87
identity: analytical framework for study of, 169; food and, 29; with food and taste, 168; Kobayashi with working women and, 196–200; minor, 29; recipes and, 183
ideophones, 43–44, 49, 52–53, 86
IHOP menu items, 2
Ikawa, Noriaki, 49
Ikeda, Takayuki, 215
Indian cuisine, 19–20
ingredients: amount and size, 76–78; cooking verbs with liquid or solid, 100; personification of, 134, 142–44; substitutions, 11

internet, social media and, 180–81, 201n8
iru$_1$ ("parch/dry roast"), [-Water] [-Fat] cooking verb, 102, 114, 115, 116
iru$_2$ ("parch/dry roast"), [-Water] [-Fat] cooking verb, 102, 114, 115, 116
Irwin, Mark, 12, 16, 20, 21, 30–31, 36n6, 36n10
Italian, 13, 37n20
itameru ("stir-fry"): with *saQto*, 131n11, 201n7; [-Water] [+Fat] cooking verb, 102, 110, 111–12, 113, 114
itamu ("hurt"), 70–71
"I Want to Hear Thank You [for the meal]" (*Gochisōsama-ga Kikitakute*) (Kurihara, H.), 203n25
Iwasaki, Shoichi, 191

Jackson, Peter, 180
Japan, non-alcoholic beverages, 95n8
Japanese: lexical strata, 12–14, 49; sound symbolism, 88
Japanese-style meal (*washoku*), 107, 130n4, 137, 153–54
"jelly-like texture" (*purupuru*), 63
Jiro Jo, 59
Johnson, Mark, 139–40
Jolly Times Cookbook, 206
Julier, Alice, 169
Jurafsky, Dan, 87, 96n20
juwaaQ, 60

Kakehi, Hisao, 53, 54, 95n5, 95nn10–11
Kamebuchi, Akinobu, 227, 228–30, 235
karai ("spicy, salty"), 156, 157, 162n1, 163n13, 210
karaoke, 21–22
karatō (alcohol). See *amatō* vs. *karatō*
karikari-okoshi (snack for squirrels and hamsters), 46, 47
"Katei Daigaku Kōza" (radio broadcast), 171
"Katei Kōza" (radio broadcast), 171
Kato, Keiko, 127

katsu, 22
Kawabata, Akiko, 1–2
Kawatsu, Yukiko, 163n11
Kebabalicious, 2
Kentaro, 84, 196, 234–36, 237–40, 247n18
Kidosaki, Ai, 81, 84, 137, 162n3, 182, 196
Kiesling, Scott Fabius, 169, 208
Kijima, Ryuta, 59–60
Kilian-Hatz, Christa, 44
Kindaichi, Hideho, 134
Kita, Sotaro, 44–45
kizzu aisu ("ice cream for kids"), 48
Klink, Richard R., 87
Kobayashi, Katsuyo (1937–2014), 81, 84, 176, 234; on children in kitchen, 239; Dainihon Tosho and, 203n22; gender equality and, 203n23; with identity-building and sharing, 196–200; as "Julia Child of Japan," 186, 202n14; Kurihara, Harumi, and, 203n25; legacy, 182, 200, 239; in media, 200n1; with mimetics, 182–86, 201n12, 202n15, 226, 246n15; with non-standard linguistic practice, 182–96; Osaka dialect and, 194–95, 200; politics and, 199, 203n24; speed cooking and, 197, 203n21. *See also* recipe writing, Kobayashi and
Kobayashi Katsuyo Kitchen Studio, 203n22
Koch, Shelley, 217
kogasu ("char"), [-Water] cooking verb, 102, 116
Kōkokugaisha, Danshiryō-no Okazu-kun ("Okazu at Male-only Dorm of Advertising Company") (Otokuni), 240–45
Kokubun, Taichi, 84, 196, 234–36, 237–38
kome-o taku ("cook rice [grain]"), 108, 130n6
Komori, Michihiko, 138, 162nn6–7

koNgari ("deep-frying with brown color, crisp texture"), 69
Koo, Hyun Jung, 162n1
Kopii, Jaanu, 210, 245n4
Korean, 52, 95n7, 162n1
korokoro-kōya ("cubed dehydrated tofu"), 46, 47
kotokoto (simmer) cooking, 70, 84, 88–89, 125, 189, 192
Krishna, Aradhna, 41, 94n1
Kubozono, Haruo, 16
Kuga, Mutsuko, 213, 214, 245n7
Kugler, Carol, 206
Kukkingu Papa ("Cooking Dad") (Ueyama), 230–34, 245
Kurashi-no Techō (magazine), 201n6
Kurihara, Harumi (1947–), 172, 176, 178–79, 201n7, 202n17, 203n25
Kurihara, Shinpei, 247n18
Kurosawa, Akira, 215
Kurowassan (magazine), 146
kushi-gata ("comb-shape"), 128, 129, 131n12
Kyō-no Ryōri ("Today's Cooking") (TV cooking show), 88–89, 200n1

Labov, William, 96n17
"Ladies' Friend" (*Hujin-no Tomo*) (magazine), 96n19, 245n5
Lakoff, George, 139–40
Lakoff, Robin, 13, 29, 168
languages: BMFT Kotobarabo lab, 55–56; borrowing, 4, 11, 14; cooking instructions and, 167; culture, food and, 1–7; donor, 11–12, 16, 19–24, 30, 34, 35n4; NINJAL, 12, 30; OQLF, 30; play, 27–28; recipe names and phrasing from foreign, 179–80; of recipes, 13; recipient, 11–13, 15, 23–24; regional dialects, 194–96, 200, 202n19; register and, 167; secret, 161–62, 163n19; "vegetable," 161. *See also specific languages*

Lehrer, Adrienne, 98, 99, 100, 102, 108–9, 111, 130n1, 163n8
Levin, Irwin P., 40
Lévi-Strauss, Claude, 98, 220
lexical strata, Japanese, 12–14, 49
life is cooking/dining metaphor, 149–51
Lim, Louisa, 207, 211
Lindenfeld, Laura, 169
linguistic adaptation, 11–12
linguistic adoption, 4, 11–12
linguistic patterning, 4
linguistic register, 167–68, 170, 181, 194, 199
linguistics, 7; NINJAL, 12, 30; regularity, 2; subfields, 3–4
liquids: amount of, 77–78; cooking verbs with solids and, 100; glass drink bottles, 19. *See also* alcohol; coffee; *niru*; water
loan doublets, 19, 35n3, 35n4
loanwords: adaptation, 14–29; auditory borrowing, 19–20; clipped, 17–18, 21, 22; English-based, 14, 15; with globalization and glocalization of food, 4; Japanese lexical strata, 12–14, 49; on menus, 32–35, 37n19, 37n20; mock-, 27–28; perception and culinary globalization, 29–35; polls, 30–32, 37n18; Portuguese, 13; pronunciations, 13, 34; re-borrowing, 21; recipe names, 35n4; vocabulary expansion with, 18–19
Lodge, David, 45

macaronic, 13–14, 27, 29
maccha powder, 22–23
makeup is cooking metaphor, 152–54, 163n11
marketing strategy, mimetics, 68–69, 91–92
marriage, women and, 154
Martin, Samuel, 43, 190–91
masculinity: alcohol and, 207; Child and, 202n15, 226; coffee and, 214–17; femininity and, 205–8, 214; herbivore men and weakened, 207, 211–12, 217, 234–45; multiple modes of, 208–9; vocabulary and, 222–25, 246n16. *See also* home cooking, men and
Maurer, Daphne, 96n20
Maynard, Senko K., 173
mayonnaise, 12, 17, 18, 24
Meah, Angela, 180
meat: eating, 148; gender and food, 205, 206, 245n1; sound of cooking, 42
Meiji Japan (1868–1912), 35n4
men: with bitterness and *karatō*, 210–11; herbivore, 207, 211–12, 217, 234–45; *karatō* and, 210–11; salad for, 223–25; salaryman, 207, 212, 214, 231, 232, 240, 241. *See also* home cooking, men and
Menon, Geeta, 87
men's cooking (*otoko-no ryōri*), 220–26
"Men should be in the kitchen" (*Danshi Chūbō-ni Haire*) (Nakamura), 218
"Men's Kitchen" (*Danshi-no Daidokoro*) (Tokuoka), 235
"Men's Recipes" (*Otoko-no Reshipi*) (Nishi), 222–26
menu items: IHOP, 2; OQLF with, 30; prestige, 13
menus: cafeteria, 39–40; language of, 13; loanwords on, 32–35, 37n19, 37n20; word choice on, 91–92
metaphorical extension, from food to non-food: book/reading is food, 146–48, 163n10; conceptual, 145–54; fashion is cooking/dining, 151–52; life is cooking/dining, 149–51; makeup is cooking, 152–54, 163n11; music and play, 148–49; sexism, 154–55; synesthetic, 144–45; taste adjectives, 155–59, 162n1; woman as dessert, 154
metaphorical extension, from non-food to food: argument is war, 139,

140; conceptual, 139–42; emotion is cooking, 140; personification of ingredients, 142–44; synesthetic, 136–39, 144; taste/food is human being, 141–42, 154; taste/food is living being, 140–41, 154; taste/food is moving object, 140, 142; transfer, 139

metaphors: adjectives describing taste, 134; analogizing sweet taste with personal traits, 134–35; compound terms with *niru* to convey anger, 135; compound terms with *ni-tsumeru* signifying positive outcome, 136; conceptual, 5, 136, 139–42, 144, 145–54; cooking is makeup, 163n11; cutting verbs and resulting shape by, 128, 129, 130; for food applied to non-food areas, 135; from food to non-food, 144–59; from non-food to food, 136–44; personification of ingredients, 134, 142–44; role of, 45; synesthetic, 136–39, 144–45, 155, 157; visual, 160–62; words describing taste, 133, 134; words too generic to describe taste, 133–34

Metaphors We Live By (Lakoff, G., and Johnson), 140

Mexican food, 35n1

Meyerhoff, Miriam, 169, 208

Mihune, Toshio, 215

mimetics: advertisements and, 41–42; affecto-imagistic dimension, 44–45, 52, 91; bodily sensation outside oral cavity, 66; with boldness to overcome fear of making errors, 185–86; childish undertone of, 63, 64; coined, 92–93; cookbook survey of, 80–86, 89–90, 95n13; cooking instructions, 69–80; deliciousness in food, 55–57, 67, 80, 90–92; description and evaluation of taste, 53–69; emphatic forms, 176, 183, 196; feeling of al dente pasta, 65; food packaging, 66–68; with forceful nuances, 184– 86; four senses and food-related, 54; Japanese lexical strata, 12–14, 49; Kobayashi with, 182–86, 201n12, 202n15, 226, 246n15; marketing strategy, 68–69, 91–92; negative qualities, 60; not specific for cooking instructions, 183–84; periphrastic extensions, 125–27; in recipe names, 174–76; role of, 4–5, 39–42; sound symbolism and innovation of, 86–94, 96n21; spoken food discourses, 58–60; token and type counts of, 83; touch and food-related, 53–56; vocabulary and semantic nature, 43–53; written food discourses, 60–65

minor identity, 29

miso soup, 14, 25, 71–72

Mister Donut, 13, 18

Mitsuno, Momo, 148

mizu-ni, 106

mochimochi ("chewy"), 56, 57

mock-loanwords, 27–28

modifiers, 16, 48. *See also* adjectives

"(be) moist with dew, (be) slightly damp" (*chokchok*), 52

moras, 15, 18, 68, 94

Moriguchi, Takeshi, 94n1

morphology, 2, 14, 21; mimetics and cooking instructions, 73; patterns, 51–52

motions, cooking instructions, 74–76

Murai, Gensai, 30, 35n4

Murakami, Motoko, 217, 218, 219, 246n11

murasu, [+Water] [-Fat] cooking verb, 109–10, 130n7

musu ("steam"), [+Water] [-Fat] cooking verb, 102, 104, 105, 107, 108, 109, 110

Muto, Ayaka, 54, 95n9, 95n12, 158–59, 163n12, 163n17

Nagano, Akiko, 23, 36nn11–12, 37n14

Nakahara, Ippo, 202n14, 203n21

Nakamura, Katsuhiko, 218, 246n11
names. *See* recipe names
National Institute for Japanese Language and Linguistics (NINJAL), 12, 30
National Public Radio (NPR), 207, 211, 245n3
native, Japanese lexical strata, 12, 49
native/mimetic vocabulary category, NINJAL survey, 12
nature, culture and, 220–21
negative qualities, mimetics, 60
Neuhaus, Jessamyn, 209
news outlets, written food discourse, 63–64
Ngo, Mary Kim, 87
NHK (Nippon Hōsō Kyōkai "Japan Broadcasting Corporation"), 30, 37n15, 69, 81, 200n1
Nihon Cooking Academy, 137
nikushokukei-joshi (carnivore women), 207
NINJAL (National Institute for Japanese Language and Linguistics), 12, 30
Nippon Hōsō Kyōkai "Japan Broadcasting Corporation" (NHK), 30, 37n15, 69, 81, 200n1
niru ("cook in liquid"), 70, 84, 201n7; anger conveyed with, 135; mimetics and, 126; [+Water] [-Fat] cooking verb, 102, 104–5, 106–7, 109, 110
Nishi, Jun'ichiro, 222–27, 236, 237, 246n16
Nishikawa, Osamu, 236
ni-tsumeru ("boil down"), 136
Noda, Mari, 49
non-alcoholic beverage consumption, 95n8
non-food items, 3, 5
noodles (pasta), 65, 89
notes, recipe writing and personalization, 174, 177–79
nouns: N(oun)-V(erb) compounds, 124; phrase form of X-*no* Y with recipe names, 174, 175, 176; sentence-final position without *desu* in recipe writing, 188–89
NPR (National Public Radio), 207, 211, 245n3
nurunuru, 66

Ochs, Elinor, 29, 169, 241
Oda, Nozomi, 157, 163n12
Office québécois de la langue française (OQLF), 30
Ogawa, Ito, 148
Ohala, John J., 86
Ohashi, Kyoko, 56, 57, 80, 89–90, 96n14, 170–71
oil: deep-fry and amount of, 203n21; *juwaaQ*, 60
"oil crisis" (*oiru shokku*), 196
"oily, greasy" (*aburakkoi*), 49
oiru shokku ("oil crisis"), 196
oishii, taste adjective, 157–59, 163n16
Okada, Shiori, 176, 180–81, 183, 196
"Okazu at Male-only Dorm of Advertising Company" (*Kōkokugaisha, Danshiryō-no Okazu-kun*) (Otokuni), 240–45
Okumura, Eikichi, 230
Ono, Masahiro, 95n11
onomatopoeia, 43, 69, 73, 75, 86
OQLF (Office québécois de la langue française), 30
orthography, 14, 27, 29, 35, 35n4, 37n20, 131n9
Osaka dialect, 194–95, 200
Osaka Kintetsu Railway, 41
Otoko-no Reshipi ("Men's Recipes") (Nishi), 222–26
Otoko-no Ryōri (Chiseisha), 221
otoko-no ryōri (men's cooking): cookbook themes and recipe choices, 221; family man and, 225–26; "four 'no' laws," 220, 222; simplicity in cooking process, 222–25
Otoko-no Ryōri-wa Dōgu-to Waza-ni Oku-no Te-ga Aru (Hōmuraihu Seminā), 246n16

Otokuni, 240–45
"oven baking" (*yaku₃*), 130n8

pain, touch and, 54
Parasecoli, Fabio, 202n15, 245n2
"parboil" (*yugaku*), 102, 105–6, 110, 126–27
"parch/dry roast" (*iru₁*), 102, 114, 115, 116
"parch/dry roast" (*iru₂*), 102, 114, 115, 116
paripari ("crisp texture"), 73
particles, recipe writing: sentence-final position with *ne* to soften requests, 190–91; sentence-final position with *yo* to give more information, 191
pasak pasak ("[be] crunchy, crispy"), 52
pasta (noodles): mimetics and feeling of al dente, 65; texture, 89
Pastagate, Canada, 30, 32
peanut butter, brand labels, 40
periphrastic extensions: compounding, 118–25; food preparation vocabulary and, 118–27; mimetics, 125–27
personal gustatory experience, power of, 41
personalization, headnotes and recipe writing, 174, 177–79
personification, of ingredients, 134, 142–44
phenomimes (*gitaigo* 擬態語), 43–44
phonetic segments, loanword adaptation and deletion of, 16–17
phonology, 14, 19, 21
phonomimes (*giseigo* 擬声語/*giongo* 擬音語), 43
photographs, in cookbooks, 96n18, 173–74, 221, 229
politics: food and, 245n2; Kobayashi and, 199, 203n24
polls, loanwords, 30–32, 37n18
ponzu, 21
Portnoy, Sarah, 35n1
Portuguese, 12, 13, 30

postpositions: sentence-final position without *desu* in recipe writing, 189–90; word ordering and, 23
potato chips (*gizagiza-potato*), 45, 47
potato salad (*hokuhoku-masshupoteto*), 46, 47
potato salad debate, 198
power structures, three, 41
precooked food items, 197–98
prepositions: borrowing of, 37n14; word ordering and, 23–25, 37n14
prestige, 13, 20, 29–30, 34
processed sausage (*gungun-sōsēji*), 46, 48
pronunciations, 4, 17, 19–22, 29, 37n20, 68, 95n6; borrowing language and changed, 11; loanword, 13, 34
prosaic, 41, 43, 78; analytical dimension, 44–45; expressions, 45, 47–49, 53, 56–57, 66, 74–76, 94, 95n13; words, 44–46, 50–51, 67, 69, 80, 88, 93–94, 95n9
prosaic vocabulary items: *desu/masu* style, 187; Kobayashi with recipe writing and, 186–87; reduplication, 187, 202n16
prose style, recipe writing, 171–72, 220
psychomimes (*gijōgo* 擬情語), 43–44
purupuru ("jelly-like texture"), 63

"quick cooking in liquid" (*saQto-ni*), 201n7
"quickly" (*saQto*), 69, 75, 106, 126, 201n7
"quick stir-frying" (*saQto-itame*), 201n7

radio broadcasts, cookbooks and, 171, 201n4
raisu. *See* rice
re-borrowing, loanwords, 21
recipe names (titles): abbreviated, 27, 28; compound form of X-Y, 174, 175; compound forms, 176–79; cryptic contents from personal anecdotes, 179; elided sentences,

179, 180; emphatic mimetic forms, 176; humor and, 178, 179, 180, 182, 202n18; internet and social media with, 180–81, 201n8; linguistic regularity with, 3; loanword adaptations and, 17; loanwords, 35n4; macaronic phenomena, 14; mimetics in, 174–76; noun-phrase form of X-*no* Y, 174, 175, 176; other linguistic forms, 179–80; personalization with creative style of serving, 178–79; personalization with enigmatic, 177–78; phrasing borrowed from foreign languages, 179–80; relative clauses, 179; texture, 175–76; utensils for serving and cooking, 176–77; word ordering in, 16, 23–27; writing, 174–82

recipes: format, 167; "Hand Salad with Yogurt-Lemon Dressing," 7n1; language of, 13

recipe writing: background, 170–82; cooking action verbs in numbered steps, 172–73; cooking action verbs in prose style, 171–72; *da/ru* style, 172, 173, 201nn5–6; *desu/masu* style, 172–73, 187–90, 201nn5–6, 226; names or titles, 174–82; personalization with headnotes and notes, 174, 177–79; sentence final forms, 172–73

recipe writing, Kobayashi and: elements in sentence-final position, 187–91; humorous contents, 191–93; identity-building and sharing, 196–200; linguistic register, 170; mimetics, 182–86; non-standard linguistic practice, 182–96; prosaic vocabulary items, 186–87; regional dialect, 194–96, 200, 202n19

recipient language, 11–13, 15, 23–24

Reddy, Helen, 245n1

reduplication, 183, 187, 202n16

regional dialects, recipe writing and, 194–96, 200, 202n19

register, languages and, 167

Rendaku (sequential voicing), 21, 127–28, 163n18

"Restaurant Snail" (*Shokudō-katatsumuri*) (Ogawa), 148

Rhee, Seongha, 162n1

rice (*raisu*), 20, 23–24, 26, 36n7; cooking, 55, 108–9; culture, 18, 55; gender and food, 206; *kome-o taku*, 108, 130n6; *taku*, 97, 102, 105, 107, 108, 109, 110

Ristorante Acqua Pazza, loanwords on menu, 32, 33, 34–35, 37n19

roast, 16, 35n3

"roast/broil" (*yaku₁*), 102, 107, 110, 111–12, 113–14, 116

"roast/broil" (*yaku₂*), 102, 111, 112, 114, 115, 116

Rozin, Paul, 94n1

Russian, 5, 12

ryōri-kenkyūka ("cooking experts"), 182, 196, 203n20, 203n25

"Ryōri Kondate" (radio broadcast), 171

ryōri-suru ("cook"), 100, 102

Sakamoto, Maki, 88

Sakamoto, Mitsuru, 34

saka-ni ("sake-ni"), 125, 131n10

sake, 53, 76–79, 105, 119, 138, 157, 163n13, 245n4

"sake-ni" (*saka-ni*), 125, 131n10

sakusaku ("crisp"), 56

salad, 2–3, 7n1, 37n13; gender and food, 205; for men, 223–25; potato, 46, 47, 198

salaryman, 207, 212, 214, 231, 232, 240, 241

Samarin, William, 44

saQto ("quickly"), 69, 75, 106, 126, 201n7

saQto-itame ("quick stir-frying"), 201n7

saQto-ni ("quick cooking in liquid"), 201n7

sarasara-su (fruit juice with natural black vinegar), 46, 48

Sawasaki, Umeko, 171, 172
secret languages, 161–62, 163n19
self-help cookbooks, for men, 226–30
semantic components, cooking verbs, 5
semantics, 14; narrowing, 20–21; nature of mimetic vocabulary, 43–53; shift, 20, 36n6
senses, five, 137. *See also* hearing; smell; taste; touch; vision
sensual/sensory appeal, power of, 41
sentence-final position, recipe writing: *desu/masu* style, 187–90; elliptical sentences, 189–90; end with nouns without *desu*, 188–89; end with particles without *desu*, 190–91; end with postpositions without *desu*, 189–90; end with verbs without *masu*, 189, 190; Kobayashi with elements in, 187–91; mimetic forms without ending in *desu* and *masu*, 188
sequential voicing (Rendaku), 21, 127–28, 163n18
Seto, Ken'ichi, 136, 137, 145
sexism: body parts, 3, 95n10, 154; metaphors, 154–55
shapes: comb-, 128, 129, 131n12; cutting verbs and resulting, 128, 129, 130; ingredients size and, 78
Shibatani, Masayoshi, 43
Shiki-no Ryōri ("Cooking for Four Seasons"), 171
Shimada, Masaharu, 23, 36nn11–12, 37n14
shi*Nn*ari state, of thinly sliced vegetables, 73–74
Shinohara, Kazuko, 88
Shintoism, *karatō* and, 245n4
shizuru-wādo ("sizzle word"), 55–57, 67, 80, 89–91
Shohet, Merav, 241
Shoji, Sadao, 62, 220, 222, 246n13
Shokudō-katatsumuri ("Restaurant Snail") (Ogawa), 148
Shokudōraku (Murai), 30, 35n4

Showa era (1926–1989), 62
"shrimp cutlet" (*ebi-katsu*), 36n8
Shuhu no Tomo ("The Housewife's Friend") magazine, 84, 213, 245n7
simmer (*kotokoto*) cooking, 70, 84, 88–89, 125, 189, 192
Simner, Julia, 94n1
Simon, Dolores, 81, 96n17
Sino-Japanese, 12, 13, 17, 20, 49
Siwi, 53
size, ingredients amount, 76–78
"sizzle word" (*shizuru-wādo*), 55–57, 67, 80, 89–91
sliminess, touch and, 54, 55
slow food, 146, 147
smell: to taste, 138; taste and, 41; taste to, 145
Smith, Jennifer, 19, 35n4
"smooth, melting" (*torori*), 92
snack for squirrels and hamsters (*karikari-okoshi*), 46, 47
Sobal, Jeffery, 169
social advancements, women and, 198–200
social class, taste and, 29
social media, 180–81, 198, 201n8
"soft and glutinous" (*torori*), 62, 67, 86
softness-hardness, touch and, 54
solids, cooking verbs with, 100
sōshokukei-danshi (herbivore men), 207, 211–12, 217, 234–45
sound: adaptations based on, 14, 15; auditory borrowing, 19–20; coda nasal, 15, 35n2, 94n3; Frequency Code, 86–87; of meat cooking, 42; onomatopoeia, 43, 69, 73, 75, 86; phonology, 14, 19, 21; segments with loanwords, 14, 15; symbolism and innovation of mimetics, 86–94, 96n21
source word, 11, 13–17, 19–22, 35nn3–4, 37n20
soy, negative connotations, 40
speed cooking, 197, 203n21

"spicy, salty" (*karai*), 156, 157, 162n1, 163n13, 210
spoken food discourses, 58–60
Starbucks Japan, 22–23
Starbucks VIA Matcha, 36n9
"steam" (*hukasu*), 102, 107–8, 110
"steam" (*musu*), 102, 104, 105, 107, 108, 109, 110
steaming: utensils for, 130n5; visual changes in food with, 80
stickiness, touch and, 55
"stir-fry" (*itameru*), 102, 110, 111–12, 113, 114, 131n11, 201n7
"stock" (*dashi*), 27, 68, 71, 105, 122, 153, 203n21
Strauss, Susan, 52, 95n7
stress-accent pattern, 14, 17, 22, 93–94
su (vinegar), 21, 46, 48
suffixes, 16, 17, 49, 68, 73
sukusuku-kizzu-aisu (ice cream), 46, 48
"super-creamy! potato salad topped with an egg [fried, sunny-side up]" (*chō-kurīmī! on tama pote-sara*), 37n13
Suter, Rebecca, 55, 95n8
Suzuki, Tokiko, 71–72
sweets: analogized with personal traits, 134–35; children and, 157, 207, 210; herbivore men with, 207, 212, 242–43; sugar, 213, 214, 215; women with, 157, 210. *See also amatō* vs. *karatō*
synesthetic metaphors, 136–39, 144–45, 155, 157
Szabo, Michelle, 217, 219

tabetara ("eat"), 179, 180
tableware, with gender and food, 206–7
Takai, Naoyuki, 245n6
Takamine, Hideko, 76–77
Takei, Emiko, 206–7
taku ("cook [rice]"), [+Water] [-Fat] cooking verb, 97, 102, 105, 107, 108, 109, 110
tamago-kake gohan (TKG), 27–28, 58

Tamamura, Toyo'o, 220, 246n14
Tamori, Ikuhiro, 45, 62, 64
Tanaka, Kei'ichi, 213
taste: adjectives, 134, 155–59, 162n1, 163n16, 163nn12–14; bitterness, 210–17; brand labels and, 40; colors and, 41, 138, 162n7; descriptions, 3; five, 137; food-related mimetics and, 54, 55; gender and, 57; to hearing, 145; hearing to, 138; identity and, 168; metaphors, 133–34; mimetics with description and evaluation of, 53–69; of sake, 53; to smell, 145; smell and, 41; smell to, 138; social class and, 29; taste/food is human being metaphor, 141–42, 154; taste/food is living being metaphor, 140–41, 154; taste/food is moving object metaphor, 140, 142; to touch, 145; touch to, 137; as ultimate goal, 197, 203n21; verbal descriptions of, 49; to vision, 145; vision to, 137–38. *See also* gender, food and; sweets
Tatsumi, Hamako, 84, 172, 173
Tatsumi, Yoshiko, 84
texture: crisp, 73; deep-frying with brown color, crisp, 69; food, 49, 55–63, 96n22; *guzuguzu*, 61; ideophones and, 52–53; jelly-like, 63; noodles, 89; recipe names, 175–76. *See also* touch
Thomason, Sarah, 36n10
Tierney, R. Kenji, 242
times, mimetics and cooking instructions, 72–74
titles. *See* recipe names
TKG (*tamago-kake gohan*), 27–28, 58
"Today's Cooking" (*Kyō-no Ryōri*) (TV cooking show), 88–89, 200n1
tofu, 46, 47
Tokuoka, Kunio, 227–28, 235
torori ("smooth, melting"), 92
torori ("soft and glutinous"), 62, 67, 86

touch: food-related mimetics and, 53–56; to taste, 137; taste to, 145
Tsujimoto, Tomoko, 140, 142
tsuntsun, 66

Ueyama, Tochi, 230–34, 245
Uhl, Kenneth P., 40
Ullmann, Stephen, 136
uragoshi (beginners cooking technique), 247n17
utensils: cooking, 11, 107, 109, 112, 124, 176–77; for steaming, 130n5; tableware, 206–7

"vegetable language" (*yasaigo*), 161
vegetables, *shiNnari* state of thinly sliced, 73–74. See also salad
verbal descriptions: cooking instructions with, 241; framing of, 40; of taste, 49
verbs: cutting, 127–30, 130n1; N(oun)-V(erb) compounds, 124; recipe writing in prose style and cooking action, 171–72; sentence-final position without *masu* in recipe writing, 189, 190. See also cooking verbs
vinegar (*su*), 21, 46, 48
vision: food-related mimetics and, 54–55; steam and visual changes in food, 80; to taste, 137–38; taste to, 145
visual metaphors: food products and, 160–61; secret language and, 161–62
vocabulary: expansion with loanwords, 18–19; four categories, 12; items, 3; masculinity and, 222–25, 246n16; prosaic items, 186–87, 202n16; semantic nature of mimetic, 43–53. See also food preparation, vocabulary of
Voelts, F. K. Erhard, 44
Vos, Frits, 21
vowels: consonants clusters and, 15–16; epenthesis, 15, 17; moras, 15, 18, 68, 94; sound symbolism and, 86–87

wafflicious, 2
wakasu ("boil [water]"): for bath, 130n2; [+Water] [-Fat] cooking verb, 102, 104, 110
"walk" (*aruku*), 70
Wansink, Brian, 39
Ward, Jamie, 94n1
"warm and flaky" (*hokuhoku*), 56
washoku (Japanese-style meal), 107, 130n4, 137, 153–54
Watanabe, Junji, 88
water, use of, 102
[-Water] cooking verb, *kogasu*, 102, 116
[-Water] [-Fat] cooking verbs: *aburu*, 102, 114–15, 116; componential analyses summary of, 116; iru_1, 102, 114, 115, 116; iru_2, 102, 114, 115, 116; $yaku_2$, 102, 111, 112, 114, 115, 116
[-Water] [+Fat] cooking verbs: *ageru*, 102, 107, 110, 111, 112, 114; componential analyses summary of, 114; *itameru*, 102, 110, 111–12, 113, 114; $yaku_1$, 102, 107, 110, 111–12, 113–14, 116
[+Water] [-Fat] cooking verbs: componential analyses summary of, 110; *hukasu*, 102, 107–8, 110; *murasu*, 109–10, 130n7; *musu*, 102, 104, 105, 107, 108, 109, 110; *niru*, 102, 104–5, 106–7, 109, 110; *taku*, 97, 102, 105, 107, 108, 109, 110; *wakasu*, 102, 104, 110; *yuderu*, 102, 105–7, 109, 110; *yugaku*, 102, 105–6, 110
wetness-dryness, touch and, 54
Whitman, Joan, 81, 96n17
Williams, Joseph, 138–39, 145
woman as dessert metaphor, 154
women: *amatō* and, 210, 245n4; carnivore, 207; coffee advertisements and, 213–14, 245n8; cookbooks and social roles of, 209; with gender and food, 206, 207, 209–10, 213–14; home cooking and, 236,

238–39, 246n12; "I Am Woman," 245n1; Kobayashi with identity and working, 196–200; magazines for, 170, 213–14, 245n5; "manly" mimetics and, 184, 185, 202n15, 226, 246n15; marriage and, 154; social and cultural advancements, 198–200; with sweets, 157, 210

"Women's Pictorial" (*Hujingahō*) (magazine), 213, 245n7

"The Women's Club" (*Hujin Kurabu*) (magazine), 96n19

"Women's World" (*Hujin-Sekai*) (magazine), 214

word ordering, 16, 23–27, 36n12, 37n14

words: choice on menus, 91–92; compounding, 17, 18, 20, 22, 80; power of, 41; sizzle, 55–57, 67, 80, 89–91. *See also* loanwords

writing, cookbooks, 200n2. *See also* recipe writing

written food discourses, mimetics: fiction, 64–66; new outlets, 63–64; by professionals, 60–62

wulthwung pwulthwung, "(be) bumpy," 52

Yahoo, 34

yaku$_1$ ("roast/broil"), [-Water] [+Fat] cooking verb, 102, 107, 111–12, 113–14, 116

yaku$_2$ ("roast/broil"), [-Water] [-Fat] cooking verb, 102, 111, 112, 114, 115, 116

yaku$_3$ ("oven baking"), 130n8

Yamaguchi, Haruhiko, 138, 162n7

Yamazaki, Mikio, 214

yasaigo ("vegetable language"), 161

Yonekawa, Akihiko, 160–61, 163n19

Yorkson, Eric, 87

YouTube, 59–60, 116, 120, 152, 202n13

yuderu ("boil"): compounding, 126–27; [+Water] [-Fat] cooking verb, 102, 105–7, 109, 110

Yuen, Shu Min, 209, 234, 235–36, 238, 239, 244

yugaku ("parboil"): compounding, 126–27; [+Water] [-Fat] cooking verb, 102, 105–6, 110

Zwicky, Ann, 13, 30, 39, 167, 181, 201n9

Zwicky, Arnold, 13, 30, 39, 167, 181, 201n9

About the Author

Natsuko Tsujimura is professor emerita in the Department of East Asian Languages and Cultures and adjunct professor emerita in the Department of Linguistics at Indiana University Bloomington. Her authored and edited books include *Expressing Silence: Where Language and Culture Meet in Japanese* (2022, Lexington Books); *An Introduction to Japanese Linguistics*, Third Edition (2014, Wiley Blackwell); *Japanese Linguistics: Critical Concepts*, Volumes I–III (Editor, 2005, Routledge); and *The Handbook of Japanese Linguistics* (Editor, 1999, Basil Blackwell). She also has published articles in journals including *Cognitive Linguistics, Journal of East Asian Linguistics, Natural Language and Linguistic Theory, Linguistics, Linguistic Inquiry,* and *Studies in Language*.

www.ingramcontent.com/pod-product-compliance
Lightning Source LLC
Chambersburg PA
CBHW052154300426
44115CB00011B/1663